The spatial theory of voting

The spatial theory of voting

An introduction

JAMES M. ENELOW
State University of New York at Stony Brook
MELVIN J. HINICH
University of Texas at Austin

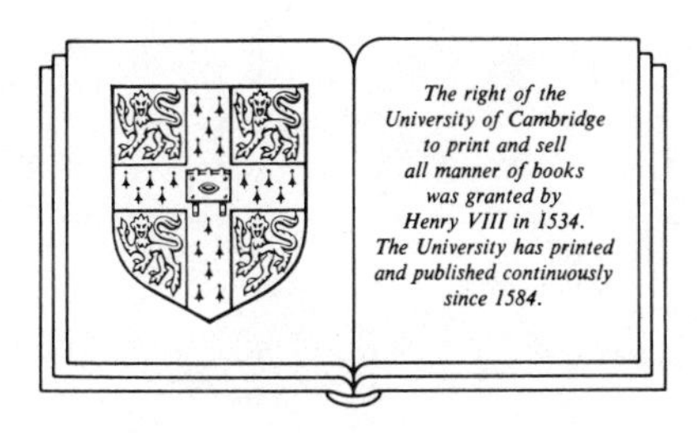

CAMBRIDGE UNIVERSITY PRESS

Cambridge
London New York New Rochelle
Melbourne Sydney

Published by the Press Syndicate of the University of Cambridge
The Pitt Building, Trumpington Street, Cambridge CB2 1RP
32 East 57th Street, New York, NY 10022, USA
296 Beaconsfield Parade, Middle Park, Melbourne 3206, Australia

First published 1984

Printed in the United States of America

Library of Congress Cataloging in Publication Data

Enelow, James M.

The spatial theory of voting.

Bibliography: p.

Includes index.

1. Voting. 2. Elections. 3. Social choice.
I. Hinich, Melvin J. II. Title.
JF1001.E53 1984 324.9 83-7758
ISBN 0 521 25507 4 hard covers
ISBN 0 521 27515 6 paperback

to

Jean, Jason, and Sarah

Sonje and Amy

Contents

Preface

This book is an effort to convey an important body of political science research to as wide an audience as possible. It is the contention of this book that the spatial theory of voting is a complete scientific theory. Spatial theory can be used to analyze systematically the behavior of voters and candidates, voting in small committees and large electorates, the impact of institutions on the voting process - in short, spatial theory can illuminate the role of any major factor relevant to the voting process. In addition, spatial theory generates deductively interrelated propositions that are susceptible to empirical testing. These are the reasons why we consider spatial theory to be a complete theory of voting.

The purpose of this book is to provide a thorough explanation of spatial theory. In fact, there are really two theories. The first is the spatial theory of committee voting, and the second is the spatial theory of elections. Chapter 1 discusses the place of spatial models in research on voting behavior. Chapters 2 and 3 introduce the unidimensional and multidimensional spatial models of committee voting. Although we do discuss a number of important results from the literature, Chapters 2 and 3 are not meant to be an exhaustive overview of the spatial theory of committees. Instead, these chapters are designed to introduce the reader to the basic concepts underlying both the theory of committee voting and the theory of elections.

Chapter 4 introduces the reader to the spatial theory of elections. Election theory, while built on the same foundations as the theory of committee voting, is concerned with a more complex phenomenon. In contrast to committee voting, elections feature candidates as the objects of voter choice. The nature of this choice is fundamentally different from that of committee voting, and we offer a new spatial model designed to reflect this difference. In explaining this new model, we bring in additional concepts important to election theory. The concept of a "predictive dimension" is introduced as well as problems that arise from differing voter perceptions of a single candidate's issue stands. Chapter 4 integrates these new concepts into the spatial theory developed in preceding chapters. In addition, the behavior of candidates is explored. The campaign tactics available to the candidates are discussed, and it is shown how these tactics can be used to affect election results.

Chapter 5 introduces two additional subjects that are important to elections. The first is candidate characteristics. Candidates are evaluated by voters not only on the basis of policy positions but also on the basis of personal attributes, party and interest group associations, and similar qualities. Chapter 5 introduces this "nonpolicy" component of the voter's evaluation into spatial theory.

Another subject treated in Chapter 5 is nonvoting or abstention. Problems of turnout continually affect mass elections, and it is important to incorporate this phenomenon into the spatial model of elections. Chapter 5 concludes with a discussion of how nonpolicy issues can upset the simple voting stability depicted in the unidimensional spatial model of Chapter 2.

Chapter 6 returns us to the committee setting to show how our new spatial model of elections can be applied to voting on budgets. This problem comes up both in legislatures and in referendum voting. Perceptual variation of how changes in total budget size will affect later changes in individual spending activities can have an important effect on the outcome of a budget vote. Chapter 6 develops a new theory of budgetary incrementalism to explain the nature of this effect.

Chapter 7 returns us to the electoral arena to discuss voter uncertainty about the candidates. This uncertainty can take several forms: uncertainty induced by candidate efforts to switch predictive labels, uncertainty created by imperfect perception of where a candidate is located on a predictive dimension, and uncertainty about future candidate behavior if the candidate is elected to office. These are important subjects for incorporation into the spatial theory of elections.

Chapter 8 discusses a recently developed topic in the spatial theory of committees, the "new institutionalism." Voting over policy alternatives usually takes place in an institutional setting. The precise choice offered the voters is usually determined exogenously by an "agenda setter." The role that an agenda setter can play in school elections is examined in Chapter 8. The main point to be made is that the agenda setter can have a significant effect on the outcomes of school budget votes, inducing voters to approve budgets that are quite different from the ones they would approve if ballot propositions were formulated by a competitive process. However, the degree to which an agenda setter can exercise control over vote outcomes is seriously complicated by factors beyond his control.[1]

[1] To avoid awkward wording, the masculine pronoun is often used in the generic sense to mean "he or she."

Legislative committee systems are another example of how institutions structure voting. Policies approved under a committee system may be quite different from those policies approved in the absence of this institution. Chapter 8 also explores this topic.

Finally, Chapter 8 returns to the subject of elections to discuss another institution: the unit rule. The electoral college is an outstanding example of this rule, and, again, we see how another type of institution biases the results of unstructured majority rule voting.

Chapter 8 also develops a new theory of particular importance in the institutional setting. This is a theory of expectations. The expectations problem arises when a multi-issue voting problem is split up into a set of one-issue pieces that are then voted on serially. We discuss and theorize about the problem of how votes on a present-day issue are affected by expectations regarding decisions on future issues.

Chapter 9 is an empirical justification for the new election theory developed in Chapters 4 and 5. It is important to know whether or not this new theory helps explain politics in the real world. We develop two methodologies designed to provide such a real-world test. Focusing on the American presidential elections of 1976 and 1980, we perform a variant of factor analysis on voter survey data to show that for both years a spatial representation of candidates and voters can be obtained that is in close conformity with theoretical expectations derived from our model. Two predictive dimensions are recovered: an economic scale and a social left–right scale. The presidential candidates are located on these scales where we expect them to be, and the average voter is located in the interior of the candidate cluster.

The scaling procedure used allows for inclusion of a valence dimension. For 1976, candidate morality is found to best represent this dimension. For 1980, leadership ability serves this role. For 1976, the voter choice model developed in Chapter 5, including a nonpolicy component as well as a policy component, predicts reported choice behavior between the two major presidential candidates better than a model based on policy alone. For 1980, the pure policy model performs better than the combined model. Prediction rates for the combined model, however, are still quite good. Chapter 9, then, is our evidence (albeit exploratory) that the new spatial theory offered in this book has real-world significance.

The emphasis of the book is on reader comprehension. Accordingly, the results in the text are usually developed in the context of examples. Most of these results can be developed at a higher level of generality, and we usually indicate where this is so. General proofs are to be found in the book's appendixes.

At the end of each chapter we provide bibliographical notes pertinent to the material in the chapter. We also mention and reference subjects that are related but ancillary to chapter material. This will provide the reader with a guide to further readings that will enhance or elaborate on the ideas discussed in the text.

We see the book as adopting a problem-oriented approach. Many of the book's arguments are carried by examples, and theorem proving is kept to a minimum in the text. Problems are included at the ends of most chapters so that the reader can test his understanding of the material. Answers to some of these problems can be found at the back of the book.

We believe that a full understanding of the spatial theory of voting is possible only if the theory's central concepts are developed in mathematical form. However, the level of mathematics needed to express the important results in this field is surprisingly modest. An understanding of simple linear and quadratic equations is required, but this knowledge is usually acquired at the high school level. Some plane geometry is also useful. Elementary (freshman) calculus makes an occasional appearance in the text. Vectors and matrices are used quite sparingly in the development of some of the results. Advanced material is confined to appendixes, which are recommended for those with additional skills. In short, we keep the math to a bare minimum and, wherever possible, provide the reader with a verbal explanation of what we are doing. We think that pictures and words are very useful, but that the reader cannot obtain a complete understanding of the spatial theory of voting without also investing time in carefully working through the basic mathematics needed to convey the major ideas that support this work.

Thus, we see this book as a middle-level introduction to an important body of theory. We hope to convince the reader that this body of theory is a major research accomplishment of political science. We believe that the effort expended in learning this theory will be rewarded by a recognition of this fact.

We have many people to thank who have helped us in our endeavor. Mrs. Vickie Carroll at Virginia Tech has been a superb typist and has, without complaint, retyped again and again almost every part of the text. Mr. Pankaj Gupta at Stony Brook has been an efficient and reliable research assistant whose excellent work has contributed significantly to Chapter 9. Mr. Michael Bloom at Virginia Tech has also made important contributions to Chapter 9, particularly through his ideas for filtering the survey data and constructing valence positions for the candidates. Finally, Ms. Lois Koh at Stony Brook has done a terrific job of transforming our sometimes sloppy pictures into professional illustrations.

We wish to thank the State University of New York at Stony Brook for a faculty grant-in-aid from the Graduate School that helped us get this book off the ground. We have also received generous support from the National Science Foundation under grants SOC-7900034 and SES-8111411. Finally, survey data for the empirical analysis of Chapter 9 were provided by the Inter-University Consortium for Political and Social Research. Needless to say, the State University of New York at Stony Brook, the National Science Foundation, and the Consortium are not responsible for any of our interpretations or conclusions.

We have also benefited from the advice of several colleagues. Professors Peter Ordeshook and Howard Rosenthal were gracious enough to give Chapters 2 and 3 a test run in their public choice course at Carnegie-Mellon University. Professors Ken Shepsle of Washington University and Peter Coughlin of the University of Maryland at College Park also provided helpful comments on several chapters. Finally, students at Stony Brook, Virginia Tech, and the University of Texas at Austin should also be thanked for their constructive comments about various aspects of the text.

Our families deserve very special thanks. They are the ones who made the greatest sacrifices for the benefit of this book. For this reason, we dedicate the book to them.

J.M.E.
M.J.H.

CHAPTER 1

Spatial voting models: the behavioral assumptions

The purpose of this book is twofold. First, we wish to introduce the reader to an important body of political science research: the spatial theory of voting. This theory has evolved over a period of about 25 years, although it can be traced back as far as the 1920s in the work of Hotelling (1929). The first major works are those of Downs (1957) and Black (1958). Since then, an enormous amount of research has been done on this subject. It is not our intent to summarize all of this research. Instead, we wish to convey the basic structure of spatial voting models. Beginning with the most elementary concepts of unidimensional spatial theory, we develop the spatial theory of voting step by step. Our goal is to present the central ideas of spatial theory in a careful and rigorous fashion, but in a way designed to maximize the reader's understanding. Once the reader has mastered the material in these chapters, he will have a full appreciation of the contributions spatial theory has made to our understanding of voting.

This brings us to the second purpose of the book. The spatial theory of voting is more than an elegant set of theoretical constructs. The purpose of this theory is to enhance our understanding of real politics. For this reason, we devote a large portion of this book to a new approach to the study of elections. This approach is grounded in the classic spatial theory to be discussed in Chapters 2 and 3, but it contains many new features designed to reflect problems of voter information and perception that are inherent in mass elections.

These problems reflect the fundamental difference between *committee voting* and *mass elections*. It is an important theme of this book that whereas these two types of voting can be analyzed spatially, two different spatial models are required to do so. Committee voting is generally characterized by a small number of well-informed voters who make choices from among a set of *policy alternatives*. Mass elections, on the other hand, feature a large number of voters who must choose from among a set of *candidates* on the basis of limited information. In Chapter 6 we discuss the case of a large committee voting over alternative total budgets without knowing for certain how a change in the total budget figure will affect individual spending activities. This type of committee voting is very much like a mass election and so can be analyzed with the same model. However, aside from this case, we treat committee voting and elections separately.

1.1 Spatial versus social-psychological models of voting

In the following section we describe the behavioral assumptions underlying the spatial theory of voting. It is important for the reader to understand this "model of man" before launching into a more technical discussion of spatial theory. All approaches to the study of voting presume a model of what causes citizens to vote as they do. This model is not directly testable, but instead serves as a basis for generating testable propositions about the behavior of voters or candidates. The ultimate test of a model lies in the quality of its predictive statements. For this reason, Chapter 9 presents some empirical results based on a test of the spatial theory of elections.

We now proceed to describe the model of man underlying the spatial theory; then we shall contrast it with a very different model of man employed in an alternative approach to the study of voting behavior. This alternative approach originates with Campbell, Converse, Miller, and Stokes (1960) and can be described as social-psychological. The social-psychological approach and the spatial approach are the two predominant paradigms used in the study of voting behavior, and it will be helpful to see how they differ.

1.2 Spatial voting models

Spatial theory describes two classes of actors: voters and candidates. Both are assumed to be motivated by self-interest. Voters can vote directly over alternative policies in the case of a committee, or they can vote over alternative candidates in the case of an election. In either case, the voter is assumed to be able to evaluate the objects (i.e., policies or candidates) competing for his vote in terms of his own self-interest and to cast his vote on this basis.

We shall give a more precise meaning to the term "self-interest" in succeeding chapters. For now, we wish to describe spatial theory in broad terms. The concept of self-interest is easily misunderstood. It is commonly thought to mean purely economic self-interest. However, self-interest can be more broadly construed. Busing may be an issue that affects a voter's self-interest even if he has no children. Abortion may also be related to self-interest, even though the issue be of theoretical concern only. Both issues may involve philosophical principles that are important to the voter. The voter may abhor a government that dictates where children will go to school or one that permits the lives of the unborn to be terminated. There is no reason to exclude such concerns from the voter's self-interest.

What spatial theory assumes is that the voter has a given stake or interest in the outcome of the vote, which he recognizes, and which leads him to vote as he does. The form of this self-interest is subjectively determined by the voter. Spatial theory does not explain the source or form that this self-interest takes. The theory merely assumes that the voter recognizes his own self-interest, evaluates alternative policies or candidates on the basis of which will best serve this self-interest, and casts his vote for the policy or candidate most favorably evaluated. In short, the voter is *rational.*

Candidates are also rational. Each candidate sees a direct connection between the "package" he offers the voters and the votes he receives. This package consists of the policy statements he makes, his own characteristics as a candidate, his past record or that of his party – in short, any of the myriad factors that voters might use as a guide to the candidate's future behavior if he is elected. Clearly, not all of these factors are under the candidate's direct control. However, the variables that are under the candidate's control (and we assume that such variables exist) are purposefully utilized in an effort to win votes. Whether the candidate wishes to attract just enough votes to win the election, as many votes as possible, or some other function of the total vote is not important here. What is important is that the candidate uses the "instruments" at his disposal in an effort to come as close as possible to achieving his campaign goal. In all cases we shall examine, this goal means winning the election. Further, the candidate proceeds on the assumption that voters are self-interested. This means that each voter will compare the package offered by the candidate with that offered by his opponent(s) and vote for the candidate whose package is most favorably evaluated.

Viewed in simplest spatial terms, the voter will cast his vote for the candidate "closest" to him in a space that describes all the factors that are of concern to the voter. These factors may include classic campaign issues such as defense spending and unemployment, as well as candidate attributes such as integrity and leadership ability. It is the purpose of succeeding chapters to define this evaluative space and the representation of voters and candidates in this space. For now, we want to introduce the analogy between preference and distance that is central to spatial theory.

1.3 Voter information in mass elections

One of the key differences between committee votes and mass elections is the problem of information costs. In mass elections there is typically an absence of incentives for voters to acquire much information about the candidates. It is unreasonable in an electorate that may number in the hundreds of millions for each individual to search out information on each candidate's positions on the many issues of the campaign. In addition, there are good reasons why candidates might be vague or ambiguous about their policy stands.

An important innovation of this book is the development of a new spatial theory of elections designed to capture this reality. Chapter 4 develops the idea that in mass elections, predictive labels that become attached to the various candidates serve as shorthand bases for estimating their positions on policy issues. Party and ideological labels are the most important predictive labels used in American politics. When a voter learns that candidate A is a conservative Republican, he acquires a basis for estimating A's positions on the issues that concern him. This procedure for gathering information is termed by Downs (1957) a "system of information acquisition." It permits voters to rationally judge the candidates competing for votes without having to invest enormous resources of time and energy that would far outweigh the consequences of one citizen's voting decision.

1.4 Social-psychological voting models

A good way to appreciate the behavioral assumptions of spatial theory is to contrast them with those of social-psychological models of voting. The most important example of such a model is the one originated by Campbell, Converse, Miller, and Stokes (1960), which we shall term the "Michigan model" of elections. That model has been expanded in the work of those who have followed that tradition, but its essential outline has remained unchanged.

The fundamental assumption of the Michigan model of elections is that voting behavior is caused by a set of social and psychological variables. These variables form a temporal chain that begins with those causal influences most distant from the actual voting act, such as the voter's social characteristics. Each set of influences in this "funnel of causality" affects succeeding influences in this chain. Thus, social characteristics affect the voter's "party identification (ID)," which measures the voter's affective orientation toward the major political parties. Party ID, in turn, affects how the voter perceives the issues and candidates of the campaign. These later variables determine how the voter reacts to the events of the campaign and how he responds to political importunings from family and friends. The individual's vote is determined by the summation of all these influences.

This model is quite different from the spatial model. Voting behavior is seen not as the result of *choice* based on self-interest but rather as the result of a set of conditioning agents. Forces largely beyond the voter's control determine his behavior. Party ID, rather than serving as a shorthand basis for evaluating candidates, is a perceptual screen that distorts the individual's view of political events. Although it does not strictly determine how the individual votes, party ID is a predisposing factor of major importance in the voter's "force field." If short-term influences specific to a single campaign are of sufficient strength, the force exerted by party ID on the individual's vote may be deflected. Thus, Eisenhower's popularity caused many Democratic voters to vote Republican. But the vote is still a resultant of a set of forces that the individual does not control.

The Michigan model is premised on determinism. The voter does not calculate which candidate will best serve his self-interest. Instead, he is conditioned to vote for one candidate or another.

1.5 A comparison between the two models

How can one tell the difference between voting behavior based on rational choice and voting behavior based on conditioning? Ultimately, one can't. However, a model of voting behavior based on rational choice is quite distinguishable from a model of conditioned voting behavior. To use an economic analogy, a model of consumer behavior that views consumer purchases as the result of "indoctrination" will ask questions very different from those asked by a model that assumes consumer decisions to involve an element of choice. The indoctrination model will focus on the source of consumer conditioning (e.g., advertising, popular culture), whereas the choice model will focus on how consumer tastes are translated into buying decisions. It may be that these tastes are based on external influences, but the element of choice remains. Tastes form the basis for choice behavior, but the two are distinct entities.

Another difference between the two consumer models lies in the assumed reasons for behavior change. The indoctrination model, by positing the malleability of taste, will view taste, and consequently behavior, as susceptible to change by direct influence. The choice model, on the other hand, will view taste as given and behavior change as due to changes in the attributes of the objects of choice.

Returning to voting behavior, many of the questions raised by the Michigan model do indeed focus on the source of voter conditioning. Viewing party ID as the major element in the voter's force field, the question arises as to the source of party ID. Studies of political socialization (e.g., Niemi and Weisberg, 1976) have concluded that party ID is acquired at an early age through a combination of influences (e.g., parents, peers) and is relatively stable throughout an individual's lifetime.

The spatial theory of elections is primarily concerned with how the self-interested choices of voters affect the behavior of candidates. Viewing voters as possessing freedom of action, as being responsive to the differential appeals made by the candidates, provides a basis by which the *candidates* can influence votes. This is the key difference between the two models. Whereas the candidates are viewed as a short-term influence affecting votes in the Michigan model, the conceptualization of candidates is passive. Rather than being viewed as active agents modifying their behavior in an effort to win votes, the candidates are conceived as fixed parameters in the voter's force field. A candidate's personal appeal or his issue stands exert a given force and direction on the individual's voting behavior. As a result, the Michigan model offers no explanation for the behavior of candidates. Without an explicit linkage between voter and candidate behavior, the candidates are relegated to an offstage role in the Michigan model.

Spatial theory sees the candidates as well as the voters as objects of analysis. As such, the origins of candidate behavior as well as voter behavior are postulated in the model. The result is a relationship of simultaneous causation. Candidates exert influence over voters, and voters exert influence over candidates. Voters give or withhold votes on the basis of what the candidates offer them, and candidates are induced to make various offers based on the desire to win votes.

In conclusion, then, the Michigan model is concerned with identifying and measuring the pattern of forces that condition the vote, whereas spatial theory is concerned with how the interaction between voters and candidates affects the choices that candidates offer the voters. Consequently, the two models, by looking at elections in very different ways, focus on very different sets of questions. In this sense, the two models are not competitive but are instead oriented around different concerns. The choice of one model over the other as a research tool depends on the interests of the investigator.

1.6 Conclusion

The spatial theory of voting is based on the premise that voters and candidates are self-interested. Voters are interested in vote outcomes, and candidates are interested in votes. This type of theory is quite different from one that posits that voting behavior is caused by a set of conditioning forces. The first type of theory focuses on candidate or policy responsiveness to voter opinion, whereas the second is concerned with identifying the strengths of various agents in the voter's force field.

Now that we have illuminated the place of spatial models in voting research, we proceed to a formal development of the subject in order to give the reader a precise idea of what these models are all about.

CHAPTER 2

The unidimensional spatial voting model

Spatial voting models have been used in a variety of theoretical and empirical analyses of political phenomena. The model presented in this section has been used as a component in (1) models of committees and legislatures and (2) models of candidate or party competition in elections where the number of voters is large. In the first area of application, the issues are often measured in monetary terms, and the alternatives are specific amounts to be spent or collected. In the second area, the alternatives are candidates or political parties, and the "issues" are related to ideological factors. Strong assumptions about voter perceptions and attitudes are required to support the application of the spatial model of committees to the study of electoral competition. In order to postpone discussion of problems having to do with voter perceptions, the model is first presented using a committee voting example where the issue is the amount to be spent on a government project. The single-issue and multi-issue committee models are explained in Chapters 2 and 3. The model is expanded to study electoral competition in Chapters 4 and 5.

2.1 The median voter

A congressional appropriations subcommittee meets to decide the amount to be spent on a military construction project during the coming fiscal year. The subcommittee consists of five members: Messrs. A, B, C, D, and E. Mr. A is dissatisfied with the current funding level of $60 million and proposes to raise it to $120 million. Mr. B also wants to raise the funding level, but only to $100 million. Mr. C believes that the project contains a significant amount of waste and fraud and proposes to lower the appropriation to $30 million. Mr. D is skeptical of the entire project and prefers a $15 million appropriation for the coming year. Mr. E prefers to maintain spending at the status quo, $60 million. All the members have established their preferences prior to the meeting, and these preferences will not be altered by further discussion.

Suppose that the decisions of this subcommittee are determined by simple majority rule. Each member is free to make proposals, and each votes according to his own preferences. We shall overlook the sociological

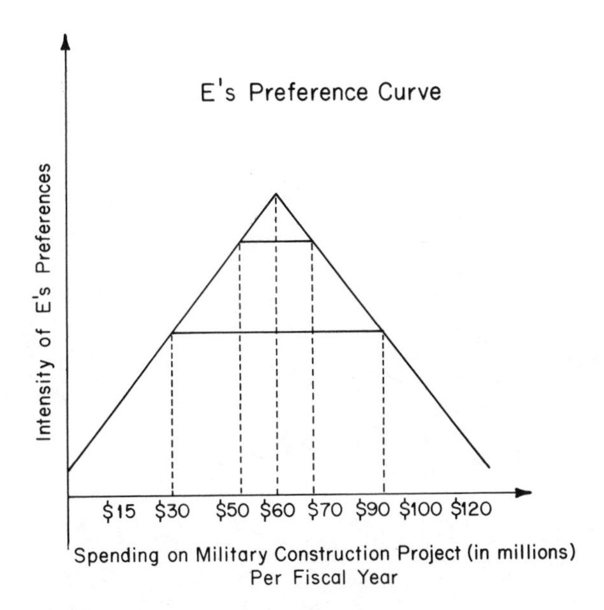

Figure 2.1. E's preference curve.

subtleties of committee decision processes to facilitate exposition of the simple median voter model.

Let us define E's preference rule first. His ideal position on the spending issue is 60 (million dollars). (Henceforth in this example, the alternatives will be stated in units of $1 million.) His preference for any other alternative (i.e., spending level) is given by the single peaked curve in Figure 2.1, which is assumed to be *symmetric* about the ideal point 60. In terms of the ideal points of the other four members, he prefers 30 to 100, 100 to 15, and 15 to 120. In other words, *the farther away an alternative is from his ideal point, the less preferred it is.* If two alternatives are equidistant from his ideal point, then he is *indifferent* between them. For example, E is indifferent between 30 and 90.

The preference curves of the other four members are shown in Figure 2.2. Each curve is also symmetric about the ideal point. Thus, C prefers 30 to 15, 15 to 60, 60 to 100, and 100 to 120. He is indifferent between 20 and 40 and between 15 and 45.

Suppose that B proposes to increase the spending level to y (million dollars); that is, $y > 60$. At most, two members out of five will prefer y to 60. If $140 > y > 60$, B and A prefer y to 60, whereas D, C, and E prefer 60 to y. Because we have assumed that all members vote according to their own preferences, the status quo wins a majority against y.

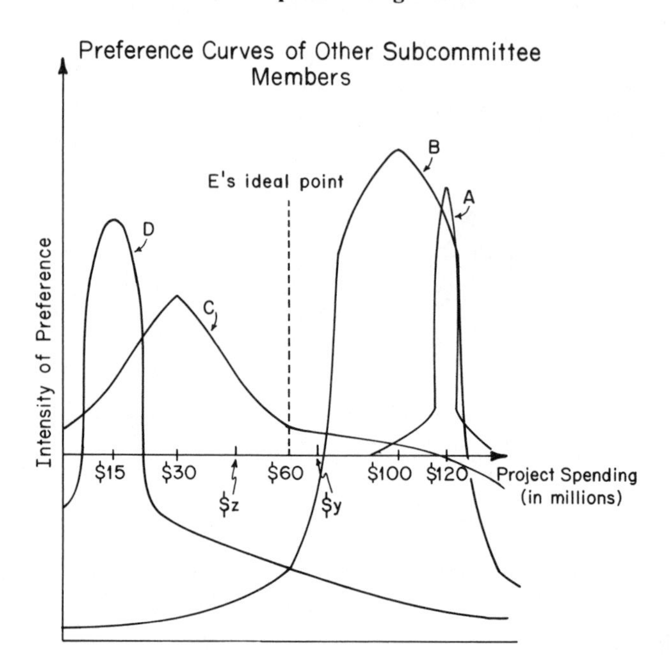

Figure 2.2. Preference curves of other subcommittee members.

Next, suppose that C proposes to decrease spending to some positive amount z; that is, $0<z<60$. Now only D and C prefer z to 60. E, B, and A prefer 60 to z, and thus 60 again wins a majority.

Even if the subcommittee members form coalitions, so long as each member votes according to his preferences, the status quo wins a majority against any other alternative. This is true even if the preference curves of members are not symmetric. So long as alternative spending levels on the same side of a member's ideal point are less preferred the farther away they are, 60 will win a majority against any other alternative.

This example serves as an introduction to an important result for majority rule decisions that involve a single issue. Suppose that a society composed of N members must decide on a collective position on a single issue and that each member votes according to his preferences. What can we say about the collective position they will adopt?

Let us now describe the preference rule of the ith member ($i=1,\ldots,N$). Assume that there exists a unique position x_i on the issue that i most prefers. This position is called the *ideal point* for voter i. Given two alternatives y and z, assume that either $y,z \geqslant x_i$ or $y,z \leqslant x_i$. Thus, y and z are on the same side of x_i. We assume that i prefers y to z if and only if

$$|y-x_i|<|z-x_i| \quad (2.1)$$

where the vertical bars denote the absolute (numerical) value of the difference. Further, if (2.1) describes i's preferences for y, z on different sides of x_i, then i's preferences are said to be *symmetric*. This is true of our subcommittee members.

If i's preferences are symmetric, then i is indifferent between y and z if and only if

$$|y-x_i|=|z-x_i| \quad (2.2)$$

If i's preferences are not symmetric, i will generally not be indifferent between two distinct alternatives equidistant from x_i. For symmetric preferences, i's preference rule is determined solely by the distances between the alternatives and x_i. The closer a position is to x_i, the more preferred it is by voter i. If preferences are not symmetric, preference is determined by distance only for alternatives on the same side of x_i.

We now must define the median position with respect to the set of voter ideal points $\{x_1, \ldots, x_N\}$ before we can present the median voter result. A position is a *median point* if there are at least $N/2$ ideal points to the right of it or equal to it and there are at least $N/2$ ideal points to the left of it or equal to it. In other words, x_{med} is a median point if $N_R \geqslant N/2$ and $N_L \geqslant N/2$, where N_R is the number of voters with $x_i \geqslant x_{\text{med}}$ and N_L is the number of voters with $x_i \leqslant x_{\text{med}}$. This definition is necessary if we want to encompass the cases in which N is odd, in which N is even, or in which there are several voters with the same ideal point. For the congressional subcommittee example, $x_{\text{med}}=60$, because three ideal points are greater than or equal to 60, three ideal points are less than or equal to 60, and $3>N/2=2\frac{1}{2}$. In this example, 60 is the only median point (i.e., there is a unique median point).

The median is not always unique. Suppose that E, whose ideal point is 60, is absent, and thus $N=4$. Then all the positions between 30 and 100 are medians. Consider, for example, $x=70$. There are $2=N/2$ ideal points greater than 70 and two less than 70. The end points of this interval (30 and 100) are also median points.

If N is odd, there is a voter whose ideal point is a unique median. For example, if $x_1=10$, $x_2=4$, $x_3=-2$, $x_4=0$, and $x_5=7$, then $x_{\text{med}}=x_2=4$ is a unique median for this five-person society. If N is even and no two voters have the same ideal position, there are two voters whose ideal points are the end points of a closed interval of medians. For example, if $x_1=-2$, $x_2=-5$, $x_3=1$, $x_4=0$, $x_5=10$, and $x_6=7$, then any point x in the interval $x_4=0 \leqslant x \leqslant 1=x_3$ is a median for this six-member society. If, however, two or more individuals share an ideal position, a unique

Table 2.1. *Median points in the unidimensional spatial model*

	Ideal points	
Voters	Not unique (shared)	Unique (not shared)
Odd number	Unique median point	Unique median point
Even number	Either unique median point or closed interval of median points	Closed interval of median points

median can exist when N is even. For example, if $x_1=2$, $x_2=x_4=3$, and $x_3=7$, then $x_{\text{med}}=3$ is a unique median for this four-member society. On the other hand, suppose for six voters that $x_1=1$, $x_2=2$, $x_3=3$, $x_4=x_5=4$, and $x_6=5$. Then an interval of medians exists, because any point x in the interval $x_3=3 \leqslant x \leqslant 4=x_4=x_5$ is a median point. Table 2.1 summarizes what we have shown. If N is odd but there is an even number of ideal points, a unique median point still exists. This statement can be proved by assuming an interval of median points and using the median voter result proved in Section 2.2 to show that N must be even. When the median is unique, $N_R>N/2$ and $N_L>N/2$; that is, there is a majority of ideal points to the right of or equal to x_{med} and a majority to the left of or equal to x_{med}.

We are now in a position to state and prove the median voter result. Then we shall state and prove a somewhat stronger result when the median is unique and voter preference curves are symmetric. Before stating the result, let us review the basic assumptions: (1) Single issue - the alternatives are points on a line. (2) Voting of preferences - given two alternatives y and z on the same side of x_i, individual i votes for y if and only if $|y-x_i|<|z-x_i|$.

2.2 Median voter result

Suppose y is a *median position* for the society. Then the number of votes for y is greater than or equal to the number of votes for any z. In other words, a median position cannot lose in a majority contest.

Proof: For sake of argument, let $z<y$. All ideal points to the right of y ($x_i>y$) are closer to y than z. Thus, because y and z are on the same side of x_i, the voters with these ideal points vote for y. All voters whose ideal points are equal to y vote for y. Because y is a median position, there are at least $N/2$ voters whose ideal points are greater than or equal to y. Thus the number of votes for y is at least $N/2$. The same proof holds if $z>y$.

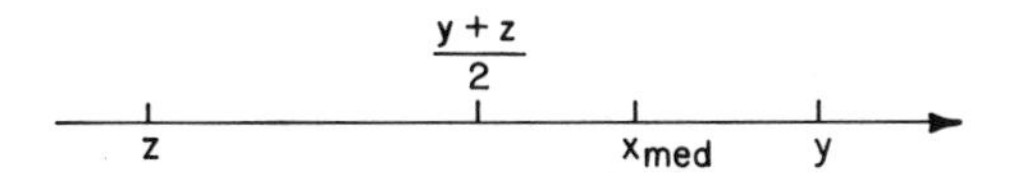

Figure 2.3. Midpoint between z and y.

2.3 Corollary to the median voter result

Suppose that there is a unique median x_{med} for the society and that preference curves are symmetric. If y is closer to x_{med} than z, then y wins a majority of the votes cast.

Proof: Once again, let $z<y$. Because y is closer to x_{med} than z, $(y+z)/2< x_{\text{med}}$ (Figure 2.3). This is true regardless of whether y and z straddle x_{med} or y and z are on the same side of x_{med}. The position $(y+z)/2$ is the point that is equidistant from y and z. Thus, all ideal points to the right of $(y+z)/2$ $[x_i>(y+z)/2]$ are closer to y than z, whereas all ideal points to the left of $(y+z)/2$ $[x_i<(y+z)/2]$ are closer to z than y.

Because x_{med} is unique, the number of ideal points to the right of x_{med} or equal to x_{med} is greater than $N/2$. These ideal points are closer to y than z, because $(y+z)/2<x_{\text{med}}$. Thus, because preferences are symmetric, y receives a majority of the votes.

This corollary is important. First, it shows under the stated conditions that the median wins a majority of the votes against any other alternative. Second, it shows that for any two points on the line, the point closest to the median wins a majority of the votes.

2.4 Conclusion

This short chapter presents basic concepts that are used throughout this book. The concept of preference as distance and the idea of preference-based voting have been defined. These ideas are generalized in the next chapter to allow preferences to be defined over more than a single issue.

The median voter result plays a very important role in spatial voting models. This result will also be generalized in the following chapter in the form of a median in all directions. However, additional assumptions are required for this generalized median to exist.

Problems

2.1 For a given issue, let $x_a=1$, $x_b=5$, $x_c=-2$, $x_d=-7$, and $x_e=7$ for a five-person committee. What is x_{med}?

2.2 Suppose that two alternatives are voted on by the foregoing committee: $y=2$ against $z=-1$. If preferences are symmetric, which alternative wins a majority?

2.3 Suppose that person c leaves the committee. What are the median positions for the remaining four persons?

2.4 (a) Suppose the remaining four vote on two alternatives: $y=2$ against $z=3$. What is the outcome of the vote?
(b) What is the outcome if z is changed to $z=-1$ and a's preferences are symmetric?

2.5 Suppose that the ideal spending level of the ith committee member is $2i$ $(i=1,\ldots,25)$. What is the median ideal spending level of the committee?

2.6 Suppose that no two individuals in a committee of n voters have the same ideal point (i.e., $x_i \neq x_j$ for all $i \neq j$). Prove that the median set is an interval if n is even.

2.7 Suppose that the preference functions of voters are not symmetric about their ideal points. This means that if y and z are on opposite sides of x_i, then i can prefer y to z or vice versa depending on the form of his preference function. To simplify the problem, suppose that the committee has an odd number of members, and thus x_{med} is unique. Show by example that an alternative y can win a majority over an alternative z even if z is closer to x_{med} than y is.

Bibliographical notes

The one-dimensional spatial model has a long history. Perhaps the earliest sources are Hotelling (1929) and Smithies (1941). Black is most responsible for the first applications of this theory to committee voting; the work contained in his papers published in the 1940s can be found in Black (1958). The application of this theory to party competition is the seminal contribution of Downs (1957). Later contributions to this theory are made by Brams (1978). Mueller (1979) also contains a discussion of the one-dimensional spatial voting model.

CHAPTER 3

A two-dimensional spatial model

Suppose that the subcommittee also has to decide the amount of spending for the upcoming fiscal year on a second project, one currently budgeted at $30 million. Member A also wants to raise the amount spent on this project, in order to finish it more quickly. He wants spending set at 100. B is afraid that such an increase would set a precedent for similar projects, and he favors a more modest increase to 50. C is satisfied to maintain the status quo. D prefers to set spending at 200, believing that any further delays in completing the project will lead to vast cost overruns. E prefers to set spending at 60. The ideal positions for the subcommittee members are summarized in Table 3.1, where the two projects are labeled in order of discussion.

It may be unreasonable to assume that the members' preferences about spending levels for these two projects are independent of one another. It may be that these two projects are perceived to some extent as duplicating each other, or that total costs on all projects are perceived as getting out of hand. Let us now model a joint preference rule for both spending issues. We shall continue to use letter subscripts to distinguish among subcommittee members, and we shall denote the two spending issues with subscripts 1 and 2 for the two projects. For example, A's ideal joint position for the two issues consists of $x_{a1}=120$ and $x_{a2}=100$. Viewing alternatives as points in a two-dimensional Euclidean space whose dimensions are the two issues, A's ideal point in this space is denoted $\mathbf{x}_a=(x_{a1}, x_{a2})=(120, 100)$. This point is the spending package that A most prefers. Any other point, such as the status quo package $(60, 30)$, is less preferred by him.

The key element of spatial models is the relationship between preference and distance. The simplest distance measure for a Euclidean space is Euclidean distance. The Euclidean distance between a point $\mathbf{y}=(y_1, y_2)$ and a point $\mathbf{z}=(z_1, z_2)$ is defined to be

$$\|\mathbf{y}-\mathbf{z}\|=[(y_1-z_1)^2+(y_2-z_2)^2]^{1/2} \tag{3.1}$$

where the superscript $\frac{1}{2}$ denotes the square root of the term in the square brackets. We shall use a generalization of this distance measure that we

Table 3.1. *Subcommittee ideal points*

	Spending on construction project 1 (in millions)	Spending on construction project 2 (in millions)
Mr. A	\$120	\$100
Mr. B	\$100	\$50
Mr. C	\$30	\$30
Mr. D	\$15	\$200
Mr. E	\$60	\$60
Status quo	\$60	\$30

call *weighted Euclidean distance* (WED). The WED between $\mathbf{y}$ and $\mathbf{z}$ is defined to be

$$\|\mathbf{y}-\mathbf{z}\|_A=[a_{11}(y_1-z_1)^2+2a_{12}(y_1-z_1)(y_2-z_2)+a_{22}(y_2-z_2)^2]^{1/2} \qquad (3.2)$$

where we require $a_{11}>0$, $a_{22}>0$, and $a_{12}^2<a_{11}a_{22}$ to ensure that $\|\mathbf{y}-\mathbf{z}\|_A>0$ for all $\mathbf{y}\neq\mathbf{z}$. The subscript A on $\|\mathbf{y}-\mathbf{z}\|_A$ denotes the set of parameters (a_{11}, a_{12}, a_{22}). For those readers familiar with matrix notation, A is the matrix

$$\begin{bmatrix} a_{11} & a_{12} \\ a_{12} & a_{22} \end{bmatrix}$$

If $a_{11}=a_{22}=1$ and $a_{12}=0$ ($A=I$, the 2×2 identity matrix), then $\|\mathbf{y}-\mathbf{z}\|_A=\|\mathbf{y}-\mathbf{z}\|$, from (3.1) and (3.2). Thus, WED is a generalization of simple Euclidean distance.

It is important to point out that WED defines a symmetric preference rule. In two dimensions, symmetry means that if two points $\mathbf{y}$ and $\mathbf{z}$ lie on a line passing through the voter's ideal point and are equidistant (in simple Euclidean distance) from this ideal point, then $\mathbf{y}$ and $\mathbf{z}$ are equally preferred by the voter.

3.1 Weighted Euclidean distance preference rule

Returning to the preferences of the subcommittee members, let us first define B's preference rule. Assume that he prefers $\mathbf{y}=(y_1, y_2)$ to $\mathbf{z}=(z_1, z_2)$ if and only if $\|\mathbf{y}-\mathbf{x}_b\|_{A_b}<\|\mathbf{z}-\mathbf{x}_b\|_{A_b}$, where $\mathbf{x}_b=(100, 50)$ is his ideal point and the parameters of A_b are a_{b11}, a_{b22}, and a_{b12}. In other words, the closer (in WED) an alternative is to his ideal point, the more he prefers it. As a consequence of this assumption, he is indifferent between all points $\mathbf{x}=(x_1, x_2)$ that lie on the curve $\|\mathbf{x}-\mathbf{x}_b\|_{A_b}=c$, where c

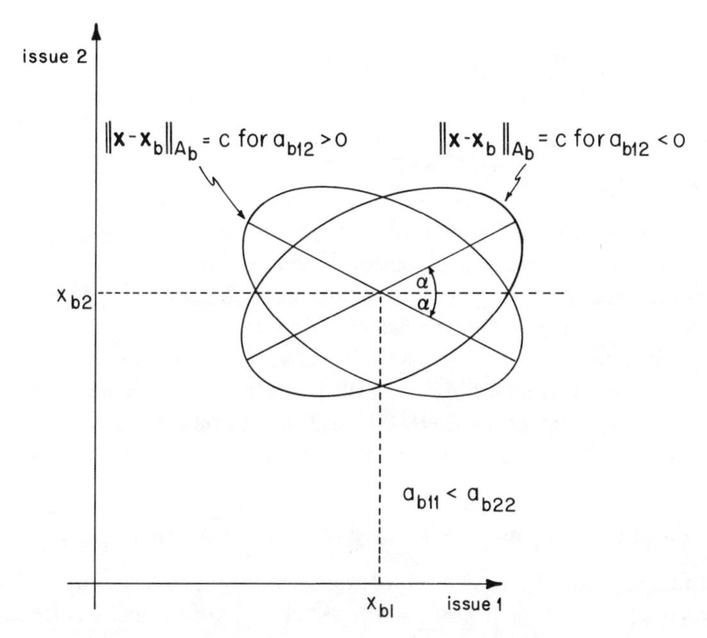

Figure 3.1. Indifference contour for a given c.

is a positive constant. Because $a_{b12}^2 < a_{b11} a_{b22}$, this curve is an ellipse centered at $\mathbf{x}_b = (x_{b1}, x_{b2})$ in the plane whose coordinates are the two issues. The "roundness" and orientation of the ellipse depend on the values of a_{b11}, a_{b22}, and a_{b12}. For example, suppose that $a_{b11} < a_{b22}$. Then the long (major) axis of the ellipse is inclined to the issue-1 axis at an angle α such that $\tan 2\alpha = -2a_{b12}/(a_{b22} - a_{b11})$ and $-45° < \alpha < 45°$. Thus, if $a_{b12} < 0$, the major axis lies along a SW-to-NE ray (Figure 3.1). If $a_{b12} > 0$, the major axis lies along a SE-to-NW ray. The ellipses shown in Figure 3.1 hold with issue 1 relabeled as issue 2 and vice versa if $a_{b11} > a_{b22}$.

In order to provide some intuitive meaning to the parameters a_{b11} and a_{b22}, consider two alternatives: $\mathbf{y} = (x_{b1} + 1, x_{b2})$ and $\mathbf{w} = (x_{b1}, x_{b2} + 1)$. From (3.2),

$$\|\mathbf{y} - \mathbf{x}_b\|_{A_b} = a_{b11}^{1/2} \tag{3.3}$$

and

$$\|\mathbf{w} - \mathbf{x}_b\|_{A_b} = a_{b22}^{1/2}$$

If $a_{b11} < a_{b22}$, it follows from (3.2) that $\|\mathbf{y} - \mathbf{x}_b\|_{A_b} < \|\mathbf{w} - \mathbf{x}_b\|_{A_b}$, and thus B prefers $\mathbf{y}$ to $\mathbf{w}$. In other words, when $a_{b11} < a_{b22}$, B prefers raising the spending level for project 1 by a dollar (or a million dollars) rather than raising the spending level on project 2 by the same amount. Similarly, B prefers $(x_{b1}-1, x_{b2})$ to $(x_{b1}, x_{b2}-1)$. These preferences hold for any value of a_{b12}. We then say that issue 2 is more salient for B than is issue 1 if $a_{b11} < a_{b22}$.

If $a_{b11} > a_{b22}$, then B prefers **w** to **y** and $(x_{b1}, x_{b2}-1)$ to $(x_{b1}-1, x_{b2})$. In this case, issue 1 is more salient for B.

To understand the meaning of the parameter a_{b12}, consider B's preferences for various amounts of spending on project 2 when spending on project 1 is fixed at some value. Suppose that spending on project 1 remains at the status quo, namely 60. What is B's ideal spending level on project 2 given that $x_1=60$? The answer seems to be 50, because $\mathbf{x}_b=(100, 50)$ is his ideal point in the space. But $\mathbf{x}_b$ is his ideal *package,* and unless $a_{b12}=0$, his ideal spending level on project 2 will depend on the fact that spending on project 1 is 60. His preferences on one issue cannot be separated from his preferences on the other unless $a_{b12}=0$.

3.2 Separability and nonseparability of voter preferences

Suppose that $a_{b12} \neq 0$. We wish to find the spending level on project 2, denoted $x_{b2}(60)$, that B most prefers when spending on project 1 is fixed at 60. Because B's preference for a package $(60, x_2)$ increases as the weighted Euclidean distance between $(60, x_2)$ and $\mathbf{x}_b$ decreases, $x_{b2}(60)$ is the value of x_2 that minimizes the function

$$f(x_2)=[a_{b11}(60-x_{b1})^2+2a_{b12}(60-x_{b1})(x_2-x_{b2})+a_{b22}(x_2-x_{b2})^2]^{1/2}$$

where $x_{b1}=100$ and $x_{b2}=50$. This minimization problem is most easily solved using elementary calculus to find the value of x_2 that minimizes the squared distance $f^2(x_2)$. The unique answer in terms of B's preference parameters is

$$x_{b2}(60)=x_{b2}-\frac{a_{b12}}{a_{b22}}(60-x_{b1}) \tag{3.4}$$

Let us study (3.4) using several numerical examples. First, let $a_{b22}=1$ and $a_{b12}=\frac{1}{2}$. Then

$$x_{b2}(60)=50-\tfrac{1}{2}(60-100)=70$$

Given that spending on project 1 is set 40 less than the spending level in his ideal package, he wants 20 more than the spending level for project 2 in his ideal package. On the other hand, if $a_{b22}=10$ and $a_{b12}=\frac{1}{2}$, then $x_{b2}(60)=50-(1/20)(60-100)=52$. The larger a_{b22} is relative to a_{b12}, the smaller the shift from his package ideal spending level for project 2.

The sign of a_{b12} determines the direction of this shift. Suppose that

$a_{b22}=1$ and $a_{b12}=-\frac{1}{2}$. Then $x_{b2}(60)=50+\frac{1}{2}(60-100)=30$. In this case he wants 20 less than his package ideal spending level for project 2. If $a_{b22}=10$ and $a_{b12}=-\frac{1}{2}$, $x_{b2}(60)=48$.

There is nothing special about 60. If the spending level on project 1 is fixed at x_1, then B's conditional ideal spending level on project 2 is given by

$$x_{b2}(x_1)=x_{b2}-\frac{a_{b12}}{a_{b22}}(x_1-x_{b1}) \tag{3.5}$$

Conversely, his conditional ideal spending level on project 1 if the spending level on project 2 is fixed at x_2 is

$$x_{b1}(x_2)=x_{b1}-\frac{a_{b12}}{a_{b11}}(x_2-x_{b2}) \tag{3.6}$$

Now let us derive B's preferences for spending on project 2 when spending on project 1 is fixed at a value x_1. Suppose that B is forced to choose between two packages containing the same project-1 spending level x_1 and different project-2 spending levels: $\mathbf{y}=(x_1,y_2)$ and $\mathbf{z}=(x_1,z_2)$. From the preference rule previously defined, B prefers $\mathbf{y}$ to $\mathbf{z}$ if and only if $\|\mathbf{y}-\mathbf{x}_b\|_{A_b}<\|\mathbf{z}-\mathbf{x}_b\|_{A_b}$. Substituting for x_{b2} from (3.5), straightforward algebraic manipulation of the terms in (3.2) (see Problem 3.1 at end of chapter) yields

$$\|\mathbf{y}-\mathbf{x}_b\|_{A_b}^2=c_b+a_{b22}[y_2-x_{b2}(x_1)]^2 \tag{3.7a}$$

where the constant c_b is defined by $c_b=(a_{b11}-a_{b12}^2/a_{b22})(x_1-x_{b1})^2$. Similarly,

$$\|\mathbf{z}-\mathbf{x}_b\|_{A_b}^2=c_b+a_{b22}[z_2-x_{b2}(x_1)]^2 \tag{3.7b}$$

and consequently B prefers y_2 to z_2 if and only if y_2 is closer than z_2 to his conditional ideal point $x_{b2}(x_1)$. The preference rule for spending on project 2 given x_1 is symmetric and single-peaked about $x_{b2}(x_1)$.

The parameter a_{b22} is the *salience* of project-2 spending to B. The smaller the value of a_{b22}, the less he cares about a given dollar difference between a proposed project-2 spending level and his conditional ideal point. Exchanging 2s for 1s in the subscripts, a_{b11} is the salience of project-1 spending to B when project-2 spending is fixed. The parameter a_{b12} gives the magnitude of interaction of these spending issues in B's preference rule.

When $a_{b12}=0$, $x_{b1}(x_2)=x_{b1}$ and $x_{b2}(x_1)=x_{b2}$. The WED between any $\mathbf{y}$ and $\mathbf{x}_b$ is simply $[a_{b11}(y_1-x_{b1})^2+a_{b22}(y_2-x_{b2})^2]^{1/2}$. There is no interaction between the issues when $a_{b12}=0$. The preference rule is called *separable* in this case.

We have concentrated on Mr. B to simplify exposition. The foregoing expressions hold for the other voters with the subscript b replaced by a, c, and so forth. We have discussed preferences on one issue given a fixed position on the other in order to illuminate the nature of the WED preference rule. In the next section we show that the median voter result becomes complicated when issues are voted on sequentially and voter preferences are not separable.

3.3 Voting one issue at a time

Suppose that the subcommittee decides to separate the issues and vote on them sequentially. We shall now show by example that the order in which the issues are voted affects the outcome when some members have nonseparable preferences. To simplify matters, let $a_{a11}=a_{a22}=a_{b11}=a_{b22}=\cdots=a_{e11}=a_{e22}=1$. Let $a_{b12}=-0.9$ and $a_{e12}=0.9$, whereas $a_{a12}=a_{c12}=a_{d12}=0$. Only B and E have nonseparable preferences.

Suppose that project-1 spending is voted on first, and then project-2 spending. Recalling expression (3.6), we see that we have to specify B's forecast of the outcome on the second vote (project-2 spending) if we are to compute B's conditional ideal point for project-1 spending. This poses a serious complication, because the median ideal point on the first issue also depends on E's forecast. At this point we make an arbitrary assumption about the forecasts in order to compute the median points. Later, in Chapter 8, we shall return to the subject of voter forecasts to offer a formal solution to this problem.

Let us begin by making the arbitrary assumption that both B and E believe that the status quo value of 30 will be the outcome of the second vote. We do not have to make any assumptions about the other three members, because their preferences on the issues are separable. Dropping the dollar signs, B's conditional ideal point for project-1 spending is

$$x_{b1}(30)=100+0.9(30-50)$$
$$=82$$

(consult Table 3.1). E's conditional ideal point on this issue is

$$x_{e1}(30)=60-0.9(30-60)$$
$$=87$$

The ideal points for the subcommittee for spending on project 1 are 15, 30, 82, 87, and 120. The median is 82, B's conditional ideal point, which is 22 more than the status quo spending level. This median value will be the outcome of the vote, because the conditions for the median voter result are met.

In the next vote, B and E know that project-1 spending has been set at 82. B's conditional ideal point for project-2 spending is

$$\begin{aligned} x_{b2}(82) &= 50 + 0.9(82 - 100) \\ &= 33.8 \end{aligned}$$

E's conditional ideal point is

$$\begin{aligned} x_{e2}(82) &= 60 - 0.9(82 - 60) \\ &= 40.2 \end{aligned}$$

The ideal points for spending on project 2 are 30, 33.8, 40.2, 100, and 200. The median is then 40.2. This is 10.2 more than the status quo on this issue.

Let us contrast these outcomes with the results obtained when project-2 is voted on first. Once again, assume that B and E believe that the status quo of 60 will not be overturned on the second vote (project-1 spending). B's conditional ideal point is

$$\begin{aligned} x_{b2}(60) &= 50 + 0.9(60 - 100) \\ &= 14 \end{aligned}$$

E's conditional ideal point is

$$\begin{aligned} x_{e2}(60) &= 60 - 0.9(60 - 60) \\ &= 60 \end{aligned}$$

The ideal points for project-2 spending are 14, 30, 60, 100, and 200. The median is then 60, which is 19.8 more than the level of spending that was voted using the other sequence.

For the project-1 vote, B's conditional ideal point is

$$\begin{aligned} x_{b1}(60) &= 100 + 0.9(60 - 50) \\ &= 109 \end{aligned}$$

E's conditional ideal point is

$$\begin{aligned} x_{e1}(60) &= 60 - 0.9(60 - 60) \\ &= 60 \end{aligned}$$

The ideal points are 15, 30, 60, 109, and 120, with a median of 60. In this case, the status quo spending level on project 1 is not changed. We have thus provided an example in which the order of voting matters.

The project-2–project-1 voting sequence for this example has a special stability property. Suppose that some member proposes that they vote again on project-2 spending. Because the status quo spending level on project 1 was not changed, the conditional ideal points of B and E on project 2 are the same as before. Thus, the median project-2 spending level remains at 60.

Contrast this stability with the result when the subcommittee revotes project-1 spending after the project-1–project-2 sequence. Project-2 spending has been set at 40.2. B's conditional ideal point for project-1 spending is

$$x_{b1}(40.2) = 100 + 0.9(40.2 - 50)$$
$$= 91.18$$

E's conditional ideal point is

$$x_{e1}(40.2) = 60 - 0.9(40.2 - 60)$$
$$= 77.82$$

The ideal points are 15, 30, 77.82, 91.18, and 120. The median is then 77.82, and thus spending on project 1 is reduced from the previous value of 82. We have once again shown that the voting sequence affects the outcome.

There are, however, cases in which the outcomes are independent of the voting sequence. For example, (3.5) and (3.6) demonstrate that the voting sequence is irrelevant if all subcommittee members have separable preferences. In this case, the outcome on each issue is the median ideal point on that issue.

Chapter 8 will return to this important subject of voting one issue at a time. For now, we wish to show how the a_{12} interaction term in the voter's preferences can affect this type of voting. The median voter result of Chapter 2 is not as simple as when only one issue is being decided.

3.4 Voting on two issues simultaneously

We have seen that when voting takes place one issue at a time and all voters have separable preferences, the voting sequence is irrelevant to the outcome. Regardless of whether project-1 or project-2 spending is voted on first, the outcome of each vote will always be the unique median ideal point on each issue (assuming the number of voters is odd). The question we now wish to pursue is whether or not this same result obtains when voting takes place on both issues simultaneously. Suppose it is admissible to introduce proposals that seek to change both project-1 and project-2 spending levels. Assuming that each committee member has separable preferences (i.e., $a_{12} = 0$), will the outcome of the voting always be the median ideal point on each issue [i.e., $\mathbf{x}_{med} = (x_{med1}, x_{med2})$]?

For simplicity, let us reconstitute our subcommittee with three members: j, k, and l. Further, let $a_{j12} = a_{k12} = a_{l12} = 0$ and $a_{j11} = a_{j22} = a_{k11} = a_{k22} = a_{l11} = a_{l22} = 1$, so that each member has *circular indifference contours*. This means that preference is based on simple Euclidean distance.

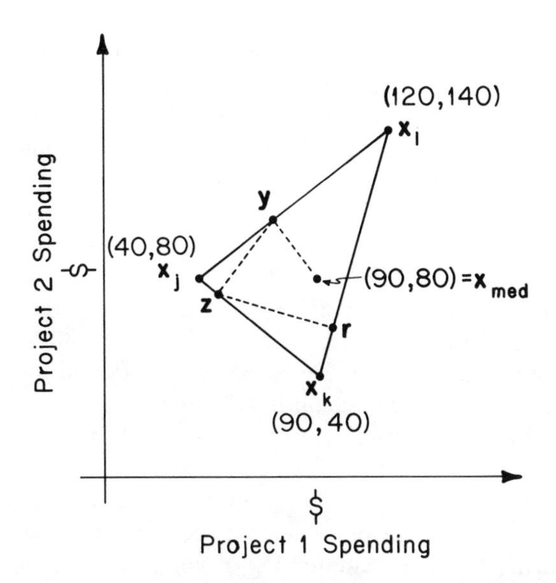

Figure 3.2. Voting on two issues simultaneously.

Also, let $\mathbf{x}_j = (40, 80)$, $\mathbf{x}_k = (90, 40)$, and $\mathbf{x}_l = (120, 140)$, so that $\mathbf{x}_{\text{med}} = (90, 80)$. Now suppose that $\mathbf{x}_{\text{med}}$ is the status quo, but that each member is free to propose any $\mathbf{y} = (y_1, y_2)$, given only that a majority must prefer $\mathbf{y}$ to $\mathbf{x}_{\text{med}}$ for it to be adopted. We know that when voting takes place one issue at a time, no proposal is preferred by a majority to $\mathbf{x}_{\text{med}}$ and that $\mathbf{x}_{\text{med}}$ is preferred by a majority to all other proposals, because the number of voters is odd. However, we are no longer limiting the subcommittee members to proposals that seek to alter only project-1 or project-2 spending. They are now free to propose simultaneous alterations of spending on both projects.

Suppose that member j proposes $\mathbf{y} = (72, 104)$ in place of $\mathbf{x}_{\text{med}} = (90, 80)$; $\mathbf{y}$ is the point of intersection between the line connecting $\mathbf{x}_j$ and $\mathbf{x}_l$ and the line perpendicular to this line containing the point $\mathbf{x}_{\text{med}}$ (Figure 3.2). The line connecting $\mathbf{x}_j$ and $\mathbf{x}_l$ is called the *contract curve* for j and l. It contains all the proposals that are *Pareto optimal* for j and l. This means that for any point not on this line, there is a point on the line preferred by both j and l.

If $\mathbf{y}$ is voted on against $\mathbf{x}_{\text{med}}$, it is clear that $\|\mathbf{x}_j - \mathbf{y}\| < \|\mathbf{x}_j - \mathbf{x}_{\text{med}}\|$ and that $\|\mathbf{x}_l - \mathbf{y}\| < \|\mathbf{x}_l - \mathbf{x}_{\text{med}}\|$, and so j and l prefer $\mathbf{y}$ to $\mathbf{x}_{\text{med}}$ (k prefers $\mathbf{x}_{\text{med}}$ to $\mathbf{y}$). Thus, $\mathbf{y}$ beats $\mathbf{x}_{\text{med}}$ in a majority contest, proving that $\mathbf{x}_{\text{med}}$ is not unbeatable when proposals are offered that differ from $\mathbf{x}_{\text{med}}$ on more than one issue.

Does this imply that $\mathbf{y}$ will be the subcommittee's ultimate choice? To the contrary, suppose that k makes a counterproposal. Dropping a line from $\mathbf{y}$ perpendicular to the line connecting $\mathbf{x}_j$ and $\mathbf{x}_k$, the point of intersection, rounded off to the nearest million dollars, is $\mathbf{z}=(48,74)$ (Figure 3.2). This point is closer to $\mathbf{x}_j$ and $\mathbf{x}_k$ than is $\mathbf{y}$. Thus, if k proposes $\mathbf{z}$, and it is voted on against $\mathbf{y}$, j and k prefer $\mathbf{z}$ to $\mathbf{y}$, so $\mathbf{z}$ is adopted.

By this point it should be clear that this process can be continued indefinitely. Dropping a line from $\mathbf{z}$ perpendicular to the line connecting $\mathbf{x}_k$ and $\mathbf{x}_l$, the point of intersection is $\mathbf{r}$ (Figure 3.2). Because $\mathbf{r}$ is closer to $\mathbf{x}_k$ and $\mathbf{x}_l$ than is $\mathbf{z}$, $\mathbf{r}$ is preferred to $\mathbf{z}$ by k and l. In fact, $\mathbf{x}_{\text{med}}$ is preferred to $\mathbf{z}$ by k and l, so there exists a majority rule cycle among $\mathbf{x}_{\text{med}}$, $\mathbf{y}$, and $\mathbf{z}$. In any event, by the same method that $\mathbf{r}$ was selected, a point can be found that beats $\mathbf{r}$, and this process can be continued indefinitely.

This result has disturbing consequences for our model. When issues were voted on separately, we found that separability of voter preferences was sufficient to produce a simple result. If $\mathbf{x}_{\text{med}}$, the vector of median ideal points, is paired against any other proposal, $\mathbf{x}_{\text{med}}$ cannot be beaten in a majority contest. Further, with an odd number of voters, the vector of median ideal points is always preferred by a majority to every other proposal. However, once both issues are voted on simultaneously, $\mathbf{x}_{\text{med}}$ possesses no such properties; $\mathbf{x}_{\text{med}}$ can be beaten in a majority contest, and furthermore there may exist no proposal that cannot be beaten. Because circular indifference contours are a special case of the more general elliptical contours, it is clear that this result is a general problem for the multidimensional spatial model.

3.5 Stability in multidimensional voting

At this point there are at least two questions to be asked. First, is there some distribution of voter ideal points for which no other proposal receives the support of a majority against $\mathbf{x}_{\text{med}}$? Second, when voter ideal points are distributed as in Figure 3.2, is there anything we can say about the proposal that is likely to emerge after a voting sequence has ended?

Let us start with the first question. Figure 3.3 shows a four-member committee represented by the voter ideal points $\mathbf{x}_1, \ldots, \mathbf{x}_4$. As before, we shall assume for simplicity that each member has circular indifference contours, and thus preference is judged by simple Euclidean distance. For an even number N of voters, a majority is $N/2+1$, so that at least three of the four voters must prefer one proposal to another for it to be victorious in a pairwise contest.

Examine the proposal $\mathbf{y}$ in Figure 3.3, and note that it is equidistant from each voter's ideal point. Note further that if each voter's indiffer-

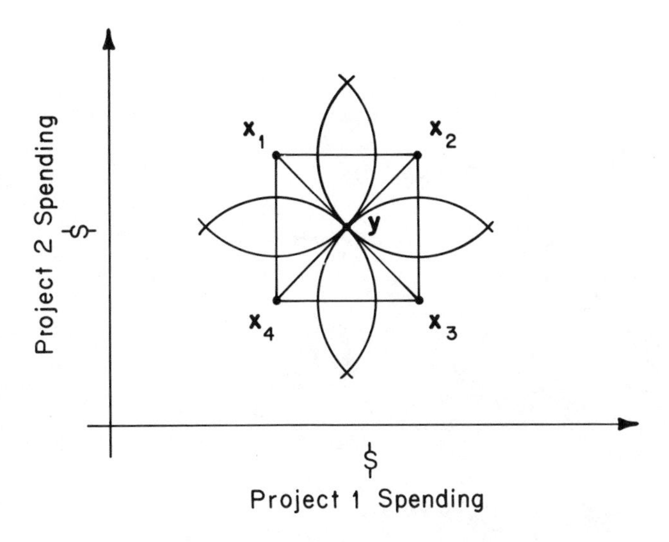

Figure 3.3. A four-member committee with a dominant point.

ence curve containing the point **y** is drawn, it is a simple geometric observation that each alternative proposal to **y** is *at most* in the interior of two of these indifference curves. In other words, there is no proposal that can beat **y** in a majority contest. Because it has this property, we shall call **y** a *dominant point*.

To satisfy ourselves that **y** is the only dominant point in Figure 3.3, we draw a line to connect each pair of ideal points. As mentioned earlier, each line contains all points that are Pareto optimal for the two voters whose ideal points are connected. Similarly, each triangle for which any three ideal points are the vertices contains all points that are Pareto optimal for those three voters. In other words, for any point outside the triangle $\mathbf{x}_1 \mathbf{x}_2 \mathbf{x}_3$ there is a point either on one of the sides of the triangle or in its interior that is preferred by voters 1, 2, and 3. Such a triangle will be termed a *Pareto set*. Now, observe that the four triangles constituting the Pareto sets for all four three-member subsets of N have one common point: **y**. In other words, every point other than **y** is exterior to some Pareto set for a majority of the committee. Thus, **y** is the only dominant point in Figure 3.3.

The existence of a dominant point **y** in Figure 3.3 is reassuring, but what is there about the distribution of these ideal points that creates this dominant point? The answer would seem to be a rather severe form of symmetry. Most important, it is possible to divide the voters into pairs such that the contract curve for each pair passes through the dominant

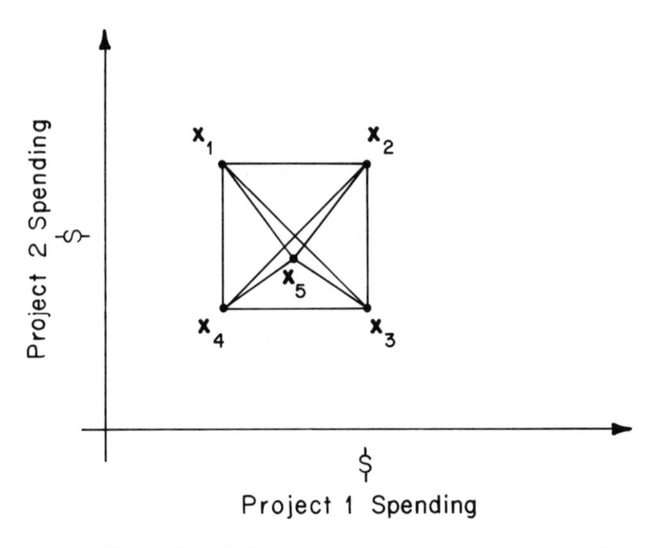

Figure 3.4. A five-member committee without a dominant point.

point. This requirement may not seem difficult to satisfy for a four-member committee. But if a fifth voter is added to the committee in Figure 3.3, the symmetry requirement becomes difficult to satisfy. The ideal point of the fifth voter must be located at the intersection of the contract curves for the two pairs of voters. In other words, the dominant point must also be the fifth voter's ideal point.

To see that this is true, consider the five-voter example in Figure 3.4, where, as before, all voters have circular indifference contours. The ideal point of the fifth voter, $\mathbf{x}_5$, is located slightly below the intersection of the pair of contract curves between voters 1 and 3 and between voters 2 and 4. The Pareto sets for all three-member majority subsets of the committee are simply the 10 triangles constructed by using the ideal points of each three-member subset as vertexes. The nonexistence of a dominant point is established by the simple observation that there is no point common to all 10 Pareto sets. Thus, $\mathbf{x}_5$, for example, is exterior to the Pareto sets for voters 1, 2, and 3 and for voters 1, 2, and 4. Thus, by definition, there exists a point in either Pareto set that is preferred by all three voters to $\mathbf{x}_5$, and thus $\mathbf{x}_5$ is not a dominant point.[1] The same argument can be used for any other point that might be considered, and so every point in

[1] A point that defeats $\mathbf{x}_5$ can easily be found by dropping a perpendicular line from $\mathbf{x}_5$ to the contract curve between either voters 2 and 4 or 1 and 3. The point of intersection is closer to the two voters on whose contract curve it lies, because it is the vertex of a right triangle and is obviously closer to the third voter (either 1 or 2).

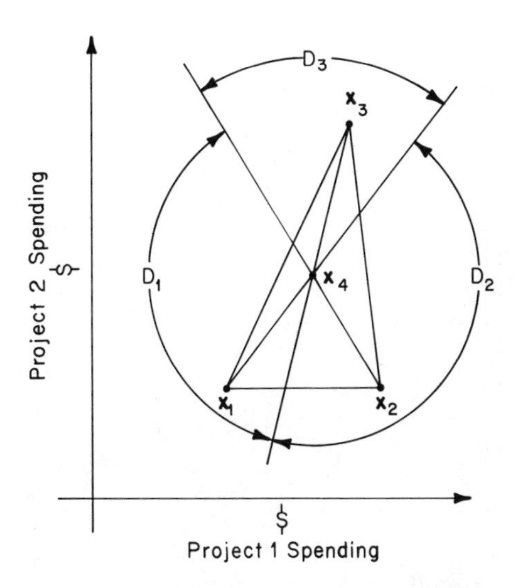

Figure 3.5. A dominant point without ideal point symmetry.

the space is defeated by some other point in a majority contest, thus establishing the nonexistence of a dominant point.

Figure 3.5 illustrates that the type of ideal-point symmetry exhibited in Figure 3.3 is not always necessary for the existence of a dominant point; $\mathbf{x}_4$ is a dominant point, but it is not possible to divide the voters into pairs such that the contract curve for each pair passes through $\mathbf{x}_4$. Thus, the ideal-point symmetry of Figure 3.3 is not necessary for a dominant point to exist. For an even number of voters, this pairwise symmetry requirement must be satisfied only if no voter's ideal point is a dominant point. For an odd number of voters, the pairwise symmetry requirement is necessary only if one voter's ideal point is a dominant point.

3.6 A median in all directions

This raises the question of what the necessary and sufficient conditions are for the existence of a dominant point. Let us redraw in Figure 3.6 the four-member committee of Figure 3.3 with its dominant point **y**. Now consider any point other than **y**, such as **z**. The set of all points equidistant from both **y** and **z** constitutes the straight line *aa*, which is the perpendicular bisector of the line joining **y** and **z**. In other words, any point on *aa* is just as far from **y** as from **z**. Further, any point on the **y** side of *aa* is closer to **y** than to **z**, whereas every point on the **z** side of *aa* is closer to **z** than to **y**. Thus, $\mathbf{x}_1$ and $\mathbf{x}_2$ are closer to **y** than to **z**, and $\mathbf{x}_3$ and $\mathbf{x}_4$ are

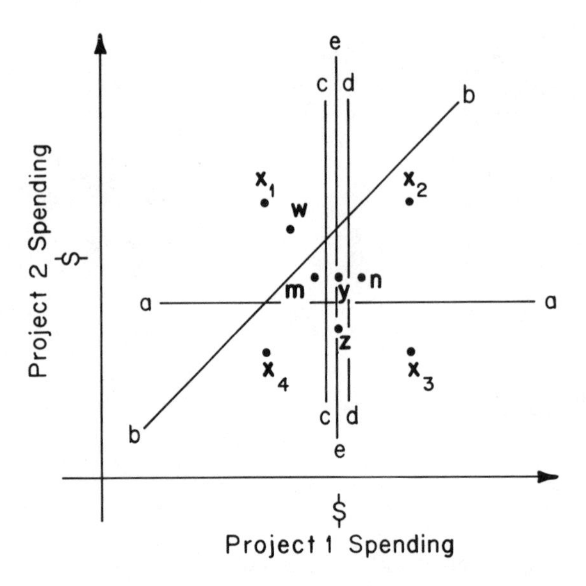

Figure 3.6. A median in all directions.

closer to **z** than to **y**. Because each committee member's preference is based on simple Euclidean distance, this is equivalent to saying that members 1 and 2 prefer **y** to **z** and members 3 and 4 prefer **z** to **y**. Thus, **z** ties **y**, but neither is preferred by a majority to the other.

If we were to pick a point other than **z** to compare with **y**, we could determine the preferences of the committee members in the same fashion. Thus, if **w** were selected, the line *bb*, which is the perpendicular bisector of the line **wy**, divides the committee into three groups: those on the **w** side of *bb* who prefer **w** to **y**, those on *bb* who are indifferent, and those on the **y** side of *bb* who prefer **y** to **w**. Clearly, member 1 falls in the first group, no one falls in the second group, and members 2, 3, and 4 fall in the last group, so a strict majority prefers **y** to **w**. Henceforth we shall call a line that divides the voters into these three preference classes with respect to two points such as **w** and **y** the **wy** *indifference line* (or *hyperplane*, more generally, when there are more than two issues).

Now, because **y** is a dominant point, it should be clear that no matter what point we pick to compare with **y**, such as **w**, a majority of ideal points will never lie on the **w** side of the **wy** indifference line. In other words, there must be at least as many ideal points on the **y** side of the **wy** indifference line as on the **w** side. Further, this must be true for every **w** that we might select. For example, we might pick two points such as **m** and **n** that are on directly opposite sides of **y** (Figure 3.6), and it must be true that at least as many ideal points are on the **y** side of the **yn** indifference line (*dd*) as are on the **n** side and that at least as many ideal points are on the **y** side of the **ym** indifference line (*cc*) as are on the **m** side. Now, if **m** and **n** are picked closer and closer to **y**, it is clear that in the limit *cc* and *dd* will both approach *ee*, so that for **y** to be a dominant point at least half the total number of ideal points must be on both sides of *ee* (with *ee* being included in each side).

Because **m** and **n** might have been selected from any line passing through **y**, *ee* might also be any line passing through **y** (perpendicular to the line **mn**). Thus, we are left with the conclusion that if **y** is a dominant point, every line passing through **y** must divide the member ideal points so that at least half are on either side of the line (with the line itself being included in each side). We call a point with this property a *median in all directions*. Thus, we see that if **y** is a dominant point, it must be a median in all directions.[2] The converse is obviously true, so we have established the sufficiency and necessity of this condition.[3] Note, however, that unlike the ideal-point symmetry condition, this condition is defined on the dominant point itself. What condition(s) the distribution of ideal points must satisfy in order for a median in all directions to exist is an open question.

As shown by Figure 3.5, ideal-point symmetry is not required for a median in all directions to exist. It is clearly impossible to pair the ideal points in Figure 3.5 so that the contract curve for each pair passes through $\mathbf{x}_4$ or, indeed, any common point. Even so, $\mathbf{x}_4$ remains a dominant point under a broad set of conditions. Suppose, for instance, that $\mathbf{x}_1$ is moved to any point in D_1, the set of all points on the $\mathbf{x}_1$ side of both the line passing through $\mathbf{x}_2$ and $\mathbf{x}_4$ and the line through $\mathbf{x}_3$ and $\mathbf{x}_4$ (the two lines being included on both sides). D_1 is shaped like a cone with its vertex at $\mathbf{x}_4$, but it is not bounded on all sides (Figure 3.5). It can be seen in Figure 3.5 that if the remaining three ideal points are fixed, $\mathbf{x}_1$ can be moved to any point in D_1, and $\mathbf{x}_4$ will still be a dominant point. In fact, the same argument applies if $\mathbf{x}_2$ is moved anywhere in D_2 or $\mathbf{x}_3$ anywhere in D_3 (D_2 and D_3 are defined in the same way as D_1, with $\mathbf{x}_4$ as a common vertex). Thus, the existence of a dominant point does not generally depend on a rigid ideal-point distribution.

We have now dealt with the question of the existence of a dominant

[2] Clearly, a median in all directions must be a median for each issue. However, if $\mathbf{x}_{\text{med}}$ is not unique, then every $\mathbf{x}_{\text{med}}$ need not be a median in all directions, when one exists. However, if $\mathbf{x}_{\text{med}}$ is unique, and a median in all directions exists, the two are identical.

[3] It is important to note that a more stringent condition, the existence of a "generalized total median," is necessary and sufficient for the existence of a dominant point if voter indifference contours are not circular and have varying shapes (Hoyer and Mayer, 1974).

point. The second question asked earlier deals with the expected outcome of a sequence of pairwise votes when a dominant point does not exist. Before taking up this question, however, it is important to note that the concept of a dominant point is a static one. If a dominant point exists, all that we are guaranteed is that no other point can beat it in a pairwise majority contest. This does not mean that a dominant point beats all others. In Figure 3.3, where the number of voters is even, $\mathbf{y}$ is tied by an infinite number of points, so that if one of these points were the status quo and $\mathbf{y}$ were proposed as an alternative to it, $\mathbf{y}$ would not beat the status quo. Further, it is possible that $\mathbf{y}$ is never proposed. However, in this case, if $\mathbf{x}_{\text{med}}$ is unique and is a median in all directions, we have the following result: If a point $\mathbf{y}$ is closer to $\mathbf{x}_{\text{med}}$ than $\mathbf{z}$, then $\mathbf{y}$ beats $\mathbf{z}$ in a majority contest. The logic of the proof is similar to that used in the one-dimensional case. Because $\mathbf{x}_{\text{med}}$ must lie on the $\mathbf{y}$ side of the $\mathbf{yz}$ indifference line, and because $\mathbf{x}_{\text{med}}$ being unique implies that a majority of the ideal points must lie on the $\mathbf{y}$ side of the $\mathbf{yz}$ indifference line, a majority must prefer $\mathbf{y}$ to $\mathbf{z}$. Thus, we have some idea of what to expect when $\mathbf{x}_{\text{med}}$ is a unique median in all directions.

3.7 Vote outcomes in the absence of a dominant point

In cases such as those shown in Figures 3.2 and 3.4 there is no median in all directions, or, equivalently, there is no dominant point. What can we say about the likely outcome of a sequence of pairwise votes in these cases? Even to attempt to answer this question we must know several things. First, who is allowed to make proposals? Can any committee member freely propose any new point, or is there a chairman who has monopoly control over this activity? Second, if there is a chairman with this authority, is he a member of the committee? We shall see shortly that this is no small matter. Finally, we have assumed up until now that each member votes in a pairwise contest for the point he prefers and that each voter casts his vote independently of the other voters. What difference does it make if we relax these assumptions? We now proceed to explore these topics.

In Figure 3.2, as we have demonstrated, it is possible to find a proposal that will beat any proposal previously adopted. Thus, if new proposals can be introduced indefinitely, it is possible for each new proposal to replace the preceding one, and the committee will never settle on a single proposal. Will this never-ending sequence of proposals be confined to some subset of the entire space? Unfortunately, the answer is no. It is possible to reach literally any point in the space through *some* sequence of votes, pairing each previously winning proposal with some

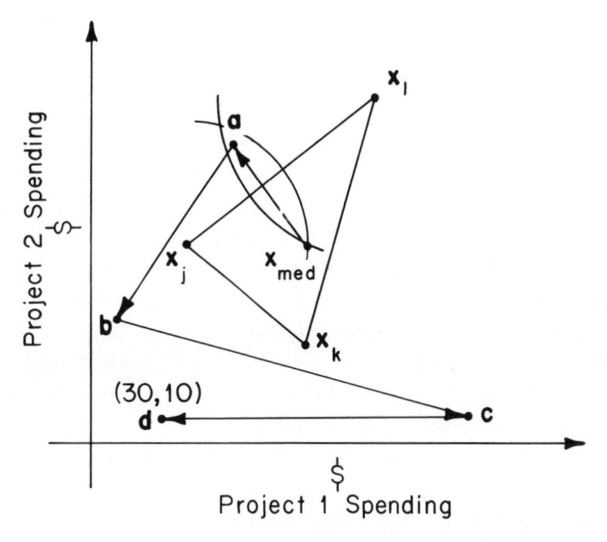

Figure 3.7. Agenda control in the absence of a dominant point.

new proposal that a majority prefers until the chosen point is finally reached. Thus, in Figure 3.2, not only is it possible for some sequence of votes starting with $\mathbf{x}_{med}$ to lead to any of the member ideal points, it is even possible to reach points outside the Pareto set (i.e., the triangle $\mathbf{x}_j \mathbf{x}_k \mathbf{x}_l$) such as (0,0) or (200,200).

The question then arises how a sequence of pairwise contests (an "agenda") might be constructed to reach some arbitrarily chosen point. This assumes that some individual is the agenda setter, because otherwise any agenda that might be constructed would be open to revision by any member proposing a point not on the agenda. Figure 3.7 is a replication of Figure 3.2, with the shortest possible agenda (in terms of number of proposals) leading from $\mathbf{x}_{med}$ to $\mathbf{d} = (30, 10)$, where **a** beats $\mathbf{x}_{med}$ by a majority, **b** beats **a**, **c** beats **b**, and **d** beats **c**. Presumably the agenda setter is not a member of the committee, because otherwise it is difficult to explain why **d** is his desired objective.

3.8 Sophisticated voting

There is an interesting feature about **d**. Every member of the committee prefers $\mathbf{x}_{med}$ to **d**! Thus, if each member always votes for the proposal he prefers (which we shall label *sincere voting*), every member ends up after this sequence of four votes being worse off than before the voting began. Presumably, any member able to foresee this eventuality would reconsider the wisdom of sincere voting. Thus, suppose the members know each other's preferences and the agenda. Then each voter will know that if **c** beats **b**, then **c** will lose to **d**. Thus, when **b** and **c** are paired for a vote, the actual contest is **b** versus **d**. Consequently, whereas sincere voting would lead members k and l to vote for **c** against **b**, *sophisticated voting* would lead members j and l to oppose **c** in such a contest. Thus, **b** would appear to be the expected outcome under the agenda we have described (we assume, for simplicity, that whenever a new proposal fails to achieve the support of a majority, the voting terminates). However, we can continue this backward reasoning to contests prior to those involving **b**, leading to the conclusion that a majority will vote to retain $\mathbf{x}_{\text{med}}$! Thus, sophisticated voting may foil the plans of our "fiendish" agenda setter.

Of course, if the agenda setter is a member of the committee, it seems unreasonable to expect him to construct an agenda leading to a unanimously inferior (Pareto-dominated) outcome. He would most likely construct an agenda leading to his ideal point. However, once again, sophisticated voting can prevent his plan from succeeding.

Once control over the agenda passes to all members of the committee, agendas such as we have described appear more implausible. Thus, in Figure 3.7, even if **d** were reached, any member would have an incentive to reintroduce $\mathbf{x}_{\text{med}}$ as a proposal. Further, if members are allowed to coordinate their voting decisions (i.e., form "coalitions"), there is no reason to expect points outside the Pareto set for j, k, and l to even be introduced, because a point inside this set can always be found that will make each member better off.

3.9 Vote trading

The possibility that voters may coordinate their voting decisions brings up another subject that relates back to our discussion of voting one issue at a time. Referring back to Figure 3.2, suppose that the two spending levels embodied in $\mathbf{y} = (72, 104)$ were introduced separately, with each being voted on in numerical order as a possible alternative to $\mathbf{x}_{\text{med}} = (90, 80)$, which we assume to be the status quo. Because all voters have separable preferences, it follows from our earlier discussion that $\mathbf{x}_{\text{med}}$ will be the outcome after both votes are taken. However, suppose voters j and l were to enter into an agreement to trade votes. Although voter l would prefer to see 90 rather than 72 spent on project 1, he would also prefer to see 104 rather than 80 spent on project 2. Voter j's preferences are exactly the opposite. Suppose, then, that j says to l, "I'll vote against the status quo on project 2 if you'll vote against the status quo on project 1." If this deal is accepted, the outcome of the two votes will be **y**, which both voters j and l prefer to the status quo.

However, there is more to this story. Voter k, determining before the votes are taken that something is afoot, may wish to approach voter j with a different offer. He may promise j that he will vote against the status quo on project 1 if j will call off his deal with l. This offer is even better for j than his deal with l, because he prefers (72, 80) to either $\mathbf{y}$ or $\mathbf{x}_{med}$.

At this point, l has no other choice but to approach k and offer to vote with him for both spending levels in $\mathbf{x}_{med}$ as l's only hope of avoiding something that, for him, is worse. Of course, now we are back where we started, and the dealing can begin all over again.

Thus, the introduction of vote trading does nothing, under these circumstances, to aid our ability to predict what the outcome of voting by this committee will be. In fact, we have shown that there is no simple answer to the question of what outcome is most likely to emerge when majority rule is employed by this three-member committee. We have, however, discussed some of the more important issues that must be addressed before this question can be answered.

3.10 Conclusion

In summary, this chapter has extended the analysis of committee voting begun in Chapter 2. We have introduced the weighted Euclidean distance preference rule and discussed its meaning. We have looked at the case in which two issues are voted on simultaneously. The concept of a dominant point was introduced, and we showed it to be equivalent to a median in all directions. Finally, we discussed several issues pertaining to vote outcomes in the absence of a dominant point.

The committee voting model introduced in the last two chapters is a good introduction to the model of elections to be discussed in Chapters 4 and 5. The basic structure of the committee voting model serves as a foundation for the more general model that will be built in these chapters. This more general model is designed to capture the additional complexity that characterizes mass elections as compared with committee voting.

Problems

3.1 From (3.2), with $\mathbf{x}_b = \mathbf{z}$,

$$\|\mathbf{y}-\mathbf{x}_b\|^2_{A_b} = a_{b11}(y_1-x_{b1})^2 + 2a_{b12}(y_1-x_{b1})(y_2-x_{b2}) + a_{b22}(y_2-x_{b2})^2 \tag{3.8}$$

From (3.5),

$$x_{b2} = x_{b2}(x_1) + \frac{a_{b12}}{a_{b22}}(x_1-x_{b1}) \tag{3.9}$$

Setting $x_1 = y_1$, substitute the right-hand side of expression (3.9) for x_{b2} in (3.8), and gather terms to prove (3.7a). As in the text, use c_b to denote $(a_{b11} - a_{b12}^2/a_{b22})(x_1 - x_{b1})^2$.

3.2 Suppose that B's salience parameters are $a_{b11} = 1$ and $a_{b22} = 100$, and his interaction parameter is $a_{b12} = 0$. Consider two alternatives: $\mathbf{y} = (100, 51)$ and $\mathbf{z} = (100 + r, 50)$, where $r > 0$. Find the value of r such that B is indifferent between $\mathbf{y}$ and $\mathbf{z}$.

3.3 Solve Problem 3.2 when $a_{b11} = 5$ and $a_{b22} = 500$ (and $a_{b12} = 0$).

3.4 Solve Problem 3.2 when $a_{b11} = 100$ and $a_{b22} = 1$ (and $a_{b12} = 0$).

3.5 Solve Problem 3.2 when $a_{b11} = a_{b22} = 1$ and $a_{b12} = -0.9$.

3.6 Suppose that Mr. B is appointed the committee chairman, with the power to set the agenda for voting. Assume that all five members believe that B's ideal spending level will prevail on the second vote. Determine the majority rule outcome for spending on both projects (using the median voter result) if B selects the following agenda: The committee first votes on project-1 spending and then votes on project-2 spending. Use the preference parameters given at the beginning of Section 3.3.

3.7 Determine the majority rule outcomes if B decides that the first vote will be on project-2 spending. As in Problem 3.6, the committee stops voting after the second vote.

3.8 Using your answers from Problems 3.6 and 3.7, decide which agenda B prefers.

3.9 Returning to Problem 3.6, determine the majority rule outcome if the committee revotes project-1 spending.

3.10 Solve Problem 3.6 under the assumption that each member assumes that his ideal position will win on the second vote. For example, E believes that the median position on the project-2 spending vote will be 60.

3.11 Solve Problem 3.7 using the naive forecasting rule defined in Problem 3.10.

3.12 What is $\mathbf{x}_{\text{med}}$ for the five-member subcommittee whose ideal points are listed in Table 3.1?

3.13 Show that for every point not on the line connecting j's and k's ideal points in Figure 3.2 there is a point on the line that they both prefer.

3.14 In Figure 3.2, prove that k and l, but not j, prefer $\mathbf{r}$ to $\mathbf{z}$.

3.15 If a sixth member is added to the committee in Figure 3.4, is it possible to locate his ideal point so as to create a dominant point? Where will his ideal point be located, and what is the dominant point?

3.16 Construct an agenda that with sincere voting will lead from $\mathbf{x}_{\text{med}}$ to $\mathbf{x}_k$ in Figure 3.7. How would sophisticated voters cast their votes under this agenda?

Bibliographical notes

The multidimensional spatial model owes its origin to Davis and Hinich (1966). Early results are contained in Davis and Hinich (1967, 1968). Tullock (1967) is also an early source in this literature. For an overview of early results, see Davis, Hinich, and Ordeshook (1970) and Riker and Ordeshook (1973).

Weighted Euclidean distance is the standard metric used in spatial voting models. However, Wendell and Thorson (1974) contains a discussion of alternative forms of distance, including the city-block norm and the sup norm.

For the literature on voting one issue at a time, Kadane (1972) is a good place to begin. The effects of nonseparable preferences on this type of voting are discussed in Mackay and Weaver (1981) and Denzau and Mackay (1981a). A very early source is Black and Newing (1951).

The median-in-all-directions result comes from Davis, DeGroot, and Hinich (1972). Contract curves and Pareto optimality are fully discussed in Henderson and Quandt (1971). The question of what conditions are necessary and/or sufficient for stability in the multidimensional spatial model is probably the single most researched question in multidimensional spatial theory. The best-known and earliest source is Plott (1967). Later studies on the subject include Davis, DeGroot, and Hinich (1972), Kramer (1973), Sloss (1973), Slutsky (1979), and Cohen and Matthews (1980).

There are solution theories designed to predict the outcome of committee voting in the absence of a dominant point. For reasons of space, we have not discussed this topic in the text, but we wish to cite a few important references. These solution theories treat committee voting as a cooperative game with or without side payments. In game-theoretic terms, a dominant point is equivalent to the existence of a core in the underlying voting game. Two concepts applicable to games without a core are the "V solution" and various forms of the "bargaining set." For a discussion of the V solution, see Riker and Ordeshook (1973). For a discussion of the bargaining set, see Owen (1968). Owen (1968) also contains a good discussion of the Shapley value and ψ stability. Finally, McKelvey, Ordeshook, and Winer (1978) offer a new solution concept termed the "competitive solution." For a general discussion of game theory, Luce and Raiffa (1957) is still the classic text.

The existence of global cycling in the absence of a dominant point is a result first developed in McKelvey (1976, 1979). Similar results can be found in Schofield (1978). Shepsle and Weingast (1981a) examine how sophisticated voting affects this result.

Sophisticated voting is a theory developed in Farquharson (1969). McKelvey and Niemi (1978) expand on this theory in the context of binary voting games. That sophisticated voting is a significant feature of congressional voting is established in Enelow and Koehler (1980) and Enelow (1981).

The literature on vote trading is large. Kadane (1972) contains many of the basic ideas. Schwartz (1977) also provides some important results.

CHAPTER 4

A general spatial model of candidate competition

4.1 The issues of the campaign

In Chapters 2 and 3 we traced a model in which each individual is presented with the following choice: He may vote to retain the status quo policy, or he may vote to replace it with another policy. Both the status quo policy and the replacement policy are known to each voter. Each policy consists of a given spending level for project 1 and project 2, and each voter bases his choice on the weighted Euclidean distance preference rule.

In this chapter we describe a model in which voters choose not between two policies but between two candidates. This is a very different type of choice. The model described in Chapters 2 and 3 is actually a model of direct democracy. The model we describe in this and the next chapter is a model of representative democracy. There are important differences between the two. In a direct democracy, voters choose directly between policies. In Chapters 2 and 3, these policies are represented by dollar amounts in order to stress that the voters share a common perception of each policy.

In a representative democracy, candidates play the role that policies play in a direct democracy. However, the choice between two candidates is not simply a choice between two policies or sets of policies. To some extent, the candidates are surrogates for policies. Each candidate has a position on the policy issues of the campaign, and the voters, to some extent, base their choice between the two candidates on these policy positions. However, the nature and range of campaign issues are far richer than the simple monetary issues discussed in the context of our committee model. Policy issues that arise in campaigns are likely to be debated in terms far more general than dollars and cents. An issue such as energy policy is likely to be discussed in broad terms that leave voters with only a general idea of what the candidate is advocating. It is frequently in the candidate's best interest to avoid being too specific, as Ronald Reagan found in 1976 when he estimated that his idea to turn federal programs back to the states would save the federal government

$90 billion. Unlike committee issues, campaign issues are likely to be phrased in less specific terms.

Added to the lack of specificity surrounding the discussion of campaign issues is the problem of information costs. Most voters in mass elections lack incentives to invest much time and energy in acquiring information about the issue positions of the candidates. When one's vote is combined with millions of other votes, it is unreasonable to expect the voter to expend the same type of energy in searching out information about the candidates as he would in learning about different brands of a consumer product. In the first case, the effect of his decision is combined with the decisions of millions of other voters, so that the individual may choose how to vote, but he does not in any real sense choose which candidate is elected. In the second case, the individual's choice is directly related to the product he consumes. There is consequently greater incentive in the second case for him to invest resources in learning about the potential objects of choice.

It is also important to note that policy issues are not the only issues that arise in campaigns. Candidates do discuss policy issues such as inflation, energy, foreign policy, the role of the courts, the Equal Rights Amendment, and the like. But the candidates themselves are also issues. The age of the candidate, the experience of the candidate, the morality of the candidate - all of these have been important issues in recent American election campaigns. We shall label issues that concern candidate characteristics such as these *nonpolicy issues.*

Nonpolicy issues are relatively fixed characteristics of the candidate that are generally beyond his control, at least for the duration of the campaign. Age, religion, party, and gender are obvious examples of nonpolicy issues. But so are issues such as war, prosperity, prestige abroad, and other conditions that are "givens" of the campaign. If the country is at war, or if its citizens are held hostage abroad, or if interest rates approach 20%, there is little, if anything, that either candidate can do to affect these conditions during the campaign. Instead, these conditions are part of the backdrop of the campaign, part of the environment in which the campaign takes place. Typically, the incumbent either defends or attempts to take credit for conditions such as these, whereas the challenger attempts either to hang the mess around the incumbent's neck or to downplay the importance of such conditions if they work in the incumbent's favor. In 1952 and 1968, the Democratic presidential candidate had the war label hung on him by the Republicans, whereas in 1960 the Democratic presidential candidate downplayed the importance of prevailing conditions under the Republicans by stressing the historical differences between the two major parties.

Policy issues are those on which the candidates have some freedom to select positions, whereas nonpolicy issues are those on which the positions of the candidate are beyond his direct control. As we shall show in Chapter 5, the inclusion of nonpolicy issues has important consequences for spatial models of candidate competition. Not only can such issues affect election outcomes, they also affect which positions on policy issues are optimal. For this reason, nonpolicy issues are incorporated into our general model of elections.

4.2 The dimensions of the campaign

How is it that voters come to know the issue positions of the candidates? The answer, typically, is by some indirect means, such as newspapers or television. Such sources typically offer simplified descriptions of the candidates. Concentrating more on nonpolicy issues, voters usually receive a disproportionate amount of information about the human qualities of the candidates (e.g., Robert Kennedy's "ruthlessness" or Barry Goldwater's mental instability). Information on policy issues is frequently scant (which may reflect what voters want to hear), with candidates being described in general terms, such as "fiscal conservative" or "New Deal liberal." However, such terms do carry substantial information for the voters on the policy positions of the candidates. A New Deal liberal may be expected to favor increases in spending on social welfare programs, oppose tax cuts for the rich, favor cuts in defense spending, favor increased government regulation of business, favor measures to aid labor unions, and a host of similar positions. Thus, political labels are convenient devices for simplifying discussion of policy issues by avoiding the alternative of listing the policy positions of the candidate on a broad range of issues. Political labeling, in fact, seems an almost inescapable feature of elections, allowing policy debates to be carried on in a form of shorthand that frees voters from the need to be highly informed about each candidate's positions on a broad range of issues. Given the lack of incentive for voters to acquire additional information about the candidates, political labels become an ideal method of communicating with the voters.

These labels that we have been referring to are an integral part of our model of elections. What we shall assume is that these labels can be arrayed on one or more *predictive dimensions* that represent the underlying space in which electoral competition takes place. Assume for a moment a single such predictive dimension. This dimension *may* be the

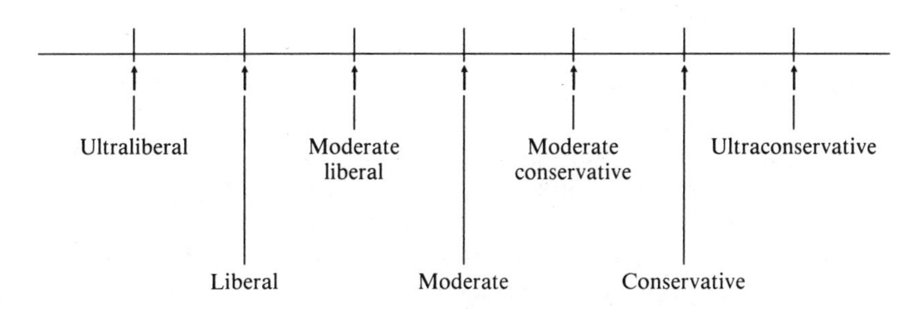

Figure 4.1. Hypothetical predictive dimension.

classic left–right ideological dimension discussed by Downs (1957). What we are assuming in such a context is that each candidate can be given one of the set of labels that exist along this dimension. An illustrative example is given in Figure 4.1. More adjectives could be attached to each of these terms, creating additional categories. What is important is neither the number of such labels nor the names by which they are denoted; the essential requirement is that these labels can be arranged in a natural linear order, such as numbers on the real line. However, no absolute origin or unit of measurement is required. Any point on the dimension can be defined as the origin, and the absolute difference between any two points (such as that between two labels) can be used to measure deviations from the origin.

We shall also assume that the label (or labels, if there are two or more predictive dimensions) by which each candidate is known to the voters cannot be changed within a single election period. Whether or not a "new Nixon" existed in 1968, we certainly cannot say that a "newer" Nixon took shape during the campaign. It was difficult enough for John Anderson to shed the conservative label that was affixed to him 15 years before he ran for president. It is vastly more difficult to conceive of a candidate changing from one political ideology to another in a period of less than a year. Nelson Rockefeller attempted for over 10 years to modify his label as a liberal Republican, with little or no success.

4.3 Perceptual variation of candidate issue positions

Although we have not yet spelled out the connection in the voters' minds between a candidate's positions on the policy issues of the campaign and his position on a predictive dimension or dimensions, we need to address a prior topic. As we have discussed, policy issues prevalent in campaigns are likely to be more general in nature than the monetary issues of our committee example. This lack of specificity is only compounded by the need to simplify political discussion by relying on a set of predictive labels. In short, the signals given to the voters on the policy positions of the candidates are too diffuse to expect voters to arrive at identical estimates of the policy positions of a single candidate. In short, unlike our committee example, perceptual variation appears endemic to elections. Although voters may all perceive that Ronald Reagan is a "conservative," it is too much to expect that each voter will arrive at the same estimate of what positions the "Reagan team" will adopt on all the policy issues of the 1980 presidential campaign if Reagan is elected president. What the term "conservative" indicates to one voter is typically different from what it indicates to another. One voter might think that a conservative like Reagan would maintain spending on all social welfare programs at current levels, whereas another voter might think that he would cut such spending by 20%. The same may be said for other issues, such as foreign policy and social issues. Different voters are likely to draw different inferences concerning the policy meanings of a given predictive label.

What we shall assume as part of our model of elections is that a common set of predictive labels is used to describe political candidates, but that each label may suggest different policy positions to different voters. Thus, political debate is framed in terms of a common set of predictive labels, but each label is given a subjective interpretation by each voter.

Predictive labels include any term or set of terms that suggest clearly defined policy positions to voters. The labels associated with left–right ideology are, perhaps, the first that come to mind. However, other predictive dimensions exist, or have existed, in democratic societies. Language, religion, and social class have all been the basis for predictive dimensions in Western democracies. To label a political candidate in Northern Ireland a Catholic, or a Canadian candidate a Québecois, is to suggest a long list of policy positions. Thus, it is important to emphasize that predictive labels are any widely used set of terms that are shorthand devices for communicating policy information to voters.

4.4 The link between issues and dimensions

We shall now address the question of how predictive dimensions are linked to policy positions in the minds of the voters. For simplicity, let us assume a single predictive dimension, denoted Π. Elements of Π will be denoted by lower-case π and subscripted according to the candidate. We shall limit our attention for the rest of Chapter 4 to the policy issues of the campaign, which will be indexed numerically from 1 to n. Nonpolicy issues will be discussed in Chapter 5.

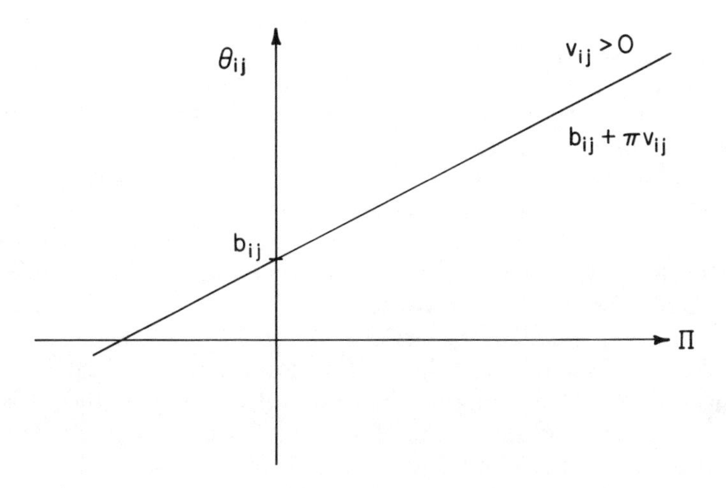

Figure 4.2. Linear mapping from predictive dimension Π to issue j.

If we are given two candidates, Theta and Psi, the predictive labels of these candidates on Π will be denoted π_θ and π_ψ, respectively. All voters know these labels, which are fixed for the duration of the campaign, but they may not agree about what policy positions correspond to these labels. However, all voters agree on the location of π_θ and π_ψ in Π.

Suppose that θ_{ij} is voter i's estimate of Theta's position on policy issue j. How might i arrive at this estimate? The simplest model is based on the assumption that Theta's policy position is a linear function of his position on the predictive dimension. Let $w_{ij}(\pi)$ denote voter i's estimate of a candidate's position on issue j as a function of the predictive label π. The simplest functional form for $w_{ij}(\pi)$ is

$$w_{ij}(\pi) = b_{ij} + \pi v_{ij} \tag{4.1}$$

where b_{ij} and v_{ij} are the coefficients of this linear function. Figure 4.2 is one example of such a function. Given this linear prediction rule,

$$\theta_{ij} = b_{ij} + \pi_\theta v_{ij}$$

If policy positions are a function only of a candidate's predictive label, then it follows that voter i estimates Psi's position on policy issue j using the same coefficients b_{ij} and v_{ij}, and thus

$$\psi_{ij} = b_{ij} + \pi_\psi v_{ij}$$

where ψ_{ij} is voter i's estimate of this policy position.

As noted earlier, there is no absolute origin or unit of measurement on Π. We might set any point equal to the origin and use the absolute difference between any two points as a unit of measurement. Accordingly, we shall set the origin equal to the position of the incumbent on Π (if one exists). Likewise, if there are two candidates, we shall use the absolute difference between them on Π as a unit of measurement (assuming these are two different points).

Suppose that Psi is the incumbent and Theta the challenger. Then, $\pi_\psi = 0$ and $\psi_{ij} = b_{ij}$, so b_{ij} is the incumbent's policy position on issue j as seen by voter i. We might also refer to b_{ij} as the status quo on this issue, as seen by i, because the incumbent's policy position is the prevailing one at the time of the election. Because we are using $|\pi_\psi - \pi_\theta|$ as a unit of measurement (assuming $\pi_\theta \neq \pi_\psi$), $\pi_\theta = 1$ or -1. The choice of either is strictly a matter of convenience. However, if we view the predictive dimension as representing liberal–conservative ideology, then it is customary to view positions to the left of the origin as more liberal and positions to the right as more conservative. Thus, if $\pi_\theta = -1$, Theta is more liberal than Psi, whereas if $\pi_\theta = 1$, Theta is more conservative.

Suppose, then, that $\pi_\theta = 1$, so that i's perception of Theta's position on issue j is $b_{ij} + v_{ij}$. What might we expect the sign of v_{ij} to be? This depends on what issue j is and how voter i translates the conservative difference between Theta and Psi into a policy difference on issue j. Suppose that issue j is defense spending. Then v_{ij} may be positive. Suppose that issue j is welfare spending. Then v_{ij} may be negative. Suppose that issue j represents NATO policy. Then v_{ij} may be zero, which implies that voter i believes that Theta will adopt the status quo policy on this issue. In short, there is no way to answer this question without knowing both the nature of the campaign issue and the meaning the voter attaches to the predictive dimension.

4.5 A two-issue, one-dimensional example

Suppose, then, that there are two policy issues in the campaign. Continuing our previous assumptions, $\pi_\psi = 0$ and $\pi_\theta = 1$ represent the labels of the two candidates on the underlying left–right dimension. Let issue 1 represent spending on social welfare programs and issue 2 spending on defense, measured as percentage increases (or decreases) in the status quo. A set of positions on more than one issue or dimension is a vector. We shall henceforth assume all vectors to be column vectors but typically write them as row vectors. Thus, a two-dimensional vector

$$\mathbf{a} = \begin{bmatrix} a_1 \\ a_2 \end{bmatrix}$$

will be written $\mathbf{a}' = (a_1, a_2)$, where the prime denotes the transpose of the vector. Equivalently, $\mathbf{a} = (a_1, a_2)'$.

Assume three voters, i, j, and k, with ideal points $\mathbf{x}_i'=(.2,0)$, $\mathbf{x}_j'=(-.2,.2)$, and $\mathbf{x}_k'=(0,.1)$. Thus, for example, voter i most prefers a 20% increase in spending on social welfare programs and a 0% increase (decrease) in defense spending (observe that the desired changes need not add to zero). For simplicity, we assume that all voters' preferences are based on simple Euclidean distance, so that $a_{11}=a_{22}=1$ and $a_{12}=0$ for all voters. In other words, each voter weights the two issues equally, and his preferences are separable across the two issues.

We need, now, to know each voter's estimation coefficients. Assume that all voters have a common perception of the status quo policies on social welfare and defense. We can then set $b_1=b_2=0$ for all voters. Thus, $\psi_{i1}=\psi_{i2}=\psi_{j1}=\psi_{j2}=\psi_{k1}=\psi_{k2}=0$, and $\theta_{i1}=v_{i1}$, $\theta_{i2}=v_{i2}$, $\theta_{j1}=v_{j1}$, $\theta_{j2}=v_{j2}$, $\theta_{k1}=v_{k1}$, and $\theta_{k2}=v_{k2}$. Suppose that i believes that Theta, being more conservative than Psi, would decrease social welfare spending by 40% and increase defense spending by 20%. Then $v_{i1}=-.4$ and $v_{i2}=.2$. Similarly, suppose that $v_{j1}=-.3$ and $v_{j2}=.1$, and $v_{k1}=-.1$ and $v_{k2}=.2$.

Using the weighted Euclidean distance preference rule, voter i prefers Theta to Psi if and only if

$$\|\boldsymbol{\theta}_i-\mathbf{x}_i\|_{A_i}<\|\boldsymbol{\psi}_i-\mathbf{x}_i\|_{A_i} \tag{4.2}$$

where $\boldsymbol{\theta}_i'=(-.4,.2)$, $\boldsymbol{\psi}_i'=(0,0)$, $\mathbf{x}_i'=(.2,0)$, and

$$A_i=\begin{bmatrix} a_{11} & a_{12} \\ a_{12} & a_{22} \end{bmatrix}=\begin{bmatrix} 1 & 0 \\ 0 & 1 \end{bmatrix}$$

Thus, from (3.2), i prefers Theta to Psi if and only if

$$[(-.6)^2+0(-.6)(.2)+(.2)^2]^{1/2}<[(-.2)^2+0(-.2)(0)+(0)^2]^{1/2}$$

which reduces to $.63<.2$ (a contradiction), so that i prefers Psi to Theta.

We can also determine i's candidate preference on the basis of the two candidates' positions on the predictive dimension. Recalling that $\boldsymbol{\theta}_i'=(\theta_{i1},\theta_{i2})=\mathbf{b}_i+\pi_\theta\mathbf{v}_i=(b_{i1}+\pi_\theta v_{i1}, b_{i2}+\pi_\theta v_{i2})$, the weighted Euclidean distance between $\boldsymbol{\theta}_i$ and $\mathbf{x}_i$ can be expressed alternatively as

$$\begin{aligned}&[a_{i11}(b_{i1}+\pi_\theta v_{i1}-x_{i1})^2+2a_{i12}(b_{i1}+\pi_\theta v_{i1}-x_{i1})\\ &\quad\cdot(b_{i2}+\pi_\theta v_{i2}-x_{i2})+a_{i22}(b_{i2}+\pi_\theta v_{i2}-x_{i2})^2]^{1/2}\end{aligned} \tag{4.3}$$

The weighted Euclidean distance between $\boldsymbol{\psi}_i$ and $\mathbf{x}_i$ can be expressed similarly. Squaring both sides, multiplying through, and gathering terms, it is also the case that voter i prefers Theta to Psi if and only if

$$\begin{aligned}&(\pi_\theta^2-\pi_\psi^2)(a_{i11}v_{i1}^2+2a_{i12}v_{i1}v_{i2}+a_{i22}v_{i2}^2)\\ &\quad<2(\pi_\psi-\pi_\theta)(a_{i11}b_{i1}v_{i1}+a_{i12}b_{i1}v_{i2}+a_{i12}v_{i1}b_{i2}+a_{i22}b_{i2}v_{i2}\\ &\qquad-a_{i11}v_{i1}x_{i1}-a_{i12}v_{i1}x_{i2}-a_{i12}v_{i2}x_{i1}-a_{i22}v_{i2}x_{i2})\end{aligned} \tag{4.4}$$

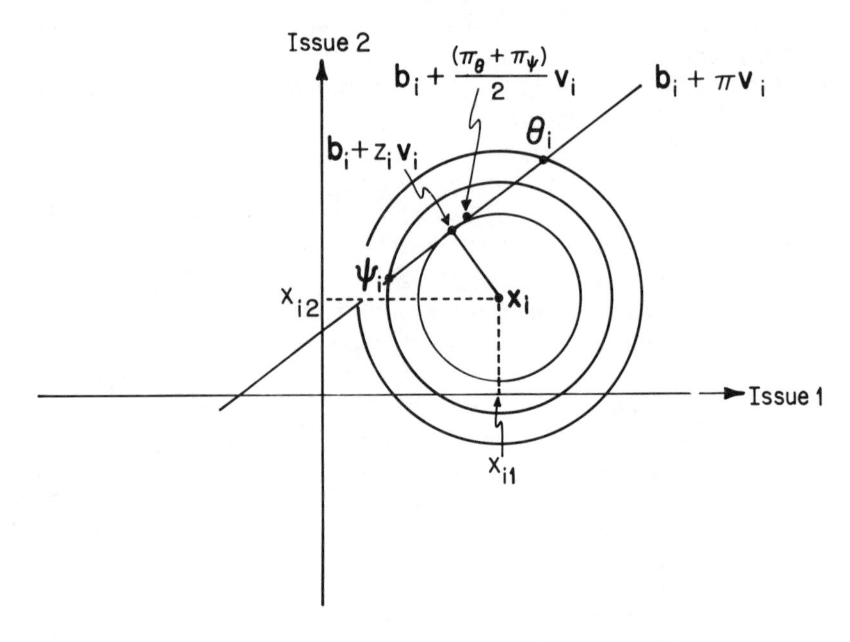

Figure 4.3. Voter i's policy estimates on issues 1 and 2.

Factoring $(\pi_\theta - \pi_\psi)$ from both sides, gathering more terms, and dividing through leaves

$$\frac{a_{i11}v_{i1}(x_{i1}-b_{i1})+a_{i12}v_{i1}(x_{i2}-b_{i2})+a_{i12}v_{i2}(x_{i1}-b_{i1})+a_{i22}v_{i2}(x_{i2}-b_{i2})}{a_{i11}v_{i1}^2+2a_{i12}v_{i1}v_{i2}+a_{i22}v_{i2}^2}$$

$$> \frac{\pi_\theta + \pi_\psi}{2} \tag{4.5}$$

assuming that $\pi_\theta > \pi_\psi$ and the denominator on the left-hand side of the inequality is not zero. Recalling (3.2), this denominator is equal to $\|\mathbf{v}_i\|_{A_i}^2$. Thus, the denominator is positive unless $\mathbf{v}_i = \mathbf{0}$. If $a_{i11} = a_{i22} = 1$ and $a_{i12} = 0$, this inequality reduces to

$$\frac{v_{i1}(x_{i1}-b_{i1})+v_{i2}(x_{i2}-b_{i2})}{v_{i1}^2+v_{i2}^2} > \frac{\pi_\theta + \pi_\psi}{2} \tag{4.6}$$

We shall label the left-hand side of (4.5) and (4.6) z_i, which will play the same role as that of the voter ideal point in the unidimensional spatial model of Chapter 2. As shown in Figure 4.3, the set of all policy estimates by some voter i based on the predictive dimension Π is the line $\mathbf{b}_i + \pi\mathbf{v}_i$. The two estimates ψ_i and θ_i correspond to the two points $\mathbf{b}_i + \pi_\psi\mathbf{v}_i$ and $\mathbf{b}_i + \pi_\theta\mathbf{v}_i$, respectively; $\mathbf{b}_i + z_i\mathbf{v}_i$ is the point where a line drawn from $\mathbf{x}_i$ perpendicular to $\mathbf{b}_i + \pi \mathbf{v}_i$ intersects the line. Because in Figure 4.3 this point of intersection is closer to ψ_i than to θ_i, $z_i < (\pi_\theta + \pi_\psi)/2$, and voter i prefers Psi to Theta.

Figure 4.3 illustrates why the term "most preferred point" (on Π) better applies to z_i than the term "ideal point," used to describe $\mathbf{x}_i$. The issue positions associated with z_i, which is a point on the predictive dimension Π, are $b_{i1} + z_i v_{i1}$ and $b_{i2} + z_i v_{i2}$ for issues 1 and 2. These positions are distinct in Figure 4.3 from x_{i1} and x_{i2}. Thus, the point $\mathbf{b}_i + z_i \mathbf{v}_i$ is closer to $\mathbf{x}_i$ than any other point on the line $\mathbf{b}_i + \pi \mathbf{v}_i$, but the two points will be the same only when $\mathbf{x}_i$ lies on this same line. In summary, z_i is i's most preferred point on Π, but it will generally not translate into his ideal issue positions.

This observation raises another point. We deliberately do not refer to z_i as voter i's ideology. Voters are not assumed to be ideological. Ideology is a predictive device that voters apply to candidates, not necessarily to themselves. A voter may like a conservative candidate more than a liberal candidate without any implication that the voter's own issue positions are derived from ideological principles. Again, looking at Figure 4.3, $\mathbf{x}_i$ is not represented by any of the points on the line $\mathbf{b}_i + \pi \mathbf{v}_i$. Thus, while we assume that voters think about candidates in ideological terms, we do not assume that they can describe themselves with an ideological label. Furthermore, we shall show how the z_i's of the voters can be changed by actions of the candidates, so that unlike the π's associated with the candidates, the most preferred points of the voters can move around during the campaign.

It is also important to note that the linear estimation process induces single-peaked preferences for each voter on Π. This can be seen in Figure 4.3, where points on $\mathbf{b}_i + \pi \mathbf{v}_i$ are less preferred the more distant they are from $\mathbf{b}_i + z_i \mathbf{v}_i$. Recalling our preference rule for voting on a single issue, defined in Chapter 2, it is readily apparent that (4.5) and (4.6) are identical to this rule, with z_i playing the role of x_i in our single-issue committee. Thus, i prefers Theta to Psi if and only if $|\pi_\theta - z_i| < |\pi_\psi - z_i|$.

The importance of this observation is that for the case of a single predictive dimension, we can utilize a form of the median voter result to determine which candidate will either tie or win the election. Just as we did with the ideal points of Chapter 2, we can define a median for the set of most preferred points z_i on the underlying predictive dimension. In the case of our example,

$$z_i = \frac{-.4(.2-0) + .2(0-0)}{.16 + .04} = -.4$$

$$z_j = \frac{-.3(-.2-0) + .1(.2-0)}{.09 + .01} = .8$$

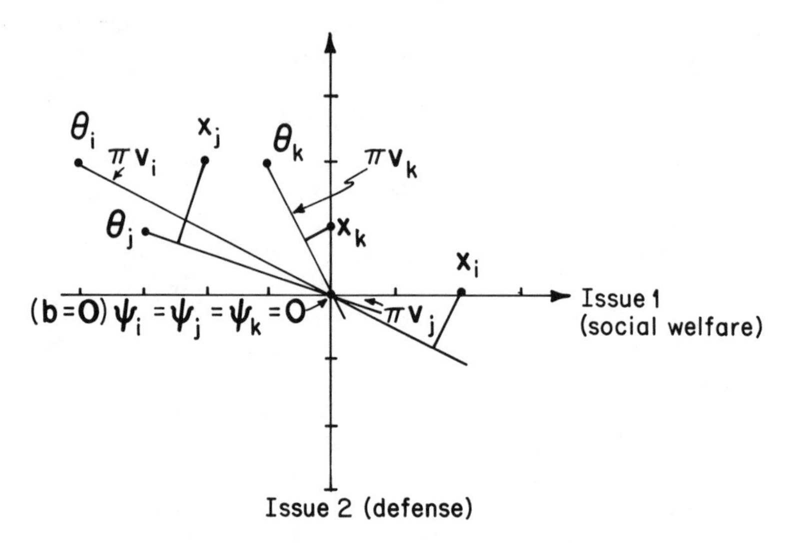

Figure 4.4. Linear policy predictions for three voters with Psi the incumbent and Theta the challenger (case 1).

$$z_k = \frac{-.1(0-0)+.2(.1-0)}{.01+.04} = .4$$

so $z_{\text{med}} = z_k = .4$. Consequently, because $.4 < (\pi_\theta + \pi_\psi)/2 = .5$, z_{med} is closer to $\pi_\psi = 0$. Thus, because z_{med} is unique, Psi will win a majority of the votes (i.e., those of voters i and k).

Figure 4.4 illustrates our three-voter example. Because $\pi_\psi = 0$ and $\pi_\theta = 1$, $\|\boldsymbol{\theta}_i - \boldsymbol{\psi}_i\|^2 = \|\mathbf{b}_i + \mathbf{v}_i - \mathbf{b}_i\|^2 = \|\mathbf{v}_i\|^2$. Similarly, $\|\boldsymbol{\theta}_j - \boldsymbol{\psi}_j\|^2 = \|\mathbf{v}_j\|^2$ and $\|\boldsymbol{\theta}_k - \boldsymbol{\psi}_k\|^2 = \|\mathbf{v}_k\|^2$.

4.6 The significance of z_{med} and the tactics of the campaign

With a single underlying dimension, the candidate whose position on the dimension is closer to z_{med} either ties or wins the election. However, because the π's attached to the candidates are fixed, candidate competition must consist of trying to move z_{med} toward the candidate's position. This means that candidate competition consists of efforts to alter the v_{ij}'s and b_{ij}'s and thereby the z_i's of individual voters. When two candidates argue about what each one's policy positions actually are, the candidates are attempting to alter the coefficients of the translation function by which policy positions are assigned to positions on the predictive dimension. Thus, Figure 4.5 illustrates how campaign tactics might alter a voter's perception of how much a liberal candidate and conservative

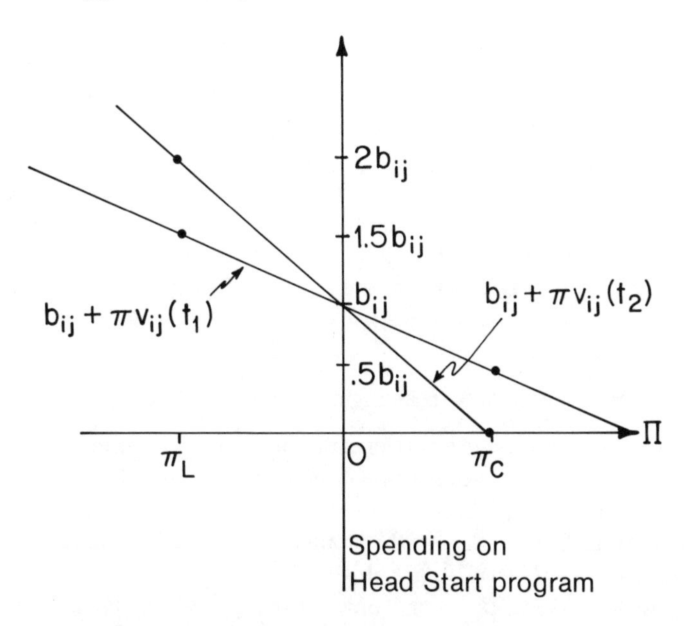

Figure 4.5. Altering v_{ij}.

candidate would spend on the Head Start program, if each were elected. Initially, at time t_1, the voter believes that the liberal (π_L) would increase spending by 50% over the existing level (b_{ij}), whereas the conservative (π_C) would cut spending by half. However, by time t_2, the voter is convinced that each candidate would enact more drastic changes. He then believes that the liberal would double spending on the program, whereas the conservative would cut out the program altogether. However, his estimate of b_{ij} remains unchanged. From (4.6), it is clear that for one issue, $z_i=(x_{i1}-b_{i1})/v_{i1}$. Thus, if Head Start were the only issue in the campaign, then z_i at time t_1, $z_i(t_1)$, would equal $(x_{i1}-b_{i1})/v_{i1}(t_1)=(x_{i1}-b_{i1})/(-.5b_{i1})$, if we set $\pi_C=1$. Thus, $z_i(t_2)=(x_{i1}-b_{i1})/-b_{i1}=z_i(t_1)/2$, so that the voter's changed perception of v_{i1} moves his most preferred point on the underlying dimension 50% of the way toward the origin. If all most preferred points were affected this way, the median $z_i(t_2)$ would equal $\frac{1}{2}$ median $z_i(t_1)$.

We assume that changes in the b_{ij}'s and v_{ij}'s of individual voters are the result of purposeful behavior by the candidates in an effort to affect the location of z_{med}. Whichever candidate is farther from z_{med} is attempting to alter the b_{ij}'s and v_{ij}'s of enough voters to move z_{med} closer to him than it is to his opponent. Likewise, his opponent is attempting to make sure that this does not happen.

In the following sections we shall describe various ways by which candidates may seek to alter the translation coefficients of the voters in order to win votes. The point of this discussion is not to suggest that candidates can alter voter perceptions in any manner they choose. Voter perceptions cannot be changed that easily. Rather, we wish to suggest certain tactics that candidates may use in an *effort* to change voter perceptions. Whether or not these tactics succeed will, of course, determine the outcome of the campaign. However, if we are interested in how candidates behave, we need to know the arsenal of weapons that is available to them if they are to try to wage a successful campaign.

4.7 Candidate efforts to change voter perceptions

Let us give an example of how the candidates might attempt to influence voter perceptions. In the example we have been discussing, $z_{med}=.4$, which is closer to the position of the incumbent on the underlying predictive dimension. Clearly, it is in the challenger's (Theta's) interest to move z_{med} closer to $\pi_\theta=1$. How might this be done?

Suppose that Theta can exert some influence over the v_{ij}'s of the individual voters. Further, suppose that v_{ij} can be expressed as the sum of a constant effect (controllable by the candidates) and a random effect (less subject to candidate control). If this constant effect is equal to the average v_{ij} across i and the residual term is i's perceptual bias with respect to v_j, we can express v_{ij} as

$$v_{ij}=v_j+\epsilon_{ij}$$

where v_j is the average v_{ij} and ϵ_{ij} is the residual term, representing i's perceptual bias on the issue.

Suppose that ϵ_{ij} is independent of v_j and that Theta can exert some influence over v_j. How might Theta wish to alter v_j in order to move z_{med} closer to 1?

Given our data,

$$v_1=\frac{(-.1-.3-.4)}{3}=-.267, \quad \text{and} \quad v_2=\frac{(.2+.2+.1)}{3}=.167$$

so that $\epsilon_{i1}=-.4+.267=-.133$, $\epsilon_{j1}=-.3+.267=-.033$, and $\epsilon_{k1}=-.1+.267=.167$. Likewise, $\epsilon_{i2}=.033$, $\epsilon_{j2}=-.067$, and $\epsilon_{k2}=.033$.

If Theta were to possess this information, at what values should he try to set v_1 and v_2? Because $\mathbf{x}_i$, $\mathbf{x}_j$, and $\mathbf{x}_k$ all lie on the same line (Figure 4.4), $\mathbf{x}_{med}=\mathbf{x}_k$ is a unique dominant point, just like a unique median ideal point in the type of single-issue voting discussed in Chapter 2. It would therefore seem advisable for Theta to attempt to alter v_1 and v_2 so

Table 4.1. *Perceptual changes in* v_{ij}*'s of voters*

		Case 1 (Figure 4.4); original values	Case 2 (Figure 4.6); change average $\mathbf{v}=(v_1, v_2)$	Case 3 (Figure 4.7); change v_1, eliminate perceptual bias on issue 1	Case 4; shrinker	Case 5; confuse voter j on issue 1, voter k on issue 2
$x_{i1}=$ .2	$v_{i1}=$	−.4	−.3	−.3	−.03	−.3
$x_{j1}=$ −.2	$v_{j1}=$	−.3	−.2	−.3	−.03	.1
$x_{k1}=$ 0	$v_{k1}=$	−.1	0	−.3	−.03	0
$x_{i2}=$ 0	$v_{i2}=$	.2	.1	.1	.01	.1
$x_{j2}=$ .2	$v_{j2}=$	.1	0	0	0	0
$x_{k2}=$ .1	$v_{k2}=$	.2	.1	.1	.01	−.2

as to move perceptions of his policy positions as close to $\mathbf{x}_k=(0,.1)$ as possible. Thus, because $\theta_i'=(v_{i1}, v_{i2})=(v_1+\epsilon_{i1}, v_2+\epsilon_{i2})$, $\theta_j'=(v_{j1}, v_{j2})=(v_1+\epsilon_{j1}, v_2+\epsilon_{j2})$, and $\theta_k'=(v_{k1}, v_{k2})=(v_1+\epsilon_{k1}, v_2+\epsilon_{k2})$, setting $(v_1, v_2)=(-.167,.067)$ will change θ_i' from $(-.4,.2)$ to $(-.3,.1)$, θ_j' from $(-.3,.1)$ to $(-.2,0)$, and θ_k' from $(-.1,.2)$ to $(0,.1)$. These changes will move z_i to $-.6$ and both z_j and z_k to 1. Thus, if Theta can convince the voters that, on average, the sizes of the changes he would make on social welfare and defense spending would be less than they originally thought, he can win the votes of two-thirds of the electorate. These changed perceptions are depicted in Figure 4.6. Table 4.1 lists the revised v_{ij}'s, as well as those for all subsequent perceptual changes to be described in this section.

The incumbent, of course, is advantaged by opposite changes in v_1 and v_2. Thus, suppose that v_2 is left at .067, but that v_1 is set at $-.3$. Further, suppose that perceptual bias on issue 1 is eliminated, so that $v_{i1}=v_{j1}=v_{k1}=-.3$. Thus, each voter believes that Theta would cut social welfare spending by 30%. Figure 4.7 shows the revised perceptions of Theta's policy positions, which are also listed in Table 4.1.

Now, $z_i=-.6$, $z_j=.67$, and $z_k=.1$, so the incumbent receives the votes of i and k, a majority of the voters. What has happened is that the meanings of the predictive labels employed by the voters have changed. The voters have become convinced that Theta's conservatism translates into deep cuts in social welfare spending. This particularly horrifies voter k, who favors the status quo on this issue. The attempt to convince voters

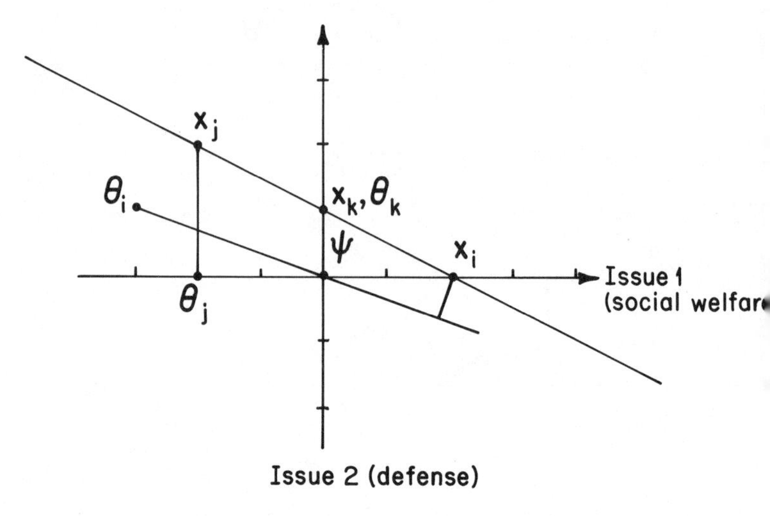

Figure 4.6. Changes in voter perceptions of policy positions (case 2).

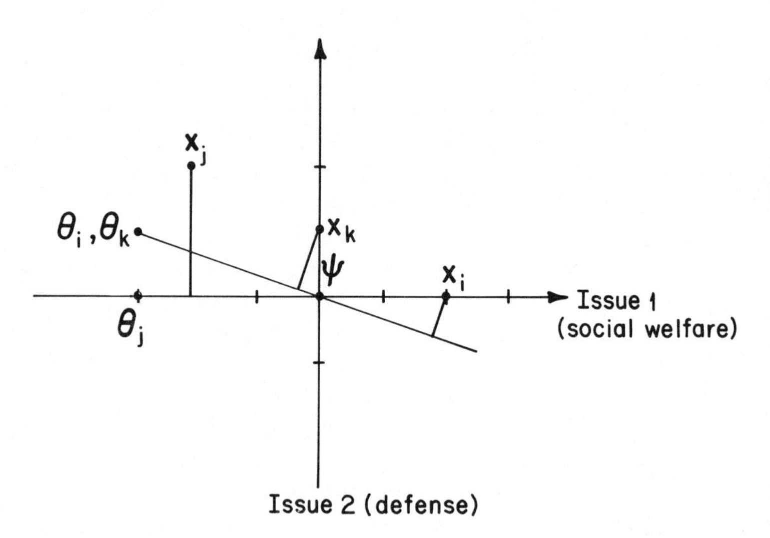

Figure 4.7. Revised voter perceptions (case 3).

who are basically sympathetic toward the status quo that candidates who are to the "left" or "right" of the incumbent will seek to enact drastic changes in policy is a favorite tactic that incumbents use in an effort to win votes.

Table 4.2. *How changes in* $\|\mathbf{v}_i\|$ *affect* z_i

	Case 1	Case 2	Case 3	Case 4	Case 5
$\|\mathbf{v}_i\|$	.45	.32	.32	.03	.32
$\|\mathbf{v}_j\|$	.32	.2	.3	.03	.1
$\|\mathbf{v}_k\|$	.22	.1	.32	.03	.2
z_i	−.4	−.6	−.6	−6	−.6[a]
z_j	.8	1[a]	.67	6.7	−2
z_k	.4[a]	1[a]	.1[a]	1[a]	−.5

[a]Median z_i.

4.8 The power of incumbency

Interestingly, the more voters are convinced of Theta's intention to make drastic alterations in the status quo, the more supportive of the incumbent the voters become. To see this, recall that $z_i = (v_{i1}x_{i1} + v_{i2}x_{i2})/(v_{i1}^2 + v_{i2}^2)$. Thus,

$$|z_i| = \frac{|v_{i1}x_{i1} + v_{i2}x_{i2}|}{v_{i1}^2 + v_{i2}^2} \tag{4.7}$$

But, by the Schwarz inequality for a scalar product of two vectors,

$$|v_{i1}x_{i1} + v_{i2}x_{i2}| \leqslant (v_{i1}^2 + v_{i2}^2)^{1/2} \cdot (x_{i1}^2 + x_{i2}^2)^{1/2} \tag{4.8}$$

so that, from (4.7),

$$|z_i| \leqslant \left(\frac{x_{i1}^2 + x_{i2}^2}{v_{i1}^2 + v_{i2}^2}\right)^{1/2} \tag{4.9}$$

Thus, as $\|v_i\| = (v_{i1}^2 + v_{i2}^2)^{1/2}$ increases, z_i shrinks to zero, which is the ideological position of the incumbent Psi. To the extent, then, that "left" and "right" are defined as departures from the ideological position of the incumbent, increasing the perceived policy distance between the candidates results in the voters increasingly favoring the incumbent.

This phenomenon is seen most clearly in Table 4.2, where $\|\mathbf{v}_i\|$ and z_i are listed for each of the five cases discussed in this section. In only two instances out of 30 pairwise comparisons does an increase in $\|\mathbf{v}_i\|$ not lead to a decrease in $|z_i|$. In these two cases ($\|\mathbf{v}_j\|$ for case 3 versus case 1 and $\|\mathbf{v}_k\|$ for case 4 versus case 2) the upper bound for $|z_i|$ on the right-hand side of (4.9) must, of course, decrease as $\|\mathbf{v}_i\|$ increases. However, in these two instances this decrease is not large enough to squeeze $|z_i|$ closer to zero. Continuing to increase $\|\mathbf{v}_i\|$, however, will accomplish this objective.

Thus, we see an important connection between the electoral prospects of the incumbent (i.e., the candidate whose position on Π is at the origin) and the perceived policy distance between him and the challenger. The greater the perceived distance, the better his chances are. If neither candidate is the incumbent, this advantage accrues to the candidate closest to the origin of the ideological scale. (If the incumbent is retiring, his ideological position can still be used as the origin.)[1]

In the 1980 American presidential election, Jimmy Carter attempted to persuade voters that Ronald Reagan, if elected, would enact drastic changes in the status quo. Our model explains why he attempted to do this. We shall have more to say on this point in Section 4.15.

4.9 The weakness of incumbency

On the other hand, shrinking the perceived policy distance between the candidates can aid the challenger. If voters are convinced that the ideological distance between the candidates translates into "small" adjustments in policy, the challenger can capitalize on even minimal dissatisfaction with the incumbent. Thus, returning to the data accompanying Figure 4.7, suppose that perceptions of the ratio of cuts or increases between issues 1 and 2 remain the same, but that the total size of these changes is reduced. Thus, the absolute value of nonzero v's decreases while maintaining the ratio for each voter between v_{i1} and v_{i2}. For example, in Figure 4.7, $v_{i2}/v_{i1}=v_{k2}/v_{k1}=-\frac{1}{3}$, while $v_{j2}/v_{j1}=0$. Preserving these ratios, but shrinking all numerators and denominators except v_{j2}, it is clear that z_{med} increases from .1. Thus, if $v_{i2}=v_{k2}=.01$, $v_{j2}=0$ and $v_{i1}=v_{j1}=v_{k1}=-.03$; then $z_i=-6$, $z_j=6.7$, and $z_k=1$, so that $z_{\text{med}}=1$ instead of .1.

We can state this phenomenon more generally. Expressing $\mathbf{v}_i'=(v_{i1}, v_{i2})$ as the product of a constant vector $\mathbf{e}_i$ and a scalar $c>0$, $\mathbf{v}_i=c\mathbf{e}_i$. Thus,

$$z_i=\frac{c(e_{i1}x_{i1}+e_{i2}x_{i2})}{c^2(e_{i1}^2+e_{i2}^2)}=\frac{e_{i1}x_{i1}+e_{i2}x_{i2}}{c(e_{i1}^2+e_{i2}^2)} \tag{4.10}$$

[1] There is a good rationale for always using the incumbent's ideological position (whether or not he is running again) as the origin in the predictive space. If b_{ij} is distributed independent of v_{ij} for each issue j, then $\text{Var}(\psi_{ij})=\text{Var}(b_{ij})+\pi_\psi^2\,\text{Var}(v_{ij})$. The variance of ψ_{ij} will then be least when $\pi_\psi=0$. In short, π_ψ can be set equal to zero on the grounds that perceptual variance of the status quo policy on issue j should be least compared to the perceptual variance of any other candidate's policy on the same issue.

Because c is the only nonconstant term left on the right-hand side of the equality ($\mathbf{x}_i$ is assumed fixed), as c decreases $|z_i|$ increases, moving z_{med} away from the ideological position of the incumbent. Observe that unlike (4.9), (4.10) is an equality. Thus, shrinking c must increase $|z_i|$.

This result has important implications for ideologically extreme candidates. Shrinking the length of $\mathbf{v}_i$ is equivalent to collapsing the perceived policy distance between the challenger (Theta) and the incumbent (Psi). If the ideological difference between Theta and Psi is $|\pi_\theta - \pi_\psi| = D$, this policy distance is $\|(\mathbf{b}_i + \pi_\theta \mathbf{v}_i) - (\mathbf{b}_i + \pi_\psi \mathbf{v}_i)\| = D\|\mathbf{v}_i\|$. Thus, shrinking $\|\mathbf{v}_i\|$ can have the effect of wiping out an enormous ideological difference between Theta and Psi.

For example, suppose that Theta is actually an ultra-right-winger, but voters believe that if elected he will make only the very small adjustments in policy just cited. If they are right, then all is well, but history is replete with examples where such expectations were replaced by shock when sharply different policies were actually enacted. The radical policies followed after Hitler was elected Reich chancellor provide one example. Disastrous results may follow if voters are unable to associate policy differences with ideologies that are quite different.

4.10 More incumbent tactics

We shall mention two more tactics favorable to the incumbent. The incumbent, Psi, may find it profitable to attempt to muddy the waters by deliberately trying to confuse the voters concerning what the issue positions of his opponent are. In short, he may attempt to weaken the link between ideology and policy. Returning to Figure 4.6, Psi may attempt to increase the variance of the $\mathbf{v}_i$'s on one or more issues by pointing out inconsistencies in the challenger's statements and, through whatever other means are available, attempting to create confusion in the voters' minds about Theta's policy positions. Thus, suppose voter k becomes convinced that Theta will decrease rather than increase defense spending, and j becomes convinced that social welfare spending will actually increase if Theta is elected. Then, if all other perceptions remain constant, Psi will win the election.

To see this, suppose in Figure 4.6 that $\theta_{k2} = -.2$, $\theta_{j1} = .1$, and all other parameters remain the same (Table 4.1). Then $z_i = -.6$, $z_j = -2$, and $z_k = -.5$, so Psi will beat Theta. Of course, Theta would benefit from eliminating this confusion. Notice that z_i is now the median z_i, whereas z_k previously held this designation. Altering the v_{ij}'s of the voters not only can alter the location of the median z_i but also can alter which voter is identified with the median z_i.

We should also mention efforts to alter the b_{ij}'s of the voters. Although both issues are measured in terms of departures from the incumbent's policies, the incumbent can always attempt to convince voters that, if reelected, he will make changes in these policies. Thus, he might claim that he will increase defense spending by 10% over the status quo. If all voters believe him, and all other perceptions represented in Figure 4.6 remain constant, the voters will all perceive Psi's position in the policy space to be $\mathbf{x}_k$, a unique dominant point. Clearly, this is a safe position for the incumbent.

Finally, we should also mention that $|z_i - \pi_\theta|$ and $|z_i - \pi_\psi|$ are direct measures of how voter *i* "feels" toward candidates Theta and Psi. Thus, anything that either candidate can do to affect these feelings will have a direct effect on the candidates' electoral prospects.

We have shown in the last four sections certain ways by which z_{med} can move on the underlying predictive dimension, because of the dynamics of a competitive campaign. In the following section we shall assume that two predictive dimensions underlie the policy issues of the campaign. Our purpose in doing this is to begin development of a broader theory of American parties and elections that will be tested in Chapter 9. This theory is designed to illuminate the connections between voter perceptions of parties, issues, and candidates. The purpose of Chapter 9 is to present some empirical results that support this theory.

4.11 Multiple predictive dimensions

So far, we have developed a model of candidate competition in which voters estimate the issue positions of each candidate by translating the candidate's position on an underlying predictive dimension into a set of positions on the policy issues of the campaign. Perceptual variation of the candidate's policy positions derives from the idiosyncratic nature of this translation process. In short, the predictive label of the candidate might imply different policy positions to different voters.

In order to simplify the exposition, the model was developed assuming a single predictive dimension. In the example in Section 4.5, this dimension was assumed to represent left–right ideology, which in turn was assumed to predict each candidate's positions on two policy issues – social welfare and defense spending. In this section we shall develop an example in which voters estimate candidate issue positions on the basis of their positions on *two* predictive dimensions. The first is an economic left–right dimension and the second a social left–right dimension. It has been noted in studies of American elections that in recent years the terms "liberal" and "conservative" have each taken on two distinct meanings.

In terms of economic issues, liberals and conservatives differ over the degree to which government should control or regulate the economy, with liberals favoring more government intervention and conservatives less. However, on social issues, liberalism and conservatism take on different meanings, with liberals favoring government intervention on certain issues, such as busing to achieve racial balance, bilingual education, or affirmative action, but not on issues such as drug control, public morality, and free speech. Social conservatives also have mixed feelings about government's role in the domain of social issues. On issues such as gay rights, abortion, and pornography, conservatives favor strict government regulation (i.e., proscription), whereas on issues such as school prayer and busing they favor a hands-off policy on the part of the federal government, allowing such policies to be made at the local level. At the root of these disputes is a desire on the part of conservatives to preserve traditional social values, such as the traditional family structure, and the desire of liberals for government to implement or at least not impede social change.

Thus, it is important to recognize the existence of multiple predictive dimensions in American politics. From time to time, foreign policy has been the basis for a third predictive dimension in American politics, with toughness toward the Soviets being a frequently used method of identifying candidates on this dimension. However, as we shall show in Chapter 9, recent American politics is best characterized by two left–right dimensions representing social and economic policy issues. It is for this reason that we explore the consequences of two predictive dimensions for our model of candidate competition.

To keep the mathematics simple, the example we shall now present assumes only two campaign issues, one based on an economic left–right predictive dimension and the other based on a social left–right dimension. The economic issue of the campaign we shall call "tax cut," which represents the extent to which individual tax relief of a given amount is targeted either toward the upper or lower end of the income scale. The social issue of the campaign is "busing," which represents the extent to which government should use busing as a tool to achieve racial balance in the public schools.

In the one-dimensional example, the two issues (social welfare and defense) were defined as public spending issues. An issue such as a tax cut is easily defined in monetary terms. However, social issues such as busing, abortion, and school prayer are not monetary issues. This does not mean that these issues cannot be represented by a continuum of some sort. If an issue can be characterized by a spectrum of alternative policies that can be arranged in either increasing or decreasing order with respect

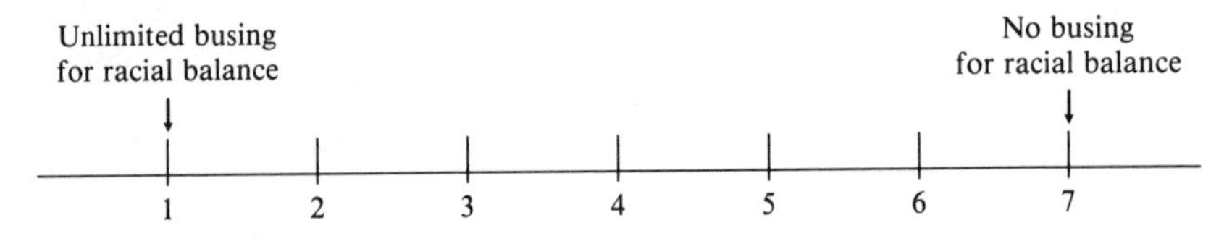

Figure 4.8. Busing.

to some common characteristic, the issue can be represented spatially. A possible representation of the busing issue (similar to the one used in the Michigan SRC/CPS election studies) is shown in Figure 4.8. Thus, there is a range of alternative policy positions that might be taken on this issue, with two policies that are extreme opposites and intermediate policies that are relatively moderate by comparison. Such intermediate policies might involve limited busing between adjacent school districts, busing only when "intent" to segregate can be shown, or other partial approaches to dealing with racially unbalanced schools. Seven alternative policy positions are shown, but we may regard these seven points as bench marks on a policy continuum. Thus, these seven points serve to divide the policy continuum into six equal subintervals, just as integers do on the real line.

We assume that this is an "objective" policy scale, so that the range of policies represented by the seven-point scale is commonly perceived by the voters. For example, a position of 3 on busing is assumed to indicate the same policy to all the voters. It is possible to assume that a seven-point scale on a given issue represents a personal issue space, unique to each individual. However, this poses insurmountable obstacles to the candidates, who are then forced to estimate the perceptual translation from the candidate's issue space into each voter's issue space. The assumption of an objective policy scale is implicit in aggregate level analyses of SRC/CPS seven-point data. If a given scale position were to mean different policies to different voters, no purpose would be served by knowing the distribution of scale scores across voters.

Figure 4.9 represents the tax cut issue. At one extreme it may be proposed that all tax relief (of a fixed amount) go to those with incomes less than $50,000, whereas at the other extreme it may be proposed that all tax relief go to those with incomes over $50,000. Intermediate policies consist of various mixtures, with some relief going to individuals in both groups. There is no significance attached to the use of seven points to divide the policy interval. As in Figure 4.8, the purpose of attaching numbers to certain policies is to allow examples to be constructed. Ultimately, the task of attaching numbers to policies on an interval scale is a scaling question to be answered empirically.

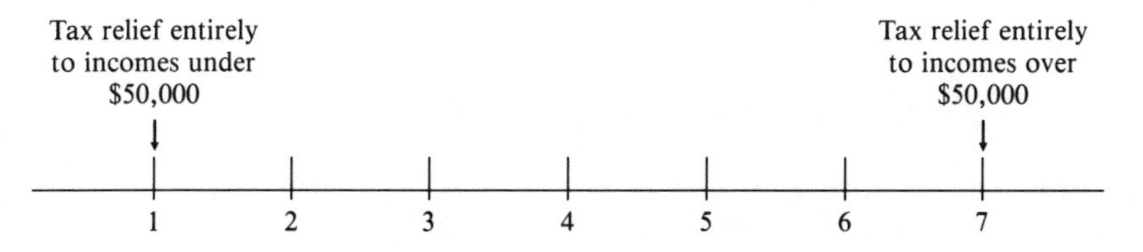

Figure 4.9. Tax cut.

We shall assume that voters estimate the position of each candidate on the issue of busing on the basis of his position on a social predictive dimension. Likewise, the position of each candidate on the tax cut issue is estimated on the basis of the candidate's position on an economic predictive dimension. The translation process from dimensions to issues has been previously described. Here we shall simply employ that mechanism to show how our model operates when voters' perceptions of candidate issue positions are based on two underlying dimensions of evaluation. We limit ourselves to one issue per dimension to simplify the mathematics and to allow for a geometric representation of voter perceptions of the candidates' issue positions.

4.12 Voter perceptions based on two predictive dimensions

As before, let Psi be the incumbent and Theta the challenger. The economic and social predictive dimensions will be labeled dimensions 1 and 2, respectively. Psi's positions on dimensions 1 and 2 will be $\boldsymbol{\pi}_\psi' = (\pi_{\psi 1}, \pi_{\psi 2}) = (0, 0)$, and Theta's will be $\boldsymbol{\pi}_\theta' = (\pi_{\theta 1}, \pi_{\theta 2}) = (1, 1)$. We interpret Theta as being more conservative than Psi on both dimensions.

Label the tax cut issue *issue 1* and the busing issue *issue 2*. Then, voter i's perception of Theta's positions on the two issues of the campaign is

$$\begin{aligned} \boldsymbol{\theta}_i' &= (\theta_{i1}, \theta_{i2}) \\ &= (b_{i1} + v_{i11}\pi_{\theta 1} + v_{i21}\pi_{\theta 2},\, b_{i2} + v_{i12}\pi_{\theta 1} + v_{i22}\pi_{\theta 2}) \end{aligned} \tag{4.11}$$

where b_{ik} is i's perception of the incumbent's policy on issue k ($k=1$ or 2) and v_{ijk} is the perceptual change on the kth issue given a unit change on the jth dimension. Thus, v_{i11} is the marginal change in θ_{i1} given a unit change in $\pi_{\theta 1}$, and v_{i21} is the marginal change in θ_{i1} given a unit change in $\pi_{\theta 2}$. Such a relationship would imply that the tax cut issue is, to some extent, a social one. Although this may be the case for a few voters, we assume that the tax cut issue is strictly economic. For similar reasons, we assume that busing is strictly a social issue. This means that $v_{i21} = v_{i12} = 0$. Because $\boldsymbol{\pi}_\theta' = (1, 1)$, it follows from (4.11) that

$$\boldsymbol{\theta}_i' = (\theta_{i1}, \theta_{i2}) = (b_{i1} + v_{i11}, b_{i2} + v_{i22})$$

and

$$\boldsymbol{\psi}_i' = (\psi_{i1}, \psi_{i2}) = (b_{i1}, b_{i2})$$

Using the weighted Euclidean distance preference rule and squaring both sides, voter i prefers Theta to Psi if and only if

$$\|\boldsymbol{\theta}_i - \mathbf{x}_i\|_{A_i}^2 < \|\boldsymbol{\psi}_i - \mathbf{x}_i\|_{A_i}^2$$

or, equivalently, if and only if

$$\begin{aligned} & a_{i11}(v_{i11} - x_{i1} + b_{i1})^2 + 2a_{i12}(v_{i11} - x_{i1} + b_{i1})(v_{i22} - x_{i2} + b_{i2}) \\ & \quad + a_{i22}(v_{i22} - x_{i2} + b_{i2})^2 \\ & < a_{i11}(-x_{i1} + b_{i1})^2 + 2a_{i12}(-x_{i1} + b_{i1})(-x_{i2} + b_{i2}) \\ & \quad + a_{i22}(-x_{i2} + b_{i2})^2 \end{aligned} \tag{4.12}$$

which reduces to

$$\begin{aligned} & a_{i11} v_{i11}^2 - 2a_{i11} v_{i11}^2 z_{i1} + 2a_{i12} v_{i11} v_{i22} - 2a_{i12} v_{i11} v_{i22}(z_{i1} + z_{i2}) \\ & \quad + a_{i22} v_{i22}^2 - 2a_{i22} v_{i22}^2 z_{i2} < 0 \end{aligned} \tag{4.13}$$

where $z_{i1} = (x_{i1} - b_{i1})/v_{i11}$ and $z_{i2} = (x_{i2} - b_{i2})/v_{i22}$ are points on dimensions 1 and 2, respectively. In matrix notation, we can express (4.13) as

$$\mathbf{1}'V_i'A_i V_i \mathbf{1} - 2\mathbf{z}_i'V_i'A_i V_i \mathbf{1} < 0$$

where $\mathbf{1}' = (1, 1)$,

$$V_i' = \begin{bmatrix} v_{i11} & 0 \\ 0 & v_{i22} \end{bmatrix}, \quad \text{and} \quad A_i = \begin{bmatrix} a_{i11} & a_{i12} \\ a_{i12} & a_{i22} \end{bmatrix}$$

In appendix 4.2 we show that, in general,

$$\begin{aligned} & \|\boldsymbol{\theta}_i - \mathbf{x}_i\|_{A_i} < \|\boldsymbol{\psi}_i - \mathbf{x}_i\|_{A_i} \\ & \qquad \text{if and only if } \|\boldsymbol{\pi}_\theta - \mathbf{z}_i\|_{V_i'A_i V_i} < \|\boldsymbol{\pi}_\psi - \mathbf{z}_i\|_{V_i'A_i V_i} \end{aligned} \tag{4.14}$$

$V_i'A_i V_i$ plays the role of A_i in the policy space, measuring how i weights and makes trade-offs between the two predictive dimensions. If $\boldsymbol{\pi}_\theta' = (1, 1)$ and $\boldsymbol{\pi}_\psi' = (0, 0)$, then (4.14) reduces to (4.13). Thus, we earlier showed that when there exists a single predictive dimension,

$$\|\boldsymbol{\theta}_i - \mathbf{x}_i\|_{A_i} < \|\boldsymbol{\psi}_i - \mathbf{x}_i\|_{A_i} \quad \text{if and only if } |\pi_\theta - z_i| < |\pi_\psi - z_i|$$

We now have a generalization of this equivalence for the case of multiple predictive dimensions.

4.13 A dominant point in a multidimensional predictive space

This raises an important point. In Chapter 3 we showed that for the committee voting model, the existence of a median in all directions was necessary and sufficient for the existence of a dominant point (i.e., a point that could not be defeated in a majority contest). In the case of candidate competition with multiple predictive dimensions, a median in all directions is also necessary and sufficient for the existence of a dominant point. Now a dominant point is defined in the predictive space, with $\mathbf{z}_{\text{med}}$ playing the role of $\mathbf{x}_{\text{med}}$ in the committee model. If $\mathbf{z}_{\text{med}}$ is a median in all directions, then a candidate identified with $\mathbf{z}_{\text{med}}$ cannot be defeated in a majority contest.

It is important to remember that the median-in-all-directions result derived in Chapter 3 was based on the assumption that $A_i = I$ for all voters (or, more generally, that A_i is the same for all i). The distance function expressed by (4.14), on the other hand, is based on $V_i'A_iV_i$. Thus, the dominant-point–median-in-all-directions equivalence holds in the predictive space if and only if $V_i'A_iV_i = I$ for all i (or, more generally, if and only if $V_i'A_iV_i$ is the same for all i). As was pointed out in footnote 3 in Chapter 3, if voters have differing salience matrices, then a more stringent condition, a generalized total median, is necessary and sufficient for the existence of a dominant point in the committee voting model. Thus, in our candidate model, if $V_i'A_iV_i$ varies across voters, this more stringent condition is also necessary and sufficient for the existence of a dominant point.

The requirement that $V_i'A_iV_i$ be the same for all voters is more stringent than the requirement that A_i not vary, and as a consequence, the requirements for a median in all directions to exist under conditions of candidate competition are even more severe than under conditions of committee voting.

This does not mean that in the absence of these requirements we are unable to make predictive statements about election outcomes or candidate behavior. As we shall show, the results obtained for the case of a single predictive dimension, based on stretching or shrinking the perceived policy distance between the two candidates, continue to hold when there are multiple predictive dimensions. In addition, even in the absence of a dominant point, we can still talk about how candidates will seek to alter the b_{ij}'s and v_{ijk}'s of the voters in order to preserve a winning position in the predictive space or translate a losing position into a winning position. We can gain insights into electoral events *without the need for a dominant point.*

Returning to the mathematical development, if $a_{i11} = a_{i22} = 1$ and $a_{i12} = 0$, then (4.13) can finally be expressed as

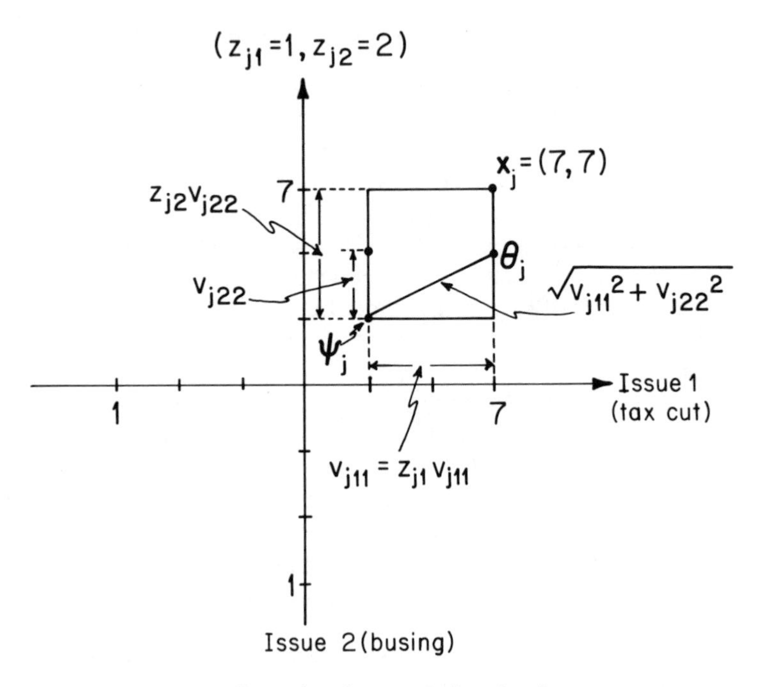

Figure 4.10. A two-dimensional most preferred point.

$$\frac{v_{i11}(x_{i1}-b_{i1})+v_{i22}(x_{i2}-b_{i2})}{v_{i11}^2+v_{i22}^2} > \frac{1}{2} \tag{4.15}$$

so that i prefers Theta to Psi if and only if (4.15) holds. Observe that because $v_{i11}(x_{i1}-b_{i1})=v_{i11}^2 z_{i1}$ and $v_{i22}(x_{i2}-b_{i2})=v_{i22}^2 z_{i2}$, an alternative representation of the left-hand side of (4.15) is $(v_{i11}^2 z_{i1}+v_{i22}^2 z_{i2})/(v_{i11}^2+v_{i22}^2)$.

Comparing $\mathbf{z}_i'=(z_{i1}, z_{i2})$ with the z_i defined in (4.5) and simplified in (4.6), it is clear that $\mathbf{z}_i$ is simply a two-dimensional generalization of z_i. If there were only one issue in the campaign, z_i would equal $(x_{i1}-b_{i1})/v_{i1}$, which is equivalent to z_{i1}, given the assumption in our example that each of the two underlying dimensions predicts positions on a single issue. Observe that whereas the left-hand side of (4.15) appears to be identical with the left-hand side of (4.6), the left-hand side of (4.15) is based on the two-dimensional projection of $\mathbf{x}_i$ onto the predictive space instead of the one-dimensional projection of (4.6).

Figure 4.10 clarifies this point. The most preferred point of voter j is the vector $\mathbf{z}_j=(z_{j1}, z_{j2})'$ based on the projection of $\mathbf{x}_j$ along each of the two issue axes. A one-dimensional analogy would consist of a single issue and a single predictive dimension, in which case the most preferred point

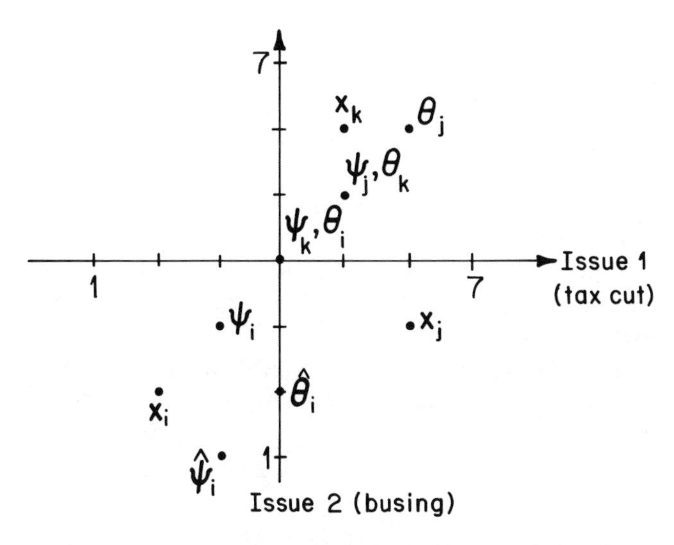

Figure 4.11. A three-voter example with two predictive dimensions.

is $(x_i - b_i)/v_i$, which is merely the ratio of two differences on a single issue axis.

4.14 A two-issue, two-dimensional example

Continuing our discussion with an example, assume three voters, i, j, and k, with ideal points $\mathbf{x}_i' = (2,2)$, $\mathbf{x}_j' = (6,3)$, and $\mathbf{x}_k' = (5,6)$. Thus, voter i most prefers the tax cut policy labeled 2 and the busing policy labeled 2. We shall assume that all three voters have circular indifference contours, so that $a_{11} = a_{22} = 1$ and $a_{12} = 0$ for all voters. Unlike our earlier example, we shall not assume common perception of the incumbent's policies. Thus, suppose that $\mathbf{b}_i' = \psi_i' = (3,3)$, $\mathbf{b}_j' = \psi_j' = (5,5)$, and $\mathbf{b}_k' = \psi_k' = (4,4)$. Finally, suppose that $v_{i11} = v_{i22} = v_{j11} = v_{j22} = v_{k11} = v_{k22} = 1$. Then, $\theta_i' = (b_{i1} + v_{i11}, b_{i2} + v_{i22}) = (4,4)$, $\theta_j' = (b_{j1} + v_{j11}, b_{j2} + v_{j22}) = (6,6)$, and $\theta_k' = (b_{k1} + v_{k11}, b_{k2} + v_{k22}) = (5,5)$. Figure 4.11 represents the data for all three voters.

From equation (4.15) it is easy to compute that

$$\frac{v_{i11}(x_{i1} - b_{i1}) + v_{i22}(x_{i2} - b_{i2})}{v_{i11}^2 + v_{i22}^2} = \frac{1(-1) + 1(-1)}{2} = -1 \not> .5$$

so that i prefers Psi to Theta. Likewise,

$$\frac{v_{j11}(x_{j1} - b_{j1}) + v_{j22}(x_{j2} - b_{j2})}{v_{j11}^2 + v_{j22}^2} = \frac{1(1) + 1(-2)}{2} = -.5 \not> .5$$

so that j prefers Psi to Theta. Lastly,

$$\frac{v_{k11}(x_{k1}-b_{k1})+v_{k22}(x_{k2}-b_{k2})}{v_{k11}^2+v_{k22}^2}=\frac{1(1)+1(2)}{2}=1.5>.5$$

so that k prefers Theta to Psi. Thus, under majority rule, Psi will win the election.

To compete for votes, Theta might employ one of the tactics previously discussed, in order to move $\mathbf{z}_{\text{med}}$ toward $\boldsymbol{\pi}_\theta$. However, unless $\mathbf{z}_{\text{med}}$ is a unique median in all directions, this tactic is no guarantee of success (observe in our example that $V_i'A_iV_i=I$ for all voters). We can prove this point with an example.

Given our data, $\mathbf{z}_i'=(-1,-1)$, $\mathbf{z}_j'=(1,-2)$, and $\mathbf{z}_k'=(1,2)$. Thus, $\mathbf{z}_{\text{med}}'=(1,-1)$. The squared distance between $\mathbf{z}_{\text{med}}$ and $\boldsymbol{\pi}_\theta=(1,1)'$, as defined by (4.14), is thus

$$\begin{aligned}\|\mathbf{z}_{\text{med}}-\boldsymbol{\pi}_\theta\|^2_{V_i'A_iV_i}&=(\mathbf{z}_{\text{med}}-\boldsymbol{\pi}_\theta)'V_i'A_iV_i(\mathbf{z}_{\text{med}}-\boldsymbol{\pi}_\theta)\\&=(0,-2)\begin{bmatrix}1&0\\0&1\end{bmatrix}\begin{bmatrix}0\\-2\end{bmatrix}=4\end{aligned}$$

and so the distance between $\mathbf{z}_{\text{med}}$ and $\boldsymbol{\pi}_\theta$ is 2. Likewise, the distance between $\mathbf{z}_{\text{med}}$ and $\boldsymbol{\pi}_\psi=(0,0)'$ is $\sqrt{2}$, so $\mathbf{z}_{\text{med}}$ is closer to $\boldsymbol{\pi}_\psi$ than to $\boldsymbol{\pi}_\theta$.

Now suppose that Theta is able to change $\psi_i'=(3,3)$ to $\hat{\psi}_i'=(3,1)$ and $\theta_i'=(4,4)$ to $\hat{\theta}_i'=(4,2)$. In other words, Theta alters i's perception of the status quo policy on busing from 3 to 1, and because $v_{i22}=1$ is unchanged, also alters i's perception of Theta's busing policy from 4 to 2. He might do this by highlighting past statements made by his opponent that indicate strong support for busing to achieve racial balance. Figure 4.11 shows i's revised perceptions of the candidates.

If Theta can accomplish this goal, $z_{i2}=1$, so $\mathbf{z}_{\text{med}}$ now equals $(1,1)'$ and $\boldsymbol{\pi}_\theta=\mathbf{z}_{\text{med}}$. However, candidate preference among the voters remains the same, because i still prefers Psi to Theta, and so Theta still loses the election. On the other hand, suppose that Theta is able to alter j's perception of the status quo policy on busing from 5 to 2, and the busing policy advocated by Theta from 6 to 3. Then $\boldsymbol{\pi}_\theta=\mathbf{z}_{\text{med}}$, and Theta wins the election, two votes to one. Thus, just as in the committee example with two issues being voted on at once (where $\mathbf{x}_{\text{med}}$ plays the role of $\mathbf{z}_{\text{med}}$), proximity to $\mathbf{z}_{\text{med}}$ is not generally advantageous to either candidate.

Perceptual variation of candidate issue positions complicates efforts to locate an optimal set of policy positions for either candidate. Suppose that in our example there exist five voters with ideal points $(2,4)$, $(4,4)$, $(6,4)$, $(4,2)$, and $(4,6)$. Clearly, in our committee voting model, $(4,4)$ is an optimal set of issue positions, because under majority rule it defeats all other points in the space in a pairwise vote and so is a dominant point.

In our candidate model, on the other hand, the incumbent may be commonly perceived at (4, 4) and still lose! If the challenger were perceived by three (or four) voters with ideal points other than (4, 4) as being closer to all of these ideal points than the incumbent, the challenger would win. Of course, common perception of the challenger's issue positions makes this event impossible. However, voter rationalization of where favorite candidates are located may lead to this result in an electoral setting.

4.15 Candidate tactics with two predictive dimensions

The tactics of lengthening and shrinking $\|\theta_i - \psi_i\|$ discussed in Section 4.6 are still useful for the incumbent and challenger, respectively, when there are multiple underlying dimensions. From the Schwarz inequality, it is clear that

$$|v_{i11}(x_{i1}-b_{i1}) + v_{i22}(x_{i2}-b_{i2})| / (v_{i11}^2 + v_{i22}^2) < \{[(x_{i1}-b_{i1})^2 + (x_{i2}-b_{i2})^2] / (v_{i11}^2 + v_{i22}^2)\}^{1/2} \quad (4.16)$$

and because i prefers Psi to Theta if the left-hand side of the inequality is less than one-half, the greater $(v_{i11}^2 + v_{i22}^2)^{1/2} = \|\theta_i - \psi_i\|$ becomes, the more likely this is to be true.

As explained in Section 4.8, this is an important result for understanding electoral politics. The ability of incumbents (or challengers) to convince voters that replacing the incumbent will result in drastic policy changes is an important factor in explaining election outcomes. Inequality (4.16), which is generalized in Appendix 4.3, extends this finding to the case of two predictive dimensions.

In 1964, many voters were convinced that if Barry Goldwater were elected president, drastic changes in domestic and foreign policy would result. Although Goldwater might still have lost the election even without that perception, the decision of many Republicans to vote for Lyndon Johnson is best explained by a deep concern on their part about how far Goldwater would go in carrying out policy changes. A perception that those changes would not have been drastic clearly would have increased his support.

As mentioned earlier, in the 1980 election, Jimmy Carter attempted to persuade voters that Ronald Reagan would make radical policy changes if he were elected president. On economic issues, Carter assailed Reagan for supporting the Kemp–Roth tax cut plan in an attempt to convince voters that Reagan would make reckless changes in the status quo. On social issues, Carter attempted to underscore Reagan's association with the Moral Majority, right-to-life lobbyists, and other extremist groups on the social "right" in order to convince voters that Reagan would make drastic changes on such issues as abortion and school prayer. As stated earlier, our model reveals the logic behind this tactic. Of course, Reagan's soft-spoken, congenial image had a great deal to do with the public's unwillingness to accept these charges. The perception of Goldwater, on the other hand, as impulsive and easily set off only made it easier to believe that he would make reckless policy changes.

We can also extend our earlier result based on the effect of shrinking the perceived policy distance between incumbent and challenger. If (v_{i11}, v_{i22}) is expressed as the product of a constant vector (e_{i11}, e_{i22}) and a scalar $c>0$, then $(v_{i11}, v_{i22})=c(e_{i11}, e_{i22})$, and

$$\frac{v_{i11}(x_{i1}-b_{i1})+v_{i22}(x_{i2}-b_{i2})}{v_{i11}^2+v_{i22}^2}=\frac{e_{i11}(x_{i1}-b_{i1})+e_{i22}(x_{i2}-b_{i2})}{c(e_{i11}^2+e_{i22}^2)} \tag{4.17}$$

Consequently, as c shrinks to zero, the left-hand side of (4.15) approaches either positive or negative infinity, depending on its initial sign. Thus, if the left-hand side of (4.15) is positive for a majority of voters, shrinking $\|\theta_i-\psi_i\|$ in this fashion for all voters will help the challenger, Theta. This result is also generalized in Appendix 4.3.

The importance of the result lies in the insights it provides for understanding the appeal of extremist candidates. The electoral success of an extremist over a centrist candidate is usually taken as proof that voters are endorsing policies quite different from those offered by the centrist candidate. Those who have described Reagan's victory over Carter in 1980 as proof that a majority of voters gave their assent to far-reaching policy changes accept this argument.

Our result indicates that this argument is specious. A belief on the part of most voters that Reagan would actually make only marginal policy adjustments is a more likely explanation of why he won. Survey data support the contention that the policy views of voters do not undergo enormous swings every few years. Thus, it is unlikely that the same voters who had previously supported policies close to the status quo suddenly shifted their support to the policies enunciated by Reagan during the 1980 campaign. It is more likely that what led many voters to support Reagan was intense dissatisfaction with Carter, coupled with the belief that a government impervious to the reform efforts of previous Republicans really would not change too much under Ronald Reagan.

4.16 Conclusion

We have laid out the basic elements of our model of candidate competition and discussed some of the tactics that might be employed in the campaign. In the following chapter we shall add nonpolicy issues to our model and show how they affect voter evaluations of the candidates. We shall also discuss how abstention affects our model of candidate competition. Chapter 7 will introduce the subject of voter uncertainty about candidates. Chapter 9 will then present empirical results designed to demonstrate the ability of our candidate model to explain the underlying basis of American presidential elections.

Appendix 4.1

A.1 Single-peaked indirect preferences

In this appendix we shall develop general conditions under which voters' indirect preferences are single-peaked when there is a single predictive dimension. A voter's indirect preference is induced on the predictive dimension Π based on the voter's preferences in $X \subset E^m$, the space of policy issues, and the predictive map w_i that associates for each point in Π a point in this policy space X. This appendix is adapted directly from Coughlin and Hinich (in press).

Let $X \subset E^m$ denote a convex set of possible positions on m policy issues (contained in an m-dimensional Euclidean space). All topological statements concerned with this space will be with respect to the usual (relative) Euclidean topology. We assume a common policy space for simplicity only, because all statements are proved for an individual voter.

The society's voters are indexed by the elements, i, in the set $N = \{1, 2, \ldots, n\}$, where n is finite. The preferences of any individual (or voter) i on the set X will be specified by the subset $R_i \subset X \times X$. We assume that each R_i is reflexive, connected, transitive, regular, weakly convex, and convex.[1] $P(R_i)$ is used for the asymmetric part[2] of R_i, and $I(R_i)$ is used for the symmetric part[3] of R_i. The n-tuple $(R_1, \ldots, R_n)$ of individual preferences in a particular society is that society's "profile on X." The collection of all *possible* profiles that satisfy the foregoing assumptions (for a particular n) is denoted by $R(n)$.

Let Π denote a set of "predictive elements" for the voters (such as a

[1] Let $R \subset X \times X$ be a preference relation on X. Then R is (a) "reflexive" if and only if $(x,x) \in R$, $\forall x, y \in X$; (b) "connected" if and only if $(x,y) \in R$ or $(y,x) \in R$, $\forall x, y \in X$; (c) "transitive" if and only if $(x,y) \in R$ and $(y,z) \in R$ imply $(x,z) \in R$, $\forall x, y, z \in X$; (d) "regular" if and only if $\{y \in X: (y,x) \in R\}$ is closed, $\forall x \in X$; (e) "weakly convex" if and only if $(x,y) \in R$ implies $[\lambda x + (1-\lambda)y, y] \in R$, $\forall x, y \in X$ and $\lambda \in (0,1)$; (f) "convex" if and only if $(x,y) \in P(R)$ implies $[\lambda x + (1-\lambda)y, y] \in P(R)$, $\forall x, y \in X$ and $\lambda \in (0,1)$.

[2] That is, $(x,y) \in P(R_i)$ if and only if $(x,y) \in R_i$ and $(y,x) \notin R_i$.

[3] That is, $(x,y) \in I(R_i)$ if and only if $(x,y) \in R_i$ and $(y,x) \in R_i$.

left–right ideological dimension). We shall assume that Π has at least three elements. The symbol $\leqslant_o$ will denote a natural linear order[4] on Π. The asymmetric part of $\leqslant_0$, in particular, will be written as $<_o$. The existence of such an ordering means, of course, that Π is essentially one-dimensional in nature [e.g., see the closely related discussion of strong orderings in Chapter 7 of Arrow (1963)].

All topological statements about Π are made with respect to the order topology[5] on this set that corresponds to the natural linear order $\leqslant_o$ [as in Denzau and Parks (1975)]. Assume that Π is compact.

We also assume throughout that all of the voters agree on the location in Π that corresponds to any particular candidate, but they may disagree about the policies that will follow if the candidate is elected. We formulate this by assuming that each voter has a "predictive map," $w_i(\pi)$, that is a continuous[6] function from Π into X. This, in turn, implies that "indirect preferences on Π" are defined for each $i \in N$ by the relation

$$(\pi_1, \pi_2) \in Q_i \quad \text{if and only if} \quad [w_i(\pi_1), w_i(\pi_2)] \in R_i \qquad \text{(A4.1)}$$

for any $\pi_1, \pi_2 \in \Pi$. We use $P(Q_i)$ for the asymmetric part of Q_i, and $I(Q_i)$ for the symmetric part of Q_i. The n-tuple $(Q_1, \ldots, Q_n)$ that occurs in a particular society is its "indirect profile" or "profile on Π."

An indirect profile on Π is said to be "single-peaked"[7] with respect to the linear order $\leqslant_o$ if and only if, for each $i \in N$, there are unique $a_i, b_i \in \Pi$ with $a_i \leqslant_o b_i$ such that

(a) $\pi_1 <_o \pi_2 \leqslant_o a_i \rightarrow (\pi_2, \pi_1) \in P(Q_i)$

(b) $a_i \leqslant_o \pi_1 \leqslant_o \pi_2 \leqslant_o b_i \rightarrow (\pi_2, \pi_1) \in I(Q_i)$

(c) $b_i \leqslant_o \pi_2 <_o \pi_1 \rightarrow (\pi_2, \pi_1) \in P(Q_i)$

and

(d) $\pi_1 <_o a_i$, or $b_i <_o \pi_1$, and $a_i \leqslant_o \pi_2 \leqslant_o b_i \rightarrow (\pi_2, \pi_1) \in P(Q_i)$ (A4.2)

4 A binary relation $\leqslant_o$ on Π is a "linear order" if and only if $\leqslant_o$ is transitive, connected, and antisymmetric (i.e., $\pi_1 \leqslant_o \pi_2$ and $\pi_2 \leqslant_o \pi_1$ imply $\pi_1 = \pi_2$ for any $\pi_1, \pi_2 \in \Pi$).

5 The "order topology" on a linearly ordered set Π is defined by the subbase of open sets $\{\pi \in \Pi: \pi < \pi_1\}$, $\{\pi \in \Pi: \pi > \pi_1\}$, $\pi_1 \in \Pi$.

6 It should be observed that when Π is a finite set, the continuity assumption on $w(\pi)$ does not impose any restriction at all. In this case, each singleton set in Π (and, hence, every subset of Π) is both open and closed.

7 This definition is based on the earlier definitions due to Black (1958), Arrow (1963), and Fishburn (1973). It differs from the Arrow definition because there can be more than two maximal elements when Π is finite and more than one maximal element when Π is convex. For a careful discussion of how it differs from Fishburn's definition, see Denzau and Parks (1975).

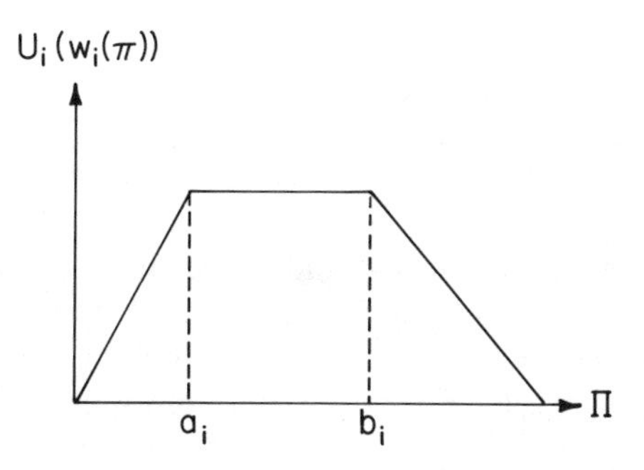

Figure A4.1. Single-peaked indirect preferences.

For a standard representation of preferences that satisfy these requirements, see Figure A4.1. The symbol U_i represents voter i's utility function, where $\forall x, y \in X$, $U_i(x) \geqslant U_i(y)$ if and only if $(x, y) \in R_i$.

We shall now state and discuss a theorem that specifies restrictions on the predictive maps of the voters that are both necessary and sufficient to be able to conclude that every indirect profile on Π is single-peaked with respect to the linear order $\leqslant_o$. In order to be able to state this theorem precisely, we shall have to provide a few more definitions.

First of all, recall that for a given pair of elements x, y in a convex set $X \subset E^m$, the set of points in X, $I(x, y)$, such that $\alpha x + (1-\alpha)y$ for $0 \leqslant \alpha \leqslant 1$ is called "*the* linear interval connecting the points x and y." Therefore, any set of points that is the linear interval connecting the points x and y for some pair $x, y \in X$ is called "*a* linear interval in X." Any linear interval $I(x, y)$ is, of course, naturally ordered by α, that is, by the relation $\geqslant_\alpha$ that is specified by

$$[z_1 = \alpha_1 x + (1-\alpha_1)y \geqslant_\alpha z_2 = \alpha_2 x + (1-\alpha_2)y] \leftrightarrow \alpha_1 \geqslant \alpha_2 \qquad \text{(A4.3)}$$

for $\alpha_1, \alpha_2 \in [0, 1]$. Furthermore, any linear interval $I(x, y) = I(y, x)$ has two such orderings. Therefore, a predictive map, $w_i(\pi)$, whose range is contained in a linear interval, $I(x, y)$, is said to be "strictly monotonic on this interval" if and only if

$$\pi_1 <_o \pi_2 \rightarrow w_i(\pi_1) <_\alpha w_i(\pi_2), \quad \forall \pi_1, \pi_2 \in \Pi \qquad \text{(A4.4a)}$$

or

$$\pi_1 <_o \pi_2 \rightarrow w_i(\pi_1) >_\alpha w_i(\pi_2), \quad \forall \pi_1, \pi_2 \in \Pi \qquad \text{(A4.4b)}$$

It should be observed that these range restrictions (which appear as condition 2 in the theorem that follows) are satisfied by a predictive map, $w_i(\pi)$, if and only if there exist vectors $\mathbf{c}_i, \mathbf{d}_i \in X$ and a strictly monotonic (real-valued) function, $f_i(\pi)$, such that

$$w_i(\pi) = \mathbf{c}_i + f_i(\pi) \cdot \mathbf{d}_i, \quad \forall \pi \in \Pi \tag{A4.5}$$

Finally, we shall also use the notation $\bar{W}(n)$ to denote a subset of the class of all possible n-tuples of predictive maps $[w_1(\pi), \ldots, w_n(\pi)]$. Using these definitions, we can now state our first theorem:

Theorem 1: Every pair in $R(n) \times \bar{W}(n)$ has an indirect profile on Π that is single-peaked with respect to $\leqslant_o$ if and only if each n-tuple in $\bar{W}(n)$ is such that each voter's predictive map either (1) is constant or (2) has its range contained in a linear interval[8] and is strictly monotonic on this interval.

Proof: For the "if" statement, we shall proceed by showing that the indirect preferences for each $i \in N$ must satisfy the conditions given by (A4.2).

Suppose that $w_i(\pi)$ is constant for a particular $i \in N$. Then i is indifferent over all of the alternatives in Π. Therefore, because Π is compact, the minimal and maximal elements of Π (with respect to $\leqslant_o$) will serve as an a_i and as a b_i, respectively, for the peak of his preference relation [see (A4.2)]. Because of the antisymmetry of $\leqslant_o$, these elements are unique.

Alternatively, consider any $i \in N$ whose predictive map, $w_i(\pi)$, is such that its range is contained in a linear interval and is strictly monotonic on this interval. Transitivity, reflexivity, and connectedness follow immediately for Q_i. We shall show that Q_i also inherits regularity and certain other properties (which are extensions for linearly ordered sets of the concepts of convexity and weak convexity, respectively). First, regularity: For any $\pi_1 \in \Pi$, the upper contour set $Q_i(\pi_1)$ is defined by $Q_i(\pi_1) = \{\pi \in \Pi: (\pi, \pi_1) \in Q_i\}$. Therefore, $Q_i(\pi_1) = \{\pi \in \Pi: [w_i(\pi), w_i(\pi_1)] \in R_i\}$. Let $C(w_i)$ be the range (or co-domain) of w_i. Then, using the notation $w_i^{-1}(A) = \{\pi \in \Pi: w_i(\pi) \in A\}$ [for $A \subseteq C(w_i)$], we have $Q_i(\pi_1) = w_i^{-1}(\{x \in C(w_i): [x, w_i(\pi_1)] \in R_i\})$. But because R_i is regular, the upper contour set $R_i[w_i(\pi_1)] = \{x \in X: [x, w_i(\pi_1)] \in R_i\}$ is closed. Furthermore, because $w_i(\pi)$ is continuous and Π is compact, $C(w_i)$ is compact. Hence,

$$\{x \in C(w_i): [x, w_i(\pi_1)] \in R_i\} = R_i[w_i(\pi_1)] \cap C(w_i)$$

is closed. Therefore, because $w_i(\pi)$ is continuous, $Q_i(\pi_1)$ is closed. Thus, Q_i is regular.

Next we shall show that for any $\pi_1, \pi_2, \pi_3 \in \Pi$,

$$[(\pi_3, \pi_1) \in P(Q_i) \quad \text{and} \quad \pi_1 <_o \pi_2 <_o \pi_3] \rightarrow [(\pi_2, \pi_1) \in P(Q_i)] \tag{A4.6}$$

[8] These linear intervals may vary from voter to voter.

Suppose that $(\pi_3, \pi_1) \in P(Q_i)$ and $\pi_1 <_o \pi_2 <_o \pi_3$ for some $\pi_1, \pi_2, \pi_3 \in \Pi$. Then $[w_i(\pi_3), w_i(\pi_1)] \in P(R_i)$. Also, because $w_i(\pi)$ has its range contained in a closed linear interval and is strictly monotonic on that interval, there must be some $\alpha \in (0,1)$ such that $w_i(\pi_2) = \alpha w_i(\pi_1) + (1-\alpha) w_i(\pi_3)$. But, by the convexity of R_i,

$$[w_i(\pi_3), w_i(\pi_1)] \in P(R_i)$$

implies

$$[\alpha w_i(\pi_1) + (1-\alpha) w_i(\pi_3), w_i(\pi_1)] \in P(R_i)$$

Therefore, $[w_i(\pi_2), w_i(\pi_1)] \in P(R_i)$. Hence, $(\pi_2, \pi_1) \in P(Q_i)$.

Finally, a similar argument (using the weak convexity of R_i) establishes that for any $\pi_1, \pi_2, \pi_3 \in \Pi$,

$$[(\pi_3, \pi_1) \in Q_i \quad \text{and} \quad \pi_1 <_o \pi_2 <_o \pi_3] \rightarrow [(\pi_2, \pi_1) \in Q_i] \qquad \text{(A4.7)}$$

We shall now show that these properties imply that i's indirect preferences on Π satisfy the conditions that each individual's preferences must satisfy for single-peakedness with respect to the order $\leqslant_o$ to hold. First, the inherited properties of Q_i together with the compactness of Π imply that there is at least one maximal element in Π (with respect to Q_i); that is, $M_i = \{\pi \in \Pi: (\pi, \pi_1) \in Q_i, \ \forall \pi_1 \in \Pi\}$ is nonempty (e.g., Bergstrom, 1975, p. 403, Lemma). The inherited properties also imply that $M_i = \{\pi \in \Pi: (\pi, \pi_1) \in Q_i\}$ for any $\pi_1 \in M_i$. Therefore, by the regularity of Q_i, M_i is closed. Hence, because Π is compact, M_i is also compact. Therefore, because (A4.7) also holds,[9] there exist $a_i, b_i \in \Pi$ with $a_i \leqslant_o b_i$ such that $M_i = \{\pi \in \Pi: a_i \leqslant_o \pi \leqslant_o b_i\}$. Because $\leqslant_o$ is antisymmetric, these "end points" are unique.

We now turn to the specific conditions given in (A4.2).

(a) Suppose that $\pi_1 <_o \pi_2 \leqslant_o a_i$. Then $\pi_1 \notin M_i$. Therefore, $(\pi_1, a_i) \notin Q_i$. Therefore, by connectedness, $(a_i, \pi_1) \in P(Q_i)$. Consequently, if $\pi_2 = a_i$, we have $(\pi_2, \pi_1) \in P(Q_i)$ immediately. Alternatively, if $\pi_2 \neq a_i$, then $\pi_1 <_o \pi_2 <_o a_i$. Therefore, by (A4.6), $(\pi_2, \pi_1) \in P(Q_i)$.

(b) Suppose that $a_i \leqslant_o \pi_1 \leqslant_o \pi_2 \leqslant_o b_i$. Then $\pi_1, \pi_2 \in M_i$. Therefore, $(\pi_1, \pi_2) \in Q_i$ and $(\pi_2, \pi_1) \in Q_i$. Hence, $(\pi_1, \pi_2) \in I(Q_i)$.

(c) Similar to (a).

[9] To illustrate the role of (A4.7), we include the following examples: (1) $\Pi = \{0, \frac{1}{2}, 1\}$, $0 <_o \frac{1}{2} <_o 1$, and $U_i(0) = 1$, $U_i(\frac{1}{2}) = 0$, $U_i(1) = 1$ for some $i \in N$; (2) $\Pi = [0,1]$, $\leqslant_o$ is the linear ordering given by the numerical values of the $\pi \in \Pi$, and $U_i(\pi)$ equals π for $0 < \pi \leqslant 1$ and equals 1 for $\pi = 0$. In both examples, the individual's preferences satisfy (A4.6), but not (A4.7). They also satisfy reflexivity, connectedness, transitivity, and regularity. But in both cases the set of maximal elements for i is $\{0, 1\}$. Therefore, preferences are not single-peaked along the given linear orders for Π.

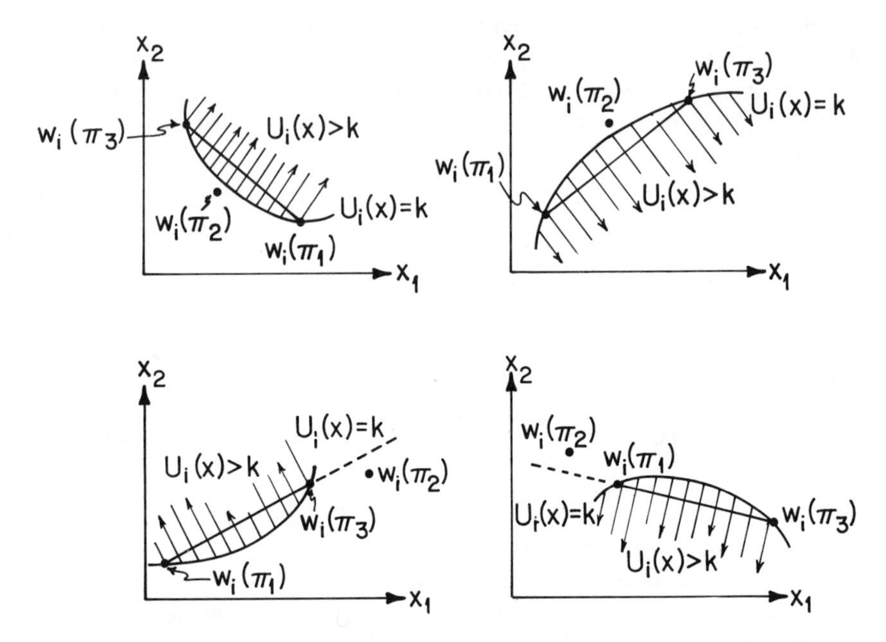

Figure A4.2. Predictive maps with ranges not contained in a linear interval.

(d) Suppose that $\pi_1 <_o a_i$ and $a_i \leqslant_o \pi_2 \leqslant_o b_i$. Then $\pi_2 \in M_i$ and $\pi_1 \notin M_i$. Therefore, $(\pi_1, \pi_2) \notin Q_i$. Hence, by the connectedness of Q_i, $(\pi_2, \pi_1) \in P(Q_i)$.

A similar argument holds for $\pi_1 <_o b_i$ and $a_i \leqslant_o \pi_2 \leqslant_o b_i$.

For the "only if" statement, we shall proceed by considering a sequence of possible assumptions about the voters' predictive maps. We shall show that each of these assumptions, in turn, allows the theorem's single-peakedness requirement to be violated at some profile in $R(n)$. In particular, because single-peakedness is a condition that requires certain properties to be satisfied by *each* voter's preferences, we shall be able to show this in each case by showing that there is at least one profile such that at least one voter's indirect preferences will violate the conditions in (A4.2). This successive elimination of alternative assumptions will establish our result.

We shall begin by showing that the range of each $w_i(\pi)$ must be contained in a linear interval. Consider any three elements in Π such that $\pi_1 <_o \pi_2 <_o \pi_3$. We shall show, more specifically, that $w_i(\pi_2)$ must be a linear combination of $w_i(\pi_1)$ and $w_i(\pi_3)$. Suppose not. Then there exist profiles in each $R(n)$ such that $w_i(\pi_1)$ and $w_i(\pi_3)$ lie on a common indifference curve, while $w_i(\pi_2)$ is in the strict lower contour set for this curve

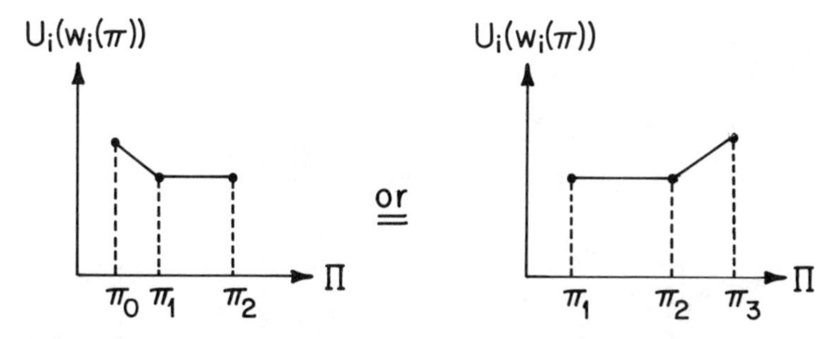

Figure A4.3. Predictive maps constant on a strict subset of Π.

(for examples with $X \subset E^2$, see Figure A4.2). But then $(\pi_1, \pi_2) \in P(Q_i)$ and $(\pi_3, \pi_2) \in P(Q_i)$, which imply that single-peakedness cannot be satisfied by the corresponding indirect profiles on Π. Our claim now follows, because, as noted before, the range of $w_i(\pi)$ must be compact.

Finally, suppose that for some $i \in N$, $w_i(\pi)$ is neither constant nor strictly monotonic. We consider first whether or not $w_i(\pi)$ can be constant on any strict subset of Π that is connected (with respect to the order topology on Π) and has at least two elements. Suppose that there is such a set, A. Let $\pi_1, \pi_2 \in A$, with $\pi_1 <_o \pi_2$. Then there will also be some profile in each $R(n)$ for which i has (1) $[x, w_i(\pi_1)] \in P(R_i)$ for some $x = w_i(\pi_0)$, with $\pi_0 \in \Pi - A$ and $\pi_0 <_o \pi_1$, or (2) $[x, w_i(\pi_2)] \in P(R_i)$ for some $x = w_i(\pi_3)$, with $\pi_3 \in \Pi - A$ and $\pi_3 >_o \pi_2$ (because A is a strict subset of Π). Finally, suppose that the indirect profile on Π is single-peaked. Then we must have, for these cases, (1) $b_i <_o \pi_1 <_o \pi_2$ or (2) $\pi_1 <_o \pi_2 <_o a_i$ [see (A4.2)]. But $w_i(\pi_1) = w_i(\pi_2)$, so we must have $(\pi_1, \pi_2) \in I(Q_i)$ as well, a contradiction. For an illustration, see Figure A4.3 versus Figure A4.1.

Therefore, for $w_i(\pi)$ not to be strictly monotonic, there must exist three elements $\pi_1, \pi_2, \pi_3 \in \Pi$, with $\pi_1 <_o \pi_2 <_o \pi_3$ and either (1) $w_i(\pi_1) >_\alpha w_i(\pi_2)$ and $w_i(\pi_3) >_\alpha w_i(\pi_2)$ or (2) $w_i(\pi_2) >_\alpha w_i(\pi_1)$ and $w_i(\pi_2) >_\alpha w_i(\pi_3)$. Suppose that the first holds. Then there also exists some profile in each $R(n)$ such that for all $x, y \in C(w_i)$, $(x, y) \in R_i$ if and only if $x \geqslant_\alpha y$. But then $(\pi_1, \pi_2) \in P(Q_i)$ and $(\pi_3, \pi_2) \in P(Q_i)$, and the indirect profile on Π cannot be single-peaked along $\leqslant_o$. Alternatively, suppose that the second holds. Then there also exists some profile in R such that for all $x, y \in C(w_i)$, $(x, y) \in R_i$ if and only if $y \geqslant_\alpha x$. But then $(\pi_1, \pi_2) \in P(Q_i)$ and $(\pi_3, \pi_2) \in P(Q_i)$ again. For an illustration with $X \subset E^2$, see Figure A4.4.

Therefore, $w_i(\pi)$ is either constant or strictly monotonic. Q.E.D.

An example of a predictive map that satisfies condition (2) of the theorem is given by the linear map specified in Section 4.4. However, the

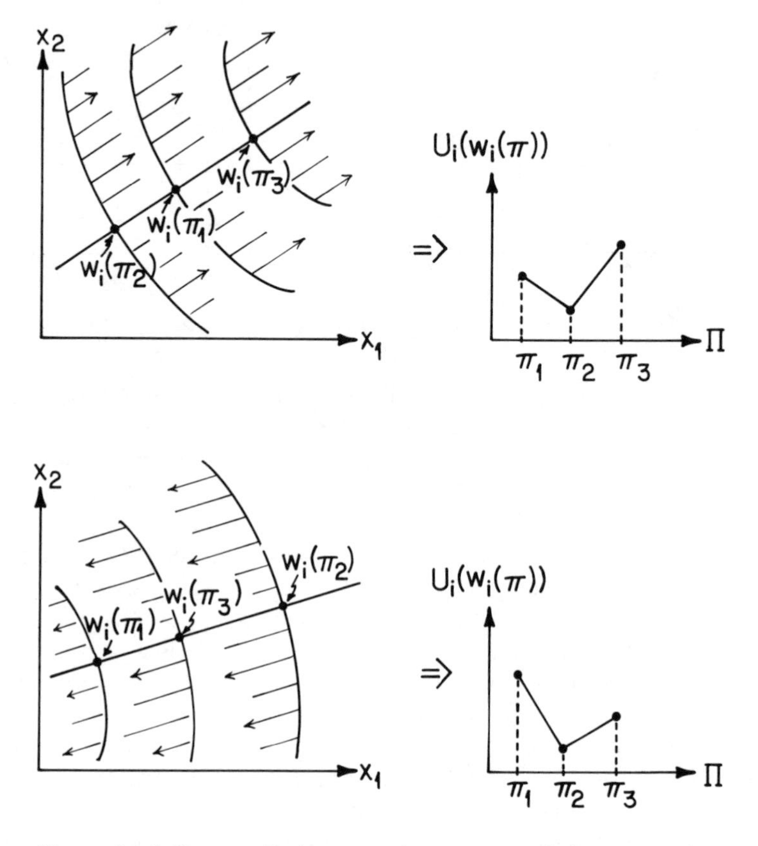

Figure A4.4. Two predictive maps that are not strictly monotonic.

restrictions on the voters' predictive maps specified by this theorem are strictly weaker than the restrictions on voters' predictive maps specified by this class of functions. Hence, it also reveals that certain piecewise linear functions (e.g., Figure A4.5) or nonlinear functions (e.g., Figure A4.6) are also sufficient for the preferences of voters to always lead to indirect preferences on Π that are single-peaked with respect to $\leqslant_o$. Furthermore, by its necessity statement, it establishes that the conditions that have been specified here are ones that are minimally sufficient[10] for societies with such voters.

When the society's policy space is unidimensional, Theorem 1 simplifies to the following.

[10] That is, there is no strictly weaker condition on the predictive maps that will be sufficient for single-peakedness with respect to $\leqslant_o$ to occur for every pair in $R(n) \times \bar{W}(n)$.

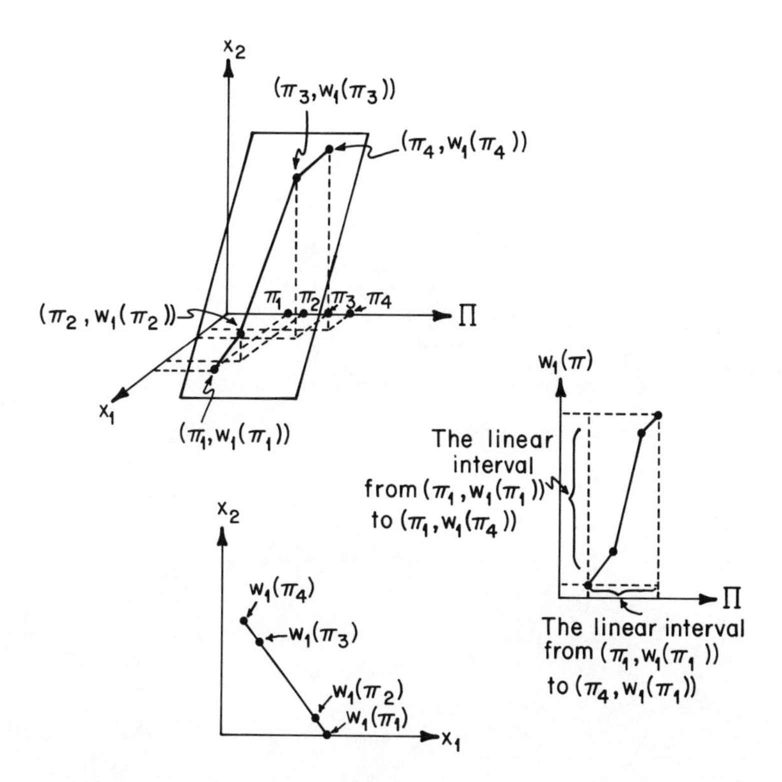

Figure A4.5. Three views of a single predictive map, $w_1 : \Pi \rightarrow X \subset E^2$.

Corollary 1: Suppose that $X \subset E^1$. Then the indirect profile on Π is single-peaked with respect to $\leqslant_o$ for every profile in $R(n)$ if and only if each voter's predictive map is either (1) constant or (2) strictly monotonic.

Theorem 1 and Corollary 1 contain both possibility and impossibility results in their "if" and "only if" statements, respectively. These results specify exact limits for spatial voting models that posit a linearly ordered set of predictive elements and the type of voter preferences we have assumed. In the next section we shall take advantage of this theorem by obtaining the median voter results that follow within these limits.

A.2 Median voter results

We say that a candidate is "identified with" a particular $\pi \in \Pi$ whenever this element of the predictive set is one that (all voters agree) specifies the

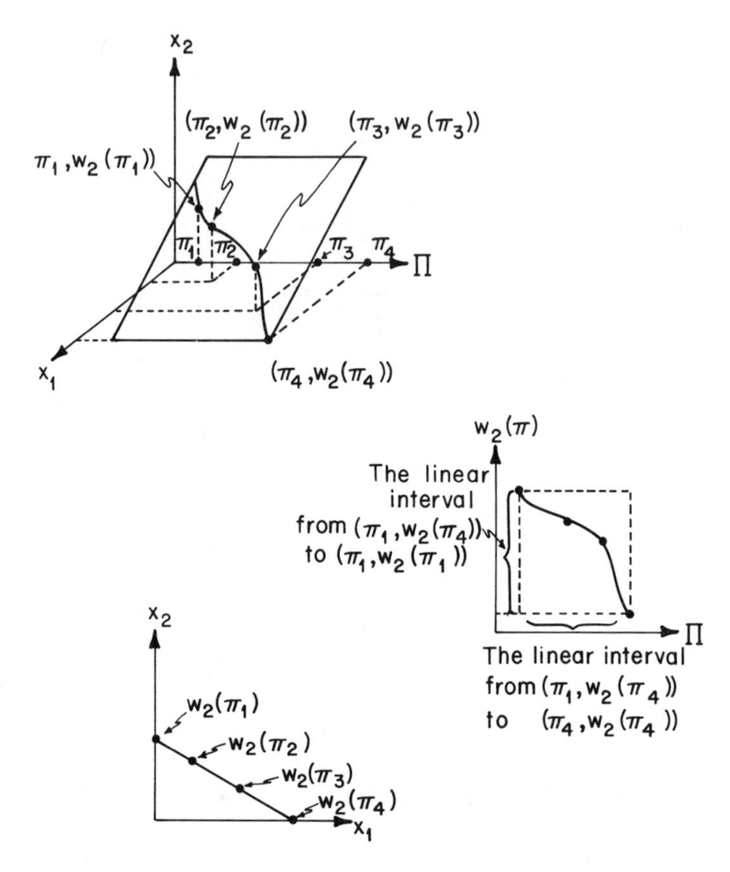

Figure A4.6. Three views of a single predictive map, $w_2: \Pi \to X \subset E^2$.

candidate's location in Π. In addition, we say that a candidate Theta identified with $\pi_\theta \in \Pi$ receives at least as many votes as a candidate Psi identified with $\pi_\psi \in \Pi$ if and only if

$$\#\{i \in N \mid (\pi_\theta, \pi_\psi) \in P(Q_i)\} \geqslant \#\{i \in N \mid (\pi_\psi, \pi_\theta) \in P(Q_i)\} \qquad \text{(A4.8)}$$

This is appropriate whenever every voter is one who casts a ballot if and only if he strictly prefers one of the candidates to the other (and he votes for the one he prefers). It is also appropriate (in terms of expected votes) when, alternatively, indifferent individuals vote but there is a probability of one-half of their voting for each candidate (and individuals with strict preferences vote for their preferred alternative).

To apply results due to Denzau and Parks (1975), we now have only to let $c_1, \ldots, c_{2k}$ be a rearrangement of the sequence $a_1, b_1, a_2, b_2, \ldots, a_k, b_k$ such that $c_1 \leqslant c_2 \leqslant \cdots \leqslant c_{2k}$. Then we have the following.

Theorem 2: Suppose that $(R_1, \ldots, R_n) \in R(n)$ and that every voter's predictive map either (1) is constant or (2) has its range contained in a linear interval and is strictly monotonic on this interval. Then a candidate Theta identified with $\pi_\theta \in \Pi$ receives at least as many votes as any other candidate Psi identified with a $\pi_\theta \in \Pi$ if and only if $c_k \leqslant \pi_\theta \leqslant c_{k+1}$.

Proof: The proof of Theorem 2 follows from our preceding Theorem 1 and from Theorem 2 of Denzau and Parks (1975).

As in Section A.1, when the society's policy space is unidimensional, this result simplifies. In this case we have the following.

Corollary 2: Suppose that $X \subset E^1$, $(R_1, \ldots, R_n) \in R(n)$, and every voter's predictive map is either constant or strictly monotonic. Then a candidate Theta identified with $\pi_\theta \in \Pi$ receives at least as many votes as any other candidate Psi identified with a $\pi_\psi \in \Pi$ if and only if $c_k \leqslant \pi_\theta \leqslant c_{k+1}$.

In either case, there is (necessarily) some π_θ that satisfies the given inequality. Furthermore, any such π_θ is, by its very definition, a median for the distribution of c_j's. Therefore, Theorem 2 and Corollary 2 provide both existence and location results for "nonlosing identifications" in the set of predictive elements.

Appendix 4.2

In this appendix we develop the general form of the equivalence between voter preferences in the space of policy issues and voter preferences induced from such policy preferences on the space defined by the underlying set of predictive dimensions. All spaces are assumed to be Euclidean.

Let $\boldsymbol{\theta}_i = (\theta_{i1}, \ldots, \theta_{in})'$ be voter i's perception of Theta's positions on the n policy issues of the campaign $(1, \ldots, n)$. $\boldsymbol{\psi}_i = (\psi_{i1}, \ldots, \psi_{in})'$ is i's perception of Psi's positions on these same issues. $\mathbf{x}_i$ is i's ideal point on these n issues, and A_i is the symmetric $n \times n$ positive semidefinite matrix of salience weights that defines the roundness and orientation of i's ellipsoidal indifference contours (see Section 3.1).

By the weighted Euclidean distance preference rule, voter i prefers candidate Theta to candidate Psi if and only if (squaring both sides)

$$\|\boldsymbol{\theta}_i - \mathbf{x}_i\|_{A_i}^2 < \|\boldsymbol{\psi}_i - \mathbf{x}_i\|_{A_i}^2 \qquad \text{(A4.9)}$$

which can also be written in quadratic form as

$$(\boldsymbol{\theta}_i-\mathbf{x}_i)'A_i(\boldsymbol{\theta}_i-\mathbf{x}_i)<(\boldsymbol{\psi}_i-\mathbf{x}_i)'A_i(\boldsymbol{\psi}_i-\mathbf{x}_i)$$

However, by the linear predictive map defined in Section 4.4 and generalized in Section 4.12, we can express $\boldsymbol{\theta}_i$ as $\mathbf{b}_i+V_i\boldsymbol{\pi}_\theta$, where $\mathbf{b}_i'=(b_{i1},\ldots,b_{in})$ is the intercept term in i's linear predictive map, $\boldsymbol{\pi}_\theta'=(\pi_{\theta1},\ldots,\pi_{\theta p})$ is Theta's position in the underlying predictive space of dimension $p\leqslant n$, and V_i is an $n\times p$ matrix of translation weights. An element v_{ijk} of the matrix V_i represents the marginal change in θ_{ik} given a unit increase in $\pi_{\theta j}$. Finally, $\boldsymbol{\psi}_i=\mathbf{b}_i+V_i\boldsymbol{\pi}_\psi$ is the equivalent expression for candidate Psi, $\boldsymbol{\pi}_\psi'=(\pi_{\psi1},\ldots,\pi_{\psi p})$ being Psi's position in the p-dimensional predictive space.

Substituting in (A4.9), we then have

$$\|\mathbf{b}_i+V_i\boldsymbol{\pi}_\theta-\mathbf{x}_i\|_{A_i}^2<\|\mathbf{b}_i+V_i\boldsymbol{\pi}_\psi-\mathbf{x}_i\|_{A_i}^2 \tag{A4.10}$$

Setting $\mathbf{y}_i=\mathbf{x}_i-\mathbf{b}_i$, we can express (A4.10) in quadratic form as

$$(V_i\boldsymbol{\pi}_\theta-\mathbf{y}_i)'A_i(V_i\boldsymbol{\pi}_\theta-\mathbf{y}_i)<(V_i\boldsymbol{\pi}_\psi-\mathbf{y}_i)'A_i(V_i\boldsymbol{\pi}_\psi-\mathbf{y}_i)$$

Expanding this expression, we have

$$\begin{aligned}&\boldsymbol{\pi}_\theta'V_i'A_iV_i\boldsymbol{\pi}_\theta-\boldsymbol{\pi}_\theta'V_i'A_i\mathbf{y}_i-\mathbf{y}_i'A_iV_i\boldsymbol{\pi}_\theta\\&\quad<\boldsymbol{\pi}_\psi'V_i'A_iV_i\boldsymbol{\pi}_\psi-\boldsymbol{\pi}_\psi'V_i'A_i\mathbf{y}_i-\mathbf{y}_i'A_iV_i\boldsymbol{\pi}_\psi\end{aligned} \tag{A4.11}$$

We shall now show that (A4.11) holds if and only if

$$\|\boldsymbol{\pi}_\theta-\mathbf{z}_i\|_{V_i'A_iV_i}^2<\|\boldsymbol{\pi}_\psi-\mathbf{z}_i\|_{V_i'A_iV_i}^2 \tag{A4.12}$$

where $\mathbf{z}_i=(V_i'A_iV_i)^{-1}(V_i'A_i\mathbf{y}_i)$. This establishes the equivalence we are seeking.

Because $\mathbf{z}_i=(V_i'A_iV_i)^{-1}(V_i'A_i\mathbf{y}_i)$, (A4.12) can be rewritten in quadratic form:

$$\begin{aligned}&[\boldsymbol{\pi}_\theta-(V_i'A_iV_i)^{-1}(V_i'A_i\mathbf{y}_i)]'V_i'A_iV_i[\boldsymbol{\pi}_\theta-(V_i'A_iV_i)^{-1}(V_i'A_i\mathbf{y}_i)]\\&\quad<[\boldsymbol{\pi}_\psi-(V_i'A_iV_i)^{-1}(V_i'A_i\mathbf{y}_i)]'V_i'A_iV_i[\boldsymbol{\pi}_\psi-(V_i'A_iV_i)^{-1}(V_i'A_i\mathbf{y}_i)]\end{aligned} \tag{A4.13}$$

Expanding both sides of (A4.13) and gathering terms, we have

$$\begin{aligned}&\boldsymbol{\pi}_\theta'V_i'A_iV_i\boldsymbol{\pi}_\theta-\boldsymbol{\pi}_\theta'V_i'A_i\mathbf{y}_i-\mathbf{y}_i'A_iV_i\boldsymbol{\pi}_\theta\\&\quad<\boldsymbol{\pi}_\psi'V_i'A_iV_i\boldsymbol{\pi}_\psi-\boldsymbol{\pi}_\psi'V_i'A_i\mathbf{y}_i-\mathbf{y}_i'A_iV_i\boldsymbol{\pi}_\psi\end{aligned}$$

which is identical with (A4.11). Thus, the equivalence between (A4.9) and (A4.12) establishes the connection between voter preferences defined on the policy issues of the campaign and voter preferences induced by these policy preferences onto the underlying space defined by the predictive dimensions of the campaign.

Appendix 4.3

In this appendix we shall generalize the results represented by (4.16) and (4.17).

Assume p predictive dimensions and n policy issues, where $p \leqslant n$. For simplicity, we set $A_i = I$, but this is not necessary for our results. We also set $\boldsymbol{\pi}_\theta = \mathbf{1}$ and $\boldsymbol{\pi}_\psi = \mathbf{0}$, but this is also strictly for convenience. Thus, Theta is the challenger and Psi the incumbent.

For p predictive dimensions, $\boldsymbol{\theta}_i = \mathbf{b}_i + V_i \boldsymbol{\pi}_\theta$ and $\boldsymbol{\psi}_i = \mathbf{b}_i + V_i \boldsymbol{\pi}_\psi$, where $\boldsymbol{\theta}_i = (\theta_{i1}, \ldots, \theta_{in})'$, $\boldsymbol{\psi}_i = (\psi_{i1}, \ldots, \psi_{in})'$, $\mathbf{b}_i = (b_{i1}, \ldots, b_{in})'$, and V_i is an $n \times p$ matrix of translation weights, with v_{ijk} being the perceptual change on the kth issue given a unit change on the jth dimension. $\boldsymbol{\pi}'_\theta = (\pi_{\theta 1}, \ldots, \pi_{\theta p})$ and $\boldsymbol{\pi}'_\psi = (\pi_{\psi 1}, \ldots, \pi_{\psi p})$ are the positions of Theta and Psi on the p predictive dimensions.

It then follows that voter i prefers Theta to Psi if and only if

$$\|\mathbf{b}_i + V_i \boldsymbol{\pi}_\theta - \mathbf{x}_i\|^2_{A_i} < \|\mathbf{b}_i + V_i \boldsymbol{\pi}_\psi - \mathbf{x}_i\|^2_{A_i} \qquad \text{(A4.14)}$$

Because $\boldsymbol{\pi}_\theta = \mathbf{1}$, $\boldsymbol{\pi}_\psi = \mathbf{0}$, and $A_i = I$, (A4.14) reduces to

$$\|V_i \mathbf{1} - \mathbf{y}_i\|^2 < \|-\mathbf{y}_i\|^2 \qquad \text{(A4.15)}$$

where $\mathbf{y}_i = \mathbf{x}_i - \mathbf{b}_i$. We can rewrite (A4.15) as

$$\|\mathbf{v}_i - \mathbf{y}_i\|^2 < \|-\mathbf{y}_i\|^2 \qquad \text{(A4.16)}$$

where $\mathbf{v}_i = (v_{i11} + \ldots + v_{ip1}, \ldots, v_{i1n} + \ldots + v_{ipn})' = V_i \mathbf{1}$. Expanding (A4.16) and collecting terms yields

$$\mathbf{v}'_i \mathbf{y}_i / \mathbf{v}'_i \mathbf{v}_i > \tfrac{1}{2} \qquad \text{(A4.17)}$$

so that i prefers the challenger (Theta) to the incumbent (Psi) if and only if (A4.17) holds; (A4.17) is an n-issue generalization of (4.15). However, from the Schwarz inequality,

$$|\mathbf{v}'_i \mathbf{y}_i| \leqslant \|\mathbf{v}_i\| \, \|\mathbf{y}_i\|$$

so that

$$\|\mathbf{y}_i\| / \|\mathbf{v}_i\| \geqslant \mathbf{v}'_i \mathbf{y}_i / \mathbf{v}'_i \mathbf{v}_i \qquad \text{(A4.18)}$$

From (A4.17), i prefers the challenger (Theta) to the incumbent (Psi) if and only if the right-hand side of (A4.18) exceeds one-half. Thus, as $\|\mathbf{v}_i\|$ increases, the upper bound $\|\mathbf{y}_i\| / \|\mathbf{v}_i\|$ approaches zero, forcing the right-hand side of (A4.18) to be less than one-half. Thus, increasing $\|\mathbf{v}_i\|$ increases support for the incumbent.

If $\mathbf{v}_i$ is expressed as the product of a scalar $c>0$ and a constant vector $\mathbf{e}_i$, then, from (A4.17), i prefers Theta to Psi if and only if

$$c\mathbf{e}_i'\mathbf{y}_i/c^2\mathbf{e}_i'\mathbf{e}_i=\mathbf{e}_i'\mathbf{y}_i/c\mathbf{e}_i'\mathbf{e}_i>\tfrac{1}{2} \qquad \text{(A4.19)}$$

Consequently, shrinking $\mathbf{v}_i$ by decreasing c increases the left-hand side of (A4.19) and increases support for Theta. If $\mathbf{v}_i'\mathbf{y}_i>0$, the left-hand side will approach positive infinity as c approaches zero. If $\mathbf{v}_i'\mathbf{y}_i<0$, the left-hand side will approach negative infinity as c approaches zero. Thus, if $\mathbf{v}_i'\mathbf{y}_i>0$ for a majority of voters, decreasing c sufficiently will ensure victory for the challenger.

Problems

4.1 Suppose that there are only two policy issues linked to positions on one predictive dimension by the linear rules (for voter i):

$$w_{i1}(\pi)=b_{i1}+\pi v_{i1}, \quad w_{i2}(\pi)=b_{i2}+\pi v_{i2}$$

These equations describe a line in the plane whose axes are the policy issues.

(a) Draw the line for $b_{i1}=b_{i2}=0$, $v_{i1}=1$, and $v_{i2}=-1$.
(b) Draw the line for $b_{i1}=b_{i2}=0$, $v_{i1}=5$, and $v_{i2}=-5$.
(c) Draw the line for $b_{i1}=b_{i2}=2$, $v_{i1}=1$, and $v_{i2}=-1$.
(d) Draw the line for $b_{i1}=b_{i2}=2$, $v_{i1}=1$, and $v_{i2}=0$.

Hint: Compute the points $[w_{i1}(0), w_{i2}(0)]$ and $[w_{i1}(1), w_{i2}(1)]$. Draw the line connecting these points.

4.2 Show that the slope of the line described by $w_{i1}(\pi)$ and $w_{i2}(\pi)$ in Problem 4.1 is v_{i2}/v_{i1}.

4.3 Express π_θ in terms of θ_{ij}, b_{ij}, and v_{ij}.

4.4 Suppose in the example in Section 4.5 that $b_{i1}=.4$. What is θ_{i1}?

4.5 Assume three voters r, s, and t with ideal points $\mathbf{x}_r=(.3,.1)$, $\mathbf{x}_s=(0,-.2)$, and $\mathbf{x}_t=(-.3,.4)$. If $\mathbf{b}_r=\mathbf{b}_s=\mathbf{b}_t=0$, and $\mathbf{v}_r=\mathbf{x}_r$, $\mathbf{v}_s=\mathbf{x}_s$, and $\mathbf{v}_t=\mathbf{x}_t$, derive z_r, z_s, and z_t.

4.6 If $\pi_\psi=0$ and $\pi_\theta=-1$, what are $\boldsymbol{\theta}_r$, $\boldsymbol{\theta}_s$, and $\boldsymbol{\theta}_t$ in Problem 4.5? What if $\pi_\theta=1$?

4.7 Given the data of Figure 4.4, if $\mathbf{v}=(v_1, v_2)$ changes from $(-.267, .167)$ to $(-.2, .1)$, derive $\boldsymbol{\theta}_i$, $\boldsymbol{\theta}_j$, $\boldsymbol{\theta}_k$, z_i, z_j, and z_k.

4.8 Given the data of Figure 4.4, if θ_{i2}, θ_{j2}, and θ_{k2} are all changed to .3, derive z_i, z_j, and z_k.

4.9 Given the data of Figure 4.4, if $\mathbf{v}_k=c\mathbf{1}$, how large must c be if k is to be indifferent between Theta and Psi?

4.10 Given the data of Figure 4.6, what is the smallest change in θ_{k2} required to make Psi the election winner?

4.11 Suppose that a two-dimensional predictive space maps into a three-dimensional issue space. The linear map for voter i of a point $\boldsymbol{\pi}_\theta'=(\pi_{\theta 1}, \pi_{\theta 2})$ in the predictive space to a point on issue j is $\theta_{ij}=b_{ij}+v_{i1j}\pi_{\theta 1}+v_{i2j}\pi_{\theta 2}$. Suppose that $A_i=I$, the 3×3 identity matrix, and

$$V_i' = \begin{bmatrix} 1/2 & 1/2 & 0 \\ 0 & 0 & \sqrt{2}/2 \end{bmatrix}$$

for a voter whose ideal point is $\mathbf{x}_i' = (1, 2, 0)$. If $\mathbf{b}_i = \mathbf{0}$, find $\mathbf{z}_i$ using the result derived in Appendix 4.2. Show that the indifference contours in the issue space are spheres centered at $\mathbf{x}_i$.

4.12 For the general linear mapping model discussed in Appendix 4.2, show that each voter whose ideal point satisfies the linear system of equations $V_i' A_i (\mathbf{x}_i - \mathbf{b}_i) = 0$ prefers $\boldsymbol{\pi} = \mathbf{0}$ to any other point in the predictive space.

Bibliographical notes

The theory developed in this chapter is of very recent vintage. Building on the work of Downs (1957) and Davis and Hinich (1966), this new theory is explicitly designed to rebuild the multidimensional spatial theory of candidate competition in mass elections. The argument underlying this enterprise is that the standard multidimensional theory outlined in Chapter 3 is more appropriate in the context of committee voting, because it is based on very strong assumptions about the source and level of voter information.

For this reason, we develop a more complete spatial theory of candidate competition. The first efforts in this regard are Hinich (1978a) and Hinich and Pollard (1981). Enelow and Hinich (1982b) develop the perceptual stretching and shrinking results contained in Sections 4.8 and 4.9, which are generalized in Appendix 4.3. Conditions necessary and sufficient for single-peaked indirect preferences in a multi-issue campaign are developed in Coughlin and Hinich (in press).

CHAPTER 5

The influence of candidate characteristics and abstention on election outcomes

5.1 Utility functions

So far, we have discussed candidate competition when all issues of the campaign are policy issues. In Section 4.5, the two issues of the campaign were public spending issues. In Section 4.11, the two issues of the campaign involved social and economic policies. In each case, alternative issue positions were measured on a policy scale that arranged these positions according to the magnitude of some underlying variable, such as degree of government intervention.

However, when we consider nonpolicy issues, we are dealing with fixed attributes of the candidates that voters measure on an affective scale. Further, a candidate who is perceived by voter i as dishonest does not select his degree of honesty from among a range of alternative choices. All voters want elected officials to be honest. Thus, in judging each candidate, each voter estimates the extent to which the candidate possesses a desired or (for an attribute such as incompetence) undesired quality and increases (or decreases) his estimation of the candidate accordingly.

For a nonpolicy issue such as religion or ethnic background, similar considerations apply. Thus, some voters (presumably of the same religion or ethnic group) increase their liking for a candidate because, for example, he is a Catholic or an Italian. Or a candidate may be given a lower rating by some voter because of his skin color. In either case, a voter may prefer one candidate to another partly because of fixed characteristics of this type.

We shall now introduce a single measure to represent the value placed by a voter on the policy aspects and nonpolicy aspects of each candidate. This measure is called a *utility function*, which is an interval-level measure of preference. Up to now, we have determined voter preference by the weighted Euclidean distance preference rule. Under this rule, one candidate is preferred to another by some voter if and only if the candidate's position in the issue space is closer to that voter's ideal point. We shall consider this distance to represent (negatively) the *policy value* of the candidate to the voter. The *nonpolicy value* of the candidate to the

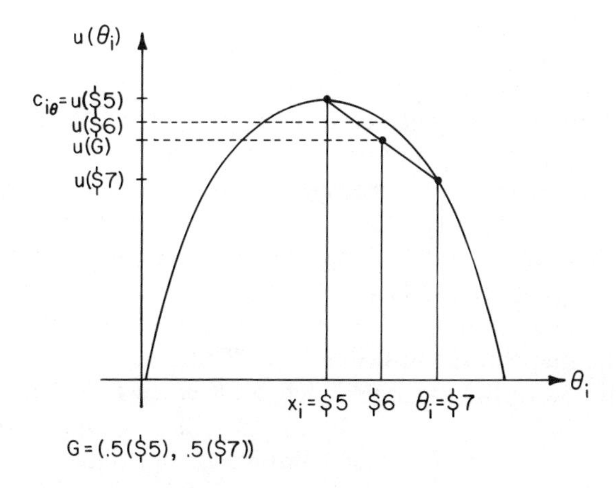

Figure 5.1. A risk-averse utility function $u(\theta_i) = c_{i\theta} - |\theta_i - x_i|^2$.

voter will be represented by a single term $c_{i\theta}$ or $c_{i\psi}$, depending on the candidate. These $c_{i\theta}$ and $c_{i\psi}$ are real numbers, like weighted Euclidean distance, and they measure the value to voter i of Theta's and Psi's nonpolicy characteristics. These characteristics are the subjectively perceived positions of the candidates on the nonpolicy issues of the campaign. If there are two or more such issues, we assume that $c_{i\theta}$ and $c_{i\psi}$ can be additively decomposed across these issues, so that $c_{i\theta}$ or $c_{i\psi}$ is the sum of a set of terms, each term representing the value placed by voter i on a single nonpolicy characteristic.

We now define a voter preference rule on candidates Theta and Psi based on this utility measure. Let $u(\boldsymbol{\theta}_i)$ represent voter i's utility for candidate Theta, and let $u(\boldsymbol{\psi}_i)$ represent i's utility for candidate Psi. Voter i prefers Theta to Psi if and only if

$$u(\boldsymbol{\theta}_i) > u(\boldsymbol{\psi}_i) \tag{5.1}$$

where $u(\boldsymbol{\theta}_i) = c_{i\theta} - \|\boldsymbol{\theta}_i - \mathbf{x}_i\|_{A_i}^2$ and $u(\boldsymbol{\psi}_i) = c_{i\psi} - \|\boldsymbol{\psi}_i - \mathbf{x}_i\|_{A_i}^2$. It is easy to see that if $c_{i\theta} = c_{i\psi} = 0$, then (5.1) reduces to the weighted Euclidean distance preference rule. Consequently, (5.1) is a generalization of the weighted Euclidean distance rule when nonpolicy characteristics of the candidates matter to the voters.

Figure 5.1 is a sample representation of the utility function we have defined, when $\boldsymbol{\theta}_i = \theta_i$ is defined on a single policy issue. Inequality (5.1) is invariant to any positive linear transformation. That is, if both sides of (5.1) are multiplied by a positive real number and any real number is added to both sides, then (5.1) is unchanged.

Observe in Figure 5.1 that utility is maximized when $x_i = \theta_i$, at which point $u(\theta_i) = c_{i\theta}$. Utility is symmetric about x_i, because utility is a function only of $|\theta_i - x_i|^2$. The shape of the utility curve is concave, meaning that as $|\theta_i - x_i|$ increases, utility decreases at an increasing rate. This type of utility function is sometimes referred to as representing *risk aversion*. Thus, suppose that θ_i and x_i are measured in dollars. Let $x_i = \$5$ and $\theta_i = \$7$. The average of these two amounts is \$6. Compare this average with a gamble taken over x_i and θ_i that yields each with probability one-half. Assume that i's utility for such a gamble is the sum of his utilities for the two amounts, each weighted by the probability given to it in the gamble. From the shape of the utility curve in Figure 5.1, it is clear that voter i will prefer \$6 to the gamble, which on average yields the same amount. Thus, he is averse to risk. In contrast, if $u(\theta_i)$ were convex over some interval, any gamble over amounts in that interval would be preferred to the average yield of that gamble. Such a voter would consequently be termed *risk-acceptant*. The utility function $u(\theta_i) = c_{i\theta} - |\theta_i - x_i|^{1/2}$ is convex over any interval that does not contain x_i in its interior. If utility were linear over some interval, the voter would be *risk-neutral* with respect to gambles over amounts in that interval, because he would be indifferent when faced with a choice between such a gamble and the gamble's average yield. The utility function $u(\theta_i) = c_{i\theta} - |\theta_i - x_i|$ is linear over any interval that does not contain x_i in its interior. These concepts will be employed more fully in Chapter 7.

5.2 Nonpolicy issues and the optimal location of party nominees

Nonpolicy issues are frequently important to voters. In this section we shall develop a theory of two-party competition designed to answer the question of how nonpolicy issues affect which candidate will maximize his party's chances of winning in the general election. We shall return to this question in our chapter on American presidential elections. Our theory of candidate behavior assumes that the position of each candidate on the underlying dimension(s) of the campaign is fixed. For simplicity, let us assume a single dimension for the remainder of this chapter. The alternative candidates for each party are then distributed along the single underlying dimension. We shall call the two parties Theta and Psi.

Which candidate will be the best representative for his party? Not surprisingly, the answer depends on the candidate who wins the nomination of the opposition party. Suppose that the best representative for each party is the candidate who will receive the largest possible plurality. Assuming that everyone votes, maximizing plurality is equivalent to maximizing total vote. The best representative for each party, then, is the candidate whose total vote is as large as possible.

Suppose that the electorate consists of K homogeneous groups. Each group k $(k=1,\ldots,K)$ consists of a set of voters with the same ideal point $\mathbf{x}_k$, the same matrix of salience weights A_k, and the same perceptions of candidates Theta and Psi (named after their respective parties):

$$\boldsymbol{\theta}_k=\mathbf{b}_k+\pi_\theta\mathbf{v}_k \quad \text{and} \quad \boldsymbol{\psi}_k=\mathbf{b}_k+\pi_\psi\mathbf{v}_k$$

where $\boldsymbol{\theta}_k=(\theta_{k1},\ldots,\theta_{kn})'$ and $\boldsymbol{\psi}_k=(\psi_{k1},\ldots,\psi_{kn})'$ are the perceived positions of the two candidates on the n policy issues of the campaign. For simplicity, let $n=2$.

These K homogeneous groups can be thought of as the politically salient interest groups in the electorate. Each interest group has a common set of policy concerns and looks at the candidates the same way. Thus, for example, a group like the Sierra Club or Friends of the Earth has a common set of concerns with respect to environmental issues and has a unified view of where candidates stand on such issues. An opposing group such as the Mountain States Legal Foundation (James Watt, former president), the American Mining Congress, or the Business Roundtable also has a common set of concerns with respect to these same issues and has a unified perception of candidate positions on such issues.

This conception of an interest group is particularly appropriate from the point of view of the candidates. It is a common practice in campaigns to view the electorate as being composed of homogeneous issue groups (e.g., farmers, blacks, senior citizens). This practice is a shorthand device that permits candidates to plan campaign strategies without becoming lost in the complexities of individual voter attitudes.

Suppose that the salient policy issues of the campaign are public land use and pollution control. Suppose further that $K=2$, with group 1 labeled the "no-growth" group and group 2 the "pro-growth" group. Let issue 1 (public land use) be measured on a scale that represents the proportion of all federally owned lands that can conceivably be opened to private development. Let issue 2 (pollution control) be measured on a scale that represents the proportion of some ideal level of air quality (defined in terms of the amounts of various types of pollutants) that government can conceivably mandate for all plants and factories. Thus, the vector of positions $(0,1)$ represents a pure no-growth set of attitudes, and the vector $(1,0)$ is a pure pro-growth set of positions.

Let the ideal point of group 1 be $(.2,.8)$ and that of group 2 $(.35,.65)$. Thus, group 1 most prefers that 20% of available federal lands be opened to private development (they recognize that an energy shortage does exist and that jobs would be created) and, in addition, that government should set emission limits for plants and factories at 80% of the maximum limits attainable (they do not want to throw everyone out of work). Group 2, on the other hand, most prefers that 35% of available federal lands be opened to development (they do derive some pleasure from national parks) and that government should set emission limits to meet 65% of what is maximally attainable (they do, after all, have to breathe the air).

Suppose that nonpolicy issues also matter to these voters. Then, from (5.1), a voter from group k $(k=1,2)$ will prefer candidate Theta to candidate Psi if and only if

$$c_{k\theta} - \|\boldsymbol{\theta}_k - \mathbf{x}_k\|^2_{A_k} > c_{k\psi} - \|\boldsymbol{\psi}_k - \mathbf{x}_k\|^2_{A_k} \tag{5.2}$$

or if and only if

$$D_k(\pi_\theta, \pi_\psi) > c_{k\psi} - c_{k\theta} \tag{5.3}$$

where

$$\begin{aligned} D_k(\pi_\theta, \pi_\psi) &= \|\boldsymbol{\psi}_k - \mathbf{x}_k\|^2_{A_k} - \|\boldsymbol{\theta}_k - \mathbf{x}_k\|^2_{A_k} \\ &= (\pi_\psi^2 - \pi_\theta^2)(a_{k11} v_{k1}^2 + 2a_{k12} v_{k1} v_{k2} + a_{k22} v_{k2}^2) - 2(\pi_\psi - \pi_\theta) \\ &\quad \times [a_{k11} v_{k1}(x_{k1} - b_{k1}) + a_{k12} v_{k2}(x_{k1} - b_{k1}) \\ &\quad + a_{k12} v_{k1}(x_{k2} - b_{k2}) + a_{k22} v_{k2}(x_{k2} - b_{k2})] \end{aligned} \tag{5.4}$$

For a group of voters such as group 1, $c_{1\psi} - c_{1\theta}$ can be expected to vary. The nonpolicy value difference between Psi and Theta is not something that all members of group 1 can be expected to agree on. Some group-1 members, for example, may perceive that Psi is very much like Theta on the nonpolicy issues that matter (like honesty or competence). Other group-1 members may believe that differences in educational background make the nonpolicy values of the two candidates quite different. Thus, (5.3) will be satisfied for some voters in group 1 but not others. If we can assume a specific distribution for the random variable $c_{1\psi} - c_{1\theta}$, we can then say what proportion of group 1 will prefer Theta to Psi. Suppose that $c_{1\psi} - c_{1\theta}$ is distributed normally. Because Theta and Psi are, as yet, unknown to the voters, we shall assume that the mean of this variable is zero (i.e., the average value of $c_{1\psi}$ and the average value of $c_{1\theta}$ are the same). For now, let the variance of $c_{1\psi} - c_{1\theta}$ simply be denoted σ_1^2. Assume that $c_{2\psi} - c_{2\theta}$ is normally distributed, with zero mean and variance σ_2^2.

The proportion of group k $(k=1,2)$ who will prefer Theta to Psi is then

$$P_k[D_k(\pi_\theta, \pi_\psi)] = \int_{-\infty}^{D_k(\pi_\theta, \pi_\psi)} (\sqrt{2\pi}\,\sigma_k)^{-1} \exp - (y^2/2\sigma_k^2)\, dy \tag{5.5}$$

The right-hand side of (5.5) is the value of the standard normal distribution function Φ evaluated at the point $D_k(\pi_\theta, \pi_\psi)/\sigma_k$.

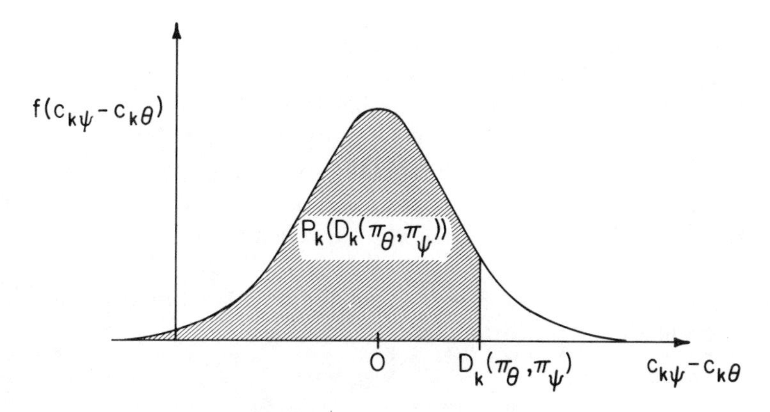

Figure 5.2. Normal density function for $c_{k\psi}-c_{k\theta}$.

Figure 5.2 is an illustrative example of (5.5). $P_k[D_k(\pi_\theta, \pi_\psi)]$ is the shaded area under the normal density function. Because $D_k(\pi_\theta, \pi_\psi)>0$, more than half of group k will vote for Theta. If there are N_k voters in group k, Theta's vote from group k will be

$$V_k(\pi_\theta, \pi_\psi)=N_k P_k[D_k(\pi_\theta, \pi_\psi)]$$

Theta's total vote is then

$$V(\pi_\theta, \pi_\psi)=N_1 P_1[D_1(\pi_\theta, \pi_\psi)]+N_2 P_2[D_2(\pi_\theta, \pi_\psi)] \qquad (5.6)$$

and, because everyone votes, if $N_1+N_2=N$, Psi's vote is $N-V(\pi_\theta, \pi_\psi)$.

The best representative for party Theta is the candidate who will do as well (in terms of votes) as possible against the opposition party candidate. This question would be much easier to answer if party Theta's selection process began after party Psi's process had been completed. However, suppose that the selections of both parties must be made simultaneously (i.e., without advance knowledge of who the other party's representative will be). It might be argued that the best candidate is the one who can guarantee the largest possible vote against any candidate nominated by the other party. This is a reasonable criterion, because the goals of the two parties are diametrically opposed.

On the basis of this reasoning, we shall show that if σ_1 and σ_2 are sufficiently large, there is a unique location $\pi^*\in\Pi$ that is best for both parties. In other words, a candidate identified with π^* will guarantee the largest vote of any candidate. No matter which candidate represents the other party, π^* will produce a win or a tie for the opposing candidate. In short,

$$V(\pi^*, \pi_\psi)>V(\pi^*, \pi^*)>V(\pi_\theta, \pi^*) \qquad (5.7)$$

for all $\pi_\theta, \pi_\psi \neq \pi^*$. The meaning of (5.7) is that a candidate located at π^* will beat any candidate not located at π^*. If both candidates are located at π^*, the election result will be a tie.

We can find π^* by differentiating $V(\pi_\theta, \pi_\psi)$ with respect to π_θ and $N-V(\pi_\theta, \pi_\psi)$ with respect to π_ψ and setting both derivatives equal to zero. Suppose that $\pi_\theta^* = \pi_\psi^* = \pi^*$ is the solution to these first-order (first-derivative) conditions. Then, if we can show that $V(\pi_\theta, \pi^*)$ is a concave function of π_θ and $N-V(\pi^*, \pi_\psi)$ is a concave function of π_ψ, (5.7) will be satisfied.

Let us start with the first-order conditions. For simplicity, let A_k be a 2×2 identity matrix for all voters. Then,

$$\begin{aligned}\frac{\partial V(\pi_\theta, \pi_\psi)}{\partial \pi_\theta} &= N_1 f_1[D_1(\pi_\theta, \pi_\psi)]\{-2\pi_\theta(v_{11}^2 + v_{12}^2) + 2[v_{11}(x_{11}-b_{11}) + v_{12}(x_{12}-b_{12})]\} \\ &\quad + N_2 f_2[D_2(\pi_\theta, \pi_\psi)]\{-2\pi_\theta(v_{21}^2 + v_{22}^2) \\ &\qquad + 2[v_{21}(x_{21}-b_{21}) + v_{22}(x_{22}-b_{22})]\} = 0 \end{aligned} \tag{5.8}$$

is the first-order condition for party Theta, where f_1 and f_2 are normal density functions, with means zero and variances σ_1^2 and σ_2^2, respectively. Solving for π_θ,

$$\begin{aligned}\pi^* = \{&N_1 f_1[D_1(\pi_\theta, \pi_\psi)][v_{11}(x_{11}-b_{11}) + v_{12}(x_{12}-b_{12})] \\ &+ N_2 f_2[D_2(\pi_\theta, \pi_\psi)][v_{21}(x_{21}-b_{21}) + v_{22}(x_{22}-b_{22})]\}/ \\ &\{N_1 f_1[D_1(\pi_\theta, \pi_\psi)](v_{11}^2 + v_{12}^2) + N_2 f_2[D_2(\pi_\theta, \pi_\psi)](v_{21}^2 + v_{22}^2)\}\end{aligned} \tag{5.9}$$

The first-order condition for party Psi is $\partial[N-V(\pi_\theta, \pi_\psi)]/\partial\pi_\psi = 0$. However, it is easy to see that this condition is the same as Theta's with π_ψ in place of π_θ on the left-hand side of (5.9). Thus, if π_θ^* and π_ψ^* are the solutions to the parties' first-order conditions, then $\pi_\theta^* = \pi_\psi^* = \pi^*$. In this case, $f_k[D_k(\pi_\theta, \pi_\psi)] = f_k[D_k(\pi^*, \pi^*)] = f_k(0) = (\sqrt{2\pi}\,\sigma_k)^{-1}$. Thus, (5.9) simplifies to

$$\begin{aligned}\pi^* = \{&N_1 \sigma_1^{-1}[v_{11}(x_{11}-b_{11}) + v_{12}(x_{12}-b_{12})] \\ &+ N_2 \sigma_2^{-1}[v_{21}(x_{21}-b_{21}) + v_{22}(x_{22}-b_{22})]\}/ \\ &[N_1 \sigma_1^{-1}(v_{11}^2 + v_{12}^2) + N_2 \sigma_2^{-1}(v_{21}^2 + v_{22}^2)]\end{aligned}$$

or, in vector notation,

$$\pi^* = \frac{N_1 \sigma_1^{-1} \mathbf{v}_1' \mathbf{y}_1 + N_2 \sigma_2^{-1} \mathbf{v}_2' \mathbf{y}_2}{N_1 \sigma_1^{-1} \mathbf{v}_1' \mathbf{v}_1 + N_2 \sigma_2^{-1} \mathbf{v}_2' \mathbf{v}_2} \tag{5.10}$$

where $\mathbf{y}_k = \mathbf{x}_k - \mathbf{b}_k$.

It remains to be shown that $V(\pi_\theta, \pi^*)$ is concave in π_θ and that $N - V(\pi^*, \pi_\psi)$ is concave in π_ψ. This is done in Appendix 5.1, where we establish lower bounds on σ_1 and σ_2, the standard deviations of $c_{1\psi} - c_{1\theta}$ and $c_{2\psi} - c_{2\theta}$, that make these claims true.

We thus have the following result. Suppose we wish to know which candidate will guarantee his party the largest possible vote. Suppose also that voters who are identical in other respects are expected to have differing views about the relative attractiveness of the candidates' positions on nonpolicy issues. Then both parties should seek to nominate candidates who are as close to π^* as possible, where π^* is defined either by (5.9) or by (5.10).

If π^* is the position of both candidates on the underlying dimension, because the mean of $c_{k\psi} - c_{k\theta}$ is zero across both groups, the election will be a tie. Further, the strict concavity of V in π_θ and $N - V$ in π_ψ means that if the nominee of one party is a candidate whose position is π^* and the nominee of the other party is a candidate whose position is something else, the candidate of the first party will win. Thus, π^* guarantees both parties at least a tie, and possibly a win. No other position guarantees either party as much, and so there is good reason to conclude that a candidate whose position is π^* is the best nominee for either party.

Let us give an example to show how π^* depends on the ideal points and translation parameters of the voters, the relative sizes of the two homogeneous groups, and the standard deviations of $c_{k\psi} - c_{k\theta}$ for each group. Although our results were derived under the assumption that $K = 2$, we could extend them to any number K if our lower bound on σ_k were satisfied for all $k = 1, \ldots, K$. The vote maximizing π^* would then be a sum in both numerator and denominator of K terms like those in (5.9) or (5.10).

Recall that the ideal point for group-1 members is (.2, .8), and the ideal point for group-2 members is (.35, .65). For simplicity, assume

$$A_k = \begin{bmatrix} 1 & 0 \\ 0 & 1 \end{bmatrix} = I$$

for all voters, so that each voter has circular indifference contours. Further, assume that $\mathbf{b}_1' = (.3, .7)$ and $\mathbf{b}_2' = (.2, .8)$, so that the no-growth group (group 1) believes that present policies are closer to a pure pro-growth set of policies [i.e., (1, 0)] than does the pro-growth group (group 2). Finally, assume that $\mathbf{v}_1 = (.2, -.2)'$ and $\mathbf{v}_2 = (.3, -.3)'$. Thus, if the challenger is one unit to the right of the incumbent position on the predictive dimension, group-1 members associate with him the policy positions (.5, .5); that is, they believe he wishes to open up an additional 20% of all available federally owned lands to private development and decrease emission limits for plants and factories by an additional 20%

measured with respect to maximum attainable limits. Given these data, it is easy to compute from (4.6) that $z_1 = -\frac{1}{2}$ and $z_2 = \frac{1}{2}$.

Now, suppose that $N_1 = 2N_2$, so that twice as many voters have ideal points at (.2, .8) as at (.35, .65). Thus, if nonpolicy issues make no difference to the voters (either because $c_{k\psi} = c_{k\theta}$ for all k or because there are no such issues in the campaign), then the optimal candidates for both parties are candidates whose positions on the underlying dimension are as close as possible to $-\frac{1}{2}$, the median z_k.

However, suppose that nonpolicy issues do matter to the voters, and $\sigma_1 > 3(1.5)^{1/2}B_1^2 = .294$, and $\sigma_2 > 3(1.5)^{1/2}B_2^2 = .661$. Remember that σ describes the standard deviation of $c_{k\psi} - c_{k\theta}$ for members of a given group, and $\sigma_k > 3(1.5)^{1/2}B_k^2$ for $k = 1, 2$ is the lower bound derived in Appendix 5.1 sufficient for (5.7) to hold. B_k is the upper bound for both $(v_{k1}^2 + v_{k2}^2)^{1/2}$ and $[(x_{k1} - b_{k1})^2 + (x_{k2} - b_{k2})^2]^{1/2}$. Then the best candidates for both parties are those whose positions are as close as possible to $\pi^* = (-.08\sigma_1^{-1} + .09\sigma_2^{-1})/(.16\sigma_1^{-1} + .18\sigma_2^{-1})$. If $\sigma_1 = \sigma_2$, then $\pi^* = .03$, which is not the median z_k. This shows that if nonpolicy issues matter to voters, the median z_k is not an optimal position for both candidates.

Rewriting (5.10) as

$$\pi^* = \frac{N_1 \sigma_1^{-1} z_1 \mathbf{v}_1' \mathbf{v}_1 + N_2 \sigma_2^{-1} z_2 \mathbf{v}_2' \mathbf{v}_2}{N_1 \sigma_1^{-1} \mathbf{v}_1' \mathbf{v}_1 + N_2 \sigma_2^{-1} \mathbf{v}_2' \mathbf{v}_2}$$

it is clear that if $\mathbf{v}_1 = \mathbf{v}_2$,

$$\pi^* = \frac{N_1 \sigma_1^{-1} z_1 + N_2 \sigma_2^{-1} z_2}{N_1 \sigma_1^{-1} + N_2 \sigma_2^{-1}}$$

If, in addition, $\sigma_1 = \sigma_2$, then π^* is the *mean* z_k, which in our case is $-\frac{1}{6}$.

Observe from (5.10) that π^* is sensitive to σ_1, σ_2, $\mathbf{v}_1$, $\mathbf{v}_2$, $\mathbf{y}_1$, and $\mathbf{y}_2$. Let us concentrate our attention on how changes in σ_1 and σ_2 affect π^*. Fixing $\mathbf{v}_1$, $\mathbf{y}_1$, $\mathbf{v}_2$, and $\mathbf{y}_2$, suppose that we set $\sigma_1 = 2\sigma_2$. Then $\pi^* = .19$, which is closer to $z_2 = \frac{1}{2}$ than when σ_1 and σ_2 were the same. Likewise, if $\sigma_2 = 2\sigma_1$, then $\pi^* = -.14$, which is closer to $z_1 = -\frac{1}{2}$ than when $\sigma_1 = \sigma_2$. What happens, other things being equal, is that as one group's σ becomes smaller than the other's, fewer voters in the first group will vote for the candidate who is not closest to them in terms of policy issues. As σ shrinks, the size of $c_{k\psi} - c_{k\theta}$ shrinks for increasing numbers of voters in the group, making $D(\pi_\theta, \pi_\psi)$, the policy difference between the candidates, the determinative criterion in casting a vote.

One way of interpreting a shrinkage of σ is that it indicates a lessening of the importance of nonpolicy issues for members of the associated group and/or an increase in the importance of policy issues. Thus, if $c_{k\psi} - c_{k\theta}$ takes on values in a decreased range or $|D_k(\pi_\theta, \pi_\psi)|$ becomes so large (possibly via A_k) that $P_k[D_k(\pi_\theta, \pi_\psi)]$ approaches either 0 or 1, all members of group k will vote for the candidate closest to them in policy terms. The effect of this decline in the importance of nonpolicy issues is to move the optimal locations for both candidates closer to the most preferred point of group k on the policy dimensions. Other things being equal, a group "intense" about its policy preferences (as compared with its nonpolicy preferences) can exert a greater influence over policy outcomes than a group that cares more about nonpolicy issues.

In terms of our example, suppose that the no-growth group placed little or no value on nonpolicy issues, whereas the pro-growth group valued such nonpolicy issues as executive capacity and managerial experience. Then the optimal locations for both candidates will be closer to the most preferred point of the no-growth group than would be the case if both groups placed the same weight on nonpolicy issues.

There are further political implications that grow out of our approach to modeling nonpolicy issues. As we have shown, a candidate who might otherwise have won an election may lose if voters who prefer him on policy issues find his opponent more attractive in other respects. If one party's candidates are continually less attractive than the candidates of the other party in these nonpolicy respects, then the mean of $c_{k\psi} - c_{k\theta}$ may be nonzero. Because the optimal location for both candidates on the predictive dimension will still be the same position, this means that one party's candidates may habitually lose, even though there is no difference between the candidates on the predictive dimension. Thus, if the mean of $c_{k\psi} - c_{k\theta} = \mu_k$ is positive across both groups, then the proportion of group k who will vote for party Theta is $\Phi(-\mu_k/\sigma_k) < \frac{1}{2}$, and so party Theta will lose. Thus, a series of candidates unattractive to the voters in nonpolicy respects may leave a party unable to win elections. To some extent this has happened to the Democrats in American presidential elections. Similarly, a party that has an unattractive record in office may find that even though it offers candidates identical with those of the opposition in policy terms, it still cannot win. Offering "me too" candidates may provide a party no guarantee against defeat.

As we shall show in Chapter 9, nonpolicy considerations have played an important role for voters in recent American presidential elections. Thus, the result derived in this section is important to our understanding of American politics.

There is another way of viewing our findings about the effects of nonpolicy issues on electoral competition. Recall that for our example, $N_1 = 2N_2$, and so the median $z_k = -\frac{1}{2}$. Thus, if nonpolicy issues do not matter to the voters, the no-growth group will see the candidate it most prefers elected to office (assuming that at least one of the parties nominates its best candidate). In a sense, the views of the minority (group 2) will be completely ignored, an example of what James Madison termed in *The Federalist,* No. 10, "majority tyranny." However, given diverse views of the nonpolicy difference between the candidates, a weighted form of the mean z_k is optimal for both parties. This result confirms Madison's hypothesis that in a large republic a majority with the same "passions" will be less likely to form to "oppress" the minority. The no-growth majority, if sufficiently divided in its assessments of the nonpolicy difference between the candidates, ceases to exert a "tyrannical" influence over the two parties, and thereby the electorate. A broad diversity of views concerning $c_{k\psi} - c_{k\theta}$ is something we expect in mass electorates, as opposed to small voting bodies. Thus, we have theoretical confirmation for Madison's thesis that large republics are superior to "pure democracies" (i.e., small societies employing direct democracy) in offering a cure for the "mischiefs of faction." In the following section we shall examine another such cure.

5.3 Abstention

Until now we have assumed that everyone votes. We shall now examine the effects of abstention on the optimal locations of Theta and Psi on the predictive dimension.

There are two policy-related reasons why citizens may not vote. Suppose the utility difference between the two candidates is very small for a given voter. This voter may then abstain from voting because it simply does not make much difference to him who wins. There are usually costs associated with the act of voting, such as the time involved, transportation costs, and the like. If the utility difference between the candidates is very small, these costs may outweigh this difference. We shall label this type of nonvoting *abstention from indifference.*

A second policy-related reason for nonvoting arises when a voter's utility for his favorite candidate fails to exceed a certain positive threshold. We shall call this type of nonvoting *abstention from alienation.* Abstention from indifference occurs when the utility difference between the two candidates fails to exceed a certain positive threshold. When a voter abstains from alienation, the utility difference between the two candidates may be great, but neither candidate is liked.

Figure 5.3 is a spatial depiction of these two types of abstention. The band of indifference describes all points that are "nearly" equidistant to $\boldsymbol{\theta}_i$ and $\boldsymbol{\psi}_i$, and the region of alienation outside the (convex) union of two circles with centers $\boldsymbol{\theta}_i$ and $\boldsymbol{\psi}_i$ and equal radii describes all points that are "too far away" from $\boldsymbol{\theta}_i$ and $\boldsymbol{\psi}_i$. Notice that it is possible to abstain both from indifference and from alienation.

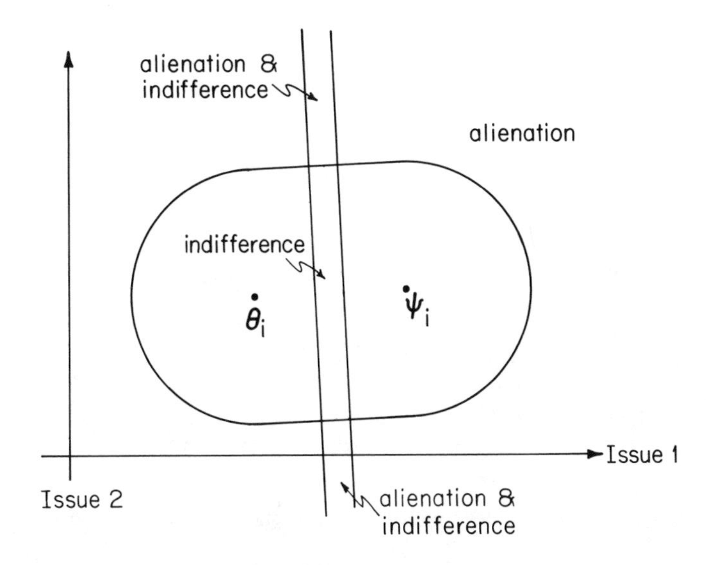

Figure 5.3. Deterministic view of abstention from alienation and indifference.

We shall now formalize abstention from alienation and from indifference with an explicit set of functions. Figure 5.3 is a deterministic view of abstention. The probability of voting is either 0 or 1, depending on the location of the voter's ideal point. Instead, assume a probabilistic view of nonvoting. Let $p_{i\theta}[u(\theta_i), u(\psi_i)]$ represent the probability that voter i will vote for Theta and $p_{i\psi}[u(\theta_i), u(\psi_i)]$ represent the probability that i will vote for Psi $(0 \leqslant p_{i\theta}, p_{i\psi} \leqslant 1)$. Then, abstention from alienation can be formalized by letting

$$p_{i\theta} = a_i[u(\theta_i)] \quad \text{and} \quad p_{i\psi} = a_i[u(\psi_i)] \tag{5.11}$$

$(\partial a_i / \partial u \geqslant 0,\ \partial^2 a_i / \partial u^2 \leqslant 0)$, with a_i either a function that increases at a decreasing rate or a positive constant.

To see how (5.11) captures the idea behind alienation from abstention, observe that $p_{i\theta}$ decreases (increases) as $u(\theta_i)$ decreases (increases); $p_{i\psi}$ exhibits the same type of behavior. The sum $p_{i\theta} + p_{i\psi}$ is the probability that i votes. If $u(\theta_i) = u(\psi_i)$, then $p_{i\theta} = p_{i\psi}$. Because $p_{i\theta} + p_{i\psi} \leqslant 1$, this implies that $p_{i\theta}, p_{i\psi} \leqslant \frac{1}{2}$. In addition, note that i has a positive probability of voting for his less preferred candidate. This allowance may be justified on the basis of measurement error by the voter regarding the candidates' positions on either policy or nonpolicy issues. Figure 5.4 is a depiction of $p_{i\theta}$ for the case of a single issue.

Abstention from indifference can also be formalized. Suppose that

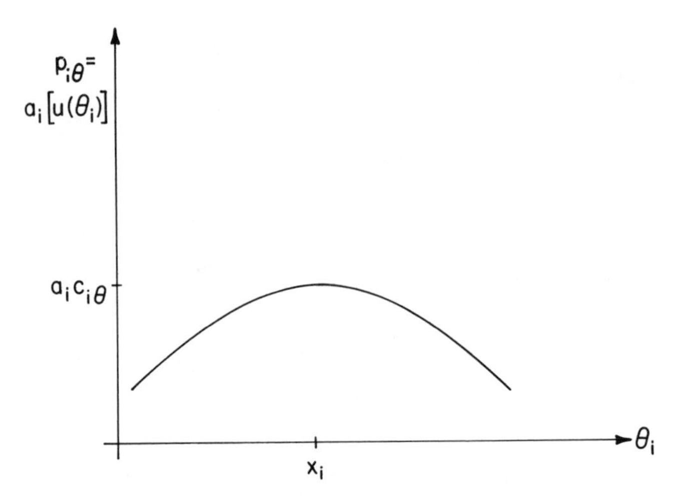

Figure 5.4. Probabilistic voting with abstention from alienation.

$$
\begin{aligned}
p_{i\theta} &= b_i[u(\theta_i)-u(\psi_i)] \quad \text{if } u(\theta_i)>u(\psi_i) \\
&= 0 \quad \text{otherwise} \\
p_{i\psi} &= b_i[u(\psi_i)-u(\theta_i)] \quad \text{if } u(\psi_i)>u(\theta_i) \\
&= 0 \quad \text{otherwise}
\end{aligned} \tag{5.12}
$$

(b_i is a positive constant). Now, assuming $u(\theta_i)>u(\psi_i)$, the probability $p_{i\theta}$ increases (decreases) as $u(\theta_i)-u(\psi_i)$ increases (decreases). Note that we now assume a zero probability of voting for a less preferred candidate. Thus, either $p_{i\theta}$ or $p_{i\psi}$ is i's overall probability of voting. Figure 5.5 depicts $p_{i\theta}$ for the case of a single issue and $c_{i\theta}=c_{i\psi}$. Because, for $u(\theta_i)>u(\psi_i)$ and unit issue salience, $p_{i\theta}=b_i[(\psi_i-x_i)^2-(\theta_i-x_i)^2]$, it is clear that for fixed θ_i, the farther ψ_i is from x_i, the greater $p_{i\theta}$.

We shall now combine (5.11) and (5.12) into a single assumption that voter i may abstain either from alienation or from indifference. If ϵ_i ($0\leqslant\epsilon_i\leqslant 1$) is the importance i attaches to alienation as a cause of nonvoting, let

$$
\begin{aligned}
p_{i\theta} &= \epsilon_i a_i[u(\theta_i)]+(1-\epsilon_i)b_i[u(\theta_i)-u(\psi_i)] \quad \text{if } u(\theta_i)>u(\psi_i) \\
&= \epsilon_i a_i[u(\theta_i)] \quad \text{otherwise} \\
p_{i\psi} &= \epsilon_i a_i[u(\psi_i)]+(1-\epsilon_i)b_i[u(\psi_i)-u(\theta_i)] \quad \text{if } u(\psi_i)>u(\theta_i) \\
&= \epsilon_i a_i[u(\psi_i)] \quad \text{otherwise}
\end{aligned} \tag{5.13}
$$

If $u(\theta_i)>u(\psi_i)$, then i's total probability of voting is $p_{i\theta}+p_{i\psi}=\epsilon_i a_i[u(\theta_i)+u(\psi_i)]+(1-\epsilon_i)b_i[u(\theta_i)-u(\psi_i)]$.

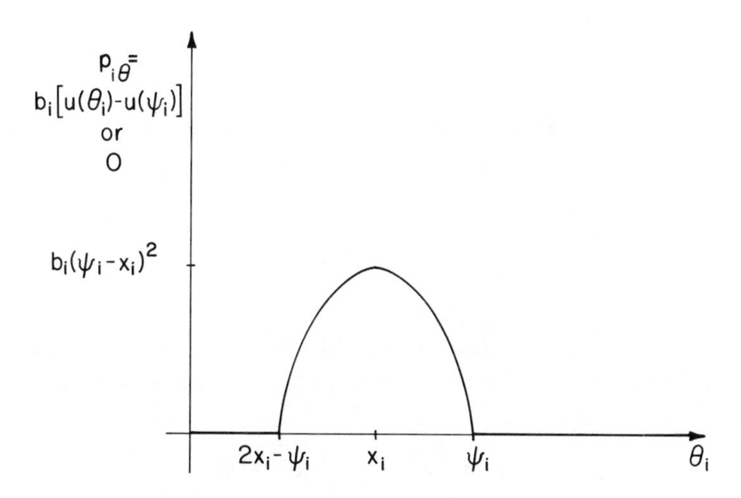

Figure 5.5. Probabilistic voting with abstention from indifference.

Define $p_{i\theta}-p_{i\psi}$ as i's *bias* for Theta over Psi. From (5.13) it is clear that $p_{i\theta}-p_{i\psi}=\epsilon_i a_i[u(\theta_i)-u(\psi_i)]+(1-\epsilon_i)b_i[u(\theta_i)-u(\psi_i)]$ regardless of which candidate is more preferred. Likewise, i's bias for Psi over Theta is $p_{i\psi}-p_{i\theta}=\epsilon_i a_i[u(\psi_i)-u(\theta_i)]+(1-\epsilon_i)b_i[u(\psi_i)-u(\theta_i)]$ regardless of which candidate is more preferred. In short, if $f_i=\epsilon_i a_i+(1-\epsilon_i)b_i$, then i's bias for Theta over Psi is $f_i u(\theta_i)-f_i u(\psi_i)$, and i's bias for Psi over Theta is $f_i u(\psi_i)-f_i u(\theta_i)$.

We call this type of bias function *separable*. If each voter's bias function is separable, it is not difficult to show that there is an optimal position on the predictive dimension for the candidate of each party (this result also holds for multiple predictive dimensions). In fact, if all voters have separable bias functions, positions in the predictive space can be ordered from best to worst in terms of the expected bias associated with any two positions. This means that the optimal position for either candidate is independent of the position of the other candidate in the predictive space. To see this more concretely, let us return to our two-group example from Section 5.2. Let ϵ_i, a_i, and b_i be the same for all voters, and let a_i and b_i be positive constants. Suppose that the optimal candidate for each party is the one whose expected bias over his opponent is greatest (which is the same as expected plurality). Then the best candidate for party Theta is the one whose position on the predictive dimension maximizes $E(p_{i\theta}-p_{i\psi})$. Recall that for the no-growth group (group 1), $\mathbf{x}_1=(.2,.8)'$, $\mathbf{b}_1=(.3,.7)'$, and $\mathbf{v}_1=(.2,-.2)'$; for the pro-growth group (group 2), $\mathbf{x}_2=(.35,.65)'$, $\mathbf{b}_2=(.2,.8)'$, and $\mathbf{v}_2=(.3,-.3)'$. Letting $c_{i\theta}=c_{i\psi}$ for simplicity,

$$\begin{aligned}E(p_{i\theta}-p_{i\psi}) &= E[f_i u(\theta_i)-f_i u(\psi_i)]\\ &= f_i E[u(\theta_i)-u(\psi_i)]\\ &= f_i E[(\pi_\psi^2-\pi_\theta^2)(v_{i1}^2+v_{i2}^2)\\ &\qquad +2(\pi_\psi-\pi_\theta)(b_{i1}v_{i1}+b_{i2}v_{i2}-v_{i1}x_{i1}-v_{i2}x_{i2})]\\ &= f_i\{N_1[(\pi_\psi^2-\pi_\theta^2)(v_{11}^2+v_{12}^2)-2(\pi_\psi-\pi_\theta)(v_{11}y_{11}+v_{12}y_{12})]\\ &\qquad +N_2[(\pi_\psi^2-\pi_\theta^2)(v_{21}^2+v_{22}^2)-2(\pi_\psi-\pi_\theta)(v_{21}y_{21}+v_{22}y_{22})]\}\end{aligned} \tag{5.14}$$

where $\mathbf{y}_i=\mathbf{x}_i-\mathbf{b}_i$. Differentiating (5.14) with respect to π_θ and setting the result equal to zero, we obtain the optimal π^*, which is easily shown to be

$$\pi^*=\frac{N_1(v_{11}y_{11}+v_{12}y_{12})+N_2(v_{21}y_{21}+v_{22}y_{22})}{N_1(v_{11}^2+v_{12}^2)+N_2(v_{21}^2+v_{22}^2)} \tag{5.15}$$

(observe that $\partial^2E/\partial\pi_\theta^2<0$). It is not difficult to see that π^* is also the optimal location for the candidate of party Psi. Refer back to (5.9), which specifies the optimal π^* for both candidates when everyone votes but there are diverse views concerning the nonpolicy difference between the candidates. Observe that π^* is a function of both candidates' predictive labels, so that the optimal location for each party's candidate is a function of the location of the other candidate. However, observe that in (5.15), π^* is independent of the other candidate's predictive label. Thus, π^* is unconditionally best for both parties, not merely a best defense.

Plugging the values from our example into (5.15) and letting $N_1=2N_2$, we see that $\pi^*=.03$. This is an interesting result. Recall that we are assuming that $c_{i\theta}=c_{i\psi}$ for all voters. If everyone votes, the median $z_i=-\frac{1}{2}$ is optimal for both candidates. Thus, we see that nonvoting can have the same moderating effect on election outcomes as nonpolicy issues can have.

Observe the close similarity between (5.15) and (5.10). Rewriting (5.15) as

$$\pi^*=\frac{N_1z_1\mathbf{v}_1'\mathbf{v}_1+N_2z_2\mathbf{v}_2'\mathbf{v}_2}{N_1\mathbf{v}_1'\mathbf{v}_1+N_2\mathbf{v}_2'\mathbf{v}_2}$$

it is clear that if $\mathbf{v}_1=\mathbf{v}_2$, then π^* is the mean z_i. As in (5.10), the optimal candidate location expressed by (5.15) is not merely a function of relative group size. The optimal π^* is also dependent on the $\mathbf{v}$'s of the two groups. Suppose, for instance, that $N_1=N_2$. The optimal π^* for both candidates is not zero but is instead .19. The reason why this occurs is that $\|\mathbf{v}_2\|$, the policy significance of ideology to group 2, is significantly greater than

$\|\mathbf{v}_1\|$. In fact, $\|\mathbf{v}_2\|=1.5\|\mathbf{v}_1\|$, so that the policy significance of ideology is 50% greater for group 2. If this discrepancy continued to grow, π^* would approach .5, the most preferred position of group 2 on the predictive dimension. To see this, we can reexpress π^* as

$$\pi^* = \frac{N_1 z_1 \|\mathbf{v}_1\|^2 + N_2 z_2 c^2 \|\mathbf{v}_1\|^2}{N_1 \|\mathbf{v}_1\|^2 + N_2 c^2 \|\mathbf{v}_1\|^2}$$

$$= \frac{N_1 z_1 + N_2 z_2 c^2}{N_1 + N_2 c^2}$$

where $c=1.5$. Suppose that $c=3$ and $N_1=N_2$. Then $\pi^*=.4$. If $c=6$ and $N_1=N_2$, then $\pi^*=.47$. Thus, π^* is biased toward the most preferred position of the group that attaches the greatest policy significance to differences in candidate ideology.

To provide some insight as to why (5.15) and (5.10) are so similar, refer back to (5.5), which is the distribution function for the nonpolicy model. Refer, now, to (5.12), which formalizes abstention from indifference. Setting $c_{i\theta}=c_{i\psi}$, and substituting for $u(\theta_i)$ and $u(\psi_i)$, we can rewrite $p_{i\theta}$ for the case in which $u(\theta_i)>u(\psi_i)$ as

$$b_i[\|\psi_i - \mathbf{x}_i\|^2_{A_i} - \|\theta_i - \mathbf{x}_i\|^2_{A_i}]$$

Since b_i is a positive constant, $p_{i\theta}$ will approximate (5.5) when the standard deviation of $c_{k\psi}-c_{k\theta}$ is very large. In short, $p_{i\theta}$ as defined in (5.12) is very much like the distribution function for the nonpolicy model.

Viewing the results of our abstention model from a Madisonian perspective, there are several points we can make. First, nonvoting can diminish the likelihood of majority tyranny. The optimal candidate location will reflect the views of the minority as well as those of the majority. In fact, minority influence increases if the policy significance of ideology is greater for the minority than it is for the majority. If this difference is too great, a form of "minority tyranny" can result. It appears more likely, though, that perceptions of the policy significance of ideology will not vary too greatly across interest groups. Thus, it is safe to conclude that nonvoting will generally increase the chances that the winning candidate will represent the ideological center of the electorate.

Both nonvoting and the presence of nonpolicy issues can have moderating effects on election outcomes. Both phenomena are pervasive in election contests, and they point to some of the key differences between mass elections and committee voting. In the next section we shall return to the subject of nonpolicy issues to discuss a type of electoral instability.

5.4 Breakdown of equilibrium

Up to this point, there appears to be one finding that is indisputably true. If a single predictive dimension underlies electoral competition, an optimal candidate position on this dimension always exists. If everyone votes and policy issues are the only issues of the campaign, the median z_i is optimal for both candidates. If voters abstain from alienation or indifference or if nonpolicy issues divide the voters, a weighted form of the mean z_i is optimal for both candidates.

In this section we shall show that instability can characterize the electoral process *even if there is a single predictive dimension.* The reason for showing this result is to demonstrate that spatial models do not neatly divide into two categories. We have given the impression so far that one-dimensional or one-issue spatial models are characterized by stability and predictability of outcomes, whereas multidimensional or multi-issue spatial models have exactly the opposite characteristics. Whereas it is true that the conditions required for the existence of a dominant point in multiple dimensions are more severe than they are for the case of a single dimension, there is one condition necessary for the median voter result that is typically violated in election contests. This condition is that the voter cast his vote for the candidate nearest his most preferred point on the predictive dimension. The introduction of nonpolicy issues leads to the possibility that a voter may not vote for the candidate who is nearest his most preferred point. Consequently, the median voter result breaks down, but we develop new conditions under which a weighted mean voter result takes its place.

We have yet to address the question of whether or not the median voter result can break down completely. Is it possible that nonpolicy issues can destabilize election contests in the sense that no position on the predictive dimension is optimal? If this is possible, we gain an important insight into election contests. If the empirical pattern of views concerning nonpolicy issues can create or destroy electoral stability, it is important to know which patterns are associated with each event.

For this reason, we proceed to examine a case in which nonpolicy issues do destroy electoral stability. The case we examine is one in which σ, the standard deviation of $c_\psi - c_\theta$, is zero for one group but not for the other. This case describes a situation in which nonpolicy issues matter to one group of voters but not to another. What we can show is that if the nonzero σ lies in a specific interval, no position on the underlying dimension is optimal. For each position on the dimension, there exists another that yields a positive plurality against that position. Thus, no matter which candidate is nominated by either party, if the other party has a sufficiently rich supply of candidates, it can find one who will win. Put differently, no position can guarantee either party anything but a loss.

Continuing with our example from Section 5.2, suppose that $\sigma_2=0$ but $\sigma_1 \neq 0$. Thus, all members of group 2 prefer the candidate whose π is closer to $z_2=\frac{1}{2}$. Assuming that $N_1=2N_2$, which candidate will be the best representative for his party? If both candidates are identified with the same position, the election result will be a tie. In Section 5.2 we showed that if π^* was this position, a tie was guaranteed for any candidate identified with π^* under the assumption that $\sigma_k>3(1.5)^{1/2}B_k^2>0$ for $k=1,2$. Now, $\sigma_2=0$. Where, then, is the best location(s) for the candidates of both parties?

Let us assume that party leaders, or those entrusted with selecting a nominee, are interested in answering this question. To reach an answer, they might engage in the following process of reasoning. They might ask which candidate will do best against various possible nominees of the opposing party. Determining who this candidate is, they might then ask how he will do against other possible opponents the other side might put up.

Suppose, then, that party Theta's decision makers ask themselves which of their potential nominees will do best against an opponent identified with the median z_i. Because $N_1=2N_2$, the median $z_i=-\frac{1}{2}$, which is the most preferred point of the no-growth group. Suppose that one of Theta's candidates is identified with $-\frac{1}{2}$. If he is nominated, the election result will be a tie. However, suppose that Theta's other candidates are located at $-\frac{1}{3}$, $-\frac{1}{6}$, 0, $\frac{1}{6}$, $\frac{1}{3}$, and $\frac{1}{2}$. Will one of these candidates do better against an opponent located at z_{med}?

Suppose that the candidate located at $-\frac{1}{3}$ is put up against Psi's candidate. Then the vote for Theta's candidate will be

$$V(\pi_\theta,\pi_\psi)=V(-\tfrac{1}{3},-\tfrac{1}{2})=N_2+2N_2P_1[D_1(-\tfrac{1}{3},-\tfrac{1}{2})] \tag{5.16}$$

In words, Theta will receive all of group 2's vote and the proportion $P_1[D_1(-\frac{1}{3},-\frac{1}{2})]$ of group 1's vote. Assuming that $A_i=I$ for all voters, and our data given earlier that $\mathbf{v}_1=(.2,-.2)'$ and $\mathbf{y}_1=(-.1,.1)'$, we can reexpress (5.4) as

$$D_k(\pi_\theta,\pi_\psi)=(\pi_\psi^2-\pi_\theta^2)(v_{k1}^2+v_{k2}^2)-2(\pi_\psi-\pi_\theta)(v_{k1}y_{k1}+v_{k2}y_{k2})$$

Consequently, $D_1(-\frac{1}{3},-\frac{1}{2})=-.002$. We can then reexpress (5.16) as

$$V(-\tfrac{1}{3},-\tfrac{1}{2})=N_2+2N_2\Phi(-.002\sigma_1^{-1}) \tag{5.17}$$

Assuming that $\sigma_1>.003$, then $\Phi(-.002\sigma_1^{-1})>.25$, and the right-hand side of (5.17) is greater than $N_2+N_2/2=3N_2/2=(N_1+N_2)/2$. Thus, a candidate located at $-\frac{1}{3}$ will beat an opponent at $-\frac{1}{2}$. Further, because

$D_1(\pi_\theta, -\frac{1}{2})$ is a decreasing function of π_θ, the candidate located at $-\frac{1}{3}$ will be Theta's best candidate against the candidate located at z_{med}.

Thus, a candidate located at $-\frac{1}{3}$ is the best representative for party Theta against an opponent located at $-\frac{1}{2}$. However, suppose party Psi's decision makers are engaged in the same type of reasoning process as the one used by the decision makers of party Theta. They then anticipate that if their candidate is identified with z_{med}, he will lose, because the opposing candidate will be located at $-\frac{1}{3}$. If they also have candidates located at $-\frac{1}{3}$, $-\frac{1}{6}$, 0, $\frac{1}{6}$, $\frac{1}{3}$, and $\frac{1}{2}$, which one should they put up against an opponent located at $-\frac{1}{3}$? If they select their candidate also located at $-\frac{1}{3}$, the result will be a tie. But if they choose the candidate located at $-\frac{1}{6}$, the vote for Psi will be

$$N-V(-\tfrac{1}{3}, -\tfrac{1}{6}) = N-2N_2P_1[D_1(-\tfrac{1}{3}, -\tfrac{1}{6})] = N-2N_2\Phi(.007\sigma_1^{-1})$$

If $\sigma_1 > .01$, then $\Phi(.007\sigma_1^{-1}) < \frac{3}{4}$, and thus

$$N-2N_2\Phi(.007\sigma_1^{-1}) > \frac{3N_2}{2} = \frac{N_1+N_2}{2}$$

So the candidate located at $-\frac{1}{6}$ will beat the candidate located at $-\frac{1}{3}$. Further, this candidate will do best against $-\frac{1}{3}$.

This process of reasoning will continue until one party (Theta) considers putting up its candidate located at $\frac{1}{3}$. Note that if any of the lower bounds for σ_1 is not met, the best candidate for both parties may be the candidate located at the last position for which this bound is met. Thus, if $\sigma_1 = .005$, then both parties should nominate candidates located at $-\frac{1}{3}$.

Assume, however, that all lower bounds on σ_1 are met and that Psi considers what its best move will be if Theta puts up its candidate located at $\frac{1}{3}$. It might seem tempting for Psi to go back to z_{med}. However, this may not be a vote-maximizing (or plurality-maximizing) strategy. If Psi chooses its candidate at $-\frac{1}{2}$, its vote will be

$$\begin{aligned} N-V(\tfrac{1}{3}, -\tfrac{1}{2}) &= N-N_2-2N_2\Phi(-.056\sigma_1^{-1}) \\ &= 2N_2[1-\Phi(-.056\sigma_1^{-1})] \end{aligned} \tag{5.18}$$

On the other hand, if Psi nominates its candidate located at $\frac{1}{2}$, the vote for Psi will be

$$N-V(\tfrac{1}{3}, \tfrac{1}{2}) = N_2+2N_2[1-\Phi(.025\sigma_1^{-1})] \tag{5.19}$$

Assume that $\sigma_1 > .06$. Then (5.19) is greater than (5.18), because

$$\tfrac{1}{2} > \Phi(.025/.06) - \Phi(-.056/.06) = .487 \tag{5.20}$$

and the right-hand side of (5.20) decreases for $\sigma_1 > .06$. Thus, so long as σ_1 is sufficiently large, each party should attempt to nominate the candidate as close as possible to, but to the right of, the candidate of the opposing party. Ultimately, of course, this reasoning will lead both parties to the conclusion that they should nominate a candidate located at $\frac{1}{2}$.

Will both parties stick with this decision? Once again, the answer depends on the size of σ_1. Suppose that Theta, for instance, considers running a candidate whose position is $z_{med} = -\frac{1}{2}$ against a candidate located at $\frac{1}{2}$. The vote for Theta will be

$$V(-\tfrac{1}{2}, \tfrac{1}{2}) = 2N_2 P_1[D_1(-\tfrac{1}{2}, \tfrac{1}{2})] = 2N_2 \Phi(.08\sigma_1^{-1})$$

which will exceed a tie if $\sigma_1 < .12$. If $\sigma_1 \geqslant .12$, "jumping back" to z_{med} will cost party Theta more votes (i.e., $N_2/2$) than it will gain by being identified with the most preferred point of group 1. This happens because the proportion $1 - P_1[D_1(-\frac{1}{2}, \frac{1}{2})]$ of group 1 will vote for Psi's candidate even though Theta's candidate is located at their most preferred point. If $\sigma_1 = .16$, 31% of group 1 will vote for Psi's candidate, and so Psi's candidate will receive 54% of the total vote.

On the other hand, if $\sigma_1 < .12$ but exceeds the lower bounds necessary for both parties not to "stick" at some location between $-\frac{1}{2}$ and $\frac{1}{2}$, the process of trying to second-guess the other party is hopeless. For each possible opponent, the other party should nominate a different candidate, but, given this candidate, the first party should nominate a different opponent. Thus, under these circumstances, the nomination process for both parties will be fraught with uncertainties, and it will be difficult to predict the eventual nominees.

It is interesting to note that if $\sigma_1 \geqslant .12$, both parties should attempt to nominate candidates located at $\frac{1}{2}$. If either party selects another candidate, it will lose. However, $\frac{1}{2}$ is the most preferred point of the smaller of the two groups, which is only one-half the size of the larger group. As with the possibility alluded to in the previous section on nonvoting, we have another example of "minority tyranny." If the majority is "too divided" over nonpolicy issues, the minority can exert complete control over the election outcome. If the pro-growth group are "pure policy" voters but the no-growth group have broadly differing views about the relative nonpolicy values of the candidates, it will not be surprising for both parties to nominate candidates whose position on the underlying dimension of the campaign is exactly the same as that of the much smaller group.

There is an alternative representation of the jumping process we have described. Suppose we are describing the American presidential nomination system, which in recent years has been highly decentralized. The party nominee may then view the process of choosing a running mate from the standpoint of "moving" the location of the ticket on the predictive dimension. Thus, if both nominees are located at the same position, each nominee may wish to pick a running mate whose position is slightly to the right of him in order to "move" the ticket some small distance in that direction. The theory we have developed will then predict whether there is an optimal location for the ticket or whether the instability described earlier will complicate the process of choosing a running mate. Concrete examples of efforts on the part of American presidential candidates to move the predictive locations of their tickets include Ford's choice of Dole as a running mate in 1976 (moving the ticket slightly to the "right") and Reagan's choice of Bush in 1980 (moving the ticket slightly to the "left").

To summarize the results obtained in this section, it is clear that nonpolicy issues can have a variety of effects on election contests. If one group of voters is solely interested in policies, whereas another group is also concerned about nonpolicy issues, a number of results can occur. If the standard deviation of $c_{\psi} - c_{\theta}$ is nonzero but "very small," the median voter result will continue to hold. If this standard deviation is slightly larger, there may not be an optimal candidate position on the predictive dimension. Finally, if this standard deviation is too large, the most preferred position of the pure policy voters will be optimal for both candidates.

5.5 Conclusion

This chapter has covered a number of topics. First, utility functions were introduced to allow nonpolicy issues to enter into the voter's evaluations of the candidates. We then discussed the effects that nonpolicy issues can have on optimal candidate location, demonstrating that nonpolicy issues can have a moderating effect on election outcomes.

Abstention is another important topic we have discussed. Like nonpolicy issues, abstention can also produce moderate election outcomes. Finally, to throw a little cold water on this depiction of stability and moderation, we showed how nonpolicy issues can destabilize election contests. The importance of this result lies in the insights it offers concerning the causes of electoral instability. What we see is that elections can be far more complex than committee voting. Even one-dimensional elections can be plagued with difficulties for the parties. Optimal candidate locations may not exist, and it may be necessary to attempt to outguess the opposition.

Chapter 9 will present empirical results designed to test some of the theoretical propositions in this chapter. What we shall see is that the results of this chapter are highly relevant to recent American presidential elections.

Appendix 5.1

This appendix derives the second-order conditions for (5.9) or (5.10) to be a vote-maximizing position for the candidates of both parties.

To show that $V(\pi_\theta, \pi^*)$ is concave in π_θ is to show that

$$\frac{\partial^2 V(\pi_\theta, \pi^*)}{\partial \pi_\theta^2} < 0$$

for all possible π_θ. Without loss of generality, we can assume that π_θ is contained in some closed interval, such as $[-\frac{1}{2}, \frac{1}{2}]$. Any closed interval will suffice. Then, if

$$\begin{aligned} D_k^* &= D_k(\pi_\theta, \pi^*) \\ &= 2(\pi^* - \pi_\theta)\left\{\frac{\pi^* + \pi_\theta}{2}(v_{k1}^2 + v_{k2}^2) - [v_{k1}(x_{k1} - b_{k1}) + v_{k2}(x_{k2} - b_{k2})]\right\} \end{aligned}$$

restated from the initial definition of $D_k(\pi_\theta, \pi_\psi)$,

$$\begin{aligned} \frac{\partial^2 V(\pi_\theta, \pi^*)}{\partial \pi_\theta^2} &= N_1\Big[f_1(D_1^*)(-2)(v_{11}^2 + v_{12}^2) \\ &\qquad - 2\{\pi_\theta(v_{11}^2 + v_{12}^2) - [v_{11}(x_{11} - b_{11}) + v_{12}(x_{12} - b_{12})]\}^2 \\ &\qquad \times f_1(D_1^*)\left(\frac{-D_1^*}{\sigma_1^2}\right)(-2)\Big] \\ &\quad + N_2\Big[f_2(D_2^*)(-2)(v_{21}^2 + v_{22}^2) \\ &\qquad - 2\{\pi_\theta(v_{21}^2 + v_{22}^2) - [v_{21}(x_{21} - b_{21}) + v_{22}(x_{22} - b_{22})]\}^2 \\ &\qquad \times f_2(D_2^*)\left(\frac{-D_2^*}{\sigma_2^2}\right)(-2)\Big] \\ &= N_1\left\{-2 - \frac{4D_1^*}{\sigma_1^2}\left[\pi_\theta(v_{11}^2 + v_{12}^2)^{1/2} \right.\right. \\ &\qquad \left.\left. - \frac{v_{11}(x_{11} - b_{11}) + v_{12}(x_{12} - b_{12})}{(v_{11}^2 + v_{12}^2)^{1/2}}\right]^2\right\} \\ &\quad \times (v_{11}^2 + v_{12}^2) f_1(D_1^*) \\ &\quad + N_2\left\{-2 - \frac{4D_2^*}{\sigma_2^2}\left[\pi_\theta(v_{21}^2 + v_{22}^2)^{1/2} \right.\right. \\ &\qquad \left.\left. - \frac{v_{21}(x_{21} - b_{21}) + v_{22}(x_{22} - b_{22})}{(v_{21}^2 + v_{22}^2)^{1/2}}\right]^2\right\} \\ &\quad \times (v_{21}^2 + v_{22}^2) f_2(D_2^*) \end{aligned} \tag{A5.1}$$

Because $f_k(D_k^*)>0$ for all D_k^*, if the two terms in braces on the right-hand side are negative, the second derivative will be negative also. Thus, for $k=1,2$, if

$$1+\frac{2D_k^*}{\sigma_k^2}\left[\pi_\theta(v_{k1}^2+v_{k2}^2)^{1/2}-\frac{v_{k1}(x_{k1}-b_{k1})+v_{k2}(x_{k2}-b_{k2})}{(v_{k1}^2+v_{k2}^2)^{1/2}}\right]^2>0 \quad \text{(A5.2)}$$

then $V(\pi_\theta,\pi^*)$ is concave in π_θ.

To obtain a condition that makes (A5.2) hold, let us assume that there exists an upper bound B_k for both

$$(v_{k1}^2+v_{k2}^2)^{1/2} \quad \text{and} \quad [(x_{k1}-b_{k1})^2+(x_{k2}-b_{k2})^2]^{1/2}$$

Then, by the Schwarz inequality,

$$\left|\frac{v_{k1}(x_{k1}-b_{k1})+v_{k2}(x_{k2}-b_{k2})}{(v_{k1}^2+v_{k2}^2)^{1/2}}\right| \leqslant \frac{(v_{k1}^2+v_{k2}^2)^{1/2}[(x_{k1}-b_{k1})^2+(x_{k2}-b_{k2})^2]^{1/2}}{(v_{k1}^2+v_{k2}^2)^{1/2}} \leqslant B_k \quad \text{(A5.3)}$$

Thus,

$$\left[\pi_\theta(v_{k1}^2+v_{k2}^2)^{1/2}-\frac{v_{k1}(x_{k1}-b_{k1})+v_{k2}(x_{k2}-b_{k2})}{(v_{k1}^2+v_{k2}^2)^{1/2}}\right]^2$$

is less than or equal to either $(\pi_\theta B_k+B_k)^2$ or $(\pi_\theta B_k-B_k)^2$, depending on the sign of π_θ. However, because $-\frac{1}{2}\leqslant\pi_\theta\leqslant\frac{1}{2}$, it follows that $(\pi_\theta B_k\pm B_k)^2\leqslant\frac{9}{4}B_k^2$. We now need a bound for D_k^*. From our definition,

$$D_k^*\geqslant-2[\tfrac{1}{2}(v_{k1}^2+v_{k2}^2)+|v_{k1}(x_{k1}-b_{k1})+v_{k2}(x_{k2}-b_{k2})|]$$
$$\geqslant-2[\tfrac{1}{2}B_k^2+B_k^2]=-3B_k^2$$

Thus,

$$1+\frac{2D_k^*}{\sigma_k^2}\left[\pi_\theta(v_{k1}^2+v_{k2}^2)^{1/2}-\frac{v_{k1}(x_{k1}-b_{k1})+v_{k2}(x_{k2}-b_{k2})}{(v_{k1}^2+v_{k2}^2)^{1/2}}\right]^2$$
$$\geqslant 1-\frac{6B_k^2}{\sigma_k^2}\left(\frac{9B_k^2}{4}\right)=1-\frac{27B_k^4}{2\sigma_k^2} \quad \text{(A5.4)}$$

So, if $\sigma_k>3(1.5)^{1/2}B_k^2$, then inequality (A5.2) holds, and thus $V(\pi_\theta,\pi^*)$ will be concave in π_θ for all $\pi_\theta\in[-\frac{1}{2},\frac{1}{2}]$. An almost identical proof establishes that this same lower bound ensures that $N-V(\pi^*,\pi_\psi)$ is concave in π_ψ.

Problems

5.1 Assume that a person has the following quadratic utility for θ on a single policy dimension: $u(\theta)=7-(\theta-5)^2$. This person must choose between two gambles: (a) $\theta=5$ with probability $\frac{1}{2}$ and $\theta=7$ with probability $\frac{1}{2}$ and (b) $\theta=4$ with probability $\frac{1}{2}$ and $\theta=8$ with probability $\frac{1}{2}$. The expected values of both gambles are equal to 6. Compute the variances of these gambles. Verify that the person's expected utility for the lower-variance gamble is higher than the expected utility of the other.

5.2 Assume that a person has the quadratic utility function $u(\theta)=c-(\theta-x)^2$. Let $\tilde{\theta}$ and $\tilde{\psi}$ denote two gambles with the same expected value μ; that is, $\tilde{\theta}$ and $\tilde{\psi}$ are random variables with $\mu=E(\tilde{\theta})=E(\tilde{\psi})$. Show that the person's expected utility for the gamble with the smaller variance is higher than the expected utility of the other.

5.3 Use $a_{k11}=a_{k22}=2$, $a_{k12}=1$, $v_{k1}=4$, $v_{k2}=2$, $y_{k1}=x_{k1}-b_{k1}=1$, and $y_{k2}=x_{k2}-b_{k2}=6$ in equation (5.4) to obtain $D_k(\pi_\theta,\pi_\psi)$ as a function of π_θ and π_ψ. Then compute $D_k(0,1)$ and $D_k(0,-1)$.

5.4 Let $\sigma_k=100$ in (5.5). Using the results from Problem 5.3 and a standard normal distribution table from any statistics text, find $P_k[D_k(0,1)]$ and $P_k[D_k(0,-1)]$.

5.5 Letting $N_1=3N_2$, $v_{11}=v_{22}=2$, $v_{12}=v_{21}=0$, $y_{11}=y_{21}=6$, $y_{22}=y_{12}=-6$, and $\sigma_2=3\sigma_1$ in (5.10), find the stable point π^*. Compute π^* for $\sigma_1=3\sigma_2$.

5.6 Use the values of y_{ij}, N_1, N_2, and the v_{ij} in Problem 5.5 to compute π^* for our abstention model [equation (5.15)]. Why is the result independent of σ_1 and σ_2?

5.7 Simplify expression (5.4) by setting $a_{k12}=0$ and $b_{k1}=b_{k2}=0$. Assume that $-1\leqslant\pi_\theta\leqslant 1$, $-1\leqslant\pi_\psi\leqslant 1$, and that a_{k11}, a_{k22}, v_{k1}, v_{k2}, x_{k1}, and x_{k2} are between 0 and 1. Verify that $|D_k(\pi_\theta,\pi_\psi)|<10$. Assume that $c_{k\psi}-c_{k\theta}$ has a uniform distribution on the range $-10<c_{k\psi}-c_{k\theta}<10$. Show that the proportion of group k that prefers Theta to Psi is then $P_k[D_k(\pi_\theta,\pi_\psi)]=D_k(\pi_\theta,\pi_\psi)/20$.

Bibliographical notes

The introduction of nonspatial candidate characteristics into voter utility functions and an examination of their effects on candidate competition can be found in Enelow and Hinich (1982a). A discussion of the shape of voter utility functions is contained in Shepsle (1972).

The equivalence and nonequivalence of candidate objective functions, alluded to at the beginning of Section 5.2, are important subjects about which there is much more to say. Aranson, Hinich, and Ordeshook (1974) is an important reference in this regard.

The results on abstention are based on Hinich, Ledyard, and Ordeshook (1973) and Hinich and Ordeshook (1973). The seminal articles on abstention from alienation and from indifference are Hinich and Ordeshook (1969, 1970). The central result of Section 5.3 appears in Enelow and Hinich (1983a).

The instability results of Section 5.4 are an outgrowth of findings contained in Hinich (1977). There is a sizable literature concerned with candidate optimality defined in terms other than a point location. McKelvey and Ordeshook (1976) and Kramer (1978) derive results concerning the existence and characteristics of mixed-strategy equilibria. A mixed strategy is defined over a set of points, one of which is ultimately selected by a random device.

CHAPTER 6

Voting on budgets

6.1 Introduction

In Chapter 4 we developed a model of elections in which voters estimate candidate positions on policy issues based on each candidate's location on an underlying predictive dimension. In this chapter we wish to show that this model is also useful in the committee setting. We shall examine the case in which a legislative committee must decide the total budget for a set of activities, and we shall show how our model of elections can be adapted to this type of decision making. This type of problem is equivalent to a referendum in which voters must decide such issues as total budgetary ceilings or aggregate levels of taxation. Thus, whereas we develop the case of legislative decision making on total budget sizes, this equivalence should be kept in mind.

What primarily characterizes this problem is that each legislator must vote on a total dollar figure for the entire budget without knowing for certain how this total figure will be translated into spending changes in the various line items that constitute the basic set of activities to be funded. This situation arises in the U.S. Congress when budget ceilings are voted on through the budget resolutions established by the 1974 Congressional Budget Act. Congressmen vote on total budget ceilings, and only afterward do committees decide how to reconcile spending on individual programs with the constraint imposed by this budgetary limit.

We assume that each legislator's preferences are defined on packages of spending figures for the individual programs or activities to be funded. If there are n of these activities, then each legislator's preferences are defined over n-tuples of monetary allocations among these n activities. For spending packages other than his ideal, each legislator's preferences are described by ellipsoidal indifference contours, so that the class of all spending packages over which he is indifferent is an ellipse of some type, centered at his ideal spending package. In short, each legislator judges alternative spending packages according to the weighted Euclidean distance preference rule defined in Chapter 3.

Although each legislator's preferences are defined over alternative spending packages, he must vote on total budget figures before the adjustments among spending activities are made. In other words, he must vote between two aggregate budget figures, without being certain of how changes in budget size will affect changes in spending on each of the n activities.

6.2 The model

Let us now see how the model of Chapter 4 can be adapted to help answer the question of what total budget size will be decided on.

Let $L=\{1,\ldots,M\}$ be the set of legislators, with $I=\{1,\ldots,N\}$ being the set of activities to be funded. The set of all possible total budget sizes is a segment of the real line, which we shall label Π. We define the *origin* of Π as the total size of the *current budget* (i.e., the status quo). Thus, alternative total budget sizes are measured as either increases or decreases in the total size of the current budget. Let π denote one such alternative budget (henceforth, the term "budget" will refer to total budget size). Various π's will be subscripted to identify different alternative budgets. The current budget will be denoted by $\pi_o=0$.

Suppose that the budget $\pi_\theta \neq 0$ is voted on as a replacement for the current budget in the next fiscal year. Because each legislator's preferences are defined over alternative spending packages, the legislator must be able to translate alternative *budget proposals* into anticipated *spending packages*. Suppose that legislator i believes that budget changes will translate linearly into spending changes on activity j. Then, if θ_{ij} is the spending level on activity j anticipated by i if π_θ is adopted,

$$\theta_{ij}=b_{ij}+\pi_\theta v_{ij} \tag{6.1}$$

where b_{ij} is the anticipated level of spending on activity j in the absence of budgetary change, and $\pi_\theta v_{ij}$ is the spending change on activity j due to the budgetary change represented by π_θ. Note that b_{ij} is subscripted by legislator, allowing varying perceptions of how much will be spent on activity j even without any change in total budget size. This presumes the possibility that total spending may increase or decrease compared to its previous level even without budgetary change. Or total spending may remain the same, but spending may be reallocated among individual activities.

It is important to distinguish between total budget size and total spending. What (6.1) assumes is that budget changes translate linearly into spending changes on individual activities. This does not imply that current spending equals current budget size or that future spending will equal future budget size. Given what we know of congressional practices, we see no reason to assume balanced budgets.

An example will allow us to see these points more clearly. Suppose that $N=2$, so that there are only two spending activities. These activities may be the two military construction projects described in Chapter 2. Suppose that legislator i believes that future spending on each activity will be the same as during the current fiscal year if there is no budgetary change. Let $b_{i1}=\$10$ million be the current spending level on project 1 and $b_{i2}=\$70$ million be the current spending level on project 2. Total current spending is then \$80 million. For argument's sake, let the current total budget be \$60 million. Cost overruns covered by supplemental appropriations may explain the \$20 million discrepancy.

Suppose that a budget cut of \$30 million is proposed. The question that legislator i must answer is how he thinks this budget cut will affect project spending cuts. He may believe that, as in the previous year, final spending will exceed what the budget initially authorizes. If he does, he may think that $v_{i1}=.2$ and $v_{i2}=.6$. In other words, he believes that actual spending will decrease by $.8(\$30)=\$24$ million even though the budget is cut by \$30 million. Given these estimates, his anticipation is that a \$30 million budget cut will result in $\$10+.2(-\$30)=\$4$ million spending on project 1 and $\$70+.6(-\$30)=\$52$ million spending on project 2 during the next fiscal year. This implies that actual spending will exceed the total budget figure by $\$56-(\$60-\$30)=\$26$ million in the next fiscal year. Thus, the budget is unbalanced in both fiscal years.

We can now state a preference rule for legislator i that determines how he will vote between two budgets. He will vote for π_θ over π_ψ if and only if

$$\|(\mathbf{b}_i+\pi_\theta \mathbf{v}_i)-\mathbf{x}_i\|_{A_i}<\|(\mathbf{b}_i+\pi_\psi \mathbf{v}_i)-\mathbf{x}_i\|_{A_i} \tag{6.2}$$

where $\mathbf{b}_i=(b_{i1},\ldots,b_{iN})'$ are i's estimates of future spending levels in the absence of budget change, $\mathbf{v}_i=(v_{i1},\ldots,v_{iN})'$ are i's estimates of the rate at which budget changes will be translated into spending changes, $\mathbf{x}_i=(x_{i1},\ldots,x_{iN})'$ is i's ideal spending package, and A_i is an $N\times N$ symmetric positive definite matrix of salience weights. This salience matrix describes the precise form of i's indifference contours with respect to alternative spending packages.

Setting $A_i=I$, we can state (6.2) for our two-project example (squaring both sides) as

$$(\pi_\theta v_{i1}-y_{i1})^2+(\pi_\theta v_{i2}-y_{i2})^2<(\pi_\psi v_{i1}-y_{i1})^2+(\pi_\psi v_{i2}-y_{i2})^2 \tag{6.3}$$

where $y_{i1}=x_{i1}-b_{i1}$ and $y_{i2}=x_{i2}-b_{i2}$. Assuming that $\pi_\theta>\pi_\psi$, if we collect terms, (6.3) is

$$(\pi_\theta^2-\pi_\psi^2)(v_{i1}^2+v_{i2}^2)<2(\pi_\theta-\pi_\psi)(v_{i1}y_{i1}+v_{i2}y_{i2})$$

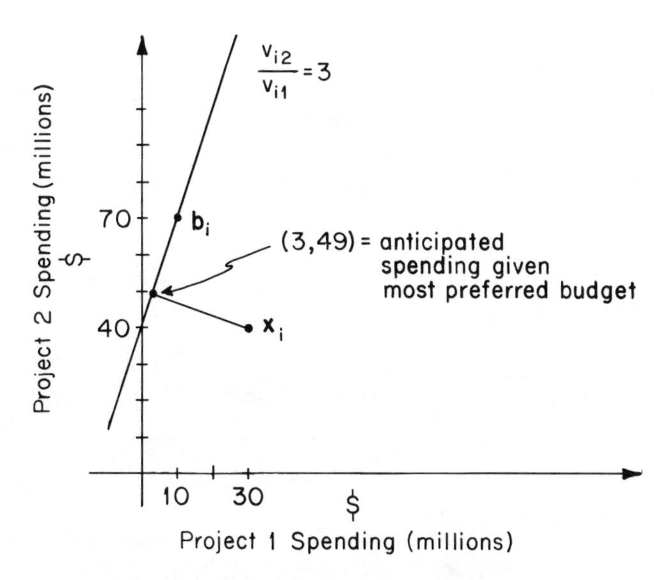

Figure 6.1. Legislator i's most preferred budget.

or

$$\frac{\pi_\theta + \pi_\psi}{2} < \frac{v_{i1} y_{i1} + v_{i2} y_{i2}}{v_{i1}^2 + v_{i2}^2} = z_i \tag{6.4}$$

which is identical with (4.6). Thus, the right-hand side of (6.4) is the same z_i (with a very different meaning) as that of Chapter 4. Now z_i represents i's most preferred budget, defined on the basis of his ideal spending package on projects 1 and 2 and the translation coefficients b_{i1}, b_{i2}, v_{i1}, and v_{i2}, which represent his estimation of future spending in the absence of budget change as well as the rate at which budget changes will be translated into future spending changes on these two projects.

Whereas we allow that $v_{i1} + v_{i2} \neq 1$, there is also no need for $0 \leqslant v_{i1}$, $v_{i2} \leqslant 1$. If $v_{i1} = -1$ and $v_{i2} = 3$, this would imply that a dollar budgetary increase would result in three more dollars being spent on project 2 and one less dollar on project 1.

Figure 6.1 illustrates legislator i's preferences over alternative budgets for our two-project example. Recall that $b_{i1} = \$10$ million, $b_{i2} = \$70$ million, $v_{i1} = .2$, and $v_{i2} = .6$. Then, if $x_{i1} = \$30$ million and $x_{i2} = \$40$ million,

$$z_i = \frac{.2(\$20) + .6(-\$30)}{.04 + .36} = -\$35 \text{ million}$$

is i's most preferred budget. Recalling that alternative budgets are measured as changes in the current budget, i most prefers cutting the budget by \$35 million from its current level. He anticipates that if the budget is cut by this amount, $\$10+.2(-\$35)=\$3$ million will be spent on project 1 and $\$70+.6(-\$35)=\$49$ million will be spent on project 2. Thus, he anticipates that total spending will decline from \$80 million to \$52 million, and the budget will decline from \$60 million to \$25 million. In other words, a \$35 million budget cut will translate into a \$28 million spending cut. Total spending will then exceed the budget by $\$52-\$25=$ \$27 million, as compared with \$20 million during the previous fiscal year.

6.3 A theory of budgetary incrementalism

As implied by (6.4), if π_θ and π_ψ are voted on, the one closer to the median z_i will win a majority of the votes, if this median is unique. In this section we shall develop conditions on the v_{ij}'s of the legislators that will ensure that the expected vote for the budget proposal closer to $\pi_o=0$ will be a majority. Therefore, when these conditions are met, the status quo budget will have an expected majority against any alternative budget. What we shall show for our two-project example is proved in exactly the same way for the general case.

Suppose that we wish to predict the outcome of the vote when we do not know for sure the preference and perception parameters of the legislators. A sensible way to model this uncertainty about the parameters is to assume that x_{ij}, b_{ij}, and v_{ij} are independently distributed random variables for each $j=1$ or 2. All the information about the legislators' voting behavior is then summarized by the distributions of these random variables. The total number of legislators is M, so that if all of them vote, the expected vote for π_θ (assuming $\pi_\theta>\pi_\psi$) is

$$EV_\theta=M\,\Pr\left(z_i>\frac{\pi_\theta+\pi_\psi}{2}\right) \tag{6.5}$$

where Pr denotes the probability of the event contained in parentheses. If $\Pr[z_i>(\pi_\theta+\pi_\psi)/2]>\frac{1}{2}$, then $EV_\theta>M/2$, which means that π_θ receives an expected majority of the vote against π_ψ.

Let μ_z and σ_z^2 denote the mean and variance of z_i. Suppose that π_θ *is closer to zero than* π_ψ. We shall now prove the following result: If

$$\frac{|\pi_\theta+\pi_\psi|}{2}>|\mu_z|+\sigma_z \tag{6.6}$$

them $EV_\theta>M/2$.

Because π_θ is closer to zero than π_ψ and $\pi_\theta>\pi_\psi$, it follows that $\pi_\psi<0$

and $(\pi_\theta+\pi_\psi)/2<0$. From (6.6), $-|\mu_z|-\sigma_z>-|\pi_\theta+\pi_\psi|/2=(\pi_\theta+\pi_\psi)/2$, so that

$$\Pr\left(z_i>\frac{\pi_\theta+\pi_\psi}{2}\right)>\Pr(z_i\geqslant-|\mu_z|-\sigma_z)$$
$$\geqslant\Pr(z_i\geqslant\mu_z-\sigma_z)=\Pr(z_i-\mu_z\geqslant-\sigma_z) \qquad (6.7)$$

because $\mu_z\geqslant-|\mu_z|$. We now show that the right-hand side of (6.7) is at least $\frac{1}{2}$, and thus $EV_\theta=M\Pr[z_i>(\pi_\theta+\pi_\psi)/2]>M/2$.

The one-sided Chebyshev inequality states that if z_i is a random variable with mean μ_z and variance σ_z^2, then for $\lambda<0$,

$$\Pr(z_i-\mu_z\leqslant\lambda)\leqslant\frac{1}{1+(\lambda/\sigma_z)^2}$$

Thus, if $\lambda=-\sigma_z$,

$$\Pr(z_i-\mu_z\leqslant-\sigma_z)\leqslant\frac{1}{1+(\sigma_z/\sigma_z)^2}=\frac{1}{2}$$

Consequently, the right-hand side of (6.7) is at least $\frac{1}{2}$, and so $EV_\theta>M/2$.

We have thus shown that when π_θ is closer to zero than π_ψ, inequality (6.6) is sufficient for π_θ to receive an expected majority of the vote against π_ψ. Furthermore, π_θ need not be greater than π_ψ. A modified form of the foregoing proof establishes that (6.6) also implies that $EV_\theta>M/2$ when $\pi_\psi>\pi_\theta$.

It remains to be established when (6.6) will hold. Clearly, as σ_z^2 and $|\mu_z|$ shrink toward zero, the likelihood that (6.6) will hold increases. What this means, of course, is that the distribution of z_i is being squeezed toward zero from both sides, moving z_{med} closer to zero. It is no surprise, therefore, that as σ_z and $|\mu_z|$ get smaller, the budget closer to the status quo will receive an expected majority of the votes against one farther away.

To gain further insight into how the v_{ij}'s of the legislators are related to the fulfillment of (6.6), we again focus on our two-project example. From (6.4),

$$z_i=\frac{v_{i1}y_{i1}+v_{i2}y_{i2}}{v_{i1}^2+v_{i2}^2}$$

Consequently, because $\sigma_z^2=E(z_i^2)-[E(z_i)]^2$, and v_{ij} is distributed independent of y_{ij} for $j=1$ and 2,

$$\sigma_z^2\leqslant E(z_i^2)=E[(v_{i1}y_{i1}+v_{i2}y_{i2})/(v_{i1}^2+v_{i2}^2)]^2$$
$$=E\,\frac{v_{i1}^2\sigma_1^2+2v_{i1}v_{i2}\sigma_{12}+v_{i2}^2\sigma_2^2+v_{i1}^2\mu_{y1}^2+v_{i2}^2\mu_{y2}^2+2v_{i1}v_{i2}\mu_{y1}\mu_{y2}}{(v_{i1}^2+v_{i2}^2)^2} \qquad (6.8)$$

where $\sigma_1^2 = \text{Var}(y_{i1})$, $\sigma_2^2 = \text{Var}(y_{i2})$, and

$$\sigma_{12} = \text{Cov}(y_{i1}, y_{i2}) = E(y_{i1} y_{i2}) - E(y_{i1})E(y_{i2})$$

For expositional convenience, assume that y_{i1} and y_{i2} are independent random variables. Then, $E(y_{i1} y_{i2}) = E(y_{i1})E(y_{i2})$, and so $\sigma_{12} = 0$. Also for convenience, assume that $\sigma_1^2 = \sigma_2^2 = \sigma_y^2$ (i.e., the variance of the y_{ij}'s are the same). These two assumptions make it easier to prove our central result, but they are in no way necessary to do so. Given that y_{i1} and y_{i2} are independent, with equal variance σ_y^2, then (6.8) can be rewritten as

$$\sigma_z^2 \leqslant E\frac{\sigma_y^2}{v_{i1}^2 + v_{i2}^2} + E\frac{(v_{i1}\mu_{y1} + v_{i2}\mu_{y2})^2}{(v_{i1}^2 + v_{i2}^2)^2} \tag{6.9}$$

An upper bound for the second term on the right-hand side of (6.9) can be obtained by the Schwarz inequality, because

$$|v_{i1}\mu_{y1} + v_{i2}\mu_{y2}|^2 \leqslant \|\mathbf{v}_i\|^2 \|\boldsymbol{\mu}_y\|^2 = (v_{i1}^2 + v_{i2}^2)(\mu_{y1}^2 + \mu_{y2}^2)$$

and thus

$$E[(v_{i1}\mu_{y1} + v_{i2}\mu_{y2})^2/(v_{i1}^2 + v_{i2}^2)^2] \leqslant E[(\mu_{y1}^2 + \mu_{y2}^2)/(v_{i1}^2 + v_{i2}^2)] \tag{6.10}$$

Combining (6.9) and (6.10), we have

$$\sigma_z^2 \leqslant (\sigma_y^2 + \mu_{y1}^2 + \mu_{y2}^2)E(v_{i1}^2 + v_{i2}^2)^{-1} \tag{6.11}$$

We now want an upper bound for $|\mu_z|$. Once we have it, this bound, in conjunction with the bound established by (6.11), will allow us to see how the v_{ij}'s of the legislators are related to the fulfillment of (6.6), which is a sufficient condition for the budget closer to the status quo to receive an expected majority against a budget farther away. From the definition of μ_z,

$$\begin{aligned} \mu_z &= E[(v_{i1}y_{i1} + v_{i2}y_{i2})/(v_{i1}^2 + v_{i2}^2)] \\ &= E[(v_{i1}\mu_{y1} + v_{i2}\mu_{y2})/(v_{i1}^2 + v_{i2}^2)] \end{aligned} \tag{6.12}$$

because v_{ij} is independent of y_{ij}. From the Schwarz inequality,

$$E[(v_{i1}\mu_{y1} + v_{i2}\mu_{y2})/(v_{i1}^2 + v_{i2}^2)] \leqslant E[(\mu_{y1}^2 + \mu_{y2}^2)/(v_{i1}^2 + v_{i2}^2)]^{1/2}$$

so that

$$\mu_z^2 \leqslant \{E[(\mu_{y1}^2 + \mu_{y2}^2)/(v_{i1}^2 + v_{i2}^2)]^{1/2}\}^2$$

But, again by the Schwarz inequality,

$$\{E[(\mu_{y1}^2 + \mu_{y2}^2)/(v_{i1}^2 + v_{i2}^2)]^{1/2}\}^2 \leqslant (\mu_{y1}^2 + \mu_{y2}^2)E(v_{i1}^2 + v_{i2}^2)^{-1}$$

Thus,

$$(\mu_{y1}^2 + \mu_{y2}^2)E(v_{i1}^2 + v_{i2}^2)^{-1} \geqslant \mu_z^2 \tag{6.13}$$

Inspection of (6.11) and (6.13) reveals that $E(v_{i1}^2+v_{i2}^2)^{-1}$ appears in both expressions and that all other terms are constants. Thus, if we can find an upper bound for $E(v_{i1}^2+v_{i2}^2)^{-1}$, we can see how this upper bound might shrink, causing σ_z and $|\mu_z|$ to shrink as well.

We shall now obtain an upper bound for $E(v_{i1}^2+v_{i2}^2)^{-1}$. Assume, for convenience only, that $\text{Var}(v_{i1})=\text{Var}(v_{i2})=\sigma_v^2$. We can then express v_{i1} and v_{i2} as products of the standard deviation σ_v and a random variable t_{ij} $(j=1,2)$ with unit variance, because if $\text{Var}(v_{ij})=\sigma_v^2$ and $v_{ij}=\sigma_v t_{ij}$, then

$$\begin{aligned}\sigma_v^2 = \text{Var}(\sigma_v t_{ij}) &= E(\sigma_v^2 t_{ij}^2) - (E\sigma_v t_{ij})^2\\ &= \sigma_v^2[Et_{ij}^2 - (Et_{ij})^2]\end{aligned}$$

and so $\text{Var}(t_{ij})=1$.

We must assume that the random variable $(t_{i1}^2+t_{i2}^2)^{-1}$ has finite expectation. However, this is not unreasonable. Let $c \geqslant E(t_{i1}^2+t_{i2}^2)^{-1}$ be this positive, finite upper bound. This allows us to establish that

$$E(v_{i1}^2+v_{i2}^2)^{-1} = \sigma_v^{-2}E(t_{i1}^2+t_{i2}^2)^{-1} \leqslant c/\sigma_v^2 \tag{6.14}$$

We can now combine (6.14), (6.13), and (6.11) to see that

$$|\pi_\theta + \pi_\psi| > 2[(\mu_{y1}^2+\mu_{y2}^2)^{1/2} + (\sigma_y^2+\mu_{y1}^2+\mu_{y2}^2)^{1/2}]c^{1/2}/\sigma_v \tag{6.15}$$

is a sufficient condition for (6.6) to hold and thus for π_θ, the budget proposal closer to the status quo, to receive an expected majority of the votes against π_ψ.

Examination of (6.15) allows us to take the final step, linking the v_{ij}'s of the legislators with conditions under which π_θ will receive an expected majority. As $\sigma_v = [\text{Var}(v_{i1})]^{1/2} = [\text{Var}(v_{i2})]^{1/2}$ increases, the right-hand side of (6.15) gets smaller (the x_{ij}'s and b_{ij}'s remain fixed and so can be treated as constants). Thus, as the variance of v_{ij} increases, the right-hand side of (6.15) approaches zero, and unless π_ψ is very close to zero, π_θ will receive an expected majority of the votes.

Figure 6.2 is an example in which the actual vote and the expected vote behave in accordance with our result. Assume three legislators with ideal points $\mathbf{x}_i'=(30,100)$, $\mathbf{x}_j'=(70,90)$, and $\mathbf{x}_k'=(30,160)$. Each ideal point represents the legislator's most preferred spending package on the two projects described earlier, measured in millions of dollars. As before, assume that in the absence of budget change, all legislators anticipate spending to remain at current levels. Then, $b_{i1}=b_{j1}=b_{k1}=\$10$ million, and $b_{i2}=b_{j2}=b_{k2}=\$70$ million. Set $\mathbf{v}_i'=\mathbf{v}_j'=\mathbf{v}_k'=(.5,.5)$, so that each legislator believes that a two-dollar increase in the budget will translate into a one-dollar spending increase in each project. Finally, set $A_i = A_j = A_k = I$.

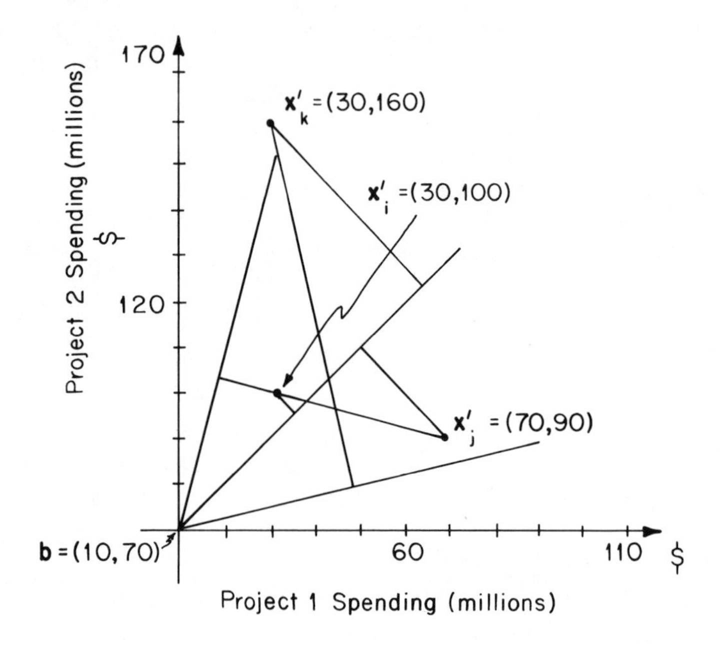

Figure 6.2. How a change in $\text{Var}(v_{ij})$ can affect $|\mu_z| + \sigma_z$.

Because the **v**'s of the legislators are identical, $\text{Var}(v_{i1}) = \text{Var}(v_{i1}) = 0$. Further,

$$z_i = \frac{v_{i1}y_{i1} + v_{i2}y_{i2}}{v_{i1}^2 + v_{i2}^2} = 50$$

$$z_j = \frac{v_{j1}y_{j1} + v_{j2}y_{j2}}{v_{j1}^2 + v_{j2}^2} = 80$$

$$z_k = \frac{v_{k1}y_{k1} + v_{k2}y_{k2}}{v_{k1}^2 + v_{k2}^2} = 110$$

so that $\mu_z = 80$ and $\text{Var}(z_i) = 600$.

Now, suppose that $\mathbf{v}_i' = (.5, .5)$ but that $\mathbf{v}_j' = (.2, .8)$ and $\mathbf{v}_k' = (.8, .2)$. $\text{Var}(v_{i1}) = \text{Var}(v_{i2}) = .06$, and $z_i = 50$, $z_j = 41$, and $z_k = 50$. Thus, $\mu_z = 47$ and $\text{Var}(z_i) = 18$. In short, increasing the variance of v_{ij} decreases both the absolute value of the mean and the variance of z_i.

If $v_{i1} + v_{i2} = 1$, the set of all possible (v_{i1}, v_{i2}) is a line intersecting the two axes at $(0, 1)$ and $(1, 0)$. Clearly, if v_{j2} and v_{k1} increase further, z_j and z_k will continue to decrease, and thus μ_z will also; σ_z does not decline, but $|\mu_z| + \sigma_z$ does, which is what actually matters in (6.6). Thus, if $\mathbf{v}_j' = (0, 1)$ and $\mathbf{v}_k' = (1, 0)$, then $|\mu_z| + \sigma_z = 44.1$, whereas previously, for $\mathbf{v}_j' = (.2, .8)$ and $\mathbf{v}_k' = (.8, .2)$, $|\mu_z| + \sigma_z = 51.2$. As perceptions of how total budget changes will affect individual project spending become more disparate, support for budget proposals closer to the status quo becomes stronger. In the case of our example, as v_{j2} and v_{k1} approach positive infinity, z_j and z_k approach zero. Thus, in the limit, no budget proposal will beat the status quo.

6.4 Conclusion

What we have done is to establish an important connection between disparity of views concerning how total budget changes will translate into spending changes on individual activities and support for small over large changes in total budget size. Other things being equal, preconceived formulas that tell all legislators beforehand how cuts or increases in the budget will affect spending on individual programs should increase support for larger cuts or increases in budget size. The sign of the median z_i determines whether it is cuts or increases in the budget that will win majority support. If this formula is itself subject to a vote, the instabilities described in Chapter 3 complicate matters. On the other hand, if this formula is commonly understood as a norm of the voting body, not something that has been decided on formally, these problems can be avoided. An informal agreement to continue past practices is an example of this type of arrangement.

In the case of referenda, the problem of decreasing perceptual variance is more difficult. Politicians and bureaucrats whose program are threatened by large tax cuts or lowered budgetary ceilings will attempt to confuse voters about how such cuts will affect individual programs. Or, what is really the same thing, an attempt will be made to convince each voter that his favorite program will be hardest hit by any cuts in budget size.

Thus, our theory indicates that committees may be more likely to support large changes in total budgetary size than mass electorates. Extreme disgust with politicians may lead voters to believe the opposite of what politicians say and thus approve measures such as California's Proposition 13. If widespread support exists for a program such as Social Security, telling all legislators exactly how much minimum Social Security benefits will be cut to balance the budget will not increase support for a balanced budget. If it is anticipated that spending cuts in popular programs are likely to be made, it may be better to vote on budget cuts one program at a time in order to avoid the risk of ending up with no budget cuts at all.

Problems

6.1 Let $v_{i1}=v_{i2}=\frac{1}{2}$, $y_{i1}=4$, and $y_{i2}=-4$. Use expression (6.4) to compute i's most preferred budget change from the status quo.

6.2 Rework Problem 6.1 with $v_{i1}=1\,(v_{i2}=0)$.

6.3 Let $v_{i1}=v_{i2}=\frac{1}{2}$ and $y_{i1}=y_{i2}=2$. Does i prefer a budget increase of 5 to an increase of 1?

6.4 To illustrate (6.14), suppose that $(v_{i1}, v_{i2})=(2,-1)$ and $(-1,2)$, each with probability $\frac{1}{2}$. Thus, $\sigma_v^2=\frac{9}{4}$ and $E(v_{i1}^2+v_{i2}^2)^{-1}=\frac{1}{5}$. Find c such that $E(v_{i1}^2+v_{i2}^2)^{-1}=c/\sigma_v^2$.

6.5 When there are n projects, voter i's most preferred budget change is $\mathbf{v}_i'A_i\mathbf{y}_i/(\mathbf{v}_iA_i\mathbf{v}_i)$, where $\mathbf{y}_i=\mathbf{x}_i-\mathbf{b}_i$. For $A_i=I$, this change is $\sum_{j=1}^n v_{ij}y_{ij}/\sum_{j=1}^n v_{ij}^2$. Find this change for $n=3$, $v_{i1}=v_{i2}=v_{i3}=\frac{1}{3}$ and $y_{i1}=y_{i2}=y_{i3}=1$. Recompute the optimal change for $v_{i1}=v_{i2}=\frac{1}{2}$ and $v_{i3}=0$, and for $v_{i1}=3$, $v_{i2}=-1$, and $v_{i3}=-\frac{1}{2}$.

6.6 Determine voter i's most preferred budget change when $v_{i1}=\ldots=v_{in}=1/n$ and $A_i=I$.

6.7 Compare the model in this chapter to the one in Chapter 4 in terms of their basic assumptions.

Bibliographical notes

The work contained in this chapter is based on Hinich and Mackay (1979). The central result of this chapter can also be proved for elections. Increasing the variance of the v_{ij}'s in the electorate increases support for the incumbent over a challenger. For details, see Hinich and Pollard (1981).

CHAPTER 7

Models of voter uncertainty

7.1 Candidate competition and the nature of uncertainty

In this chapter we shall return to the subject of candidate competition and examine an important topic. In Chapter 4 we developed a model in which each voter was assumed to know the political label of each candidate. This label was defined as a position on the predictive dimension Π. The position of candidate Theta was denoted π_θ, the position of candidate Psi was π_ψ, and so on. Each label was then used by the voter, in conjunction with the voter's translation coefficients, to assign a vector of policy positions to the candidate.

We discussed at some length the origin of the voter's translation coefficients – the b_{ij}'s and v_{ij}'s that represent how the voter predicts policy positions on the basis of predictive labels. In this chapter we shall look more closely at the candidates' predictive labels. Specifically, we shall ask how uncertainty about these labels can affect voter preferences and candidate competition.

There are three types of uncertainty that we shall examine. The first type arises from candidate movement on the predictive dimension *between* election periods. Up until now, we have concerned ourselves only with a single election period. During such an interval, we have assumed that the candidate's predictive label is fixed. This assumption reflects an important aspect of political reality: Candidate labels are not easily changed. However, candidates have attempted to change labels from one election period to the next. These attempts create uncertainty in the minds of voters. A candidate may announce a change of position on the predictive dimension – calling himself a conservative, whereas he might previously have been known as a moderate. However, voters may believe this announcement only to a limited extent. This is the first type of uncertainty we shall examine; it will be termed *candidate-induced uncertainty.*

The second type of uncertainty we shall look at is *perceptual uncertainty*. In any single election period, there are many reasons why voters may be unsure about precisely where a candidate is located on the predictive dimension. Political communication is a noisy process, and voters typically lack incentives to resolve uncertainties they may have about the candidates. Our second model of uncertainty reflects these problems and shows how our original model is affected by them.

The last type of uncertainty we shall discuss is *predictive uncertainty*. This type of uncertainty is about what will happen in terms of real policy change if a candidate is elected to office. We shall employ the perceptual uncertainty model to represent predictive uncertainty, but predictive uncertainty and perceptual uncertainty are caused by different factors. This difference leads to different conclusions concerning the consequences of these two types of voter uncertainty for our model. A central idea we shall explore is that the degree of predictive uncertainty may be related to where, on average, the candidate is seen as being located on the classic left–right dimension.

7.2 Candidate behavior between election periods

It is not unusual for a candidate who has been unsuccessful at the polls to attempt to move his position on the predictive dimension in preparation for another try at elective office. Losing candidates in American politics tend to make large-scale changes in their campaigns the next time they run for office. The election result tells them only that they did something wrong. Consequently, it is typical for a losing candidate to completely overhaul his campaign organization the next time he runs for office. This may involve an effort to change his location on the predictive dimension.

Winning candidates may face a changed electoral environment when running for reelection or higher office. A congressman who stays in touch with his constituents may come to realize that demographic changes have affected the composition of his district, or a politician running for higher office may face an electorate substantially different from the one he previously represented. In either case, the politician may wish to move his position on the predictive dimension.

As we argued in Chapter 4, the predictive label of the candidate is difficult to change. A candidate who attempts to run as a moderate one year and a conservative the next may lose credibility with the voters. His political career may ultimately be destroyed, simply because the voters no longer believe he has any predictive label at all. However, reasonable changes on the predictive dimension over a longer period of time may be possible. A candidate who argues that fundamental changes in the economy require a new approach may be able to convince voters that he is now more of an economic conservative than he was 5 or 10 years earlier. Voters may find his statement credible that a change of philosophy is dictated by the nature of the times.

But it may be impossible to erase doubts in the minds of some voters about how genuine this shift is. These voters may feel that an element of political expediency underlies the candidate's statements, leaving them with the conclusion that there is some probability that his position on the predictive dimension has not changed at all.

7.3 A model of candidate-induced uncertainty

Let us assume that two candidates, Theta and Psi, face each other in two successive elections. We shall assume that Psi received a majority of the votes in the first contest and so is the incumbent in the second race. Let π_θ and π_ψ be the respective positions of the two candidates in this first race. In the second race, π_ψ will again represent Psi's position on the predictive dimension. However, it is now Theta's claim that his position has moved to π'_θ, where $\pi'_\theta \neq \pi_\theta$. What we want to know is how this announcement will affect the outcome of the second race.

For simplicity, assume two policy issues in the second election. Further, let the status quo policy on both issues be commonly perceived, and let alternative policies on both issues be measured as departures from the status quo. Thus, $\mathbf{b}_i = (b_{i1}, b_{i2})' = \mathbf{0}$ for each voter i. Let voter preferences be measured in terms of utility, as defined in Chapter 5. Then, voter i will prefer the candidate for whom he has the highest utility.

The position of Psi on the predictive dimension is the same for both elections. Thus, because π_ψ is this position, voter i's utility for Psi is

$$u(\psi_i) = c_{i\psi} - \|\psi_i - \mathbf{x}_i\|^2_{A_i} \tag{7.1}$$

where $\psi_i = \pi_\psi \mathbf{v}_i = (\pi_\psi v_{i1}, \pi_\psi v_{i2})'$, $c_{i\psi}$ is the nonpolicy value of Psi to voter i, and $\mathbf{x}_i = (x_{i1}, x_{i2})'$ is i's ideal point on the two policy issues. We shall show that the shape of the curve representing $u(\psi_i)$ plays an important role in the theory of voter uncertainty. Consequently, we wish to reexpress (7.1) in terms of voter and candidate positions on the predictive dimension.

For simplicity, let $A_i = I$. Then, from (7.1),

$$\begin{aligned} u(\psi_i) &= c_{i\psi} - (\psi_{i1} - x_{i1})^2 - (\psi_{i2} - x_{i2})^2 \\ &= c_{i\psi} - (\pi_\psi v_{i1} - x_{i1})^2 - (\pi_\psi v_{i2} - x_{i2})^2 \\ &= c_{i\psi} - \pi_\psi^2 (v_{i1}^2 + v_{i2}^2) + 2\pi_\psi (v_{i1} x_{i1} + v_{i2} x_{i2}) - x_{i1}^2 - x_{i2}^2 \end{aligned}$$

But recall that $z_i = (v_{i1} x_{i1} + v_{i2} x_{i2}) / (v_{i1}^2 + v_{i2}^2)$, and thus

$$u(\psi_i) = c_{i\psi} - (\pi_\psi^2 - 2\pi_\psi z_i)(v_{i1}^2 + v_{i2}^2) - x_{i1}^2 - x_{i2}^2$$

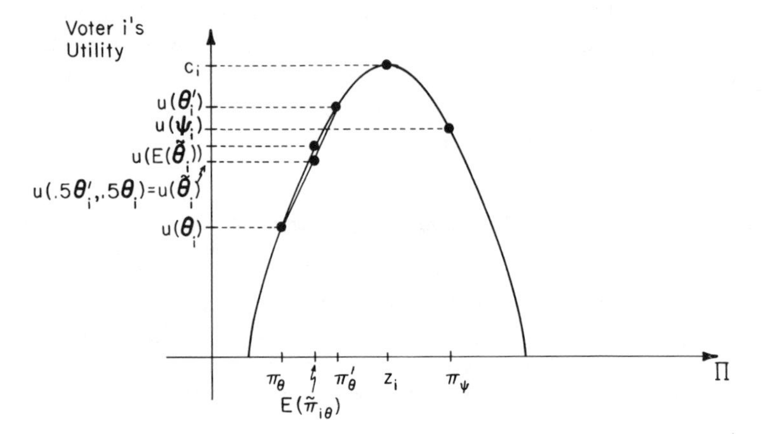

Figure 7.1. Voter utility for lottery and point positions on Π.

Completing the square,

$$u(\psi_i) = c_{i\psi} - (\pi_\psi - z_i)^2 (v_{i1}^2 + v_{i2}^2) - \frac{(x_{i1} v_{i2} - x_{i2} v_{i1})^2}{v_{i1}^2 + v_{i2}^2} \tag{7.2}$$

Figure 7.1 is a sample representation of (7.2). Clearly, because

$$\frac{\partial u(\psi_i)}{\partial \pi_\psi} = -2(\pi_\psi - z_i)(v_{i1}^2 + v_{i2}^2) \quad \text{and} \quad \frac{\partial^2 u(\psi_i)}{\partial \pi_\psi^2} = -2(v_{i1}^2 + v_{i2}^2)$$

$u(\psi_i)$ is symmetric and concave downward, as in Figure 5.1. Thus, voter i's utility for Psi decreases at an increasing rate the farther π_ψ moves from z_i.

If $c_{i\psi} = c_{i\theta} = c_i$, the curve representing $u(\psi_i)$ also represents $u(\theta_i)$. To simplify exposition, we shall assume that this is true. Thus, if π_θ is Theta's position on the predictive dimension, voter i prefers Theta to Psi if and only if π_θ is closer than π_ψ to z_i. This is the result we derived in Chapter 4.

However, the problem we face with respect to determining i's candidate preference is that we have not specified the position at which Theta is perceived on the predictive dimension. In the first election, Theta's position was π_θ. Now it is his claim that his position has moved to π_θ'. This claim is bound to produce uncertainty in the minds of the voters' owing to the resistance to change of predictive labels. It may have taken some time for π_θ to be affixed to Theta as a predictive label. It therefore seems natural to suppose that voters will give only a certain amount of credence to Theta's claim that he should be given the label π_θ' in the upcoming campaign.

To model this uncertainty about Theta's position, we shall assume that voter i estimates that there is some probability p_i that Theta's position has changed to π'_θ, but he also estimates that there is a complementary probability $(1-p_i)$ that Theta's position is still π_θ. The probability p_i is the *credibility* that Theta has with voter i in the current campaign.

What, then, is voter i's utility for Theta, given that his credibility with voter i is p_i? To answer this question, let us introduce the expected utility hypothesis in the context of our model. Given his credibility with voter i, Theta's position on the predictive dimension is perceived as a *lottery* or gamble $\tilde{\pi}_{i\theta}=[p_i\pi'_\theta, (1-p_i)\pi_\theta]$, and thus i's perception of Theta's position on the two policy issues of the campaign is a lottery of vectors $\tilde{\boldsymbol{\theta}}_i=[p_i\boldsymbol{\theta}'_i, (1-p_i)\boldsymbol{\theta}_i]$, where

$$\boldsymbol{\theta}'_i=\mathbf{b}_i+\pi'_\theta\mathbf{v}_i \quad \text{and} \quad \boldsymbol{\theta}_i=\mathbf{b}_i+\pi_\theta\mathbf{v}_i$$

The expected utility hypothesis states that i's *utility* for Theta is

$$\begin{aligned} u(\tilde{\boldsymbol{\theta}}_i)&=u[p_i\boldsymbol{\theta}'_i, (1-p_i)\boldsymbol{\theta}_i] \\ &=p_i u(\boldsymbol{\theta}'_i)+(1-p_i)u(\boldsymbol{\theta}_i) \end{aligned} \tag{7.3}$$

In short, i's utility for Theta is an average of his utility for Theta at the two different positions π'_θ and π_θ. In terms of Figure 7.1, $u(\tilde{\boldsymbol{\theta}}_i)$ is represented by a chord joining $u(\boldsymbol{\theta}_i)$ and $u(\boldsymbol{\theta}'_i)$. The exact location on this chord corresponding to $u(\tilde{\boldsymbol{\theta}}_i)$ depends on the value of p_i. If $p_i=.5$, then $u(\tilde{\boldsymbol{\theta}}_i)$ is represented by a point half the distance between $u(\boldsymbol{\theta}_i)$ and $u(\boldsymbol{\theta}'_i)$. This point is indicated in Figure 7.1.

Suppose that Theta's credibility with voter i is .5. Inspection of Figure 7.1 reveals that $u(\boldsymbol{\theta}'_i)>u(\boldsymbol{\psi}_i)$, so that if Theta's credibility with voter i were 1, then i would prefer Theta to Psi. However, because Theta's credibility with i is .5, i continues to prefer Psi to Theta.

Recall from Section 5.1 that the curve represented in Figure 7.1 characterizes risk aversion. Thus, i will prefer a candidate whose position on Π is an average of π'_θ and π_θ, $E(\tilde{\pi}_{i\theta})=p_i\pi'_\theta+(1-p_i)\pi_\theta$, to a candidate whose position on Π is the lottery between π'_θ and π_θ, $\tilde{\pi}_{i\theta}=[p_i\pi'_\theta, (1-p_i)\pi_\theta]$. This preference can be seen in Figure 7.1, where $u[E(\tilde{\boldsymbol{\theta}}_i)]$ represents i's utility for the candidate whose position on Π is $E(\tilde{\pi}_{i\theta})$, and $u(\tilde{\boldsymbol{\theta}}_i)$ represents i's utility for the candidate whose position on Π is the lottery $\tilde{\pi}_{i\theta}$.

Suppose, then, that $\pi_\psi=z_{\text{med}}$, as in Figure 7.2. If Theta's position is π_θ, voters 2 and 3 will prefer Psi to Theta. If Theta's position is π'_θ, voters 1 and 2 will prefer Psi to Theta. Either way, Theta will lose to Psi. However, suppose that Theta's position on Π is perceived by all voters as a lottery between π'_θ and π_θ. If Theta's credibility is the same with each voter, Theta will still lose the election. To see this, assume that

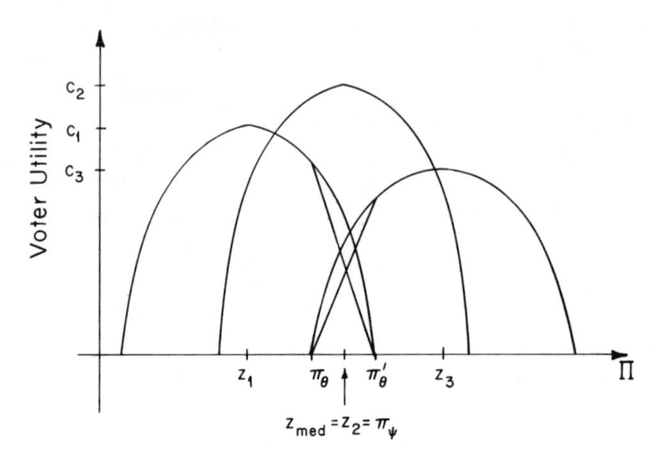

Figure 7.2. Electoral competition with one lottery candidate and risk-averse voters.

$\tilde{\pi}_{i\theta} = [p_i \pi'_\theta, (1-p_i)\pi_\theta]$ characterizes this commonly perceived lottery and that $E(\tilde{\pi}_{i\theta}) < \pi_\psi = z_{\text{med}}$. Then, because z_{med} is the unique median z_i, a majority of these most preferred points must lie to the right of $E(\tilde{\pi}_{i\theta})$. Because these voters (in Figure 7.2, voters 2 and 3) are risk-averse, $u[E(\tilde{\theta}_i)] > u(\tilde{\theta}_i)$. In addition, because the most preferred points of these voters are equal to or greater than z_{med}, their utility curves must slope downward between z_{med} and $E(\tilde{\pi}_{i\theta})$. Thus, because $z_{\text{med}} = \pi_\psi$, $u(\psi_i) > u[E(\tilde{\theta}_i)]$. This means that $u(\psi_i) > u[E(\tilde{\theta}_i)] > u(\tilde{\theta}_i)$, and so a majority of voters prefer Psi to Theta. If $E(\tilde{\pi}_{i\theta}) \geqslant z_{\text{med}}$, a similar argument establishes the same result.

However, suppose that Theta's credibility is not the same with each voter. Examining Figure 7.2, if Theta's credibility is high with voter 3, but low with voter 1, voters 1 and 3 will vote for Theta over Psi. Thus, Theta can beat Psi even when $\pi_\psi = z_{\text{med}}$ and all voters are risk-averse, if Theta's credibility varies among voters.

Theta's electoral prospects are improved under a different circumstance. If the utility curves of Figure 7.2 are convex instead of concave, Theta can beat Psi under a broader range of conditions. Figure 7.3 is a representation of three such curves, under the assumption that

$$u(\psi_i) = c_{i\psi} - \|\psi_i - \mathbf{x}_i\|_{A_i}^{1/2}$$

Now Theta can defeat Psi even if $\pi_\psi = z_{\text{med}}$ and Theta's credibility is the same for all voters. Because voters 1 and 3 are now risk-acceptant in the interval $[\pi_\theta, \pi'_\theta]$, $u(\tilde{\theta}_i) > u[E(\tilde{\theta}_i)]$ for $i = 1, 3$. Thus, in Figure 7.3, if $E(\tilde{\pi}_{i\theta}) = z_{\text{med}} = \pi_\psi$, $u(\tilde{\theta}_i) > u(\psi_i)$ for voters 1 and 3, and Theta will defeat

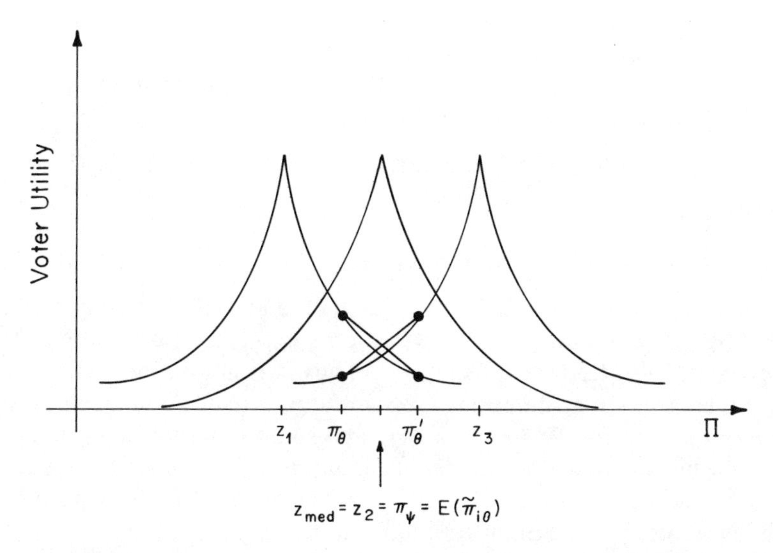

Figure 7.3. Electoral competition with one lottery candidate and risk-acceptant voters.

Psi. In general, if a majority of voters are risk-acceptant in an interval containing z_{med}, it will always be possible for Theta to defeat Psi, even if his credibility is the same among voters. However, it is possible to construct an example in which a minority of voters are risk-acceptant, Theta's credibility is the same among voters, and Theta defeats a candidate located at z_{med}.

Let us conclude Section 7.3 with one additional result. We have shown that a candidate whose position on Π is perceived as a lottery can defeat a candidate whose position is perceived as z_{med}. This event can occur when voters are risk-averse and the lottery candidate's credibility varies among voters or when some voters are risk-acceptant. The question then arises whether or not a safe position exists for a lottery candidate. Suppose that $\pi_\psi = z_{med}$ and $\tilde{\pi}_{i\theta} = [p_i\, \pi'_\theta, (1-p_i)\, \pi_\theta]$ are the two positions of Psi and Theta. Suppose Theta anticipates that Psi will attempt to change his position to a lottery position or some point position other than z_{med}. Suppose Theta does not know what this position is. Does a lottery or point position exist that can prevent Theta's defeat, no matter what Psi's new position is?

It is not difficult to show that the answer is no. Under our model, if z_{med} is not a safe position, then no point position is safe. Suppose, then, that $\tilde{\pi}_{i\theta}$ is safe for Theta. For simplicity, assume that $c_{i\theta} = c_{i\psi}$ for all voters. We shall now show that if $\tilde{\pi}_{i\theta}$ can defeat some other lottery position, $\tilde{\pi}_{i\theta}$ cannot be safe.

To see that this is true, suppose that $x=(.5\pi'_\theta, .5\pi_\theta)$ is safe for Theta. Let $y=(.4\pi'_\theta, .6\pi_\theta)$ and $t=(.9\pi'_\theta, .1\pi_\theta)$. For convenience, write $u(\tilde{\theta}_i)=u[p_i\theta'_i, (1-p_i)\theta_i]$ as $u[p_i\pi'_\theta, (1-p_i)\pi_\theta]=u(\tilde{\pi}_{i\theta})$. Then $u(x)>u(y)$ if and only if $u(.2t, .8x)>u(.2t, .8y)$. But

$$(.2t, .8x)=[.2(.9\pi'_\theta)+.8(.5\pi'_\theta), .2(.1\pi_\theta)+.8(.5\pi_\theta)]=(.58\pi'_\theta, .42\pi_\theta)=r$$

and

$$(.2t, .8y)=[.2(.9\pi'_\theta)+.8(.4\pi'_\theta), .2(.1\pi_\theta)+.8(.6\pi_\theta)]=(.5\pi'_\theta, .5\pi_\theta)=x$$

Thus, $u(x)>u(y)$ if and only if $u(r)>u(x)$, and so if a majority prefers $(.5\pi'_\theta, .5\pi_\theta)$ to $(.4\pi'_\theta, .6\pi_\theta)$, as we assume is the case, a majority also prefers $(.58\pi'_\theta, .42\pi_\theta)$ to $(.5\pi'_\theta, .5\pi_\theta)$. Thus, x is not a safe position for Theta, contrary to assumption. The same argument can be applied to any lottery position for Theta and any y, and so no lottery position is safe. This means that under our model of candidate-induced uncertainty, only z_{med} can be a safe position. If z_{med} can be defeated by a lottery position, neither a lottery nor a point position can be safe.

7.4 A model of perceptual uncertainty about candidate location on Π

We shall now discuss the second type of voter uncertainty mentioned in Section 7.1. In any single election period, there are numerous reasons why voters may be unsure of the precise locations of the candidates on a predictive dimension. Information is costly to acquire, and incentives for doing so are typically weak or nonexistent in mass elections. Consequently, voters may be left with uncertainties about where the candidates are located on a predictive dimension.

Further, the process by which information about the candidates is conveyed to voters is inherently imperfect. Voters must typically rely on newspapers or television in order to acquire information about the candidates. These sources, responding to market forces, typically supply information about nonspatial characteristics of the candidate, at the expense of more issue-oriented information. Thus, voters may be more knowledgeable about a candidate's personal characteristics than his political ideology.

It may be especially difficult for voters to attach predictive labels to lesser-known candidates. Jimmy Carter is a case in point. Virtually unknown by the American electorate in 1976 and stressing personal over issue concerns, Carter was commonly accused of being "fuzzy" on the issues. Whereas this charge may be interpreted to mean that Carter was deliberately ambiguous, a more plausible interpretation is that the voters' lack of familiarity with Carter, compounded by the personal focus of his campaign, made it extremely difficult for them to decide where he was located on the predictive dimensions of the campaign.

For these reasons, it is plausible to model voter uncertainty due to imperfect information regarding the predictive labels of the candidates. As in the previous section, we shall assume a single underlying predictive dimension in the campaign. The positions of the two candidates, Theta and Psi, are then perceived as random variables $\tilde{\pi}_\theta$ and $\tilde{\pi}_\psi$. We might subscript these random variables, as the lotteries of the previous section were subscripted, to denote idiosyncratic perception. The results we shall derive would then apply to each voter individually. However, our results are easier to interpret if we assume *common perception* of $\tilde{\pi}_\theta$ and $\tilde{\pi}_\psi$. In addition, further assumptions will be made in the next section concerning the form of $\tilde{\pi}_\theta$ and $\tilde{\pi}_\psi$ that will increase the appropriateness of assuming common perception.

We shall express each of $\tilde{\pi}_\theta$ and $\tilde{\pi}_\psi$ as the sum of its mean and a random element. Thus, if $E(\tilde{\pi}_\theta)=\pi_\theta$ and $E(\tilde{\pi}_\psi)=\pi_\psi$,

$$\tilde{\pi}_\theta=\pi_\theta+\epsilon_\theta \quad \text{and} \quad \tilde{\pi}_\psi=\pi_\psi+\epsilon_\psi$$

and so $E(\epsilon_\theta)=E(\epsilon_\psi)=0$. We shall assume that the "true" positions of candidates Theta and Psi are π_θ and π_ψ, respectively. Thus, ϵ_θ and ϵ_ψ represent the distortion or noise that results from the imperfect process of transmitting these true positions to the voters. Thus, the signal sent by Theta is π_θ, but the signal received by the voters is $\tilde{\pi}_\theta$.

What is voter i's utility for Theta if Theta's position on the predictive dimension is perceived as $\tilde{\pi}_\theta$? Because $\tilde{\pi}_\theta$ is a random variable, i's utility for Theta is his utility for a random variable. However, the expected utility hypothesis tells us that i's utility for a random variable is the utility expectation of that random variable. Thus, if $\tilde{\theta}_i=(v_{i1}\tilde{\pi}_\theta, v_{i2}\tilde{\pi}_\theta)'$ is the vector of random variables expressing how i perceives Theta on the two issues of the campaign,

$$u(\tilde{\theta}_i)=c_{i\theta}-\|\tilde{\theta}_i-\mathbf{x}_i\|^2_{A_i} \tag{7.4}$$

is i's utility for Theta. Letting $A_i=I$ and $c_{i\theta}=c_i$, (7.4) can be reexpressed as

$$\begin{aligned} u(\tilde{\theta}_i)&=c_i-(\tilde{\pi}_\theta v_{i1}-x_{i1})^2-(\tilde{\pi}_\theta v_{i2}-x_{i2})^2 \\ &=c_i-[(\pi_\theta+\epsilon_\theta)v_{i1}-x_{i1}]^2-[(\pi_\theta+\epsilon_\theta)v_{i2}-x_{i2}]^2 \end{aligned} \tag{7.5}$$

However, by the expected utility hypothesis,

$$u(\tilde{\theta}_i)=E[u(\tilde{\theta}_i)]$$

so that i's utility for Theta is

$$E[u(\tilde{\theta}_i)] = E\{c_i - [(\pi_\theta + \epsilon_\theta)v_{i1} - x_{i1}]^2 - [(\pi_\theta + \epsilon_\theta)v_{i2} - x_{i2}]^2\}$$
$$= c_i - (\pi_\theta v_{i1} - x_{i1})^2 - (\pi_\theta v_{i2} - x_{i2})^2 - (v_{i1}^2 + v_{i2}^2)E(\epsilon_\theta^2) \quad (7.6)$$

which follows because $E(\epsilon_\theta) = 0$ and π_θ, v_{i1}, v_{i2}, x_{i1}, and x_{i2} are all constants. In addition, if $\sigma_\theta^2 = \text{Var}(\epsilon_\theta)$, $E(\epsilon_\theta^2) = \sigma_\theta^2 + [E(\epsilon_\theta)]^2 = \sigma_\theta^2 + 0 = \sigma_\theta^2$, so that (7.6) can be rewritten as

$$E[u(\tilde{\theta}_i)] = c_i - (\pi_\theta v_{i1} - x_{i1})^2 - (\pi_\theta v_{i2} - x_{i2})^2 - (v_{i1}^2 + v_{i2}^2)\sigma_\theta^2 \quad (7.7)$$

It is clear from (7.7) that if perfect perception of π_θ exists, then $\sigma_\theta^2 = 0$, and (7.7) is the same as i's utility for Theta would be if his position were perceived as π_θ. However, the presence of σ_θ^2 alters i's utility if perception is imperfect. The greater σ_θ^2 is, the less i's utility is for Theta. Because i is risk-averse, this is not surprising.

It would appear from (7.7) that the $(v_{i1}^2 + v_{i2}^2)\sigma_\theta^2$ term plays the role of a constant, like c_i, in determining voter preference. Thus, because i's utility for Psi is

$$E[u(\tilde{\psi}_i)] = c_i - (\pi_\psi v_{i1} - x_{i1})^2 - (\pi_\psi v_{i2} - x_{i2})^2 - (v_{i1}^2 + v_{i2}^2)\sigma_\psi^2 \quad (7.8)$$

if $\sigma_\theta^2 = \sigma_\psi^2$, i's candidate preference is exactly the same as it would be if the candidates' positions were perfectly perceived. In other words, if the degree of perceptual distortion were the same, regardless of the candidates' true positions, perceptual uncertainty would not affect candidate competition.

On the other hand, if $\sigma_\theta^2 \neq \sigma_\psi^2$, candidate preference is a function both of true candidate location and of the amount of perceptual uncertainty associated with that position. Thus, if $\sigma_\theta^2 = 2\sigma_\psi^2$, so that the degree of perceptual uncertainty associated with π_θ is twice that associated with π_ψ, then i will prefer Theta to Psi if and only if

$$(\pi_\psi v_{i1} - x_{i1})^2 + (\pi_\psi v_{i2} - x_{i2})^2 > (\pi_\theta v_{i1} - x_{i1})^2 + (\pi_\theta v_{i2} - x_{i2})^2 + (v_{i1}^2 + v_{i2}^2)\sigma_\psi^2$$

This implies that if $\pi_\theta > \pi_\psi$, i prefers Theta to Psi if and only if

$$z_i > \frac{\pi_\theta + \pi_\psi}{2} + \frac{\sigma_\psi^2}{2(\pi_\theta - \pi_\psi)} \quad (7.9)$$

Because the right-hand side of (7.9) is greater than $(\pi_\theta + \pi_\psi)/2$, i might prefer Psi to Theta even though z_i is closer to π_θ.

Why might $\sigma_\theta^2 \neq \sigma_\psi^2$? Suppose that Psi is the incumbent. It might then be the case that $\sigma_\theta^2 > \sigma_\psi^2$. Perceptual uncertainty is usually less for incumbents than it is for challengers. Perceptual uncertainty may also be a function of campaign spending. The candidate spending the greater amount of money may transmit a clearer image to the voters of his predictive location. As mentioned earlier, a well-known candidate may generate less perceptual uncertainty than a lesser-known candidate. Although it is natural to expect the better-known candidate to be the incumbent or to be politically more experienced than his opponent, there is no need for either of these conditions to hold. The Ford–Reagan contest for the Republican presidential nomination in 1976 is a case in point.

The clarity of a candidate's predictive location appears to be primarily linked to nonspatial factors. Prior experience in elective office, endorsements from news media and interest groups, candidate articulateness, and the degree to which a candidate emphasizes nonpolicy issues in his campaign are other nonspatial factors that may influence the degree of perceptual uncertainty regarding the candidate's predictive location.

7.5 A model of predictive uncertainty about the future policies of elected officials

There is another way of looking at the question of voter uncertainty. Suppose that positions on Π are used by the voters to predict what policies will actually be implemented if the candidate is elected to the office he is seeking. Suppose, for instance, that π_θ is used by the voters to predict what will happen if Theta is elected. Prediction of future events is very hazardous, and so it seems quite reasonable to assume that voters will be uncertain in making this prediction.

One way of allowing this uncertainty to be reflected in the voter's decision making is to assume that his prediction is characterized by a random variable instead of a point prediction. In other words, the predictive mapping that takes place in the voter's mind is not a mapping into a point but is instead a mapping into a set of points, with a probability density defined over those points. However, this is equivalent to the random variable concept of positions on the predictive dimension discussed in Section 7.4. Thus, we can make use of our model of perceptual distortion to discuss this different type of voter uncertainty.

The positions of Theta and Psi on the predictive dimension are thus perceived as

$$\tilde{\pi}_\theta = \pi_\theta + \epsilon_\theta \quad \text{and} \quad \tilde{\pi}_\psi = \pi_\psi + \epsilon_\psi$$

where $E(\tilde{\pi}_\theta) = \pi_\theta$ and $E(\tilde{\pi}_\psi) = \pi_\psi$ as before. The interpretation now given to $\tilde{\pi}_\theta$ and $\tilde{\pi}_\psi$ is that the difficulty in predicting future policies under Theta or Psi means that this prediction is characterized by a random variable. Because each element $\pi_o \in \Pi$ corresponds to the point prediction $\mathbf{b}_i + \pi_o \mathbf{v}_i$, uncertainty about this prediction can be characterized by a random variable defined over Π. Thus, π_θ and π_ψ correspond to what, on average, each voter predicts will happen if Theta or Psi is elected, and ϵ_θ

and ϵ_ψ represent the random element of these two predictions. As in the case of uncertainty due to perceptual distortion, we could subscript this predictive variable by voter to allow for idiosyncratic predictions. However, the results we shall develop are more easily understood if $\tilde{\pi}_\theta$ and $\tilde{\pi}_\psi$ are commonly perceived. But because our results depend only on the mean and variance of each random variable, there is no need to assume that the functional form of the random variable is commonly perceived.

How, then, does predictive uncertainty affect our model of elections? From (7.7) and (7.8) it is clear that if $\pi_\theta > \pi_\psi$, then i will prefer Theta to Psi if and only if

$$z_i > \frac{\pi_\theta + \pi_\psi}{2} + \frac{\sigma_\theta^2 - \sigma_\psi^2}{2(\pi_\theta - \pi_\psi)} \tag{7.10}$$

so that if the predictive uncertainty surrounding Theta is greater than that surrounding Psi, z_i need not be closer to π_ψ for i to prefer Psi. Thus, if $\pi_\theta = 1$, $\pi_\psi = 0$, $\sigma_\theta^2 = \frac{1}{16}$, and $\sigma_\psi^2 = 0$, then i will prefer Theta to Psi if and only if $z_i > \frac{17}{32}$. This might occur if Psi were the incumbent and a continuation of prevailing policies were expected, and the prediction regarding Theta were a normally distributed random variable, contained in the interval $[\frac{1}{2}, \frac{3}{2}]$ with probability .95. Thus, if predictive uncertainty is always less for incumbents than for challengers, incumbents possess an absolute advantage in election contests.

Given the existence of predictive uncertainty (or perceptual uncertainty), the median z_i may no longer be an optimal location in two-candidate contests. Suppose, for three voters, that $z_i = 0$, $z_j = \frac{1}{2}$, and $z_k = 1$, so that median $z_i = \frac{1}{2}$. Suppose, further, that $\pi_\theta = \frac{1}{2}$ and $\pi_\psi = \frac{1}{3}$. Thus, Theta would beat Psi if $\tilde{\pi}_\theta$ and $\tilde{\pi}_\psi$ had zero or equal variances. However, suppose that $\sigma_\theta^2 = \frac{1}{16}$ and $\sigma_\psi^2 = 0$. Then i will prefer Theta to Psi if and only if $z_i > \frac{29}{48}$, so that i and j will prefer Psi, and Psi will beat Theta.

Predictive uncertainty can result in a shift in each voter's most preferred point. Instead of z_i, z_i^* represents the revised most preferred point on the predictive dimension. To solve for z_i^*, we differentiate the expression for voter utility given by either (7.7) or (7.8) with respect to π_θ or π_ψ and set the result equal to zero. This will tell us what average predictive value will maximize voter utility (given satisfaction of the second-order condition). If this average predictive value is known to the candidates, it will be possible for them to determine the revised most preferred points of the voters. From (7.7),

$$\frac{\partial E[u(\tilde{\theta}_i)]}{\partial \pi_\theta} = -2v_{i1}(\pi_\theta v_{i1} - x_{i1}) - 2v_{i2}(\pi_\theta v_{i2} - x_{i2}) - (v_{i1}^2 + v_{i2}^2)\frac{\partial \sigma_\theta^2}{\partial \pi_\theta} \tag{7.11}$$

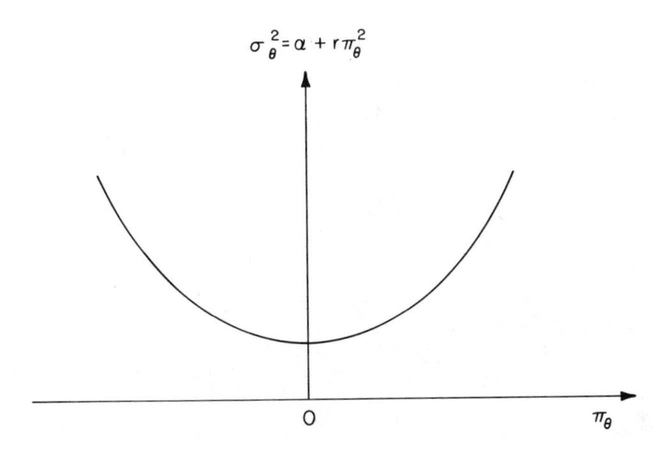

Figure 7.4. A case in which predictive uncertainty is least for $\pi_\theta = 0$.

Setting (7.11) equal to zero, and relabeling π_θ as z_i^*,

$$z_i^* = z_i - \frac{\partial \sigma_\theta^2}{2\partial \pi_\theta} \tag{7.12}$$

Thus, $\pi_\theta = z_i^*$ is the average predictive value that maximizes i's utility (assuming $\partial^2 \sigma_\theta^2 / \partial \pi_\theta^2 > -2$). Notice that this utility-maximizing value is a function of $\partial \sigma_\theta^2 / \partial \pi_\theta$. Thus, if predictive uncertainty is not a function of average predictive value, $\pi_\theta = z_i$ maximizes voter i's utility. On the other hand, spatially dependent perceptual uncertainty results in a shift of each voter's most preferred point from z_i to z_i^*.

How might a relationship exist between σ_θ^2 and π_θ, and what form might this relationship take? In American politics, middle-of-the-road or moderate candidates have traditionally been associated with the least amount of predictive uncertainty. Except for such critical election periods as the 1850s, 1890s, and 1930s, it has usually been easiest for voters to predict what will happen if centrist rather than extremist candidates are elected. Figure 7.4 is one way of representing this phenomenon. Letting $\pi = 0$ be defined as the center of the left–right political spectrum, let $\sigma_\theta^2 = \alpha + r\pi_\theta^2$ ($\alpha \geqslant 0$, $r > 0$), so that the more the average predictive value diverges from the center, the greater the degree of predictive uncertainty associated with the candidate. Thus, if $\pi_\theta = 0$, $\sigma_\theta^2 = \alpha$ is the minimum degree of predictive uncertainty, and for $\pi_\theta \neq 0$, predictive uncertainty increases at an increasing rate.

If $\sigma_\theta^2 = \alpha + r\pi_\theta^2$, then, resolving (7.11) for the average predictive value that is optimal for i, we find that $z_i^* = z_i/(1+r)$. Because $r > 0$, $|z_i^*| < |z_i|$.

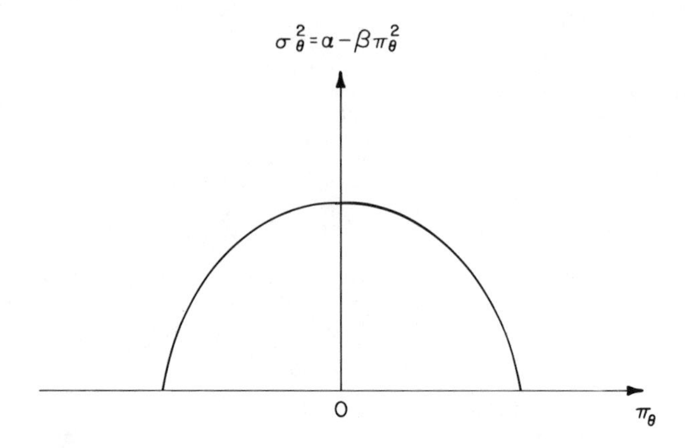

Figure 7.5. A case in which predictive uncertainty is greatest for $\pi_\theta = 0$.

In short, the revised most preferred points of the voters are shifted toward zero, this shift being in direct proportion to the size of r. Thus, a centrist candidate may beat a noncentrist candidate even if the average predictive value associated with the latter is closer to the median z_i. The optimal location for π_θ and π_ψ is now $[1/(1+r)]$ (median z_i), which is closer to zero than the median z_i.

However, in times of crisis it may be easier to predict what an extremist candidate would do if elected than a centrist candidate. As the slavery question progressively polarized the American electorate during the 1850s, it became easier to predict what extreme proslavery and antislavery candidates would try to accomplish, as compared with those who sought a compromise solution. Figure 7.5 represents a characterization of the center as the average predictive value associated with the greatest predictive uncertainty; $\sigma_\theta^2 = \alpha - \beta\pi_\theta^2$, with $\alpha, \beta > 0$, and thus $\alpha/\beta \geqslant \pi_\theta^2$, because $\sigma_\theta^2 \geqslant 0$.

If this relationship characterizes predictive uncertainty, then $z_i^* = z_i/(1-\beta)$ is i's revised most preferred point. However, to satisfy the second-order condition for utility maximization, it must be the case that $\beta < 1$. Thus, $|z_i^*| > |z_i|$, and, in contrast to the case represented by Figure 7.4, the revised most preferred points of the voters are shifted away from the center of the predictive dimension, this shift being in direct proportion to the size of β.

We have shown that predictive uncertainty can have very pronounced effects on electoral competition when the degree of uncertainty is tied to the location of the average predictive value of each candidate on the predictive dimension. Given the type of relationship characterized by Figure 7.4, candidates who, on average, are expected to be centrist possess an inherent advantage over those with noncentrist central tendencies. Given the type of relationship characterized by Figure 7.5, the advantage rests on the opposite side.

7.6 Conclusion

This chapter has dealt with three types of uncertainty: candidate-induced uncertainty due to candidate attempts to change location on the predictive dimension, perceptual uncertainty due to imperfect perception of candidate location on the predictive dimension, and predictive uncertainty due to the difficulty of predicting future policies if the candidate is elected. We have indicated what the consequences of each type of uncertainty are for our model of elections, assuming in each case that the voter copes with uncertainty by attempting to maximize his expected utility. Although we have not touched on this subject, the voter might use a different type of decision rule. In the case of the lotteries discussed in Section 7.3, he may wish to ignore the probabilities attached to π'_θ and π_θ and base his utility for Theta on whichever position gives him the least utility. If he views all candidates this way and prefers the candidate for whom the "least is best," he will be engaging in *maximin* decision making. This is just one example of a different decision rule that voters might employ.

Problems

7.1 Suppose that $c_{i\psi}=1$, $\mathbf{x}_i=(1,2)'$, $v_{i1}=1$, and $v_{i2}=-1$ in (7.2). Consider the following gamble: $\pi_\psi=7$ with probability $\frac{1}{4}$, and $\pi_\psi=0$ with probability $\frac{3}{4}$. Find the expected utility of this lottery. Compare the result with the utility for $\pi_\psi=\frac{7}{4}$.

7.2 Suppose that a voter's utility function is of the form $u(\pi_\psi)=c-|\pi_\psi-z|$, where z is his most preferred ideological position. The utility function is linear in π_ψ. Show that for all $\tilde{\pi}_\psi=[p\pi'_\psi,(1-p)\pi_\psi]$, $E[u(\tilde{\pi}_\psi)]=u[p\pi'_\psi+(1-p)\pi_\psi]$.

7.3 Using (7.7) and (7.8), find the condition for z_i similar to (7.9) that makes $E[u(\tilde{\theta}_i)]>E[u(\tilde{\psi}_i)]$ if $\sigma_\theta^2=7\sigma_\psi^2$ and $\pi_\theta>\pi_\psi$.

7.4 Let $\pi_\psi=0$, $\pi_\theta=1$, and $\sigma_\psi^2=0$. How small must σ_θ^2 be so that a voter with $z_i=1$ prefers Theta to Psi?

7.5 Rework Problem 7.4 with $\sigma_\psi^2=1$.

7.6 Suppose that $\sigma_\theta^2=b|\pi_\theta|$, where $b>0$. Thus, $\partial\sigma_\theta^2/\partial\pi_\theta=b$ if $\pi_\theta>0$, and $-b$ if $\pi_\theta<0$. Find z_i^*.

7.7 For the model in Problem 7.6, compare the median z_i^* with the median z_i.

Bibliographical notes

The theory developed in Section 7.3 is based on Shepsle (1972). Zeckhauser (1969) also contributes to this theory. Sections 7.4 and 7.5 are based on Enelow and Hinich (1981). A proof of the general instability of lottery positions can be found in Fishburn (1973).

Most studies of voter uncertainty have seen it as a candidate-induced phenomenon rather than as a result of imperfect information about the candidates. Downs (1957), Shepsle (1972), and Page (1976) are prominent examples of the candidate-based approach to modeling uncertainty.

CHAPTER 8

Institutions

8.1 Introduction

In this chapter we shall analyze an important feature of the voting environment. This feature is the institutional structure within which voting takes place. In Chapter 2 we showed that for the unidimensional spatial model, the proposal closest to the median voter's ideal point will receive a majority of the votes against any other proposal, if there is an odd number of voters. Presumably, if anyone is permitted to offer proposals to be voted on, the median voter will offer his most preferred proposal, which will beat any other proposal in a pairwise vote. However, it is frequently the case that a single individual, or a small group of individuals, is given the power to decide what is to be voted on. Public school boards usually possess this power, offering the voters a single choice: Approve the budget that the board proposes, or an "austerity" budget will take effect. A majority of the voters may prefer an alternative budget to that proposed by the school board. However, they are faced with a take-it-or-leave-it choice. Thus, control of the agenda by the school board may result in voter approval of a budget other than the one most preferred by the median voter.

It may also be possible for a school board to affect the outcome of the voting process by controlling the formula by which the total budget will be apportioned among the set of spending activities. This is another form of agenda control. Both types of agenda control are important and will be analyzed in this chapter.

A different type of institutional structure that affects vote outcomes is the committee system used in Congress and other legislative bodies. The assignment of jurisdiction over a policy domain to a subset of the voting body (i.e., a committee or subcommittee) can influence the outcome ultimately approved by the entire voting body. This topic will also be explored in this chapter.

Another type of institutional structure we shall analyze is the unit rule. In American politics there are several settings in which this rule has been or continues to be used. The electoral college is based on a winner-take-all principle at the state level, which is a form of the unit rule. Certain

Republican presidential primaries (also certain Democratic primaries, before 1976) award delegates on a winner-take-all basis, which is also a form of the unit rule. Republican national party rules permit state delegations to national party conventions to cast the votes of the entire delegation for the presidential candidate preferred by a majority of the delegation. This is also a form of the unit rule. Finally, the procedure for breaking electoral college deadlocks in the House of Representatives is a form of the unit rule. In each case, the entire vote allotted to a group is cast on the basis of the preference of a majority of the group.

Lastly, an important question that pervades the analysis of institutions is the question of expectations. When the decision-making process is broken up by institutional design into a series of steps, what voters expect will happen later on may affect their voting decisions in the present. This question will come up at several points in our discussion, and we shall show how it affects institutional analysis.

8.2 Agenda control

We shall shortly formalize the school budget example described at the beginning of this chapter. Initially we shall assume that voter preferences are defined on total spending figures, so that we can employ unidimensional spatial theory. We shall then relax this assumption and permit preferences to be defined over packages of spending figures for the individual activities or budget categories to be funded. This is the way preferences were defined in Chapter 6.

It is important to understand the difference between the type of voting on budgets we analyze here and that of Chapter 6. In Chapter 6, voters voted on total budget size, with varying perceptions of how changes in budget size would translate into changes in individual spending categories. Within this framework, the voting process was completely competitive in the sense that there were no restrictions on what total budget figure could be paired with the status quo budget for a vote.

In this chapter we shall modify these assumptions in several ways. First, we shall allow separate votes on individual spending categories (in contrast with Chapter 6, we assume in this chapter that budget figures are synonymous with spending figures). This is voting one issue at a time, which was discussed in Chapter 3, but with important differences. Second, when total budget size is voted on directly, we shall assume that the formula that translates aggregate into category-level changes is itself voted on at some stage in the voting process. However, the most important modification we shall make is to assume monopolistic control of proposed changes in the status quo. A single individual, or a like-minded

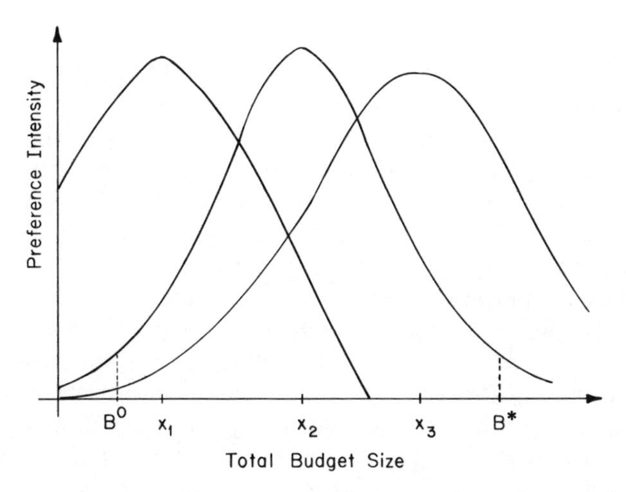

Figure 8.1. Three voters with symmetric preferences defined on total budget sizes.

group of individuals, will be assumed to control all access to the ballot or agenda by being given the power to decide what is paired against the status quo for a vote. It is the importance of this power that we wish to investigate.

8.3 A one-dimensional example

Assume three voters with single-peaked preferences defined directly on alternative total budget sizes (i.e., total spending figures). Figure 8.1 illustrates our example, with ideal points labeled x_1, x_2, and x_3 and symmetric preference curves. If all voters are given the opportunity to propose alternative budget sizes, voter 2 can propose x_2, which a majority prefers to all other proposals. Thus, x_2 is the expected budget size under an unrestricted or completely competitive voting process.

However, suppose that one of the three voters other than voter 2 is given monopoly control over budget proposals. If B^0 is the status quo budget, which is paired against any alternative proposal, a majority prefers either x_1 or x_3 to B^0, because both are closer to x_2. Thus, either x_1 or x_3 may be approved, depending on which voter is given monopoly control over budget proposals.

Alternatively, suppose that a school board proposes a budget to these three voters that must secure majority approval to replace B^0. If the school board wishes to maximize the size of the school budget, it should propose a budget just short of B^*. Because $|B^0 - x_2| = |B^* - x_2|$, voter 2 will prefer any budget in the open interval (B^0, B^*) to B^0, as will voter 3. Thus, if the school board can force this three-person electorate to accept their budget or be left with the status quo budget B^0, they can win majority approval for any budget larger than B^0, up to B^*.

A *reversion budget* is the budget that is enacted if the budget proposed by the school board fails to win majority approval. The reversion budget may not be the status quo budget. If rejection of the school board's proposal places the school district on an austerity budget, the reversion budget will probably be less than the status quo budget.

If B^0 is a reversion budget that the school board also controls, another result is clear. The lower B^0 is set, the larger the budget will be that a majority will prefer to B^0. Because voter 3 will prefer any budget to B^0 also preferred by voter 2 (for $B^0 < x_2$), voter 2's preference curve defines the relationship between B^0 and the maximum budget a majority will prefer to B^0. Thus, as B^0 decreases, voter 2 (and voter 3) will vote for larger and larger budgets against B^0. Thus, the school board should attempt to set B^0 as low as possible if they wish to maximize the school budget and the reversion budget is under their control.

8.4 A two-issue example with competitive voting

In this and the following section we shall extend the previous analysis to the case of two issues, or budgetary activities. We shall assume that the funding for each activity is voted on separately, and in the following section we shall assume that the school board controls the choice to be offered the voters on both issues. The question then arises: If the school board wishes to maximize the amount of funding for each activity, what choice should they offer the voters on each issue?

We shall construct an example to show how this question can be answered. Assume that the school district consists of three voters: A, B, and C. The school board is seeking approval to fund two programs: The first is the athletic program, and the second is a program for gifted children. Each voter has preferences defined over alternative spending packages for these two programs and bases his preferences on weighted Euclidean distance.

Voter A is a big supporter of the program for gifted children (because his child is in the program). Athletics, on the other hand, are of little interest to him. Accordingly, his ideal point (in thousands of dollars) is $\mathbf{x}_a = (35, 115)'$. Voter B is a moderate supporter of both programs and has $\mathbf{x}_b = (65, 40)'$ as his ideal point. Lastly, voter C is a big football fan and has a stupid child, so his ideal point is $\mathbf{x}_c = (160, 25)'$.

If the two issues are voted on one at a time, if any voter can make funding proposals, and if all voters have separable preferences, it is reasonable to expect that $\mathbf{x}_{\text{med}} = \mathbf{x}_b = (65, 40)'$ will be the outcome on the two issues. However, if voter preferences are not separable, then, as we showed in Section 3.3, the problem of predicting vote outcomes is more difficult. Suppose that $a_{a11} = a_{b11} = a_{c11} = a_{a22} = a_{b22} = a_{c22} = 1$, but that $a_{a12} = a_{b12} = c_{c12} = .9$. Thus, preferences are not separable by issue. For each voter, the higher the funding is set on one program, the lower he wishes to see the funding set on the other.

As shown in Section 3.2, each voter has a conditional ideal point on each issue, dependent on each value the other issue may take. Specifically, for voter A, $x_{a1}(x_2)$ and $x_{a2}(x_1)$ are these two conditional ideal points for issues 1 and 2, respectively, where

$$
\begin{aligned}
x_{a1}(x_2) &= x_{a1} - \frac{a_{a12}}{a_{a11}}(x_2 - x_{a2}) \\
x_{a2}(x_1) &= x_{a2} - \frac{a_{a12}}{a_{a22}}(x_1 - x_{a1})
\end{aligned}
\qquad (8.1)
$$

This is the result we proved in Section 3.2.

The two equations (8.1) describe a linear relationship between $x_{a1}(x_2)$ and x_2 as well as between $x_{a2}(x_1)$ and x_1. In Figure 8.2 these two lines are plotted for each voter - A, B, and C. Because each voter has the same salience weights, $x_{a1}(x_2)$, $x_{b1}(x_2)$, and $x_{c1}(x_2)$ are all parallel. The same is true for $x_{a2}(x_1)$, $x_{b2}(x_1)$, and $x_{c2}(x_1)$.

Returning to our school board, suppose they try to estimate the outcome of a completely competitive voting process. Instead of giving the voters a take-it-or-leave-it choice, suppose they allow the voters to make their own proposals, each of which can be voted up or down. Each issue is considered separately, but voting continues until no proposal can be found that a majority prefers to the last accepted proposal. At this point, the second issue is considered, and the same process takes place. When voting stops on the second issue, the first issue is taken up again, and the process is repeated until no change on either issue taken separately can win majority approval. This is a highly idealized voting process, and it should be viewed as a device for revealing the pattern of vote outcomes over time. By inspecting this pattern the school board can see where a series of votes may ultimately lead.

As explained in section 3.2, the problem each voter with nonseparable preferences faces is that he needs to know how the second issue will be decided to know what he most prefers on the first issue. This is the problem of *expectations*, about which we shall have more to say later in this chapter.

For now, let us assume that the spending levels in the last fiscal year

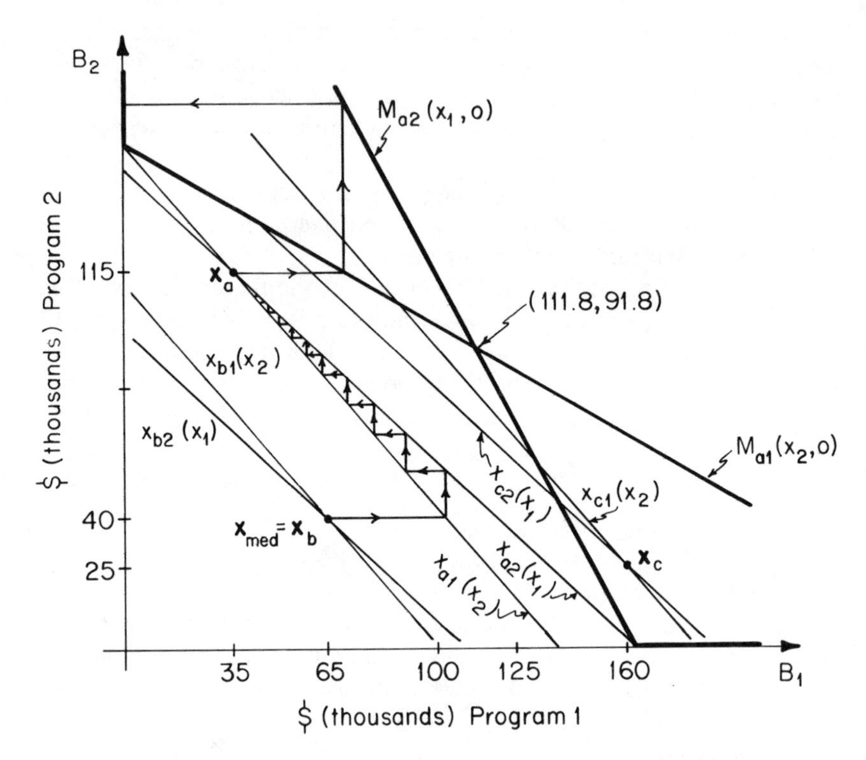

Figure 8.2. Competitive voting and agenda control over B_1 and B_2.

are used as the initially accepted proposals for both issues. Let $\mathbf{x}_b = (65, 40)'$ be this status quo point. Further, we shall assume for now that when an issue is voted on, each voter acts as if he expects the spending figure last accepted on the other issue to remain unchanged. This assumption really makes no difference at this point in the analysis.

Beginning with issue 1, if preferences are induced for each voter on issue 1, given that $x_2 = 40$, each voter has symmetric, single-peaked preferences around his conditional ideal point. To see this, for voter A, we shall show that he is indifferent between two points equidistant from $x_{a1}(40)$ on the line $x_2 = 40$. Thus, for $y_1 > 0$, we need to show that

$$\|\{x_{a1} - [x_{a1}(40) - y_1]\},\ (x_{a2} - 40)\|_{A_a}^2$$
$$= \|\{x_{a1} - [x_{a1}(40) + y_1]\},\ (x_{a2} - 40)\|_{A_a}^2 \tag{8.2}$$

Expanding (8.2) yields

$$.81(5{,}625) - 1.8y_1(75) + y_1^2 - 1.8[.9(5{,}625) - y_1(75)] + 5{,}625$$
$$= .81(5{,}625) + 1.8y_1(75) + y_1^2 - 1.8[.9(5{,}625) + y_1(75)] + 5{,}625$$

The term linear in y_1 drops out of both sides, so (8.2) is an identity. It was shown in Section 3.2 that the equivalent of (8.2) holds for the general case when preferences are induced on issue 2.

It then follows that each voter has symmetric, single-peaked preferences around his conditional ideal point. We assume that each voter votes on alternative proposals on issue 1 with the expectation that the last accepted figure on issue 2 will remain unchanged. This leads to the conclusion, based on the median voter result, that the median of the set $\{x_{a1}(40), x_{b1}(40), x_{c1}(40)\}$ will be the final decision on issue 1. Using (8.1) to solve for these conditional ideal points reveals that $x_{a1}(40) = 102.5$ is this median point.

Given $x_{a1}(40)$ as the decision on issue 1, issue 2 is then voted on. Again, the expectation is that changes on the issue under consideration will leave the last accepted spending level on the other issue unchanged. Thus, each voter compares alternative proposals on issue 2 with the expectation that spending on issue 1 will be $x_{a1}(40) = 102.5$. Because each voter's preferences for a fixed value on issue 1 are symmetric and single-peaked around his conditional ideal point on issue 2, the median of the set $\{x_{a2}(102.5), x_{b2}(102.5), x_{c2}(102.5)\}$ will be the final decision on issue 2. The second equation of (8.1) reveals that $x_{a2}(102.5) = 54.25$ is this median point.

If issue 1 is then voted on again, then issue 2, and so on, it is clear from Figure 8.2 that the voting will ultimately lead to $\mathbf{x}_a = (35, 115)'$. Further, once $\mathbf{x}_a$ is reached, further voting will not lead to any changes in either of these two figures. $\mathbf{x}_a$ is a *stable equilibrium*, because no matter which point is used as the status quo, the voting process we have described will always lead to $\mathbf{x}_a$.

8.5 A two-issue example with agenda control over budget proposals

Thus, the school board may reason that $\mathbf{x}_a = (35, 115)'$ will be the outcome of a completely competitive voting process. It then remains for them to estimate the advantages of controlling the agenda by offering the voters a take-it-or-leave-it choice. This requires a decision on the board's part as to what they should offer the voters, a decision that is based in part on how much will be spent on each program if the voters reject the board's offer. This latter set of figures is the *reversion level* for the two programs.

Suppose the reversion level for both programs is zero. If the voters turn down the figures proposed by the board, the two programs will be shut down. If the school board knows the voters' preferences, how can they take advantage of this situation?

Consider voter A. Suppose A expects 115 to be the final spending figure on issue 2; $x_{a1}(115)=35$ is the spending figure he most prefers on issue 1. However, if voter A is given a choice between some figure M on issue 1 and zero, the reversion level, how large can M be before A is indifferent between M and the reversion level? This is easy to determine. Because A's preferences are symmetric around $x_{a1}(115)=35$, he will vote for any proposal on issue 1 up to 70. Thus, if voter A must choose between any figure M on issue 1 up to 70 and the reversion level zero, he will vote for M.

For each expectation level on issue 2, it is possible to determine how large a figure each voter will vote for on issue 1, given his conditional preferences and the reversion level for issue 1. For voter A, if r_1 is the reversion level on issue 1 and x_2 is his expectation of how much will be spent on issue 2, then $M_{a1}(x_2, r_1)$ is the figure on issue 1 that leaves him indifferent between accepting or rejecting the school board's offer. Because preferences are symmetric around $x_{a1}(x_2)$,

$$M_{a1}(x_2, r_1) - x_{a1}(x_2) = x_{a1}(x_2) - r_1$$

and so

$$M_{a1}(x_2, r_1) - 2x_{a1}(x_2) - r_1 \tag{8.3}$$

Observe that for $x_{a1}(x_2) \leqslant r_1$, no proposal larger than r_1 will win A's approval. Thus, in Figure 8.2, where $r_1=0$, it is clear that if $x_{a1}(x_2) \leqslant 0$, A will vote for no figure on issue 1 larger than zero. Thus,

$$M_{a1}(x_2, r_1) = 2x_{a1}(x_2) - r_1 \quad \text{if } x_{a1}(x_2) > r_1$$

$$M_{a1}(x_2, r_1) = r_1 \quad \text{if } x_{a1}(x_2) \leqslant r_1 \tag{8.4}$$

$M_{a1}(x_2, 0)$ is plotted in Figure 8.2. $M_{a2}(x_1, r_2)$ is defined analogously as the figure on issue 2 that leaves A indifferent between accepting the school board's offer or being left with the reversion level r_2, assuming x_1 as his expectation level on issue 1. By the same reasoning,

$$M_{a2}(x_1, r_2) = 2x_{a2}(x_1) - r_2 \quad \text{if } x_{a2}(x_1) > r_2$$

$$M_{a2}(x_1, r_2) = r_2 \quad \text{if } x_{a2}(x_1) \leqslant r_2 \tag{8.5}$$

$M_{a2}(x_1, 0)$ is also plotted in Figure 8.2.

Suppose that all voters expect that 115 will be the spending level on issue 2. Then $M_{a1}(115, 0)=70$, $M_{b1}(115, 0)=0$, and $M_{c1}(115, 0)=158$. Thus, voters A and C will vote for any figure on issue 1 up to 70. On the other hand, suppose that all voters expect that 35 will be the spending level on issue 1. Then $M_{a2}(35, 0)=230$, $M_{b2}(35, 0)=134$, and $M_{c2}(35, 0)=275$, and so any figure on issue 2 up to 230 will win majority approval. It is clear that $M_{a1}(x_2, 0)$ and $M_{a2}(x_1, 0)$ describe the maximum limits to what the school board can wring out of the voters, *if all voters share the same expectations.* However, if voters have differing expectations, this may not be true. For example, if voters A and B expect 35 to be the spending level on issue 1, but voter C's expectation is 160, then $M_{c2}(160, 0) = 50$, and so 134 will be maximum limit on issue 2.

This last example raises an important issue that will be pursued at greater length in Section 8.7. Voter expectations affect the power of agenda control. Because these expectations cannot be controlled in the same way as budget proposals, there exists a "wild card" in the agenda setter's deck that may greatly complicate his task.

It should also be noted that the maximum limit on each issue is stable only in a restricted sense. The maximum limit is the most the voters will approve on a single issue, and so it is the best offer for a budget-maximizing school board to make. The voters clearly prefer to spend less. The type of stability we are discussing, therefore, is stability from the agenda setter's point of view.

In order to get a sense of how vote outcomes are affected over time by offering the voters take-it-or-leave-it choices, let us make three additional assumptions. First, let us assume common expectations. Thus, $M_{a1}(x_2, 0)$ and $M_{a2}(x_1, 0)$ describe the maximum spending limits on each issue that a majority of the voters will approve. Second, let issue 1 be voted on, then issue 2, then issue 1 again, and so on until further voting leaves spending figures unchanged. This is the same procedure we analyzed under conditions of competitive voting. Finally, let the last accepted figure on each issue be the expectation on that issue when the other issue is voted on. This is the assumption we made under competitive voting. Thus, we can make a controlled comparison between the final spending figures under this form of agenda control and the final figures under competitive voting.

Suppose the spending figures that will ultimately be reached under competitive voting are the last accepted figures on issues 1 and 2. As identified in Section 8.4, $\mathbf{x}_a = (35, 115)'$ is this set of figures. Under competitive voting, we know that $\mathbf{x}_a$ is stable, meaning that a majority will not approve a change in either figure if it is voted on separately. The question, then, is how control over budget proposals affects this result. Suppose that issue 1 is voted on with $x_2 = 115$, the common expectation on issue 2. As shown before, 70 will be the maximum amount (actually $69,999.99) the voters will approve on issue 1. Given 70 as the expectation on issue 1, $M_{a2}(70, 0) = 167$ is the most the voters will approve on issue 2. But, given 167 on issue 2, $M_{a1}(167, 0) = 0$ is the most the voters will approve on issue 1. Thus, continued voting wipes out program 1 (the athletic program). But this is not where the voting ends. $M_{a2}(0, 0) = 293$

is the amount subsequently approved on issue 2, and only now is the voting over. The point $(0, 293)$ is where the two lines $M_{a1}(x_2, 0)$ and $M_{a2}(x_1, 0)$ would cross (if they were extended) in the upper left-hand corner of Figure 8.2. Thus, we see that $(0, 293)$, not $\mathbf{x}_a = (35, 115)'$, is the final set of spending figures under this form of agenda control.

However, there is another important difference between these two types of voting. Under competitive voting, the spending figures that set initial expectation levels at the start of voting are irrelevant to the final outcome. Any point in Figure 8.2 can be used as a status quo point, and competitive voting will still converge on $\mathbf{x}_a$. The same is not true for voting under agenda control. Instead of 115, suppose that 40 is the initial expectation on issue 2. Then $M_{a1}(40, 0) = 205$ will be the amount initially approved on issue 1. $M_{a2}(205, 0) = 0$ will be the amount then adopted on issue 2, and $M_{a1}(0, 0) = 277$ will be the final amount adopted on issue 1. Thus, $(277, 0)$ will be the final set of spending figures on programs 1 and 2, and the program for gifted children will be eliminated.

In contrast to the outcome under competitive voting, the voting process under agenda control leads to a very lopsided outcome. Thus, board members may wish to think twice before attempting to manipulate the election outcome. Further, even under our highly restrictive assumptions about voter expectations, the board members are still faced with a fundamental uncertainty. The intersection of $M_{a1}(x_2, 0)$ and $M_{a2}(x_1, 0)$, shown in Figure 8.2, is at the point $(111.8, 91.8)$. These two spending figures are crucial to the ultimate outcome of the voting. If issue 1 is voted on first and the initial common expectation on issue 2 exceeds 91.8, repeated voting will ultimately destroy program 1. If the initial common expectation on issue 2 is less than 91.8, repeated voting ultimately destroys program 2. Only if the initial common expectation on issue 2 is 91.8 will the final set of spending figures remain unchanged at $(111.8, 91.8)$. The same point applies if issue 2 is voted on first. Thus, even in the very simple world we have described, board members must worry about initial voter expectations and may find them incompatible with the goal of the board members.

This assumes, of course, that the board members do have a common goal. Suppose some members wish to eliminate program 1, whereas others wish to eliminate program 2. Then an irreconcilable conflict exists between the two goals of the members. This conflict may be manifested in several ways. If, for instance, $\mathbf{x}_{\text{med}} = (65, 40)'$ is the status quo point at the start of the voting, board members will disagree about whether issue 1 or 2 should be voted on first. If issue 1 is considered first, repeated voting will result in the elimination of program 2, whereas if issue 2 is considered first, repeated voting will result in the elimination of program

1. On the other hand, if $\mathbf{x}_a = (35, 115)'$ is the initial status quo point, repeated voting will wipe out program 1 no matter which issue is voted on first. In this case, those members who oppose elimination of program 1 can be expected to oppose agenda control and fight for the use of competitive voting.

Thus, we find that agenda control is not an unmitigated blessing for the agenda setter. Voter expectations may pose serious difficulties for school board members seeking to achieve various spending goals. Even if they are fully known to the school board, these expectations may still prevent the attainment of certain outcomes.

8.6 Competitive voting over budget size and budgetary formula

In the next section we shall analyze a different type of agenda control available to our school board. We shall continue the example of the previous section, changing the preferences of the voters in one respect. The ideal points of the voters will remain the same, but we shall assume that all voters have circular indifference contours. Thus, all preferences are separable across issues, and the conditional ideal-point lines are either vertical or horizontal for each voter.

If each issue is voted on separately and the voting process is completely competitive, $\mathbf{x}_{\text{med}} = (65, 40)'$ will be the unique outcome for both issues. However, suppose that voting is not over individual spending figures. Suppose, instead, that voters vote separately on total budget size and on the formula by which the total budget figure is divided up between the two programs. In terms of Chapter 6 notation, if B_1 is the spending level on program 1, B_2 the spending level on program 2, and $B_1 + B_2 = B$ the total budget size, then

$$B_1 = Bv_1 \quad \text{and} \quad B_2 = Bv_2$$

where v_1 and v_2 are the respective fractions of B allocated to the two programs. The ratio $v_2/v_1 = B_2/B_1 = k$ is then the budgetary formula (or mix) that the voters must approve. Notice that $B_2 = B - B_1$, and so the budget line B is a line with -1 slope that crosses the B_1 and B_2 axes at B. Notice also that v_1 and v_2 are not subscripted by voter, because these fractions are commonly perceived.

Thus, voters are serially choosing B and k. To know what budget size and mix the voters will select, we must define two concepts for each voter: the most preferred budget conditional on a given mix k and the most preferred mix conditional on a given budget B. For voter B, let $B_b(k)$ and $k_b(B)$ represent, respectively, these two concepts.

To solve for $B_b(k)$, examine Figure 8.3. Given the mix k, voter B's

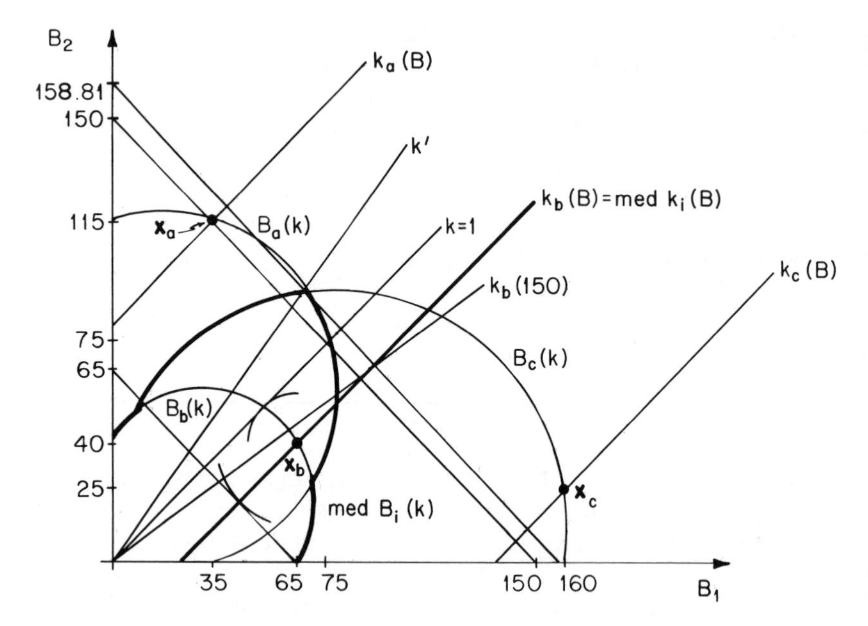

Figure 8.3. Most preferred B given k and most preferred k given B with competitive voting over B and k.

most preferred budget is the one described by the line intersecting k at the point closest to $\mathbf{x}_b$. Let us solve for this B. From the definition of k,

$$B_2 = kB_1 \tag{8.6}$$

In addition, because the point on k closest to $\mathbf{x}_b$ is found by dropping a line perpendicular to k from $\mathbf{x}_b$,

$$B_2 = -\frac{1}{k}B_1 + \left(x_{b2} + \frac{1}{k}x_{b1}\right) \tag{8.7}$$

where the two terms within parentheses on the right-hand side of (8.7) constitute the intercept term solved for by plugging $\mathbf{x}_b$ into the equation for this line.

Thus, from (8.6) and (8.7),

$$B_1 = \frac{kx_{b2} + x_{b1}}{k^2 + 1}$$

and so

$$B_b(k) = B_1 + B_2 = \frac{kx_{b2} + x_{b1} + k(kx_{b2} + x_{b1})}{k^2 + 1} = \frac{(k+1)(kx_{b2} + x_{b1})}{k^2 + 1} \tag{8.8}$$

Substituting B_2/B_1 for k yields

$$B_1^2+B_2^2=B_2x_{b2}+B_1x_{b1}$$

Completing the square yields

$$\left(B_1-\frac{x_{b1}}{2}\right)^2+\left(B_2-\frac{x_{b2}}{2}\right)^2=\left(\frac{x_{b1}}{2}\right)^2+\left(\frac{x_{b2}}{2}\right)^2 \tag{8.9}$$

which is the equation for a circle with center $(x_{b1}/2, x_{b2}/2)$ and radius $[(x_{b1}/2)^2+(x_{b2}/2)^2]^{1/2}$.

Thus, $B_b(k)$ is a circle that passes through the origin, centered halfway between the origin and the voter's ideal point. These circles are drawn for voters A, B, and C in Figure 8.3.

As for $k_b(B)$, it is easy to show that it is the equation of a line passing through $\mathbf{x}_b$ with slope 1; $k_a(B)$, $k_b(B)$, and $k_c(B)$ are also drawn in Figure 8.3. Because $k_i(B)$ is identified by the point on the budget line $B=(B_1, B_2)$ closest to $\mathbf{x}_i$, B_1 must minimize the squared distance

$$\|\mathbf{x}_i-(B_1, B-B_1)\|^2=(x_{i1}-B_1)^2+[x_{i2}-(B-B_1)]^2 \tag{8.10}$$

Minimizing (8.10) with respect to B_1 yields the result that

$$B_1=\frac{x_{i1}-x_{i2}+B}{2}$$

and so

$$k_i(B)=\frac{B_2}{B_1}=\frac{B-B_1}{B_1}=\frac{B-x_{i1}+x_{i2}}{B+x_{i1}-x_{i2}} \tag{8.11}$$

The question then is, What B and k will be selected by the voters under a completely competitive voting process? Let B be voted on and then k. As we allowed in the previous section, B and k will be voted on serially until no further changes in either B or k meet with majority approval.

As in the case of serial voting on separate budget figures, expectations are important. First, however, observe that voter preferences are single-peaked around $B(k)$ and $k(B)$. Figure 8.4 shows why this is so. Because fixing B and varying k will describe different points on the line B, whereas fixing k and varying B will describe different points on the line k, single-peaked preferences are induced in both cases. Thus, in Figure 8.4, $B=B_i(k)$ and other budgets such as B' are less preferred (holding k constant) the more they differ from B. Conversely, $k'=k_i(B)$ and other mixes such as k are less preferred (holding B constant) the more they differ from k'.

Assume that B is voted on with the common expectation that $k=1$ will be the mix. Inspecting Figure 8.3, voter A is the median voter in terms of most preferred budgets, given that $k=1$. From the equation for A corresponding to (8.8), it is simple to calculate that $B_a(1)=150$. Thus, under competitive voting, $B_a(1)=150$ is the median most preferred budget and

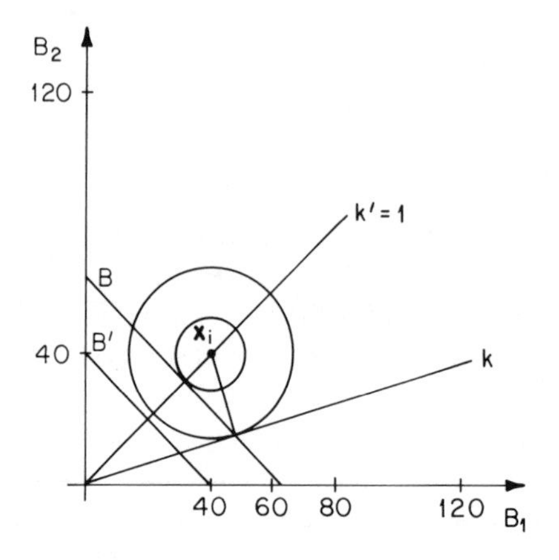

Figure 8.4. Single-peaked preferences defined by $B_i(k)$ and $k_i(B)$.

will be the equilibrium budget given that $k=1$. For any given B, voter B's most preferred mix is the median most preferred mix. Thus, $k_b(150)=.71$ is the median most preferred mix. $(B,k)=(150,.71)$ will therefore be the budget and mix selected in the first round of competitive voting.

If a second round of voting takes place, we might assume that $k=.71$ is the expected mix when the budget is voted on again. If this is so, we can see from the equation for A corresponding to (8.8) that $B_a(.71)=132.7$ is the median most preferred budget. If $B=132.7$ is the expected budget when the mix is again voted on, equation (8.11) shows that $k_b(132.7)=.683$ is the median most preferred mix. If revoting continues in this fashion and expectations continue to be the last B or k accepted in the voting, competitive voting ultimately converges to the point where median $B_i(k)$, which is shaped like a bishop's miter in Figure 8.3, intersects with median $k_i(B)$, which is $k_b(B)$ in Figure 8.3. The budget and mix corresponding to this point of intersection are $B=129.8$, $k=B_2/B_1=52.4/77.4=.677$. Thus, the school board might anticipate $(B,k)=(129.8,.677)$ as the budget and mix that the electorate will approve if the voting process is completely competitive.

Remember that the budget and mix would be $x_{med1}+x_{med2}=105$ and $40/65=.615$, respectively, if competitive voting were held over individual spending figures. Thus, a budget-maximizing school board would prefer serial voting over B and k to serial voting over B_1 and B_2, because in the first case both B_1 and B_2 would be larger. However, this result depends on voter expectations. Suppose, for instance, that B is voted on with differing expectations about k. If voters B and C expect k to be .677 but A expects k to be .25, the median most preferred budget is 105.9, not 129.8, as is the case when all voters expect k to be .677. Voter expectations are obviously important, which is why we shall defer a full discussion of the topic until Section 8.8.

8.7 Agenda control over budget size and budgetary formula

Suppose, now, that the school board exerts control over the agenda, when voting takes place over B and k. As a first case for examination, assume that the school board sets the mix and then allows competitive voting over the size of the budget. If the school board wishes to set k so as to maximize B, examination of Figure 8.3 reveals that k', which intersects median $B_i(k)$ at its largest value, is the optimal mix. Solving for this value by using (8.9), $k'=B_2/B_1=1.39$. From (8.8), defined for voter A, the maximum budget the voters will approve is $B=B_1+B_2=66.48+92.33=158.81$, which is larger than the budget of 129.8 that competitive voting will yield. Notice, however, that the budget for program 1 will decline from 77.4 to 66.48. If this concerns the school board, they can set $k=.741$. Then competitive voting will yield $B=135.1=B_1+B_2=77.6+57.5$. The largest B_1 the voters will approve is 77.6, because the center of $B_a(k)$ is $(17.5, 57.5)$, and so the median $B_i(k)$ is maximized over B_1 for $B_2=57.5$.

Let us now look at a more powerful form of agenda control. Suppose that a reversion budget B_R exists. Suppose also that the school board can set both the budget B and the mix k that the voters can either take or leave. The question then is, What k and B should the school board offer the voters if the board seeks approval of the largest possible budget?

Figure 8.5 is a continuation of the example depicted in Figure 8.3, with an extra curve drawn for each voter. This curve represents the upper bound for the maximum budget the voter will prefer to $B_R=65$ for alternative k. For example, suppose k' is the mix. For $B_R=65$, the point **a** in Figure 8.5 is the allocation of B_R between programs 1 and 2 given the mix k'. Consider voter B. Holding k' constant, voter B will prefer all budgets larger than B_R up to point **a**′, which is the same distance from $\mathbf{x}_b$ as **a** is. Thus, the budget line passing through **a**′ represents the largest budget, given k', that voter B will not reject in favor of B_R. However, for a mix such as k'', voter B will prefer no budget larger than B_R to B_R.

We can solve for this maximum B, given k, for each voter. Take voter B, for example. Let $B_b^*(B_R, k)=[B_{1b}^*(B_R, k), B_{2b}^*(B_R, k)]$ be the maximum budget that voter B will not reject, given $B_R=(B_{1R}, B_{2R})$ and k. Then,

$$B_{1R}+B_{2R}=B_R \quad \text{and} \quad k=\frac{B_{2R}}{B_{1R}}$$

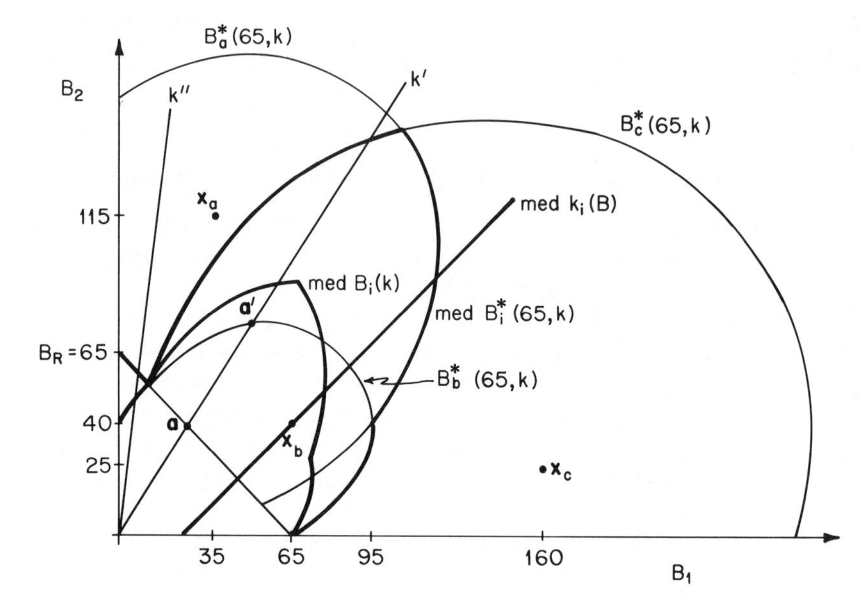

Figure 8.5. Agenda control over B and k with a reversion budget B_R.

and so

$$B_{1R}=\frac{B_R}{1+k},\quad B_{2R}=\frac{B_R k}{1+k}$$

Because voter B has circular indifference contours,

$$\left(x_{1b}-\frac{B_R}{1+k}\right)^2+\left(x_{2b}-\frac{B_R k}{1+k}\right)^2$$
$$=[x_{1b}-B_{1b}^*(B_R,k)]^2+[x_{2b}-kB_{1b}^*(B_R,k)]^2$$

Setting $B_R=65$ and $\mathbf{x}_b=(65,40)'$, we can solve for B_{1b}^*, yielding

$$B_{1b}^*(65,k)=\frac{15k^2+210k+65}{(1+k^2)(1+k)} \tag{8.12}$$

Thus,

$$B_b^*(65,k)=\frac{15k^2+210k+65}{1+k^2} \tag{8.13}$$

For example, $B_b^*(65,1)=145$, which means that if $k=1$, then B will vote for any budget larger than 65 up to 145. However, suppose that $k=12$. Then $B_b(65,12)=32.72$, which means that B will prefer only budgets less than 65. Thus, $B_b^*(65,k)$ is described by (8.13) so long as $B_b^*(65,k)>65$.

Otherwise, $B_b^*(65,k)=65$, and the school board should not offer B anything but the reversion budget. For $k \geqslant 4.2$, this will be the case for voter B.

Solving for $B_a^*(65,k)$, we find that

$$B_a^*(65,k)=\frac{165k^2+300k+5}{1+k^2} \tag{8.14}$$

if $k>.19$, and $B_a^*(65,k)=65$ otherwise. Finally,

$$B_c^*(65,k)=\frac{-15k^2+370k+255}{1+k^2} \tag{8.15}$$

if $k<5.09$, and $B_c^*(65,k)=65$ otherwise. These curves are all represented in Figure 8.5.

Returning to our earlier question, we now have the tools that will enable us to determine what B and k will lead voters to select the maximum budget. Given a choice between $(B_R=65,k)$ and (B,k), the larger miter-shaped curve in Figure 8.5, med $B_i^*(65,k)=B^*(65,k)$ describes the maximum bound for those budgets that a majority will prefer to $B_R=65$ under alternative k. Clearly, the point on this curve where $B_a^*(65,k)$ intersects $B_c^*(65,k)$ is the maximum we seek. Setting (8.14) equal to (8.15) and solving for k yields $k=1.39$ and $B^*(65,1.39)=252.63$. Thus, a majority (namely, A and C) will be indifferent between $(B,k)=(252.63,1.39)$ and $(65,1.39)$, and so any budget just short of 252.63 will win majority support, given that $k=1.39$. Completing the result, $B_1^*(65,1.39)=105.75$ and $B_2^*(65,1.39)=146.88$. This is certainly much more spending on both programs than would be approved under any type of voting we have discussed so far.

Consider, finally, one other type of agenda control. Allow the reversion mix to differ from the mix proposed by the school board. Then the board wishes to set (B,k) so as to maximize B, given the reversion budget and mix (B_R,k_R). Suppose that $B_R=65$ and $k_R=1$. In Figure 8.6, all indifference contours through $(32.5,32.5)=(B_{1R},B_{2R})$ are drawn, and it is clear that the intersection of these two contours for voters A and C defines the upper bound for the maximum budget the voters will approve. Solving for $B^*(B_R,k_R)=B^*(65,1)$ and $k^*(B_R,k_R)=k^*(65,1)$ yields 256.06 and $143.58/112.48=1.28$, respectively. Not surprisingly, giving the school board the leeway to offer a budget and a mix different from the reversion budget and reversion mix increases their ability to get larger budgets approved. If $k_R=1$ is fixed, (8.13), (8.14), and (8.15) show that the voters will approve no budget larger than $B_a^*(65,1)=235$. Thus, this last type of agenda control is the most powerful one we have described.

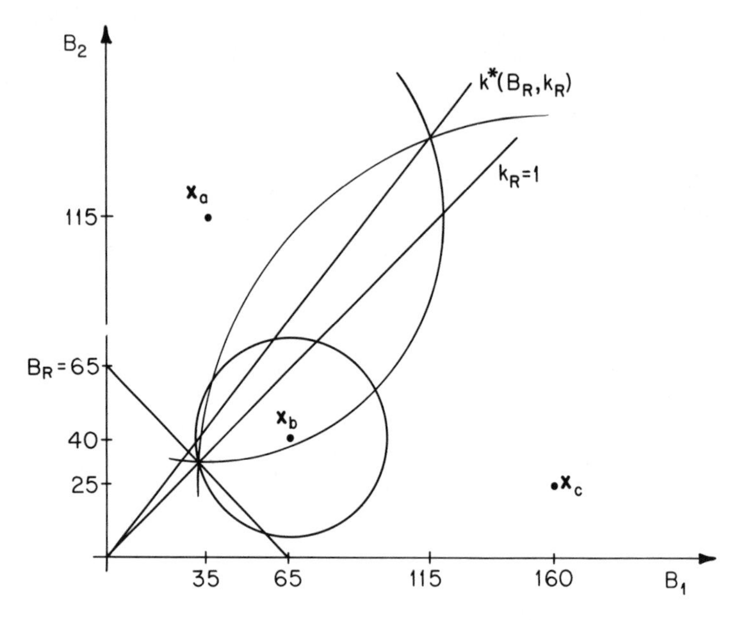

Figure 8.6. Agenda control over B and k with a reversion budget B_R and a reversion mix k_R.

8.8 Expectations

It is now time to address a question that we have heretofore skirted. As we have repeatedly pointed out, when voters have nonseparable preferences and issues are voted on one at a time, what the voter most prefers on each issue depends on what he expects will be the outcome of voting on other issues. In fact, when there is separate voting over total budget size and budgetary mix, Section 8.6 demonstrates that expectations matter even if all voters have separable preferences across issues. We have sidestepped this question of expectations up to now by assuming that the last accepted spending figure or mix is the expected value of that variable when a different variable is being voted on.

This assumption is clearly implausible, and so we shall now replace it with an alternative set of assumptions. First, however, it must be pointed out that the problem of expectations is not simply a problem of imperfect information about other voters' preferences. In fact, we shall demonstrate the surprising result that perfect information about voter preferences may *increase* the difficulty of the expectations problem.

To see this, refer to Figure 8.7, where three voters (A, B, and C) are represented. A's indifference contours are circular, with $\mathbf{x}_a$ his ideal

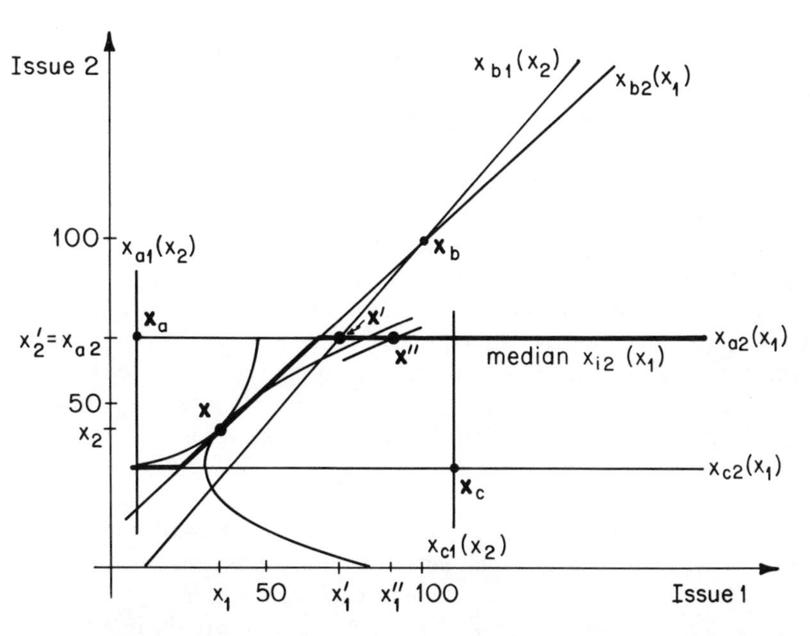

Figure 8.7. A case in which voter forecasts complicate voting one issue at a time.

point. B has nonseparable preferences, with salience weights $a_{b11} = a_{b22} = 1$, $a_{b12} = -.9$ and $\mathbf{x}_b$ his ideal point. Lastly, C has separable preferences but noncircular indifference contours, with $\mathbf{x}_c$ his ideal point.

Suppose that all preferences are known by each voter. This information provides knowledge of the median $x_{i2}(x_1)$ curve, which is marked in Figure 8.7. Voting on issue 1 is now complicated in the following way. For each value that issue 1 may take, there is an associated point on the median $x_{i2}(x_1)$ curve representing the final decision on issue 2 that will follow. Thus, as Figure 8.7 indicates, if x_1 is the decision reached on issue 1, x_2 will be the decision reached on issue 2. Suppose, now, that voting on issue 1 commences with x_1 paired against x_1' in a vote. Because x_1 will lead to a decision of x_2 on issue 2, and x_1' will lead to $x_2' = x_{a2}$, voter preferences with respect to x_1 and x_1' are determined by preferences with respect to $\mathbf{x} = (x_1, x_2)'$ and $\mathbf{x}' = (x_1', x_2')'$. Thus, because voters A and C prefer $\mathbf{x}$ to $\mathbf{x}'$, they prefer x_1 to x_1'. Accordingly, x_1 beats x_1' in a majority vote.

Suppose that x_1 is then paired against x_1''. Voters B and C prefer $\mathbf{x}''$ to $\mathbf{x}$, and so x_1'' beats x_1 in a majority contest. Thus, x_1'' appears triumphant with respect to this set of three alternatives. However, if x_1'' is paired against x_1', voters A and B prefer $\mathbf{x}'$ to $\mathbf{x}''$, and so x_1'' will lose to x_1'. In short, the majority cycle $x_1 > x_1' > x_1'' > x_1$ exists over these three alternatives. Thus, if voting takes place over these alternatives and continues until an alternative is reached that will not lose to any of the other alternatives in the set, the voting will continue indefinitely, precluding any consideration of issue 2. Thus, we are left with the surprising result that perfect information about voter preferences may not enable voters to forecast the outcome that will be reached on later issues.

In fact, imperfect information may ease the problem shown to arise in Figure 8.7. If voters have little or no information about others' preferences, it is not unreasonable for their forecasts on issue 2 to be independent of the decision reached on issue 1. If this is true, we know that preferences are single-peaked with respect to the line of conditional ideal points. Thus, preferences for A are single-peaked on issue 1 around $x_{a1}(x_2)$, and so, no matter what x_2 voter A forecasts, his preferences over the alternatives in the set $\{x_1, x_1', x_1''\}$ will be (from first to last) x_1, x_1', x_1''. In similar fashion, C's preferences will be x_1'', x_1', x_1. Inspection of these two preference orders reveals that regardless of how B ranks these three alternatives, a majority cycle will not exist. Thus, forecasting on issue 2 is easier with imperfect information about voter preferences.

We shall now proceed to develop a general approach to the question of forecasting.

8.9 A theory of expectations

Let us again take up the question of voting one issue at a time. As in Chapters 5 and 7, assume that voter *i* has the following risk-averse utility for an outcome $\mathbf{y} = (y_1, y_2)'$:

$$u_i(\mathbf{y}) = c_i - \|\mathbf{y} - \mathbf{x}_i\|_{A_i}^2 \tag{8.16}$$

The expectations problem can be framed as follows. Suppose that *i* must make a choice of voting for θ_1 or ψ_1 on issue 1 without knowing how issue 2 will be decided. Given the forecasting difficulties described earlier, let $\tilde{\theta}_2$ be a random variable representing the range of final decisions on issue 2 that *i* believes possible, as well as the probability density associated with each. $\tilde{\theta}_2$ may not be independent of θ_1, or ψ_1, but this dependence is unknown to voter *i*. Thus, we shall make the minimal assumption that the mean of $\tilde{\theta}_2, \mu_2$, and the variance of $\tilde{\theta}_2, \sigma_2^2$, are independent of θ_1 and ψ_1.

Suppose, now, that *i* is an expected utility maximizer. Then, from (8.16), he will vote for θ_1 over ψ_1 if and only if

$$E[u_i(\hat{\theta})] > E[u_i(\hat{\psi})] \tag{8.17}$$

where $\hat{\theta}=(\theta_1,\tilde{\theta}_2)$ and $\hat{\psi}=(\psi_1,\tilde{\theta}_2)$. From (8.16) we can expand both sides of (8.17) and gather terms, leaving us with

$$\theta_1\left[a_{i11}\left(\frac{\theta_1}{2}-x_{i1}\right)+a_{i12}(\mu_2-x_{i2})\right]$$
$$<\psi_1\left[a_{i11}\left(\frac{\psi_1}{2}-x_{i1}\right)+a_{i12}(\mu_2-x_{i2})\right] \tag{8.18}$$

Thus, i will vote for θ_1 over ψ_1 if and only if (8.18) holds.

We can put (8.18) into a more convenient form: Multiply both sides by 2, and divide both sides by a_{i11}. Then complete the square and take the square root of each side. This yields

$$\left|\theta_1-x_{i1}+\frac{a_{i12}}{a_{i11}}(\mu_2-x_{i2})\right|<\left|\psi_1-x_{i1}+\frac{a_{i12}}{a_{i11}}(\mu_2-x_{i2})\right| \tag{8.19}$$

Inequality (8.19) states that i will vote for θ_1 over ψ_1 on issue 1 if and only if θ_1 is closer than ψ_1 to $x_{i1}-(a_{i12}/a_{i11})(\mu_2-x_{i2})$. But, from (8.1), we know that $x_{i1}-(a_{i12}/a_{i11})(\mu_2-x_{i2})$ is i's conditional ideal point on issue 1, given μ_2 as the decision reached on issue 2. Thus, we have an important result. If i is an expected utility maximizer, has the utility function defined by (8.16), and uses a random variable forecast on issue 2, he behaves as if he expects the mean of this forecast to be the decision reached on issue 2. This result is general and is proved in Appendix 8.1 for any finite number of issues. In Appendix 8.2 we show that risk-averse utility is necessary and sufficient for issue-by-issue stability under all voter forecasts.

The preference relation defined by (8.19) is symmetric and single-peaked. Thus, if $\theta_1^*=x_{i1}-(a_{i12}/a_{i11})(\mu_2-x_{i2})$, the median θ_1^* is the predicted decision that will be reached on issue 1. If median θ_1^* is unique and a finite number of proposals are voted on, the one closest to med θ_1^* will be the final decision. Although we have not subscripted μ_2 by voter, it is important to keep in mind that this mean is idiosyncratic. Thus, the median θ_1^* may be based on a diverse set of mean forecasts.

If med θ_1^* is the final decision on issue 1, we have, from (8.1), that med θ_2^* will be the expected decision on issue 2, where

$$\theta_2^*=x_{i2}-\frac{a_{i12}}{a_{i22}}(\text{med }\theta_1^*-x_{i1}) \tag{8.20}$$

Let us now return to the example in Figure 8.2. Given competitive voting, we showed that repeated rounds of voting over issues 1 and 2 will ultimately drive spending to (35, 115). However, this result is based on the implausible assumption that when one issue is being voted on, it is commonly expected that the last accepted value on the other issue will prevail. How can we revise this assumption, given our new results on expectations?

From (8.19), it is clear that each voter must derive a mean forecast on issue 2 in order to know how to vote on issue 1. How might this be done? First, we must specify each voter's information set. Assume that a small set of proposals is to be voted on for issues 1 and 2. Let {\$25, \$60, \$75, \$100} be this set. The agenda by which these proposals will be voted on is unknown to the voters in advance of the voting. Each voter is uncertain about the preferences of other voters. Given the difficulties of forecasting decisions on future issues, the voter might then reason that any proposal in this set is equally likely to be the final decision on issue 2. If this is the case, $\$25(\frac{1}{4})+\$60(\frac{1}{4})+\$75(\frac{1}{4})+\$100(\frac{1}{4})=$ \$65 is the mean forecast on issue 2. However, recall that the voters need not arrive at the same mean forecast.

The conditional ideal points of voters A, B, and C then become

$$x_{a1}^{*}=35-.9(65-115)=\$80$$

$$x_{b1}^{*}=65-.9(65-40)=\$42.5$$

$$x_{c1}^{*}=160-.9(65-25)=\$124$$

The median $x_{i1}^{*}=\$80$, but \$80 is not one of the proposals voted on. \$75 is the proposal closest to \$80, and so, from the corollary to the median voter result (Section 2.3), \$75 will be the final decision on issue 1.

Given \$75 as the decision on issue 1, the conditional ideal points of the voters on issue 2 are

$$x_{a2}^{*}=115-.9(75-35)=\$79$$

$$x_{b2}^{*}=40-.9(75-65)=\$31$$

$$x_{c2}^{*}=25-.9(75-160)=\$101.5$$

The median $x_{i2}^{*}=\$79$, and so \$75 will also be the final decision on issue 2.

How good is a mean forecast of \$65 on issue 2 when the actual decision is \$75? Actually, pretty good. Recall that \$65 is the *mean* of the forecast. Obviously, \$65 cannot be the correct forecast, because it is never voted on. However, in the absence of certainty about the preference parameters of the other voters, it is fairly good as an average guess. Suppose that issue 1 were voted on again, and the voters used \$75 as a mean forecast on issue 2. Recalculating the conditional ideal points on issue 1, \$75 would again be the final decision on issue 1, and so \$75 would also be the final decision on issue 2. Thus, given our set of four proposals, {\$75, \$75} appears stable with respect to repeated voting. However, expectations may upset this stability. If voter A's mean forecast on issue 2 in the second round of voting is the median $x_{i2}^* = \$79$ from the first round of voting, then \$60 will be the final decision on issue 1, and \$100 the final decision on issue 2. Thus, repeated rounds of voting over issues 1 and 2 may not yield the stable equilibrium $\mathbf{x}_a$ described in Section 8.4.

It should now be clear how voter expectations hamper the efforts of an agenda setter to control the outcome of budget votes. Without perfect information about the form of voter expectations prior to each vote, the agenda setter is gambling that these expectations will aid him in the pursuit of his goal. In the case of our model of voter forecasts under uncertainty, the agenda setter must know the mean forecasts of each voter on each future issue (as well as all of his preference parameters). Otherwise he will be unsure of each voter's conditional ideal point and will be unable to calculate how large a budget figure a majority of the voters will approve in a take-it-or-leave-it vote. If he mistakenly sets this figure too high, the voters will reject his proposal and the reversion budget figure will be implemented.

As mentioned earlier, expectations are also a problem when total budget size and mix are voted on. Let us examine the simplest case in which voters have circular indifference contours. If the voter must choose between two budgets B_θ and B_ψ, he may wish to forecast k if it is subsequently voted on. Assume that $\tilde{k}$ is a random variable denoting his forecast. Then, if there are two spending activities, (8.16) is the voter's utility function, and he is an expected utility maximizer; i will vote for B_θ over B_ψ if and only if

$$E\left\|\left(\frac{B_\theta}{1+\tilde{k}}, \frac{B_\theta \tilde{k}}{1+\tilde{k}}\right) - \mathbf{x}_i\right\|^2 < E\left\|\left(\frac{B_\psi}{1+\tilde{k}}, \frac{B_\psi \tilde{k}}{1+\tilde{k}}\right) - \mathbf{x}_i\right\|^2 \tag{8.21}$$

where $B_\theta/(1+\tilde{k}) = \tilde{B}_{1\theta}$ and $B_\theta \tilde{k}/(1+\tilde{k}) = \tilde{B}_{2\theta}$ is his forecast of how B_θ will be divided between the two spending activities. Assume that $\tilde{k}$ is independent of B_θ and B_ψ. Expanding (8.21) and collecting terms, we have

$$|B_\theta^* - B_\theta| < |B_\theta^* - B_\psi| \tag{8.22}$$

where

$$B_\theta^* = \frac{x_{i1} E[1/(1+\tilde{k})] + x_{i2} E[\tilde{k}/(1+\tilde{k})]}{E[(1+\tilde{k}^2)/(1+\tilde{k})^2]} \tag{8.23}$$

is voter i's most preferred budget conditioned by $\tilde{k}$. Inequality (8.22) is easier to deal with if we assume that $\tilde{k}$ is a discrete random variable. Suppose that only two values of k are voted on, k_1 and k_2. Then $E(\tilde{k}) = pk_1 + (1-p)k_2$, where p is the voter's estimate of the probability that k_1 will beat k_2 in a majority vote. Similarly, if ϕ is a function of $\tilde{k}$, then $E(\phi) = p\phi(k_1) + (1-p)\phi(k_2)$.

Suppose, then, that $k_1=1$ and $k_2=2$. Then (8.22) will be (for $B_\theta > B_\psi$)

$$\frac{(B_\theta+B_\psi)(10-p)}{6} < x_{i1}(2+p)+x_{i2}(4-p) \tag{8.24}$$

Refer to Figure 8.4, where $x_{i1}=x_{i2}=40$. If $p=1$, which means that $\tilde{k}$ is the point forecast k_1, then i will vote for B_θ over B_ψ if and only if $x_{i1} > (B_\theta+B_\psi)/4$. Thus, if $B_\psi=40$, then i will prefer B_θ to B_ψ ($B_\theta > B_\psi$) if and only if $B_\theta < 120$.

Suppose that k is voted on first, followed by voting on B. Then the voter may wish to forecast B_1 in order to decide how to vote (once B_1 is fixed, $B_2=B_1 k$, so there is no uncertainty about B_2). If $\tilde{B}_1$ is a random variable denoting his forecast, then i will vote for k_θ over k_ψ if and only if

$$E\|(\tilde{B}_1, \tilde{B}_1 k_\theta)-\mathbf{x}_i\|^2 < E\|(\tilde{B}_1, \tilde{B}_1 k_\psi)-\mathbf{x}_i\|^2 \tag{8.25}$$

Assume that $\tilde{B}_1$ is independent of k_θ and k_ψ. Expanding (8.25) and collecting terms, we have

$$-2x_{i2}E(\tilde{B}_1)k_\theta + k_\theta^2 E(\tilde{B}_1^2) < -2x_{i2}E(\tilde{B}_1)k_\psi + k_\psi^2 E(\tilde{B}_1^2)$$

Setting $E(\tilde{B}_1)=\mu_{B_1}$ and Var $\tilde{B}_1=\sigma_{B_1}^2$ and completing the square yields

$$|k_\theta^* - k_\theta| < |k_\theta^* - k_\psi| \tag{8.26}$$

where $k_\theta^* = x_{i2}\,\mu_{B_1}/(\mu_{B_1}^2+\sigma_{B_1}^2)$ is voter i's most preferred mix conditioned by $\tilde{B}_1$. Thus, i will vote for k_θ over k_ψ if and only if (8.26) holds. Returning to Figure 8.4, assume that $\tilde{B}_1$ is a discrete random variable taking the values 40, 60, and 80 with equal probability. Then $\mu_{B_1}=60$ and $\sigma_{B_1}^2=$ 266.67, so that i will vote for k_θ over k_ψ if and only if

$$|.62-k_\theta| < |.62-k_\psi| \tag{8.27}$$

where $k_\theta^*=.62$. Thus, if $k_\psi=1$, then i will prefer all $k_\theta \in (.24, 1)$ to k_ψ.

We have shown that regardless of whether B or k is voted on first, each voter will have single-peaked preferences on both B and k under our theory of expectations. We have also shown that voter expectations about total budget size or mix are just as important to the outcome of budget and mix votes as expectations about program spending are to the outcome of program budget votes. Agenda control over total budget and mix proposals does not ensure that vote outcomes can be successfully manipulated. Not only must voter expectations (and preferences) be known, these expectations must also be compatible with the goal of the agenda setter.

Of course, we have discussed examples of agenda control in which voting takes place over only one budget or mix variable, and all other variables are either preset or predetermined by the agenda setter. In such cases there is no expectations problem, because nothing remains to be decided except the one variable under consideration. However, true one-shot votes are rare. School budgets usually are voted on every year, and expectations about future budgets may complicate the simple examples discussed in Section 8.7. Thus, we conclude that there is no easy escape from the expectations problem and that this problem can be a severe headache for agenda setters.

8.10 Committee jurisdictions

We shall now move on to a different variety of institutional structure. In Congress and other legislative bodies, a subset of the voting body is given the power to propose legislation to the entire membership. The simplest example of this practice can be understood when two issues are before the voting body, with a subset of the membership responsible for making proposals on each.

To illustrate this practice, we shall return to our committee example of Chapter 3 (see Table 3.1). Figure 8.8 represents the five committee members. For simplicity, assume that all voters have circular indifference contours. We can think of this five-member committee as being embedded within a larger voting body. If this is the case, we assume that the larger voting body is expected to approve whatever bill is reported by the committee. Or the five-member committee may be the entire membership of the voting body, in which case it is a committee of the whole.

If each project is voted on separately, then $\mathbf{x}_e = \mathbf{x}_{\text{med}} = (60, 60)'$ is the expected outcome of the voting (assuming $x_{\text{med}\,1}$ and $x_{\text{med}\,2}$ are voted on). However, suppose that the committee is broken up into two subcommittees $S_1 = \{A, B, C\}$ and $S_2 = \{C, D, E\}$ with the following jurisdictional structure. Invest S_1 with the power to make proposals on issue 1 to the full committee and S_2 the power to make proposals on issue 2. We might think of S_1 and S_2 as being delegated responsibility by the full committee over issues 1 and 2, respectively.

If we specify a reversion level on each issue, the following rule may be followed. Each subcommittee is allowed to make a proposal with respect to the issue over which it has jurisdiction. If no proposal is made, the reversion level on that issue will be adopted by the full committee. If a proposal is made, it is voted on by the full committee as a replacement for the reversion level.

Given this rule, what decisions do we expect will be made by the full committee? Consider issue 1. The ideal points of S_1 on issue 1 are $\{\$120, \$100, \$30\}$, so \$100 is the proposal that a majority of S_1 prefers to any other. Let r_1 be the reversion level on issue 1. If $\$0 \leqslant r_1 < \$20$, then S_1

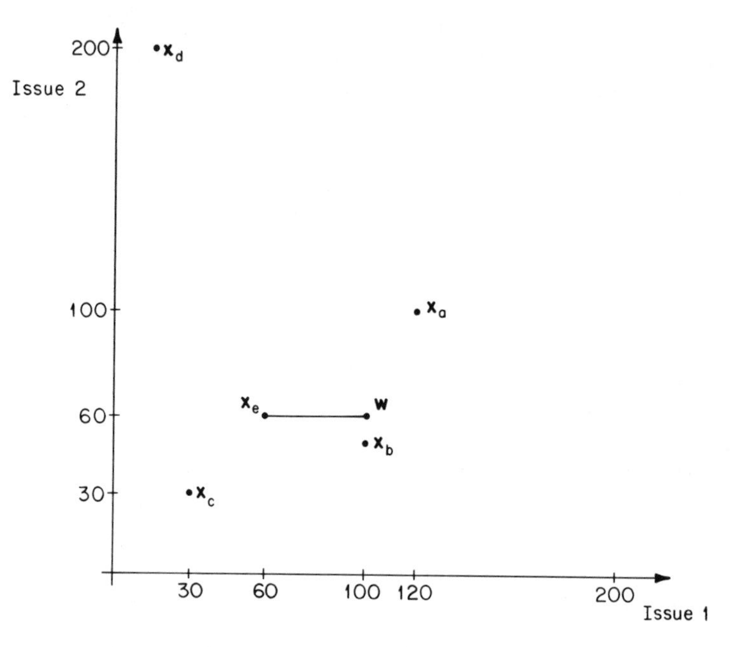

Figure 8.8. A committee with two subcommittees $S_1 = \{A, B, C\}$ and $S_2 = \{C, D, E\}$.

will propose \$100, because it is closer to $x_{\text{med}\,1} = \$60$ than r_1 and so will win. However, if $\$20 \leqslant r_1 < \$60$, r_1 will beat \$100 in the full committee (assume that r_1 prevails in case of ties). But this does not mean that S_1 should not make a proposal. Instead, S_1 should propose an amount p such that $|r_1 - 60| > |p - 60|$, with p as close to \$100 as possible. Thus, if $r_1 = 30$, p should be just less than 90. However, for $\$60 \leqslant r_1 \leqslant \$100$, it is pointless for S_1 to make a proposal, because it is possible to win only with amounts farther from \$100 than is r_1. Finally, for $r_1 > \$100$, S_1 should propose \$100, because it will win. Thus, the closed interval [\$60, \$100] is the set of final decisions on issue 1 that may be reached (depending on r_1) under the procedure we have described.

As for S_2, their ideal points on issue 2 are $\{\$30, \$200, \$60\}$, and so \$60 is S_2's median point, which is also the full committee's median point on this issue. Thus, if r_2 is the reversion level on issue 2, S_2 will propose \$60 if $r_2 \neq \$60$, and this proposal will always win. This leaves us with the conclusion that the line between $\mathbf{w} = (100, 60)'$ and $\mathbf{x}_e = (60, 60)'$ describes the set of possible decisions on both issues by the full committee.

Let us examine the effects of a different jurisdictional structure. Instead of two subcommittees within a single committee, assume two full

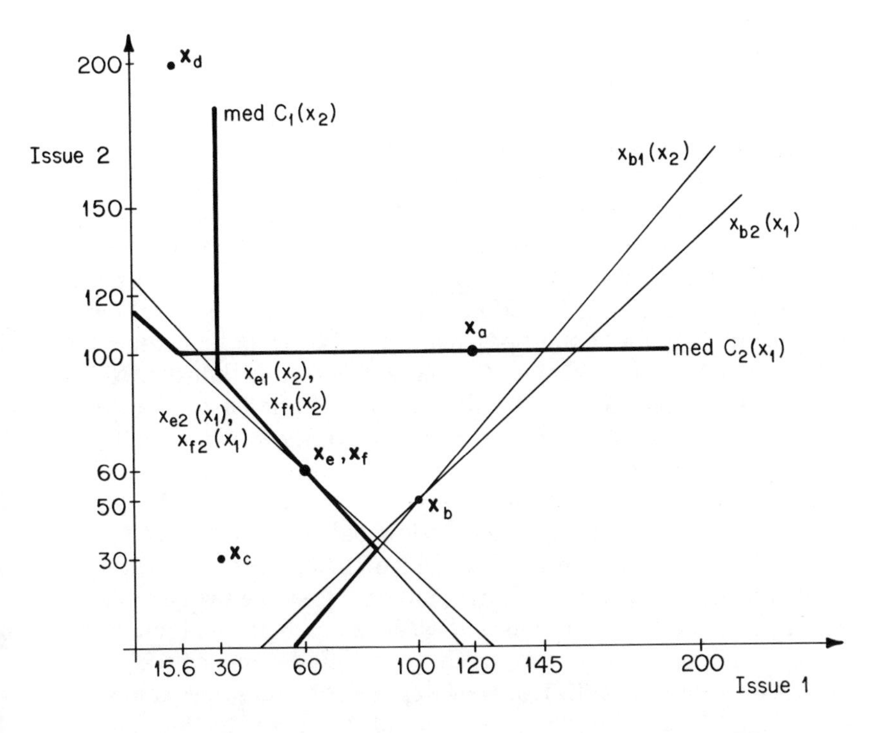

Figure 8.9. Two committees $C_1=\{B, C, E\}$ and $C_2=\{A, D, F\}$.

committees with disjoint memberships. Think of these two committees as being embedded within a larger voting body that is expected to approve whatever bill either committee reports. We shall continue with the committee example of Chapter 3, with the same preference parameters assumed in Section 3.3. Thus, voters A, C, and D have circular indifference contours, whereas for B, $a_{b11}=a_{b22}=1$, $a_{b12}=-.9$, and for E, $a_{e11}=a_{e22}=1$, $a_{e12}=.9$. In addition, assume a sixth voter F with preference parameters identical with those of voter E. Figure 8.9 represents this example.

Let $C_1=\{B, C, E\}$ be committee 1, whose task is to report a bill on issue 1. Let $C_2=\{A, D, F\}$ be committee 2, whose task is to report a bill on issue 2. Suppose C_1 and C_2 are merged into a single committee with the power to report separate bills on issues 1 and 2. As Figure 8.9 indicates, if all six voters consider each issue separately and voters B, E, and F have a (mean) forecast of 60 on whichever issue is considered second, then (\$60, \$60) is the expected decision on both issues (assuming it is voted on).

How is this result altered by having C_1 and C_2 report separate bills? Assume that each committee must report a bill prior to knowing what the other committee will do. Then each committee member with nonseparable preferences must forecast the bill that will be reported by the committee to which he does not belong.

If the members of C_1 forecast \$60 as the bill that will be reported by C_2, then \$60 is the bill they will report. Figure 8.9 indicates the median most preferred bill for each committee based on the bill reported by the other committee. Given a forecast of \$60 by C_1, {\$30, \$60, \$109} are the most preferred bills of C, E, and B, respectively. Thus, if \$60 is voted on by C_1, it will have the support of a majority of C_1 against any other bill.

Alternatively, if members of C_2 forecast \$60 as the bill that will be reported by C_1, then \$100 is the bill they will report. Thus, (\$60, \$100) may be the two bills that will be reported out of these two committees.

Suppose, however, that C_1 has some knowledge of the preferences of C_2. As shown in Figure 8.9, $\text{med}\, C_2(x_1) = \$100$ for all $x_1 > 15.6$. Thus, unless C_2 expects C_1 to report a very low bill, \$100 is the bill C_2 will report. Assuming that C_2 will report a bill of \$100, Figure 8.9 shows that \$30 is the bill C_1 will report. Thus, (\$30, \$100) will be the two bills reported by C_1 and C_2, given some knowledge of each other's preferences.

Other types of jurisdictional structures might be examined. Following the procedures of the U.S. House of Representatives, a rules committee may be introduced with the power to decide what type of floor amendments, if any, members may try to attach to a committee's bill. However, we have looked at two important structures: one that models not only subcommittee voting but also full committee voting with expectations regarding floor votes, and one that models not only committee voting but also voting by two separate houses of a single legislature with expectations by each regarding the actions of the other. Thus, we have looked at two general types of jurisdiction.

8.11 Unit rule

We now turn to one last example of an institutional setting. The electoral college is an important feature of American presidential elections. Instead of choosing winners on the basis of the direct vote, the electoral college apportions 538 votes among the 50 states and the District of Columbia on the basis of the total number of U.S. representatives and senators apportioned to each state. A presidential candidate who wins a plurality of the total vote cast in a given state wins that state's entire electoral vote. The presidential candidate winning a majority of the total number of electoral votes wins the election.

This is an example of the unit rule. The entire electoral vote of each state is awarded to the candidate who wins the most votes in that state. This is quite different from a system in which every vote in the electorate is treated equally. We shall now proceed to assess the extent of this difference.

To keep matters simple, we shall assume a small set of states. In addition, it is important to recognize that we are now back in the realm of candidate competition. Thus, we shall frame our discussion of the electoral college and the unit rule generally in terms of the predictive space developed in Chapter 4.

To start with, assume a single predictive dimension Π in the campaign. Thus, voter i can be identified by his most preferred point z_i on the single predictive dimension, and candidates Theta and Psi can be identified by their respective positions on this same dimension, π_θ and π_ψ. Recalling what we showed in Section 4.5, i prefers Theta to Psi if and only if $|z_i - \pi_\theta| < |z_i - \pi_\psi|$. As in Chapter 4, let Theta be the challenger and Psi the incumbent. Following the convention of Chapter 4, $\pi_\psi = 0$ and $\pi_\theta = 1$.

For simplicity, assume three homogeneous states. Let $z_i = 0$ for all members of state 1, $z_i = .6$ for all members of state 2, and $z_i = 1$ for all members of state 3. Further, assume that states 2 and 3 have the same numbers of voters, but that state 1 has 2.5 times as many voters as either state 2 or 3.

Clearly, under a direct majority rule contest, Psi will win the election, because five-ninths of the electorate has a most preferred point identical with Psi's location on the predictive dimension. However, assume that the election is decided by the electoral college. Every state has two senators and at least one representative. If there are nine representatives in all, then apportioning these seats among the states in proportion to size, state 1 will receive five seats and states 2 and 3 will receive two seats each. This gives state 1 seven electoral votes and states 2 and 3 four electoral votes each. Thus, seven electoral votes will be cast for Psi, but eight electoral votes will be cast for Theta, and Theta will win the election.

This example demonstrates that the electoral college can affect election results. In fact, in this example the small states are relatively advantaged, as compared with the election result under direct majority rule. However, this need not be so. If state 3 were three times larger than either state 1 or state 2, Theta would win under a direct election and under the electoral college. Because state 3's most preferred point is identical with Theta's location on Π, the largest state would not be disadvantaged by the electoral college. Increasing the size of the House in the previous example will have the same effect. Interestingly, if the House size is increased from 9 to 18 in the previous example, the two candidates will tie in the electoral college. Because electoral college deadlocks are broken in the House, where each state delegation casts one vote, the smaller states will join together to elect Theta.

It may also be true, however, that a small state may do better under direct majority rule than under the electoral college. Assume five homogeneous states with $z_i = 0$ for the voters of state 1, $z_i = .45$ for the voters of state 2, $z_i = .55$ for the voters of state 3 and the voters of state 4, and $z_i = 1$ for the voters of state 5. In addition, assume that states 1, 3, and 4 are of equal size, whereas state 5 is three times larger and state 2 five times larger than the smallest state (i.e., state 1, 3, or 4). For the entire electorate, $z_{\text{med}} = .45$, so Psi, the candidate most preferred by state 1 (one of the three smallest states), will win the election. However, under the electoral college with 11 House seats apportioned by relative population, states 1–5 will receive 3, 7, 3, 3, and 5 electoral votes, respectively, making $z_{\text{med}} = .55$ under the electoral college. Theta is now the winner, and his location on Π is identical with the most preferred position of the second largest state (state 5).

If states are not homogeneous and voters from the same state have differing z_i's, then the entire electoral vote of the state will be cast for the candidate closest to z_{med} for that state (assuming there are two candidates). Thus, under the electoral college, a heterogeneous state is behaviorally identical with a homogeneous state with the same number of voters as electoral votes and a most preferred position equal to z_{med} for that state.

Lastly, suppose that the voters care about nonpolicy issues. As in Section 5.2, assume two groups in the electorate, with $z_1 = -\frac{1}{2}$ for group 1 and $z_2 = \frac{1}{2}$ for group 2. Then, assuming that $N_1 = N_2$, $\mathbf{v}_1 = \mathbf{v}_2$, and $\sigma_1 = \sigma_2 > 3(1.5)^{1/2}B^2$, $\pi^* = 0$ is an optimal location for the candidates of both parties. However, suppose that the parties' decision makers incorporate the electoral college into their calculations. Assume that each state is composed of certain numbers of group-1 and group-2 voters. Then, if σ_{jk} is the standard deviation of $c_{i\psi} - c_{i\theta}$ for voters from state $j = 1, \ldots, 51$ and group $k = 1, 2$, it may be true that $\sigma_{jk} < 3(1.5)^{1/2}B_{jk}^2$ for all j, k, in which case an optimal candidate location may not exist. In other words, σ_1 and σ_2 may be sufficiently large, if measured over the entire electorate, to ensure equilibrium, but insufficiently large if measured over individual states. The electoral college may destroy equilibrium in this case.

The opposite may be true. Consider Figure 8.10, which represents five groups of voters in a space of two predictive dimensions. Let $N_1 = N_2 = \ldots = N_5$, and assume that $V_i'A_iV_i = I$ for all voters, so that distance in the predictive space is simple Euclidean (see Appendix 4.2). Under a direct majority election, it is not difficult to see that an optimal π (i.e., a

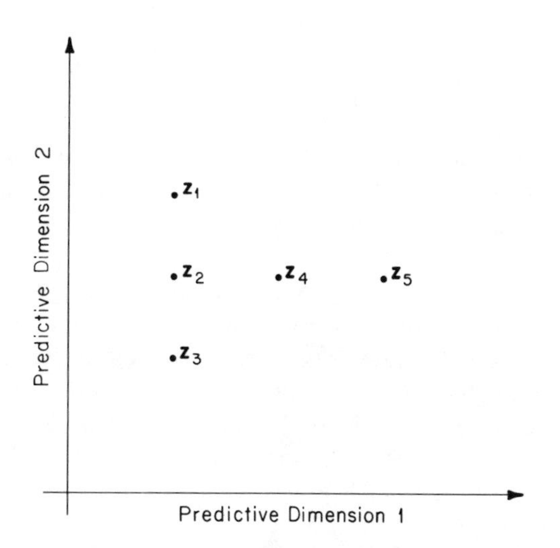

Figure 8.10. A case in which the electoral college creates equilibrium.

dominant point) does not exist. However, suppose that there are three states, the first of which is composed of groups 1, 2, and 3, the second of which is composed of group 4, and the third of which is composed of group 5. Then, under the electoral college, an optimal π does exist. If the electoral votes given states 1–3 are 5, 3, and 3, respectively, then $\mathbf{z}_4$ is a dominant point and optimal location for both candidates. On the other hand, if the House is expanded from 5 members to 20 members, then the electoral votes given states 1–3 are 14, 6, and 6, respectively, and $\mathbf{z}_2$ is an optimal location for both candidates.

Finally, suppose that group 2 is eliminated from Figure 8.10. Then, under a direct majority election, $\mathbf{z}_4$ is a dominant point. However, if there are two states, with state 1 consisting of groups 1, 3, and 4, and state 2 consisting of group 5, then under the electoral college an equilibrium will not exist.

8.12 Conclusion

This chapter has been devoted to an analysis of how institutions affect the spatial theory of voting. In both committee voting and electoral competition we have shown that institutional structures such as agenda control, committee jurisdictions, and the unit rule have important effects on voting outcomes. These results illustrate several points. First, institutions matter. If spatial theory is to illuminate real-world voting, the effects of institutional structures must be ascertained. When an institution is shown to significantly affect the calculus of the voter or the candidate, the institution must be included in the spatial voting model.

The second point, however, is that spatial theory is quite adaptable to this purpose. As we have shown in this chapter, such diverse institutions as take-it-or-leave-it voting and the electoral college can be modeled spatially. Thus, the existence of political institutions does not jeopardize the utility of spatial theory. Instead, it poses an interesting set of challenges.

Finally, after eight chapters, the reader is now fully able to appreciate the richness of spatial theory. From the minimal set of assumptions initially specified in Chapter 2, we have proceeded to build a theoretical edifice of very large proportions. We have explored many topics in the theory of committees and elections, utilizing the simple analogy between preference and distance that is the foundation of spatial theory. That such a simple analogy can produce such powerful theory is, to say the least, an impressive result.

Appendix 8.1

The purpose of this appendix is to generalize the result described in Section 8.9 concerning the role of mean forecasts in the theory of voter expectations.

First, we shall show what voter i's revised ideal point is on issues $n+1,\dots,p$ when issues $1,\dots,n$ have already been decided. Let $\boldsymbol{\theta}=(\theta_1,\dots,\theta_n)'$ represent the outcome on these first n issues. Voter i is uncertain about how issues $n+1,\dots,p$ will be decided. Let $\tilde{\boldsymbol{\theta}}=(\tilde{\theta}_{n+1},\dots,\tilde{\theta}_p)'$ represent the $(p-n)$-dimensional random variable that describes i's forecast on the remaining $p-n$ issues. Let $\Theta=(\theta_1,\dots,\theta_n,\tilde{\theta}_{n+1},\dots,\tilde{\theta}_p)'$.

Let $\tilde{\boldsymbol{\mu}}=(\mu_{n+1},\dots,\mu_p)'$ denote i's forecast of the mean of $\tilde{\boldsymbol{\theta}}$, let $\tilde{\boldsymbol{\sigma}}^2=(\sigma_{n+1}^2,\dots,\sigma_p^2)'$ denote i's forecast of the variance of $\tilde{\boldsymbol{\theta}}$, and let $\mathbf{x}=(\mathbf{x}_n,\mathbf{x}_{p-n})'$ denote i's unrevised ideal point on all p issues, where $\mathbf{x}_n=(x_1,\dots,x_n)'$ and $\mathbf{x}_{p-n}=(x_{n+1},\dots,x_p)'$. For simplicity, the voter subscript is dropped. Finally, A is i's $p\times p$ salience matrix on all p issues (A is symmetric, positive definite). Let A be partitioned into four submatrices as follows:

$$A=\begin{bmatrix} A_{11} & A_{12} \\ A_{12}' & A_{22} \end{bmatrix} \quad A_{11}=\begin{bmatrix} a_{11} & \cdots & a_{1n} \\ \vdots & & \vdots \\ a_{1n} & \cdots & a_{nn} \end{bmatrix}$$

$$A_{12}=\begin{bmatrix} a_{1n+1} & \cdots & a_{1p} \\ \vdots & & \vdots \\ a_{nn+1} & \cdots & a_{np} \end{bmatrix} \quad \text{and} \quad A_{22}=\begin{bmatrix} a_{n+1n+1} & \cdots & a_{n+1p} \\ \vdots & & \vdots \\ a_{n+1p} & \cdots & a_{pp} \end{bmatrix}$$

We shall now derive i's revised ideal point on issues $n+1,\ldots,p$. $\|\Theta-\mathbf{x}\|_A^2$ is the weighted (squared) Euclidean distance between Θ and $\mathbf{x}$. Given the foregoing notation,

$$\|\Theta-\mathbf{x}\|_A^2=[(\boldsymbol{\theta}-\mathbf{x}_n)',(\tilde{\boldsymbol{\theta}}-\mathbf{x}_{p-n})']\begin{bmatrix} A_{11} & A_{12} \\ A_{12}' & A_{22}\end{bmatrix}\begin{bmatrix}\boldsymbol{\theta}-\mathbf{x}_n \\ \tilde{\boldsymbol{\theta}}-\mathbf{x}_{p-n}\end{bmatrix}$$

$$=(\boldsymbol{\theta}-\mathbf{x}_n)'A_{11}(\boldsymbol{\theta}-\mathbf{x}_n)+2(\boldsymbol{\theta}-\mathbf{x}_n)'A_{12}(\tilde{\boldsymbol{\theta}}-\mathbf{x}_{p-n})$$
$$+(\tilde{\boldsymbol{\theta}}-\mathbf{x}_{p-n})'A_{22}(\tilde{\boldsymbol{\theta}}-\mathbf{x}_{p-n}) \qquad \text{(A8.1)}$$

If we differentiate (A8.1) with respect to $\tilde{\boldsymbol{\theta}}$ and set the result equal to zero, we can solve for i's revised ideal point on issues $n+1,\ldots,p$:

$$\frac{\partial\|\Theta-\mathbf{x}\|_A^2}{\partial\tilde{\boldsymbol{\theta}}}=2A_{12}'(\boldsymbol{\theta}-\mathbf{x}_n)+2A_{22}(\tilde{\boldsymbol{\theta}}-\mathbf{x}_{p-n})=0$$

so that $\mathbf{x}_{p-n}-A_{22}^{-1}A_{12}'(\boldsymbol{\theta}-\mathbf{x}_n)$ is i's revised ideal point (observe that the second-order condition for a minimum is met).

We can now use this result to derive a rule whereby i can determine how to vote on issue $n+1$, given $\boldsymbol{\theta}$ on issues $1,\ldots,n$, his revised ideal point on issues $n+1,\ldots,p$, and his forecast $(\tilde{\theta}_{n+2},\ldots,\tilde{\theta}_p)$ on the remaining issues. Assume that $(\mu_{n+2},\ldots,\mu_p)$ and $(\sigma_{n+2}^2,\ldots,\sigma_p^2)$ are independent of the alternatives on the $(n+1)$st issue. This assumption is reasonable, because voters are uncertain about the outcomes on later votes.

Suppose that i must decide whether to vote for θ_{n+1} or ψ_{n+1} on issue $n+1$. If he is an expected utility maximizer, he will vote for θ_{n+1} if and only if

$$E\|\hat{\boldsymbol{\theta}}-\hat{\mathbf{x}}\|_{A_{22}}^2<E\|\hat{\boldsymbol{\psi}}-\hat{\mathbf{x}}\|_{A_{22}}^2 \qquad \text{(A8.2)}$$

where $\hat{\boldsymbol{\theta}}=(\theta_{n+1},\tilde{\theta}_{n+2},\ldots,\tilde{\theta}_p)'$, $\hat{\boldsymbol{\psi}}=(\psi_{n+1},\tilde{\theta}_{n+2},\ldots,\tilde{\theta}_p)'$, and $\hat{\mathbf{x}}=\mathbf{x}_{p-n}-\mathrm{A}_{22}^{-1}A_{12}'(\boldsymbol{\theta}-\mathbf{x}_n)$ is his revised ideal point. Thus, (A8.2) can also be written

$$E\{[\hat{\boldsymbol{\theta}}-\mathbf{x}_{p-n}+A_{22}^{-1}A_{12}'(\boldsymbol{\theta}-\mathbf{x}_n)]'A_{22}[\hat{\boldsymbol{\theta}}-\mathbf{x}_{p-n}+A_{22}^{-1}A_{12}'(\boldsymbol{\theta}-\mathbf{x}_n)]\}$$
$$<E\{[\hat{\boldsymbol{\psi}}-\mathbf{x}_{p-n}+A_{22}^{-1}A_{12}'(\boldsymbol{\theta}-\mathbf{x}_n)]'A_{22}[\hat{\boldsymbol{\psi}}-\mathbf{x}_{p-n}+A_{22}^{-1}A_{12}'(\boldsymbol{\theta}-\mathbf{x}_n)]\} \qquad \text{(A8.3)}$$

Multiplying through and gathering terms, we can rewrite (A8.3) as

$$E(\hat{\boldsymbol{\theta}}'A_{22}\hat{\boldsymbol{\theta}})-2E(\hat{\boldsymbol{\theta}}'A_{22}\mathbf{x}_{p-n})+2(\boldsymbol{\theta}-\mathbf{x}_n)'A_{12}\hat{\boldsymbol{\mu}}_\theta$$
$$<E(\hat{\boldsymbol{\psi}}'A_{22}\hat{\boldsymbol{\psi}})-2E(\hat{\boldsymbol{\psi}}'A_{22}\mathbf{x}_{p-n})+2(\boldsymbol{\theta}-\mathbf{x}_n)'A_{12}\hat{\boldsymbol{\mu}}_\psi \qquad \text{(A8.4)}$$

where $\hat{\boldsymbol{\mu}}_\theta=(\theta_{n+1},\mu_{n+2},\ldots,\mu_p)'$ and $\hat{\boldsymbol{\mu}}_\psi=(\psi_{n+1},\mu_{n+2},\ldots,\mu_p)'$.

Taking the first term on the left-hand side of (A8.4),

$$E(\hat{\boldsymbol{\theta}}' A_{22} \hat{\boldsymbol{\theta}}) = E\left\{ (\theta_{n+1}, \tilde{\theta}_{n+2}, \ldots, \tilde{\theta}_p) \begin{bmatrix} a_{n+1,n+1} & \cdots & a_{n+1,p} \\ \vdots & & \vdots \\ a_{n+1,p} & \cdots & a_{pp} \end{bmatrix} \begin{bmatrix} \theta_{n+1} \\ \tilde{\theta}_{n+2} \\ \vdots \\ \tilde{\theta}_p \end{bmatrix} \right\}$$

and it is clear that the only part of this term not identical with its counterpart in the first term on the right-hand side of (A8.4) is

$$\theta_{n+1}(a_{n+1,n+1}, \ldots, a_{n+1,p})(\theta_{n+1}, 2\mu_{n+2}, \ldots, 2\mu_p)'$$

In the same way, the only part of the second term on the left-hand side of (A8.4) not identical with its counterpart in the second term on the right-hand side is

$$-2\theta_{n+1}(a_{n+1,n+1}, \ldots, a_{n+1,p})\mathbf{x}_{p-n}$$

Finally, the only part of the third term on the left-hand side of (A8.4) that does not drop out is

$$2\theta_{n+1}(\boldsymbol{\theta} - \mathbf{x}_n)'(a_{1,n+1}, \ldots, a_{n,n+1})'$$

and thus (A8.4) can finally be rewritten as

$$\theta_{n+1}\mathbf{a}'_{n+1}(\theta_1 - x_1, \ldots, \theta_n - x_n, \theta_{n+1}/2 - x_{n+1}, \mu_{n+2} - x_{n+2}, \ldots, \mu_p - x_p)'$$
$$< \psi_{n+1}\mathbf{a}'_{n+1}(\theta_1 - x_1, \ldots, \theta_n - x_n, \psi_{n+1}/2 - x_{n+1}, \mu_{n+2} - x_{n+2}, \ldots, \mu_p - x_p)' \quad \text{(A8.5)}$$

where $\mathbf{a}_{n+1} = (a_{n+1,1}, \ldots, a_{n+1,p})'$ is the $(n+1)$st column of A.

Inequality (A8.5) can be better understood by way of an example. Suppose that there is a total of three issues. The outcome of issue 1 is θ_1; the forecast on issue 3 is $\tilde{\theta}_3$. Issue 2 is being voted on, and the choice is between θ_2 and ψ_2. Then, by (A8.5), i will vote for θ_2 if and only if

$$\theta_2(a_{12}, a_{22}, a_{23})(\theta_1 - x_1, \theta_2/2 - x_2, \mu_3 - x_3)'$$
$$< \psi_2(a_{12}, a_{22}, a_{23})(\theta_1 - x_1, \psi_2/2 - x_2, \mu_3 - x_3)'$$

Multiplying both sides by 2 and dividing by a_{22} gives

$$\theta_2^2 - 2\theta_2 x_2 + 2\theta_2\left[\frac{a_{12}}{a_{22}}(\theta_1 - x_1) + \frac{a_{23}}{a_{22}}(\mu_3 - x_3)\right]$$
$$< \psi_2^2 - 2\psi_2 x_2 + 2\psi_2\left[\frac{a_{12}}{a_{22}}(\theta_1 - x_1) + \frac{a_{23}}{a_{22}}(\mu_3 - x_3)\right]$$

Completing the square and taking the square root, we obtain

$$\left|\theta_2 - x_2 + \frac{a_{12}}{a_{22}}(\theta_1 - x_1) + \frac{a_{23}}{a_{22}}(\mu_3 - x_3)\right|$$
$$< \left|\psi_2 - x_2 + \frac{a_{12}}{a_{22}}(\theta_1 - x_1) + \frac{a_{23}}{a_{22}}(\mu_3 - x_3)\right|$$

But $x_2 - (a_{12}/a_{22})(\theta_1 - x_1) - (a_{23}/a_{22})(\mu_3 - x_3)$ is i's revised ideal point on issue 2, given θ_1 as the decision on issue 1 and μ_3 as the decision forecast on issue 3. So i will vote for θ_2 if and only if it is closer than ψ_2 to this revised ideal point.

Appendix 8.2

In this appendix we shall show that concavity of the utility function (i.e., risk aversion) in each issue is necessary and sufficient for each voter to have single-peaked preferences on each issue, regardless of his forecasts on future issues. Because single-peaked preferences for all voters on each issue and preference-based voting are sufficient for an equilibrium outcome on each issue, we show that risk aversion plays a crucial role in stabilizing the effects of voter expectations. The result of Appendix 8.1 can be thought of as a special form of this stability when risk aversion is described by a particular type of concavity (i.e., quadratic utility).

Suppose that a set of voters $N = \{1, \ldots, n\}$ vote on a set of issues $P = \{1, \ldots, p\}$ one issue at a time. Each issue can be thought of as a one-dimensional continuum, with a point on this continuum labeled an alternative. Each vote consists of a contest between two alternatives, with the winning alternative receiving at least a simple majority of the votes [$(n+1)/2$ if n is odd and $n/2+1$ if n is even].

If $\boldsymbol{\theta} = (\theta_1, \ldots, \theta_p)$ is an outcome on issues $1, \ldots, p$, then voter i's utility for $\boldsymbol{\theta}$ is $u_i(\boldsymbol{\theta})$; u_i is said to be (jointly) concave if and only if for any two outcomes $\boldsymbol{\theta} = (\theta_1, \ldots, \theta_p)$ and $\boldsymbol{\psi} = (\psi_1, \ldots, \psi_p)$,

$$u_i[\alpha\boldsymbol{\theta} + (1-\alpha)\boldsymbol{\psi}] \geqslant \alpha u_i(\boldsymbol{\theta}) + (1-\alpha) u_i(\boldsymbol{\psi})$$

for all $\alpha \in [0, 1]$. Concave utility is the same as risk aversion. If u_i is concave for any two outcomes that differ only on a single issue, then u_i is concave (risk-averse) by issue. Clearly, if u_i is jointly concave, then u_i is concave by issue. However, the converse is not true.

Let us suppose that when issue 1 is voted on, $\tilde{\boldsymbol{\theta}}^{p-1} = (\tilde{\theta}_2, \tilde{\theta}_3, \ldots, \tilde{\theta}_p)$ represents i's forecast of the outcome on the remaining $p-1$ issues. $\tilde{\boldsymbol{\theta}}^{p-1}$ is a $(p-1)$-dimensional random variable that describes what i believes are the possible outcomes on issues $2, \ldots, p$ and the probability density associated with each outcome. Voter i might condition $\tilde{\boldsymbol{\theta}}^{p-1}$ on each alternative on issue 1 under consideration. In the absence of perfect information about the linkage between alternatives on issue 1 and outcomes on issues $2,\ldots,p$, the signals received by voter i that are transmitted through the votes cast on issue 1 are too confusing for i to gain even partial knowledge of how present alternatives condition future outcomes. Even knowledge of the preference parameters of the other voters is insufficient for this purpose, because future votes are also a function of the forecast variables used by the other voters. Lastly, there is no assurance that these parameters will remain unchanged between the present and the time future issues are considered. Thus, for most large committee voting situations, we argue that it is reasonable to assume that the distribution of $\tilde{\theta}^{p-1}$ is independent of the alternatives on issue 1 that are voted on. Our result also goes through if only the mean and variance of $\tilde{\theta}^{p-1}$ are independent of the alternatives on issue 1.

Let $\tilde{\theta}^{p-1}$ be a discrete random variable to simplify the exposition. $\tilde{\theta}^{p-1}$ is idiosyncratic, but, again, the subscript will be dropped for simplicity. Let $s=1,\ldots,S$ be an index for the set of values taken by $\tilde{\theta}^{p-1}$, and let π_s be the *subjective* probability that value s will occur. Then

$$V_i(\theta_1)=\sum_{s=1}^{S}\pi_s u_i(\theta_1,\tilde{\theta}_s^{p-1}) \qquad \text{(A8.6)}$$

is the expected utility for i associated with the alternative θ_1 on issue 1.

Suppose that i is an expected utility maximizer. Then he will vote for θ_1 over ψ_1 on issue 1 if and only if $V_i(\theta_1)>V_i(\psi_1)$. Suppose that u_i is concave in issue 1. If $V_i(\theta_1)$ is quasi-concave, then $V_i(\theta_1)\geqslant V_i(\psi_1)$ implies that $V_i[\alpha\theta_1+(1-\alpha)\psi_1]\geqslant V_i(\psi_1)$ for all $\alpha\in[0,1]$. But the independence of $\tilde{\theta}^{p-1}$ from the alternatives of issue 1 and the concavity of u_i in issue 1 imply that $V_i[\alpha\theta_1+(1-\alpha)\psi_1]\geqslant\alpha V_i(\theta_1)+(1-\alpha)V_i(\psi_1)$. Thus, if u_i is concave in issue 1, then V_i is quasi-concave in issue 1.

The same result holds for any other issue. Suppose that issue j is voted on. Let $\boldsymbol{\theta}_{j-1}=(\theta_1,\ldots,\theta_{j-1})$ be the decisions reached on issues $1,\ldots,j-1$, and let $\tilde{\theta}^{p-j}=(\tilde{\theta}_{j+1},\ldots,\tilde{\theta}_p)$ be the random variable forecast on issues $j+1,\ldots,p$. Then, assuming that $\tilde{\theta}^{p-j}$ is independent of alternatives on issue j, i's utility for the alternative θ_j on issue j is

$$V_i(\theta_j)=\sum_{s=1}^{S}\pi_s u_i(\boldsymbol{\theta}_{j-1},\theta_j,\tilde{\theta}_s^{p-j}) \qquad \text{(A8.7)}$$

It is important to note that $\tilde{\theta}^{p-j}$ may not be identical with the last $p-j$ random variables of $\tilde{\theta}^{p-1}$. The index s is used in both (A8.7) and (A8.6), but, again, there is no necessity for the $(p-1)$-dimensional and $(p-j)$-dimensional random variables to assume the same number of values. Forecasts on future issues may depend on past decisions. In addition, u_i may have changed since issue 1 was voted on. Still, so long as u_i is concave in issue j, $V_i(\theta_j)$ is quasi-concave.

We shall now show a more surprising result. If $V_i(\theta_j)$ is quasi-concave for *all* $\{\tilde{\theta}_s^{p-j}, \pi_s\}$, then $u_i(\boldsymbol{\theta})$ must be concave by issue. The proof of this result follows from an adaptation of a famous theorem of Arrow (1970, Chapter 4).

Theorem (Arrow): If $\frac{1}{2}[u_i(\boldsymbol{\theta})+u_i(\boldsymbol{\psi})]$ is quasi-concave in all its variables, then $u_i(\boldsymbol{\theta})$ is a concave function.

It is easy to interpret this theorem in terms of our model. If $S=2$, $\pi_s=\frac{1}{2}$, and $j=1$, let $\tilde{\theta}_s^{p-1}=\{\boldsymbol{\theta}^{p-1}, \boldsymbol{\psi}^{p-1}\}$ be the set of values taken by the forecast variable $\tilde{\theta}^{p-1}$, where $\boldsymbol{\theta}^{p-1}=(\theta_2,\dots,\theta_p)$, $\boldsymbol{\psi}^{p-1}=(\psi_2,\dots,\psi_p)$, and $\boldsymbol{\theta}^{p-1}\neq\boldsymbol{\psi}^{p-1}$. Then

$$V_i(\theta_1)=\tfrac{1}{2}[u_i(\theta_1,\boldsymbol{\theta}^{p-1})+u_i(\theta_1,\boldsymbol{\psi}^{p-1})]$$

From Arrow's theorem, if $V_i(\theta_1)$ is quasi-concave under this simple forecast of equiprobability, u_i must be a concave function. Thus, if V_i is quasi-concave under *all* possible forecasts, u_i must be a concave function, which means that u_i must be concave by issue.

Quasi concavity is equivalent to single-peakedness. Thus, we are left with the following equilibrium theorem.

Equilibrium theorem: If $\tilde{\theta}^{p-j}=(\tilde{\theta}_{j+1},\dots,\tilde{\theta}_p)$ is independent of alternatives on issue j and voter i is an expected utility maximizer, concavity of the utility function (i.e., risk aversion) in each issue is necessary and sufficient for single-peaked preferences on issue j under *all* $\tilde{\theta}^{p-j}$.

Problems

8.1 Draw the lines $x_{a1}(x_2)$ and $x_{a2}(x_1)$ using the numerical values for the parameters of voter A as given in the example in Section 8.4.

8.2 Write out the expressions for $x_{b1}(x_2)$, $x_{b2}(x_1)$, $x_{c1}(x_2)$, and $x_{c2}(x_1)$ using the parameters for voters B and C as given in Section 8.4.

8.3 Draw the lines $x_{a1}(x_2)$ and $x_{a2}(x_1)$ when $a_{a11}=3$, $a_{a22}=1$, and $a_{a12}=-0.2$.

8.4 Draw $M_{a1}(x_2, 10)$ using (8.4) for voter A in the example in Section 8.4.

8.5 Draw $M_{a2}(x_1, 10)$ for the example.

8.6 Draw $M_{b1}(x_2, 10)$ and $M_{b2}(x_1, 10)$ for voter B in the example.

8.7 Using (8.8), find $B_b(1)$ for voter B.

8.8 Determine $k_b(100)$ and $k_b(200)$ using (8.11).

8.9 Determine $B_a^*(65,\frac{1}{2})$, $B_b^*(65,\frac{1}{2})$, and $B_c^*(65,\frac{1}{2})$.

8.10 Suppose that $\tilde{k}=\frac{1}{4}$ with probability $\frac{1}{2}$ and $\tilde{k}=\frac{3}{4}$ with probability $\frac{1}{2}$. Using (8.23), find B_θ^* for this forecast and $x_{i1}=x_{i2}=40$.

8.11 Determine B_θ^* for the forecast in Problem 8.10 when $x_{i1}=30$ and $x_{i2}=7$.

8.12 Work out a comparison between direct democracy and the unit rule for a country with three states in which the electorate uses two predictive dimensions and does not care about nonpolicy issues. The different values for the parameters in the model can be freely selected.

Bibliographical notes

The theory of Section 8.3 is based on Romer and Rosenthal (1978). The extension of this theory to two issues appears in Mackay and Weaver (1981). Two-issue results in agenda control theory that are based on voting over total budget size and mix appear in Mackay and Weaver (1980).

The expectations problem is discussed in Denzau and Mackay (1981a), the source for Figure 8.7. However, the general theory of expectations is developed in Enelow and Hinich (1983b; in press).

The discussion of committee jurisdictions in Section 8.10 is inspired by Shepsle (1979). This section is also indebted to Denzau and Mackay (1981b). The discussion of the electoral college in Section 8.11 is indebted to Hinich and Ordeshook (1974).

CHAPTER 9

Empirical testing of the spatial theory of elections

9.1 Introduction

The purpose of this chapter is to offer some empirical results designed to test the general spatial model of elections developed in Chapters 4 and 5. No matter how elegant or aesthetically pleasing, a model of politics must ultimately be tested against the real world. Otherwise, it remains, at best, an interesting set of abstractions.

In this chapter we shall demonstrate that the new model of elections developed in this book offers real insights into American electoral politics. Focusing on the American presidential elections of 1976 and 1980, we use voter survey data to recover the underlying predictive space for each of these elections, as well as the positions of the candidates and voters in each space.

The results are easily interpretable in terms of the economic and social left–right dimensions postulated in Chapter 4. It is indeed the case that in the last two presidential contests, the policy issues of the campaign were largely based on one or both of these two left–right dimensions. It is interesting to see which issues belonged to each of these dimensions and which issues involved a mixture of the two.

An important feature of the methodology we employ is that it allows for inclusion of a valence dimension. This dimension measures the nonpolicy value of each candidate. We are therefore in a position to test the general choice model of Chapter 5, which postulates that voter choice is based on the policy and nonpolicy values that the voter associates with each candidate. We can see how well this model predicts voter choice as compared with the choice model of Chapter 4 based on policy alone.

Our maps of voters and candidates in the 1976 and 1980 presidential elections allow us to comment on recent trends in the American two-party system. A number of findings emerge regarding the nature of the Democratic and Republican parties, as well as the way in which voters define the terms of electoral competition. Most important, the general liberal–conservative scale in American politics has consistently been seen by voters as an economic scale when used for self-description. In addition, for at least the last two presidential elections, this scale has been strongly associated with party identification. Voters who strongly identify with the Democratic party tend to be economic liberals, and those who strongly identify with the Republican party tend to be economic conservatives. The social left–right scale is uncorrelated with party identification. However, both the social and economic left–right scales are correlated with the positions of Democratic and Republican *politicians* in the predictive space. Democratic politicians tend to be liberal on both dimensions, whereas Republican politicians tend to be conservative.

These are a few of the major findings we shall discuss. In the sections that follow, we hope to convince the reader that the model of elections developed in Chapters 4 and 5 offers interesting, nonobvious insights into American elections. It is also a model that can be used to explain elections in other democracies. The possibilities for applying the model to real elections are both numerous and exciting.

9.2 A methodology for testing the spatial theory of elections

In this section we shall outline the methodology that permits us to recover the predictive space underlying the 1976 and 1980 American presidential elections, as well as the positions of the voters and candidates in each of these two spaces. The methodology is fully explained in Appendix 9.1, and so we shall discuss only its main features in the text. A second methodology, designed to estimate the voter translation coefficients, is explained in Appendix 9.2. We present results based only on the first methodology. The two advantages of the first over the second methodology are that only the first allows for inclusion of a valence dimension and permits estimation of the angle of rotation of the voter and candidate positions in the predictive space.

The data employed by the first methodology are thermometer scores that voters give to describe their feelings toward major political figures: A political figure is named, and the voter is asked to assign a number to his feelings toward that person. The voter is instructed that scores from 50 to 100 are meant to indicate increasing warmth, whereas scores from 50 to 0 are meant to indicate increasing coldness; 50 is a neutral point, indicating neither warmth nor coldness. Only scores from 0 to 100 are permitted.

The methodology we shall employ assumes that the thermometer score a voter gives to a candidate is a measure of the distance between the voter and candidate in the predictive space plus a factor that represents the candidate's weighted position on a prespecified valence dimension. Formally, if T_{jm} is the thermometer score (t score) given by the mth voter ($m=1,\ldots,N$) to the jth politician ($j=1,\ldots,p$),

$$T_{jm} = c_{jm} - P_{jm} \tag{9.1}$$

where

$$P_{jm} = [\|\boldsymbol{\pi}_j - \mathbf{z}_m\|^2 + aV_j]^{1/r} \tag{9.2}$$

The vectors $\boldsymbol{\pi}_j$ and $\mathbf{z}_m$ are the positions of the jth politician and mth voter in the predictive space. The scalar c_{jm} represents unmeasurable, nonsystematic influences on T_{jm}. V_j is the investigator-assigned position of the jth politician on a prespecified valence dimension; a is the common weight attached by voters to this dimension; r is a parameter specifying the sensitivity of T_{jm} to differences in P_{jm}.

For our empirical results, we set $r=2$, but the methodology also handles $r=1$ or 4. What is crucial to assume is that voters have the same estimates of $\boldsymbol{\pi}_j$, a, and r. Common perception of $\boldsymbol{\pi}_j$ is part of our theory of predictive labeling. Common perception of a is necessitated by the manner in which it is estimated [see equation (A9.18) in Appendix 9.1]. A common r for all voters is clearly restrictive. Our main defense of it lies in the belief that differences in the r's of voters will average out across a large heterogeneous sample. The recovered space may then be viewed as a correct average of the different voter spaces based on varying r's.

Because c_{jm} is basically an error term, it is necessary to assume that c_{jm} is uncorrelated across politicians and also with $\mathbf{z}_m$. This is a standard assumption for this type of statistical model.

A note about t scores is in order before proceeding further. Although we have broken up P_{jm} in equation (9.2) into a policy term $\|\boldsymbol{\pi}_j - \mathbf{z}_m\|^2$ and a nonpolicy term aV_j, the nonpolicy term still may not capture all of the nonpolicy factors that may affect T_{jm}. There are three points to note in this regard. First, by analyzing a sample of Democratic, Republican, and Independent voters, any remaining bias in the t scores will to some extent be averaged out. For example, a Democratic politician may be "too favorably" evaluated by Democratic voters because of his party label, but for the same reason he may be "too negatively" evaluated by Republican voters. Second, an adjusted form of the covariance matrix of the t scores across politicians is what is actually analyzed. This point supports the averaging-out argument just made. Finally, of course, the aV_j term does extract out nonpolicy influences on the t scores, so the closer the postulated valence dimension comes to tapping the source of these influences, the less residual bias there will be. For all these reasons, we believe that (9.1) and (9.2) are reasonable assumptions about the data.

The methodology we employ is a variant of factor analysis. For this reason, we need observations that are linear in $\mathbf{z}_m$. This is accomplished by a straightforward transformation of the data. Specifically, T_{jm} is raised to the rth power, and one politician's t scores are chosen to subtract from the scores given to each of the other politicians. The covariance matrix of the adjusted scores is then factor-analyzed, yielding an estimate of an arbitrary rotation of a modified form of the matrix of candidate positions in the predictive space. Two regressions are then performed to eliminate the effects of errors on the observations and to estimate the remaining parameters of the model. These parameters include the angle of rotation in the predictive space (a result usually unobtainable in factor analysis), the positions of voters and politicians in the predictive space, the weight given by voters to the postulated valence dimension, and the standard deviations of voter most preferred points on the predictive axes.

As an aside, candidate and voter positions can be estimated only up to a reflection or an exchange of axes. For example, if $(8, 7)$ is the estimated position of a given candidate, $(8, -7)$, $(-8, 7)$, $(-8, -7)$, $(7, 8)$, $(-7, 8)$, $(7, -8)$, and $(-7, -8)$ are all equally acceptable estimates.

There are several checks that can be used to evaluate the results of the procedure. We shall discuss these checks in the context of our analysis of the 1976 and 1980 American presidential elections. We now turn to this analysis.

9.3 The 1976 American presidential election

The thermometer data described in the preceding section have been collected since 1968 by the Michigan Survey Research Center's Center for Political Studies (SRC/CPS) in its series of American National Election Studies. These studies are based on a random sample of the eligible electorate. The traditional cross-sectional study consists of an interview conducted in two waves. The first wave is administered before the election (September–October) and the second wave after (November–January). In 1976 and 1980, the thermometer questions about political figures were asked in the preelection wave. This is an advantage, because questions asked after the election are subject to rationalization by respondents "adjusting" their views in light of the election result.

The unweighted sample size in 1976 was 2,248 for the preelection wave. Of this number, 1,203 unweighted respondents were able to give thermometer scores for all 12 political figures who were scaled. The final N was 1,020 after a filter procedure was used to discard respondents whose scores suggested a less-than-serious effort to answer the questions. This filter procedure consisted of breaking up the t scores into nine groups based on the most frequently given scores. A respondent was then eliminated if he gave more scores in any of these nine ranges of scores than 97.5% of the respondents analyzed. The idea behind this filter was

Table 9.1. *1976 income distribution and education level for subsample (*N*=1,020) and population sample (*N*=2,248)*

	Percentage of population sample in each group	Percentage of subsample in each group
Income	(*N*=2,097)	(*N*=965)
Less than $1,999	25.7	19.6
$2,000–3,999	16.3	11.7
$4,000–5,999	11.5	10.8
$6,000–7,999	10.3	11.6
$8,000–9,999	6.6	7.6
$10,000–11,999	6.8	8.3
$12,000–14,999	9.1	11.3
$15,000–19,999	6.1	7.5
$20,000–24,999	3.4	4.8
$25,000 or more	4.3	6.9
Education	(*N*=2,238)	(*N*=1,019)
8 grades or less	17.2	8.5
9–12 grades	50.7	47.1
Some college or all	25.3	33.7
More than 4 years of college	6.8	10.7

to discard respondents who were unable to discriminate sufficiently among the candidates. As one example, 97.8% of the respondents gave a score of 0–7 to six or fewer candidates in the 1976 survey. A respondent giving scores in this range to seven or more candidates was consequently eliminated.

In addition, 98.1% of the respondents used at least three of the nine ranges of scores in 1976. Any respondent using less than three ranges was also discarded. This same filtering procedure was used to analyze the 1980 data.

Three candidates in 1976 were eliminated because of the large number of "don't know" responses (Brown, Jackson, Udall). Nixon was eliminated because 35% of the sample gave him a score of zero. As a test, Nixon was included in a few runs. Although not significantly altering the locations of the other candidates, Nixon's own location was so far out on the periphery of the space as to suggest that the voters were simply banishing him from politics.

Table 9.1 gives comparative demographic information about the entire sample and the subsample of respondents whose scores were used to scale the candidates.

9.4 A valence dimension

We shall discuss the various options used in running the computer program. First, however, let us explain how the valence dimension was constructed. The user must specify candidate positions on such a dimension. The program then estimates the weight voters attach to this dimension.

By definition, a valence dimension concerns an issue or set of issues about which all voters feel the same way. Integrity, executive ability, compassion, and intelligence are examples of qualities that almost all voters wish a president to have. As discussed in Chapter 5, other valence issues concern associations voters may have with the major political parties. Because there is no variation in the way voters feel toward valence issues, a valence dimension cannot be estimated in the same way as policy-related dimensions. In other words, factor analysis cannot recover a valence dimension.

On the other hand, failure to specify a valence dimension when one exists leads to serious distortions in the scaling results. For this reason, if one suspects the existence of such a dimension, it must be specified in advance of the analysis.

In 1976, candidate morality was a much-discussed quality. Jimmy Carter's candidacy for the presidency began and continued up to his election as a personal crusade to restore trust and decency to the White House. The political hangovers of Vietnam and Watergate gave Carter his most potent issue - the need to elect a president who told the truth and who had not succumbed to the evils of the Washington establishment.

Fortunately, the 1976 SRC/CPS survey included a question in the preelection wave that tapped the basic issue of candidate morality. The question asked, "Do you believe that any of these persons have higher moral or religious standards than the others?" The respondent was then shown a list of political figures and allowed to make a *first* and *second* choice. Carter was named by 765 (weighted) respondents as a first choice and by 217 as a second choice. For Ford, the corresponding figures are 307 and 270. All other candidates were named less often.

First mentions were weighted twice as heavily as second mentions. A weighted sum across respondents for whom there were no missing data was then computed for each candidate. The mean and standard deviation of these weighted sums were computed. A standardized score was then derived for each candidate by subtracting the mean from his unstandardized score and dividing by the standard deviation.

It is necessary for the candidate whose scores are subtracted from those of the other candidates to be at the origin on the valence dimension.

Table 9.2. *Means and variances of candidate thermometer scores for 1976 and candidate positions on valence dimension of candidate morality (*N=*1,020)*

Candidate	Mean	Variance	Valence position
Wallace	42.27	674.61	1.52
Carter	60.82	672.85	−1.47
Ford	62.50	482.49	.00
Humphrey	52.05	601.63	1.44
Reagan	56.33	669.45	1.40
Kennedy	54.58	738.04	1.30
Rockefeller	46.71	472.15	1.95
Mondale	53.16	353.12	1.95
McGovern	46.28	532.34	1.92
Kissinger	51.03	577.47	1.97
McCarthy	46.48	388.86	1.96
Dole	51.07	385.72	1.96

Consequently, the standardized score of this candidate is subtracted from the standardized scores of the other candidates. For 1976, the candidate so chosen was Ford. In 1980, the chosen candidate was Reagan. As a final step, each candidate's score on the valence dimension was multiplied by −1. This means that the larger the valence score, the worse the candidate's position on this dimension. The mean and variance of each candidate's thermometer scores, as well as his position on the valence dimension, are listed in Table 9.2.

Not surprisingly, Carter's position on the valence dimension is best. The clear dominance of Carter and Ford over the remaining candidates is evident. Candidate morality was a quality not widely associated with any of the remaining candidates. Kennedy is third best (as he is in total number of both first and second mentions), but he is not far ahead of the others. It is not difficult to speculate as to why this is the case.

9.5 Remaining program options and goodness-of-fit measures

There are three basic options that remain to be specified. First, the number of dimensions in the predictive space must be determined. The eigenvalues of the covariance matrix of t scores across candidates are used for this decision; 66.43% of the variance in the covariance matrix for the two-dimensional solution was explained by the first (54.74%) and second (11.69%) eigenvalues. The third eigenvalue explained 7.38% of the variance. This led to the decision to select a two-dimensional solution for 1976.

Factor analysis or the method of principal components may be used to analyze the covariance matrix. Factor analysis was selected for both the 1976 and 1980 studies because it allows for unequal error variances among the candidates.

Finally, we must choose a value for r, which measures the sensitivity of T_{jm} to differences in P_{jm} in equation (9.1). As mentioned earlier, $r=$ 1, 2, and 4 are possible specifications. We selected $r=2$ for both the 1976 and 1980 analyses for several reasons. If $a=0$ in equation (9.2), then $P_{jm}=\|\boldsymbol{\pi}_j-\mathbf{z}_m\|^{2/r}$. When valence issues do not matter to the voters, P_{jm} is simply a measure of distance between candidate and voter in the predictive space. In this case, there is no reason to expect that, on average, voters are more or less sensitive to differences among candidates near them in the predictive space, as compared with candidates who are farther away. This argument supports setting $r=2$. Running the program under $r=1$ or 4 produces candidate configurations that are quite similar to what is obtained for $r=2$. However, for $r\neq 2$, the candidate configuration is either stretched, squashed, or shifted away from the voters. For these reasons, we deemed $r=2$ to be the optimal compromise.

A few words should be said at this point about judging the statistical adequacy of the results. There are two explicit checks that are available. First, the standard deviations of the voter most preferred points (which are estimated at the same time as the remaining parameters) must be positive. Negative signs for either of the two standard deviations obtained for a two-dimensional solution indicate failure of the voters and candidates to properly scale.

Second, the explained variances for the two regressions used to correct for the effects of errors and estimate the remaining parameters must be quite high. In fact, experience suggests that the R^2 in both cases should exceed .90. The second R^2, which concerns the bulk of the estimation, is particularly important. Experience indicates that the first R^2 is invariably above .95, but that the second can vary a great deal. The second R^2 is particularly sensitive to different methods for deriving the valence positions of the candidates. This insight played a crucial role in estimating the predictive space for the 1980 election.

The standard errors of the regression coefficients are not particularly useful in judging the significance of the regression results. The underlying distribution of the errors is unknown, and so t tests are inappropriate.

The location of the mean most preferred point of the voters is another way of judging the adequacy of the results. There is no reason to expect

Table 9.3. *Related statistics for Figures 9.1 and 9.2*

	Figure 9.1 (N=1,020)	Figure 9.2 (N=798)
R^2 for second regression	.963	.907
Standard deviation on first dimension	50.12	42.14
Standard deviation on second dimension	15.30	16.89
Valence dimension weight	421.67	241.75

the mean voter to lie far away from *all* the candidates. A map that has this feature is almost certainly an artifact of misspecification.

One final point: The estimates of the candidate positions in the predictive space are far more robust than the estimates of the voter positions. Even poorly specified maps reveal essentially the same candidate configuration, though the candidates may be squashed together or stretched apart. The voter positions are not as robust, because of the small number of degrees of freedom in the regression that estimates them. However, the mean most preferred point of the voters is estimated separately and so has a smaller error.

9.6 The 1976 results

We are now ready to discuss our results for the 1976 election. Figure 9.1 is the recovered space based on the procedures and options described in the earlier sections of the chapter. Figure 9.2 includes the same candidates and four groups (Democrats, Republicans, liberals, and conservatives). Thermometer data were collected on these groups in the post-election wave of the survey. The valence question pertains to candidates, so all groups are given a valence score of zero. Figures 9.1 and 9.2 are quite similar. The N for Figure 9.2 is 798. Related statistics for both maps are listed in Table 9.3.

Several results are immediately apparent from an examination of the two maps. First, Democrats and Republicans do indeed differ from each other. Forgetting Wallace for a moment, it is possible in either map to divide the space into a left side for the Democrats (Carter, Mondale,

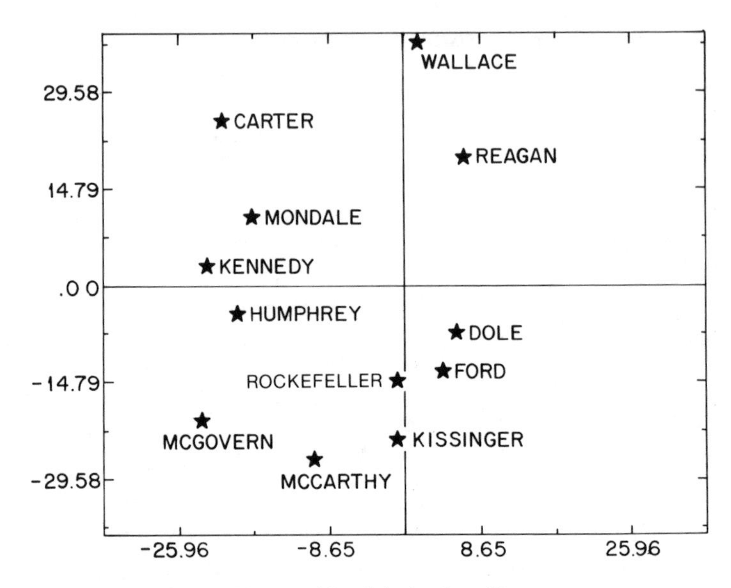

Figure 9.1. 1976 presidential election (I).

Kennedy, McGovern, Humphrey, McCarthy) and a right side for the Republicans (Reagan, Dole, Ford, Rockefeller, Kissinger). The two groups Democrats and Republicans are on the correct sides of the space. Interestingly, the two groups liberals and conservatives are on the Democratic and Republican sides, respectively. We have immediate confirmation that the terms "liberal" and "conservative" do indeed serve as a means of distinguishing the two major parties. We shall have more to say later about the meanings of these two ideologies.

There is one school of thought that maintains that the two major parties are basically alike. Our results contradict this view. Democratic and Republican politicians occupy clearly separate parts of the predictive space. Unless voter translation coefficients are zero on all issues, this difference in predictive location translates into perceived differences in candidate issue positions.

Wallace's location is somewhat problematic. As the candidate with the lowest average thermometer score, however, his location appears biased by unspecified valence factors that do not significantly affect the other candidates. Still, there is a reasonable explanation for his general location, which we shall provide in Section 9.8.

Figure 9.3 is a map of the candidates and voters in the estimated space of Figure 9.1. As listed in Table 9.3, the standard deviation of voter most preferred points on the horizontal axis is 3.28 times the standard devia-

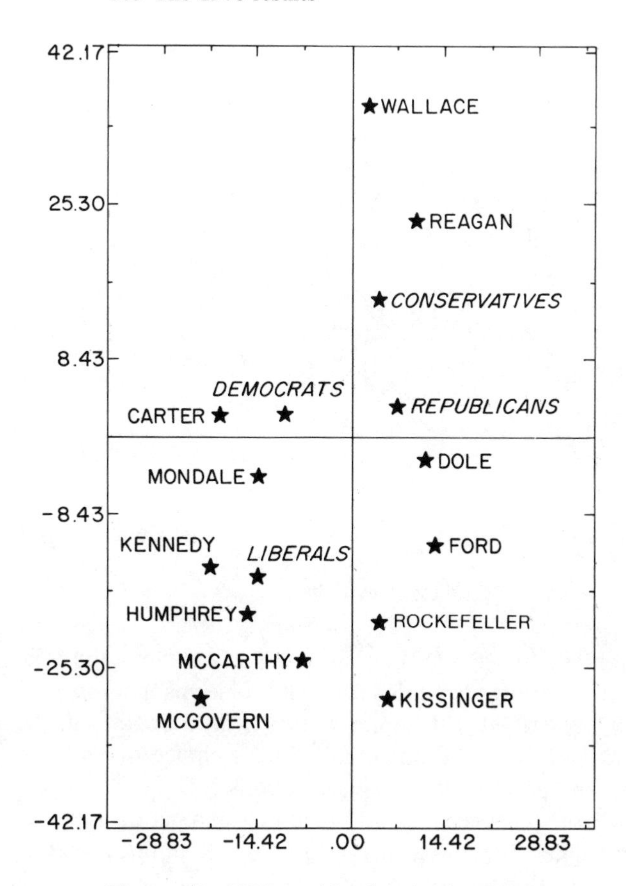

Figure 9.2. 1976 presidential election (II).

tion on the vertical axis. Figure 9.3 shows that there are a great many more voters to the left and right of the candidates than above or below them. In this sense, the horizontal axis is much more significant to the voters than the vertical axis.

The origin of the space is the *mean* most preferred point of the voters. Although we are in no position to judge whether or not the mean is an optimal location for the candidates (to do so requires additional information about the voters), the results of Chapter 5 tempt us to see who is closest to the mean, particularly between Carter and Ford.

Surprisingly enough, among all candidates, Dole is closest to the mean in both Figures 9.1 and 9.2. However, recall that Dole is evaluated quite poorly on the valence dimension, so that seeing him as a terrific candidate is a mistake. Still, there is something quite interesting about the two

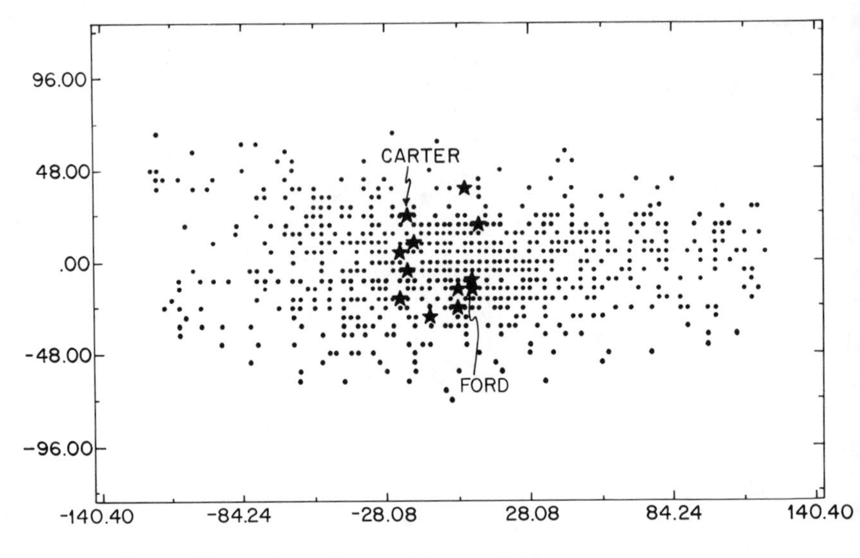

Figure 9.3. Voters and candidates in 1976.

running mates (Mondale and Dole). Each is closer to the mean than the head of his ticket (this finding also holds for 1980). It seems that the logic of ticket "moving" described in Chapter 5 does indeed operate in the real world. Carter's choice of Mondale and Ford's choice of Dole do appear to be guided by policy-related considerations.

Ford's choice of Dole has been viewed by many as an act of appeasement to the "ultra-right" (i.e., Reagan) wing of the Republican party. Our results suggest that this view is an oversimplification. Dole, though slightly to the right of Ford on the horizontal axis, is closer to the center of the electorate than Ford. His acerbity aside, Dole actually helped the ticket in terms of its predictive location.

As for the two presidential nominees, Carter is farther from the mean than Ford by a factor of 2.26 in Figure 9.1 and by a factor of 1.21 in Figure 9.2. If closeness to the mean were the sole determinant of electoral success, Carter would have lost the election. In fact, only Mondale is closer to the mean than Ford (in Figure 9.2). Of course, we have yet to incorporate the valence dimension into our analysis. Doing so substantially affects the relative advantage that Ford appears to possess over Carter.

Let us focus on Figure 9.2, where Ford's advantage is not as substantial as it is in Figure 9.1. Of the 798 voters represented in this same space, 53.38% are closer to Ford than Carter, and 46.62% are closer to Carter than Ford. In keeping with Chapter 5, let us assume that distance between voter and candidate in the predictive space negatively measures the policy value of the candidate to the voter.[1] In this case, a policy model of voter choice specifies that voter j votes for Carter (c) over Ford (f) only if

$$\|\boldsymbol{\pi}_c - \mathbf{z}_j\| < \|\boldsymbol{\pi}_f - \mathbf{z}_j\| \quad (9.3)$$

On the other hand, if the valence dimension measures the nonpolicy value of the candidate to the voter, we can postulate a model of voter choice based on both the policy value and nonpolicy value of the candidate. Because the valence dimension is negatively scaled, this policy and nonpolicy model specifies that voter j votes for Carter over Ford only if

$$aV_c + \|\boldsymbol{\pi}_c - \mathbf{z}_j\|^2 < aV_f + \|\boldsymbol{\pi}_f - \mathbf{z}_j\|^2 \quad (9.4)$$

where a is the estimated valence weight and V_p is the valence position of politician p. Policy distance is squared in accordance with the utility model postulated in Chapter 5. Because utility may be any monotone function of distance, however, this is not the only possible specification.

The question then arises whether or not (9.4) is superior to (9.3) as a model of voter choice. Interestingly, if the choices of all 798 voters are predicted on the basis of (9.4), a two-way contest between Carter and Ford yields 51.13% of the vote for Carter and 48.87% of the vote for Ford. Because the actual division of the major party vote was 51.05% for Carter and 48.95% for Ford, there is reason to think that (9.4) is a more successful model than (9.3).

However, we need more evidence. The precise question that must be asked is whether or not (9.4) is a better predictor than (9.3) of voter behavior at the individual level. Survey respondents are asked in the preelection wave which candidate they think they will vote for. In the postelection wave they are asked which candidate they actually voted for. Considering only those in either the preelection or postelection wave who named Carter or Ford, we can determine how often the two models (9.3) and (9.4) correctly predict the reported behavior of the voter. Among voters who answered Carter or Ford, the percentages are 48.32% Carter and 51.68% Ford for the preelection reported vote and 49.01% Carter and 50.99% Ford for the postelection reported vote. Table 9.4 lists the individual prediction rates for the two models for the preelection and postelection reports.

Clearly, the policy and nonpolicy model (9.4) is better at predicting

[1] If $V_i' A_i V_i = I$, the voter choice function defined on the basis of distance between voter and candidate in the predictive space is equivalent to the choice function defined on the basis of distance in the issue space. Thus, under this condition, the policy value of the candidate as defined in Chapter 5 is, for all practical purposes, the same as the definition used here.

Table 9.4. *Individual-level vote predictions for 1976 presidential election based on Figure 9.2*

	Preelection reported vote (%)	Postelection reported vote (%)
Policy model (9.3)	82.48[a]	82.44
Policy and nonpolicy model (9.4)	83.21	88.36

[a]Entry is percentage of Carter or Ford choices correctly predicted.

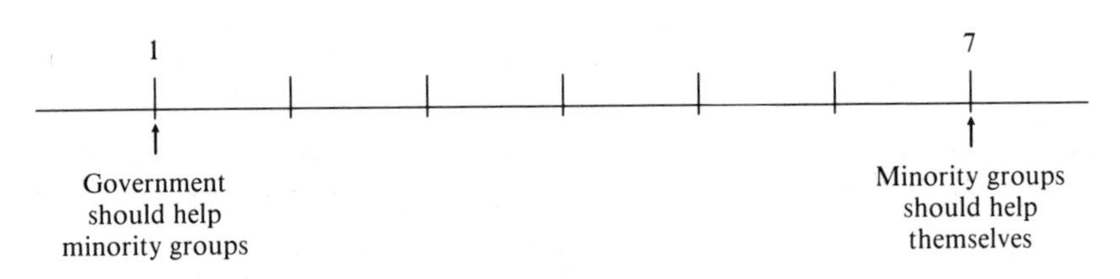

Figure 9.4. Seven-point aid-to-minorities scale.

reported voting behavior in 1976 than the simple policy model (9.3). The same analysis done on the 1,020 respondents used to estimate Figure 9.1 yields a preelection prediction rate of 82.43% for the policy model and an 85.03% prediction rate for the combined policy and nonpolicy model. Thus, we feel safe in stating that for the 1976 election, the model of voter choice expressed by (9.4) is empirically superior to the choice model expressed by (9.3). Candidate morality did indeed play an important role in affecting voters' choices in the 1976 presidential election. A model based on policy alone is not able to account for the 1976 vote as well as a model that also includes a measure of the nonpolicy value of each candidate.

9.7 Identification of the predictive dimensions for 1976

Up to this point we have been intentionally silent about the meanings of the two axes represented in Figures 9.1–9.3. Figure 9.2 indicates that liberals are negative on both axes, whereas conservatives are positive. But what do these two axes represent?

To answer this question, we constructed the following procedure. Part of the survey questionnaire consists of asking respondents to locate themselves on seven-point scales designed to measure their attitudes on various policy issues. This type of scale was described in Chapter 4. One such scale is an aid-to-minorities scale, shown in Figure 9.4. The

Table 9.5. *Number of respondents in each range of scores (1976)*

Range:	1	2	3	4	5
Party ID	157	368	105	269	119
	1–2		3–5		6–7
Liberal–conservative	103		568		167
Aid to minorities	177		470		275
Guaranteed jobs	139		424		328
Legalization of marijuana	167		313		334
Busing	60		160		740
	0–33		34–66		67–100
Women's liberation	140		509		236
	1	2		3	4
Abortion	63	357		159	291

respondent locates his own attitude at one of the seven points of the scale, which is shown to him in the form of Figure 9.4. At the time he is shown the scale in Figure 9.4, the respondent is asked: "Some people feel that the government in Washington should make every possible effort to improve the social and economic position of blacks and other minority groups. Others feel that the government should not make any special effort to help minorities because they should help themselves. Where would you place yourself on this scale, or haven't you thought much about this?"

The axis-by-axis median $\mathbf{z}_m$ among all respondents giving the *same* scale score can then be computed, and the seven medians can be printed in the predictive space to see whether or not the medians line up parallel to one of the two axes. If parallelism exists, we conclude that to some extent the seven-point scale describes what the predictive axis means to the voters. If the seven medians lie on a diagonal line in the predictive space, we conclude that the scale in question is a mixture of the meanings of the two predictive axes.

Table 9.5 lists eight scales that produced either a parallel or diagonal

Table 9.6. *End-point labels* (*1976*)

	1	7
Liberal–conservative	Extremely liberal	Extremely conservative
Aid to minorities	Government should help minorities	Minorities should help themselves
Guaranteed jobs	Government see to job and good living standard	Government let person get ahead on own
Legalization of marijuana	Make marijuana use legal	Set higher penalties
Busing	Bus to achieve integration	Keep children in neighborhood schools
	1	4
Abortion	Abortion never permitted	Abortion never forbidden

distribution of same-score voter medians. Table 9.6 identifies the end points for all but the party ID and women's liberation scales. The party ID scale is a five-point version of the usual seven-point scale (i.e., Strong Democrats = 1, Weak and Independent Democrats = 2, Pure Independents = 3, Weak and Independent Republicans = 4, Strong Republicans = 5). The women's lib scale is based on a feeling thermometer question about the women's liberation movement.

Table 9.5 shows how the scores were grouped for calculating the voter medians. This collapsing of scores does not significantly affect the results and simply facilitates their presentation. This grouping means that three medians are computed for each seven-point scale. The first median is computed for all respondents giving a 1 or 2 on the scale, the second median for those giving a 3, 4, or 5, and a third median for those giving a 6 or 7. Medians are computed for all four abortion scores. The women's lib question is grouped into three ranges (0–33, 34–66, 67–100), and a median is computed for each range.

Figure 9.5 shows that three issues (Aid to Minorities, Liberal–Conservative, and Guaranteed Jobs) exhibit parallelism with the horizontal axis. Guaranteed Jobs is a classic example of a New Deal economic issue. Aid to Minorities is a classic example of a Great Society economic issue. We are thus in a position to identify the horizontal axis of the predictive space as an economic left–right dimension. Results based on a third economic issue, "tax rate change," also support this conclusion. The medians for the two end points (increase tax rate for high incomes = 1,

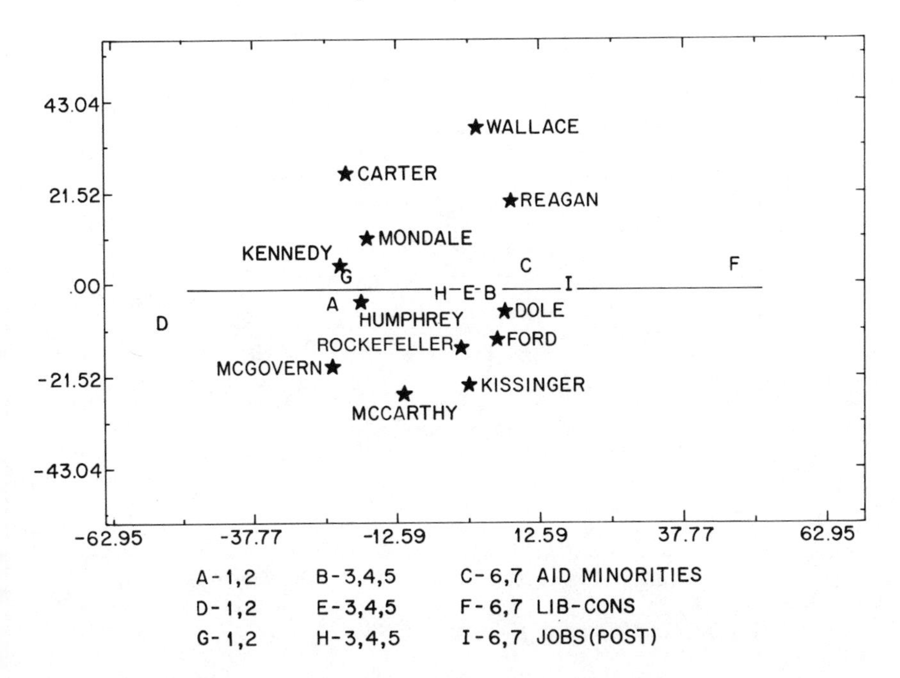

Figure 9.5. 1976 issues: aid to minorities, liberal–conservative, guaranteed jobs.

same tax rate for everyone = 7) also lie on a line parallel to the horizontal axis. Medians for intermediate scores on the tax rate change issue exhibit a muddied pattern. Because only the end points are labeled, we believe (and this holds for every scale we have examined) that a line drawn through the end-point medians provides the best way of determining the orientation of the scale in the predictive space.

That the liberal–conservative scale also lies on a line almost parallel to the horizontal axis is a most interesting result. This suggests that as a way of describing themselves, most voters interpret the terms "liberal," "moderate," and "conservative" on the basis of economic issues. This same finding is repeated in 1980, and earlier studies of 1968 and 1972 election data (Cahoon, Hinich, and Ordeshook, 1978) reach the same conclusion. This means that voter ideology has long been synonymous with attitudes toward New Deal–type economic issues. To voters, the classic left–right scale of American politics is an economic scale when used for self-description.

This does not mean that "liberalism" and "conservatism" are necessarily employed in the same way to describe politicians. In fact, the

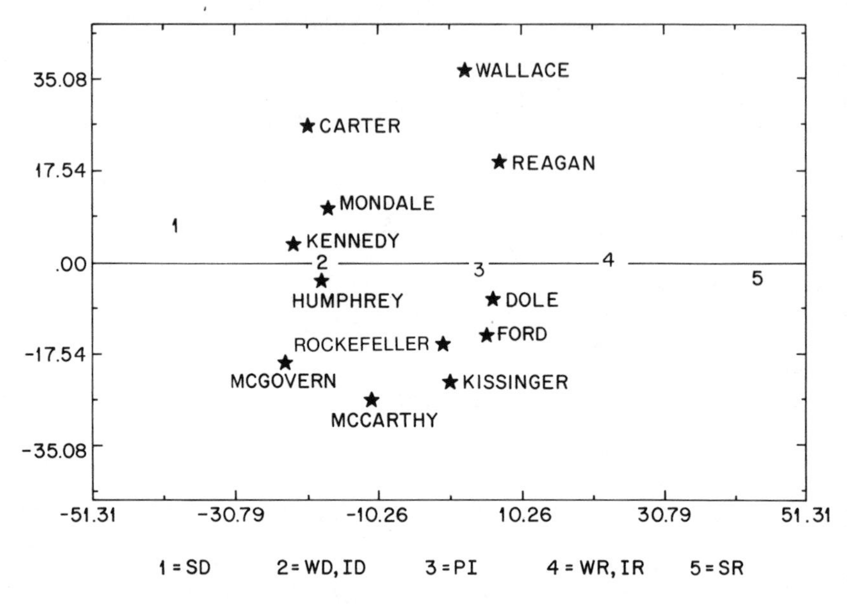

Figure 9.6. 1976 party ID.

placement of "liberals" and "conservatives" in Figure 9.2 suggests otherwise - a point we shall pursue in the next section.

Returning to our discussion of the horizontal axis, examine the party ID medians in Figure 9.6. Party ID is largely synonymous with left–right attitudes on economic issues. A line drawn through the end-point medians for party ID is slightly negative in slope, whereas the slope of such a line is slightly positive for the liberal–conservative scale. However, the two scales are largely the same. Party ID, liberal–conservative self-placement, and views on economic issues are all highly correlated with each other and the horizontal predictive axis.

The correspondence between party ID and ideology is somewhat surprising in light of results by other researchers (e.g., Levitin and Miller, 1979). Of course, by examining voter medians we are averaging out individual differences that would otherwise be apparent. Conservative Democrats and liberal Republicans obviously exist, but they are few enough in number that they do not significantly affect the location of the median for each category of party ID.

Figure 9.7 shows the four medians on the abortion issue. A line drawn through the end-point medians is parallel with the vertical axis. The medians for 2 and 3, however, are shifted to the right. An unusual feature of the abortion question is that all four scale positions are labeled

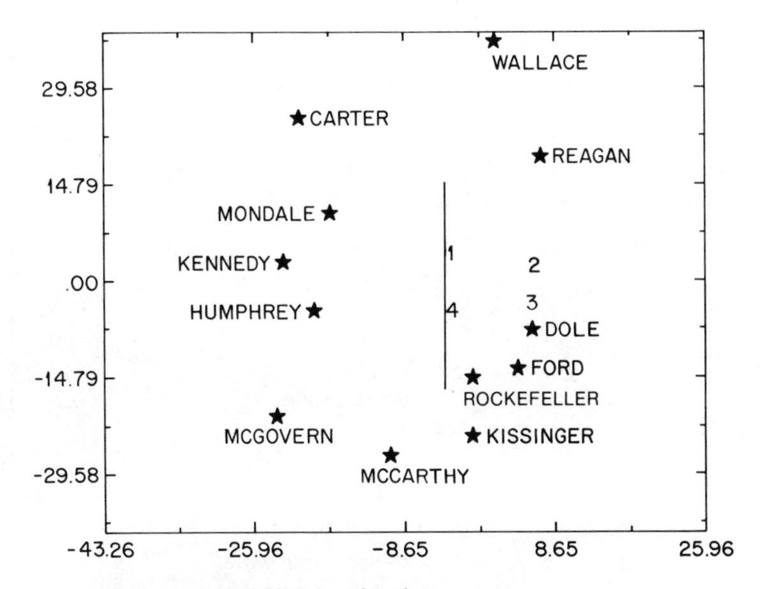

Figure 9.7. 1976 issues: abortion.

for the respondent, not just the end points (the question was asked in the same form in 1980). Positions 1 and 4 are listed in Table 9.6. Position 2 is labeled "abortion should be permitted only if the life and health of the woman is in danger." Position 3 is labeled "abortion should be permitted if, due to personal reasons, the woman would have difficulty in caring for the child." In light of the "never permitted" language of position 1 and the "never forbidden" language of position 4, it is not unreasonable to argue that, to some extent, abortion is a two-point scale (i.e., 1, 2 = 1 and 3, 4 = 2). Relatively few respondents chose position 1, and many more chose 2. The "under *no* circumstances" statement of position 1 may have persuaded many "pro-life" respondents to select position 2 even though they were in no sense moderates on this issue. Positions 3 and 4 are also somewhat similar in that it is difficult to interpret position 3 as anything but a "pro-choice" position.

If medians 1 and 2 are averaged to yield a single median and medians 3 and 4 are also averaged, the two resulting medians lie on a line parallel to the vertical axis. We are consequently convinced that the most controversial social issue of the last decade, abortion, does indeed tap the underlying meaning of the second predictive axis. In short, the vertical axis is a social left–right dimension. Abortion is the only "pure" social issue that we are able to identify for 1976. As we shall show shortly, busing, marijuana, and women's lib are all "mixed" issues (i.e., social and

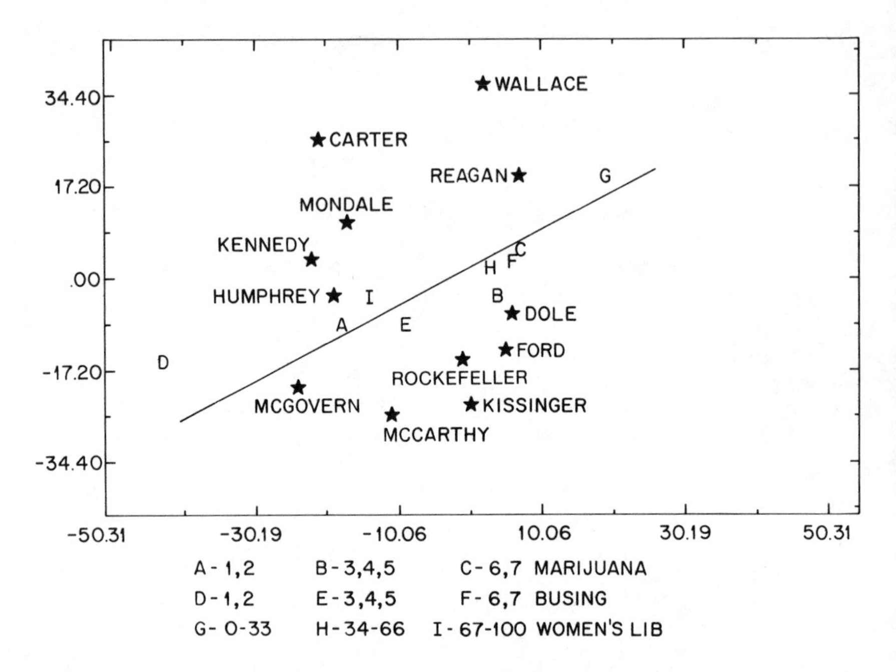

Figure 9.8. 1976 issues: marijuana, busing, women's lib.

economic). Abortion is also a pure social issue in 1980, as is "equal rights for women." Abortion, therefore, is the best measure available of the second predictive dimension in American national elections. Further support for our identification of the second axis will be given in our discussion of the locations of the political figures in the predictive space.

Figure 9.8 shows the medians for the "diagonal" issues. These issues are, to some extent, both social and economic in nature. That marijuana, busing, and women's lib are not strictly social issues may be somewhat of a surprise. However, an explanation for each issue does exist. The marijuana question, to some extent, taps attitudes toward crime, which is indeed a mixture of social and economic concerns (on a "rights of the accused" scale in the 1976 survey, the end-point medians lie on a diagonal line). The busing question also taps both economic and social concerns. Busing can be viewed as an economic tool as well as a social tool of government. Finally, women's lib can involve attitudes toward the workplace as well as the home. In short, it is not that surprising that these issues involve an economic element as well as a social element.

9.8 Interpretation of candidate and party locations in the predictive space for 1976

In this section we shall discuss the locations of the Democratic and Republican politicians in the predictive space of 1976. We shall also discuss the nature of the Democratic and Republican parties and the basis for competition within and between them.

We are now in a position to fully interpret Figures 9.1 and 9.2. All Democrats except Wallace are economic liberals (McCarthy is a strange case, because he was an independent candidate in 1976, supposedly challenging the two-party system). Democrats vary much more on the social dimension than they do on the economic dimension. Wallace, while perceived as an economic moderate, is socially quite conservative. This finding certainly fits what we know about Wallace. Starting in 1968, when he ran for president on the American Independent Party ticket, George Wallace has consistently been identified nationally with tough stands on social issues. As pointed out in Section 9.6, Wallace's location is biased to some extent by valence issues not incorporated in the candidate morality question. The low average thermometer score indicates that for many respondents, Wallace elicits a visceral reaction not captured by our valence dimension. Still, Wallace's location in the space relative to the other candidates (particularly Democrats) is quite reasonable.

Jimmy Carter is socially the most conservative of the remaining Democrats. There is some confusion, looking at Figures 9.1 and 9.2, as to whether or not Carter is socially more conservative than Reagan. Experience from extensive analysis of the data indicates that the intraparty order of the candidates on the social dimension is more robust than the order of all 12 candidates on the same axis.

However, there is good reason to believe that Carter is socially more conservative than Ford. Ford's own pollster (Robert Teeter), using a nonmetric scaling technique different from ours, reached the same conclusion (Kessel, 1980). This finding led Ford's strategists to conclude that Carter enjoyed an advantage on the social dimension. Our results do not allow us to verify this conclusion. In Figure 9.1, Carter is farther from the social mean of the voters than Ford, but in Figure 9.2 he is closer. In both figures, Carter is farther from the economic mean than Ford.

Candidate morality does relate to social issues, particularly in 1976. Defense of traditional values, such as the nuclear family and religion, is related both to social conservatism and to candidate morality. Jimmy Carter's brand of morality was heavily imbued with social conservatism.

This connection may account for some of the ambiguities that we encounter.

There is little doubt that Carter's position on the social dimension is correctly specified relative to the remaining Democrats. McGovern, the 1972 presidential candidate of "amnesty, acid, and abortion," clearly belongs at the liberal end of the social dimension. Humphrey's position is less clear, but relative to other Democrats he is a social moderate. Kennedy is perhaps more socially conservative than expected. On the other hand, whereas Kennedy's credentials as an economic liberal are beyond question, it is not obvious what his social position is. As a member of the Senate Judiciary Committee, he has sponsored tough anticrime legislation. As a Catholic, he is personally opposed to abortion. It is generally perceived that he believes in large, traditional-style families, where the mother stays at home to care for her children. It is therefore reasonable to find that Kennedy is not perceived as a social liberal.

Mondale's position on the social dimension may be somewhat biased by being Carter's running mate. All journalistic accounts of the 1976 election view Mondale as more liberal than Carter. Although it seems clear that economic liberalism is what is meant, our results indicate that Mondale's liberalism relative to Carter is social in origin.

This leads us into a discussion of what the real differences are among Democratic politicians. Our results indicate that conservative, moderate, and liberal Democrats are not divided on economic issues so much as on social issues. In fact, the same finding holds for Republicans. To choose among Democrats (or among Republicans) is to choose among social ideologies. To choose between a Democrat and a Republican may or may not involve a choice between social ideologies, but it must necessarily involve a choice between economic ideologies.

The Republicans, like the Democrats, show greater variance on the social dimension than on the economic dimension. Reagan and Rockefeller differ to a much greater extent on the social dimension than they do on the economic dimension.

Of course, Figure 9.3 shows that the electorate is more divided on the economic dimension than the social dimension. Thus, it is simultaneously true that the social dimension is more important as a way of distinguishing among a given party's politicians, but at the same time the economic dimension is more significant to the voters as a group.

The relative locations of Republican politicians are not surprising. Kissinger, a strange figure to include, because he is constitutionally ineligible to be president, is located near his mentor, Rockefeller. Rockefeller is Ford's vice-president, and Dole is Ford's 1976 running mate.

This partially explains their proximity to Ford. Rockefeller is economically the most liberal Republican in both Figures 9.1 and 9.2. This certainly fits Rockefeller's image as a big spender. What is interesting is that he is not located farther to the left on the economic dimension. This suggests that party labels are a very important determinant of candidate positions in the predictive space. Labeling a politician a "Democrat" or a "Republican" is for most voters equivalent to labeling him an "economic liberal" or "economic conservative." Figure 9.5 suggests that Rockefeller is seen as an economic moderate. But Rockefeller may have been the most liberal governor in terms of public spending in New York State's entire history. To label him an economic moderate attests to the power of party labels.

Reagan, of course, well deserves his location. Whereas Kennedy and Humphrey come closest to what most voters mean by a "liberal" politician, Reagan stands alone as the only true conservative. On both the social and economic dimensions, he is the one Republican who clearly deserves the conservative label. For reasons we have explained, Wallace's position in the predictive space may be somewhat distorted. On economic issues, his brand of populism, though not the radical style of the 1890s, still retains some of the anti-"Big Business" emphasis associated with this label. A candidate of common people, Wallace certainly cannot be called an economic royalist - a term that has been applied to Reagan.

Finally, note in Figure 9.2 that the groups "Democrats" and "Republicans" are socially moderate. This would seem to indicate that, on average, the real basis for distinguishing between the two parties is the economic dimension.

9.9 Conclusions about the 1976 election

Let us restate some of our main results. First, when voters describe themselves as liberals or conservatives, they are defining these terms on the basis of economic issues. On average, this is also the basis that voters use for distinguishing Democrats from Republicans.

However, the terms "liberal" and "conservative" as applied to individual politicians refer both to social issues and to economic issues. For example, a politician who is viewed as liberal is liberal on both the social and economic dimensions.

Carter, while economically more liberal than Ford, is socially more conservative. If distance from the voters on these two dimensions were the basis for the election outcome, Carter would have lost in 1976. His advantage on the valence dimension provided the margin of victory.

Finally, party labels play a very important role in voter estimation of candidates' predictive locations. Once a candidate adopts a party label, he is to some extent typecast by the voters on the economic dimension. A Republican who is economically liberal within his party is still likely to be perceived as more conservative than most Democrats on the same dimension. This suggests that the surest way by which a politician can change locations on the economic dimension is to switch parties.

We shall now move on to our analysis of the 1980 American presidential election to see if our conclusions about the 1976 election hold up over time.

9.10 The 1980 American presidential election

For reasons of space, we shall shorten our discussion of the 1980 election. We have already fully explained the methodology used for the analysis. All of the procedures described earlier were also employed in analyzing the 1980 election data. The same filter procedure was used for the respondents. The valence dimension, though based on a different survey question, was constructed the same way. A two-dimensional solution was specified for the factor analysis, and the sensitivity parameter r was set equal to 2.

The valence dimension posed major difficulties for the 1980 analysis. Unlike the 1976 survey, the 1980 questions about candidate personal qualities focused only on the three major presidential candidates (Carter, Reagan, and Anderson). This problem was somewhat alleviated by a separate panel study conducted by CPS. The Major Panel File of 1980 is a year-long study in which a random sample of eligible voters is reinterviewed three times to establish a four-wave study (P-1, January to February; P-2, June to July; P-3, September to October; P-4, November). The same candidate quality questions asked in the traditional preelection/postelection study were also asked in the P-1, P-2, and P-3 waves of the Major Panel File. In P-1, the voters were asked about the personal qualities of Carter, Reagan, Kennedy, Connally, Baker, and Bush. In P-2, they were asked about the qualities of Carter, Reagan, Kennedy, Anderson, and Bush. In P-3, they were asked about the qualities of Reagan, Anderson, Carter, and Kennedy.

Of the nine candidate qualities concerning which questions were asked, only two had anything to do with the major valence issues of the 1980 presidential campaign. One asked, "How well does 'weak' describe [ ] if he were president?" The other asked, "How well would 'He would provide strong leadership' describe [ ] if he were president?" Preliminary analysis showed that it made very little difference to the final results which question was used. The "strong leadership" question was consequently chosen. The four possible responses (extremely well, quite well, not too well, not well at all) were coded 3, 2, 1, and 0. A valence position was then computed for each candidate using the method described in Section 9.4.

Across all waves of the Major Panel File, data on the leadership question exist for seven candidates. A first approach to constructing valence positions was to use the latest data for each of the seven candidates (i.e., Carter P-3, Reagan P-3, Kennedy P-3, Anderson P-3, Connally P-1, Baker P-1, Bush P-2). These data were then weighted to eliminate differences in the sample sizes of different waves, and valence positions were constructed according to the standard procedure.

The statistical fit of the candidate and voter maps derived with these valence positions was poor. The R^2 for the second regression was around .45 and was relatively insensitive to additions or deletions from the set of candidates and groups (i.e., Republicans, Democrats, Conservatives, Liberals, Parties, and Independents).

The second approach to constructing valence dimension positions for the candidates was to rely simply on the four candidate scores derived from the P-3 wave (i.e., Carter, Kennedy, Reagan, and Anderson). Each of the remaining candidates scaled was then given the *average* of these four scores. Scaling of the P-3 data was statistically quite successful using this procedure for 10 candidates, with 6 candidates being given an average valence score (second $R^2 = .921$, $N = 209$). We were thus encouraged to use the same valence positions in scaling the much larger data set in the traditional pre–post study.

9.11 Information about the 1980 sample

The traditional pre–post 1980 survey includes 1,614 unweighted respondents in the preelection wave and 1,408 in the postelection wave. The two maps we present are based on 827 and 621 cases. A demographic comparison between the full sample and larger subsample is presented in Table 9.7.

The thermometer scores on the candidates were collected in the preelection wave. Table 9.8 lists the mean candidate thermometer scores, the variances of the t scores, and the valence positions for the 11 candidates who were scaled. Of the candidates scaled for 1976, Carter was, on average, the best-liked Democrat and Ford the best-liked Republican among the respondents in our subsample. For our 1980 candidates, this is not true. Mondale is, on average, better liked than Carter; Ford and Bush are both, on average, better liked than Reagan. Kennedy takes a big drop in 1980 compared with his average t score in 1976, supporting the

Table 9.7. *1980 income distribution and education level for subsample (N=827) and population sample (N=1,614)*

	Percentage of population sample in each group	Percentage of subsample in each group
Income	(*N*=1,455)	(*N*=760)
Less than $1,999	17.9	16.7
$2,000–3,999	11.3	7.8
$4,000–5,999	9.8	7.4
$6,000–7,999	8.5	8.9
$8,000–9,999	8.4	8.6
$10,000–11,999	6.8	7.1
$12,000–14,999	8.9	8.9
$15,000–19,999	10.5	11.4
$20,000–24,999	8.3	10.0
$25,000 or more	9.6	13.2
Education	(*N*=1,609)	(*N*=825)
8 grades or less	12.0	4.6
9–12 grades	51.2	46.3
Some college or all	28.2	36.6
More than 4 years of college	8.6	12.5

Table 9.8. *Means and variances of candidate thermometer scores for 1980 and candidate positions on valence dimension of presidential leadership (N=621)*

Candidate	Mean	Variance	Valence position
Carter	53.76	739.90	2.57
Reagan	56.40	652.15	.00
Kennedy	44.89	809.85	.90
Ford	59.82	540.32	1.38[a]
Brown	44.48	374.67	1.38[a]
Mondale	54.64	405.06	1.38[a]
Bush	56.63	311.67	1.38[a]
Anderson	53.43	400.22	2.05
Baker	51.69	269.26	1.38[a]
Connally	41.48	460.03	1.38[a]
McGovern	44.85	438.41	1.38[a]

[a] Average of Carter, Reagan, Kennedy, and Anderson positions.

Table 9.9. *Means and variances of group thermometer scores for 1976 (*N=*798) and 1980 (*N=*621)*

	1976		1980	
	Mean	Variance	Mean	Variance
Democrats	60.92	287.22	59.17	485.35
Republicans	58.07	294.25	57.79	447.85
Liberals	51.63	369.48	51.56	451.87
Conservatives	59.38	277.61	63.10	347.68

conclusion that he is a more popular presidential candidate when he is not running. Although the 1976 and 1980 subsamples are not strictly comparable, the 10-degree difference between Kennedy's two average scores is hardly a chance result. Even Carter shows a smaller drop from his average 1976 score to his average 1980 score.

The average t scores for "Republicans" and "Liberals" show very little change between 1976 and 1980. However, "Democrats" shows a slight decline, and "Conservatives" a noticeable increase. Table 9.9 presents these results. The high average t score for "Conservatives" is reflected in their closer location to the mean voter in 1980 as compared with 1976.

9.12 The 1980 results

Figures 9.9 and 9.10 are the two estimated maps for 1980, with related statistics in Table 9.10. For Figure 9.9, 57.42% of the variance in the co-variance matrix for the two-dimensional solution was explained by the first (46.34%) and second (11.08%) eigenvalues. The third eigenvalue explained 8.96% of the variance. This compares with 54.74%, 11.69%, and 7.38% of the variance for the first three eigenvalues of the covari-ance matrix for the two-dimensional solution in 1976 (Figure 9.1). We thus have our first indication that our 1976 solution better fits the data than our 1980 solution.

The second confirmation that the 1980 results are less reliable than the 1976 results comes from the R^2's reported in Table 9.10. Both are less than .90.

There is little we can do to improve the quality of these results. Any procedure for assigning valence positions to candidates without valence data is ad hoc. Many such procedures were tried, and none worked better than the one we used. As stated earlier, valence data in the pre–post

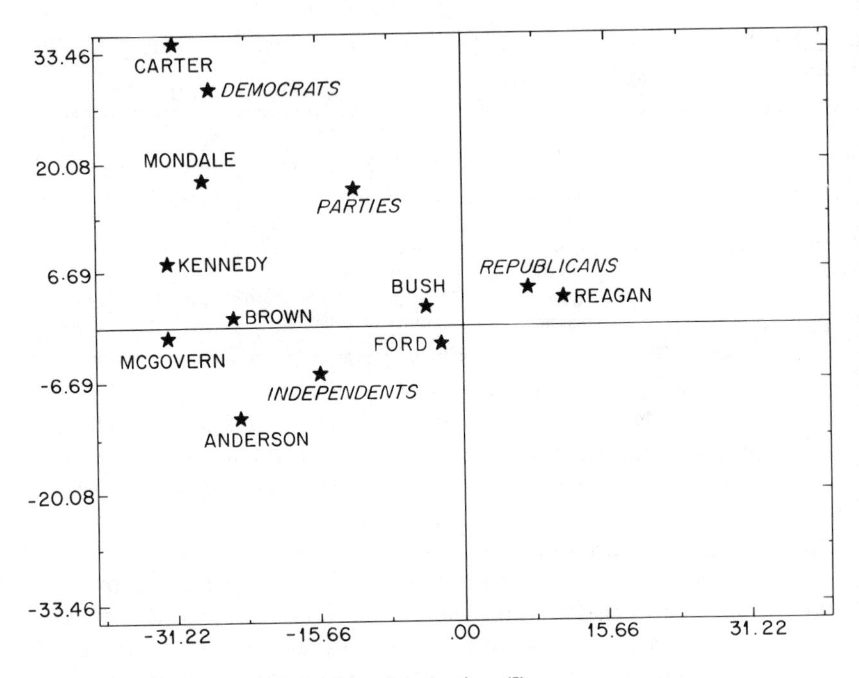

Figure 9.9. 1980 presidential election (I).

study exist only for Carter, Anderson, and Reagan. Our 1980 results, therefore, should be interpreted more cautiously than our 1976 results.

Figures 9.9 and 9.10 are quite similar (and are also quite like the map obtained from scaling the P-3 data). As in 1976, all Republicans are on the right side of the space, and all Democrats are on the left side. Further, within each party, the ordering of candidates on the two axes is almost the same in 1980 as in 1976. Among the four Democrats and two Republicans scaled in both years, there are no within-party differences in the ordering of the candidates on the vertical axis. On the horizontal axis, it appears that Carter may have moved slightly to the left between 1976 and 1980, but Figure 9.2 (1976) and Figure 9.9 (1980) have the Democratic candidates in the same order. These results support our argument in Chapter 4 that candidate positions in the predictive space are not easily altered.

As in 1976, the two groups "Liberals" and "Conservatives" are, respectively, on the Democratic and Republican sides of the predictive space. Not surprisingly, there is a large degree of continuity in comparing the 1976 and 1980 predictive maps. As in 1976, the standard

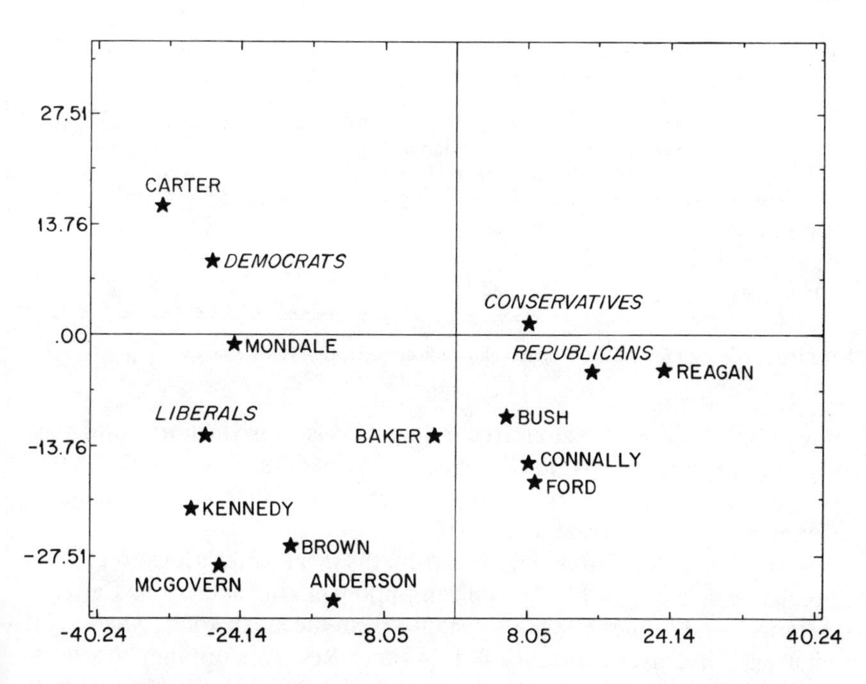

Figure 9.10. 1980 presidential election (II).

Table 9.10. *Related statistics for Figures 9.9 and 9.10*

	Figure 9.9 (N=827)	Figure 9.10 (N=621)
R^2 for second regression	.812	.725
Standard deviation on first dimension	34.596	29.794
Standard deviation on second dimension	24.868	20.111
Valence dimension weight	20.76[a]	279.96

[a] The size of the difference between the two valence weights is probably caused by errors in the specification of the valence positions.

Table 9.11. *Individual-level vote predictions for 1980 presidential election based on Figure 9.10*

	Preelection reported vote (%)	Postelection reported vote (%)
Policy model (3)	85.54[a]	92.00
Policy and nonpolicy model (4)	82.17	87.78

[a] Entry is percentage of Carter or Reagan choices correctly predicted.

deviation of voter most preferred points is greater on the horizontal axis than on the vertical axis. In this sense, the horizontal axis is more significant to voters than the vertical axis. However, the difference in standard deviations is not as great as in 1976.

Also as in 1976, Carter is farther from the mean voter's location in the predictive space than his Republican opponent. In Figure 9.9, Carter's distance is 4.17 times Reagan's distance from the mean voter, whereas in Figure 9.10, Carter's distance is 1.54 times Reagan's distance. Carter's absolute distance from the mean is roughly the same in both maps, but Reagan is about twice as far away in Figure 9.10 as compared with Figure 9.9.

In contrast to 1976, however, Carter's disadvantage in the predictive space is only made worse by his position on the valence dimension. This double disadvantage makes the policy model a better predictor of individual and aggregate-level voting behavior than the combined policy and nonpolicy model. Based on Figure 9.10, 55.72% of all 621 ideal points are closer to Reagan than to Carter on a pure policy basis. On the basis of the combined policy and nonpolicy model, Reagan receives 58.28% of the vote to 41.72% for Carter. Because Reagan actually received 55.29% of the major party vote, this is an interesting result.

On an individual basis, the policy model also performs better than the policy and nonpolicy model. In the preelection reported vote, of those naming Carter or Reagan, 47.20% named Carter and 52.80% named Reagan. In the postelection reported vote, the split was 40.75% for Carter and 59.25% for Reagan. Table 9.11 reports the individual prediction rates for both models, applied to the preelection and postelection reports.

It is plain that the policy model predicts somewhat better than the policy and nonpolicy model. Because of the problems we have discussed

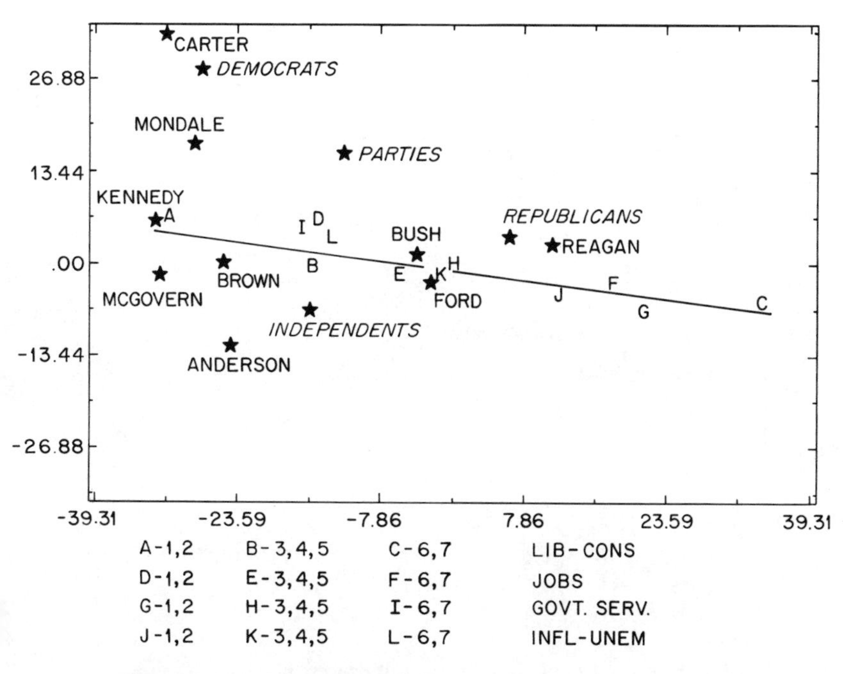

Figure 9.11. 1980 issues: liberal–conservative, jobs, government services, inflation–unemployment.

in connection with the valence dimension, we are reluctant to conclude that the policy model is the superior of the two models for predicting the 1980 vote. However, we are certainly unable to preclude this possibility.

9.13 Identification of the predictive dimensions for 1980

The meanings of the two predictive dimensions in 1980 are the same as in 1976. The horizontal axis represents economic issues, party identification, and self-placement on the liberal–conservative scale; the vertical axis represents social issues. Figures 9.11, 9.12, and 9.13 illustrate the issues that line up with the horizontal axis. Table 9.12 lists the 11 scales of Figures 9.11–9.14, with the number of cases and range of scores represented by each point in the figures. Table 9.13 identifies the end points for all scales not also used in the 1976 analysis. As Figures 9.11 and 9.12 indicate, the same issues that line up along the horizontal axis in 1976 (i.e., liberal–conservative, aid to minorities, and jobs) line up the same way in 1980. In addition, economic issues such as inflation–unemployment, government services, and tax cut also line up along the horizontal

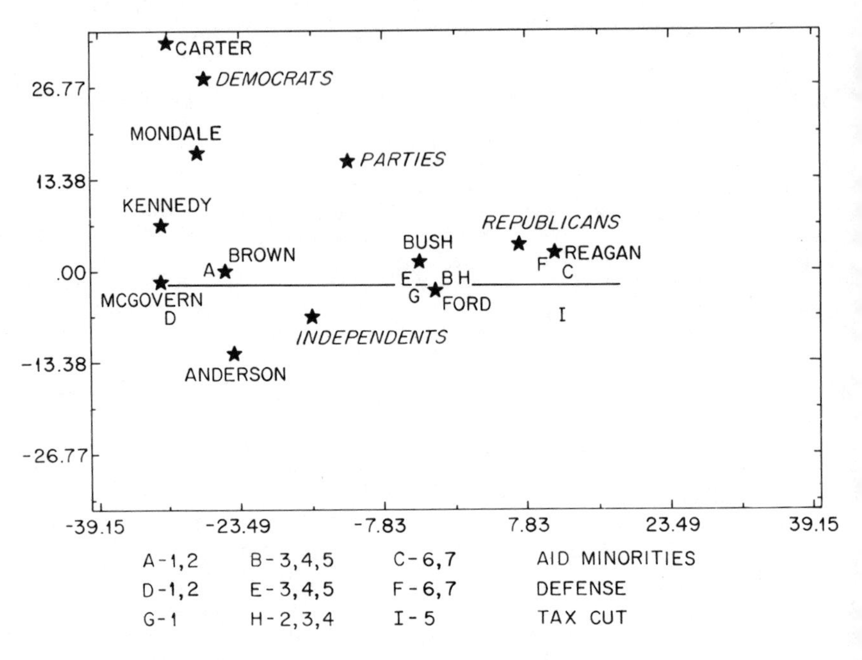

Figure 9.12. 1980 issues: aid to minorities, defense, tax cut.

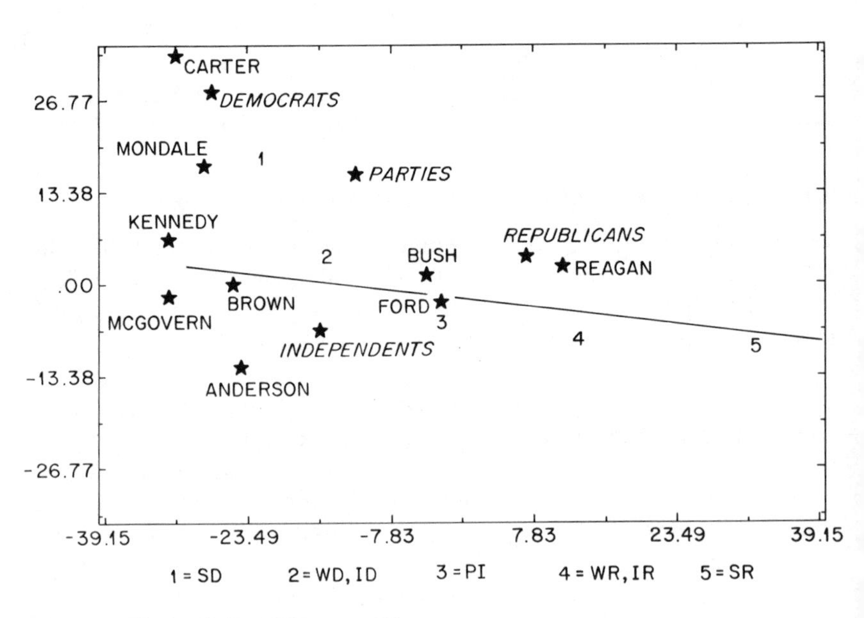

Figure 9.13. 1980 party ID.

Table 9.12. *Number of respondents in each range of scores (1980)*

Range:	1	2	3	4	5
Party ID	134	284	94	228	82
	1–2		3–5		6–7
Liberal–conservative	60		400		134
Guaranteed jobs	93		336		220
Government services	149		376		208
Inflation–unemployment	76		407		77
Aid to minorities	57		435		184
Defense	34		381		343
	1		2–4		5
Tax cut	121		371		70
	1–2		3–5		6–7
Equal women's rights	403		244		65
	1	2		3	4
Abortion (preelection)	71	243		161	330
Abortion (postelection)	46	314		132	230

axis (these last three issue scales were not included in the 1976 survey). Interestingly, defense is also an economic issue.

Figure 9.13 represents party identification. The party ID scale turns up at the point representing strong Democrats (1), but this is probably because of Carter's location in the upper left-hand corner of the map. Given the likely exaggeration of Carter's position on the vertical axis in Figure 9.13, we attach no special significance to the median location of strong Democrats on the vertical axis as compared with the vertical location of the other party group medians.

Table 9.13. *End-point labels (1980)*

	1	7
Government services	Government provide many fewer services; reduce spending a lot	Government continue to provide services; no spending reductions
Inflation–unemployment	Reduce inflation even if unemployment goes up a lot	Reduce unemployment even if inflation goes up a lot
Defense	Greatly decrease defense spending	Greatly increase defense spending
Equal women's rights	Equal role	Women's place in home
	1	5
Tax cut	Should not be cut	Should be cut by more than 30%

[a] For issues also used in the 1976 analysis, see Table 9.6.

Thus, we conclude that, as in 1976, voter self-placement on the liberal–conservative scale is substantially the same as party identification. On average, voters who identify themselves as strong Democrats also identify themselves as liberals, whereas strong Republicans identify themselves as conservatives. Further, these two scales are based on economic issues. This is exactly what we found in 1976.

Figure 9.14 identifies the vertical axis. As in 1976, the abortion issue (asked in both the preelection and postelection waves in 1980) is the best single identifier of the vertical axis. In addition, the issue of equal rights for women also lines up nearly parallel to the vertical axis. Notice that the 1980 abortion (preelection) scale is not unlike the 1976 abortion scale in that at least the second position (abortion permitted only if life and health of woman in danger) differs from the first position mainly along the horizontal axis. For reasons explained earlier, we believe that this is largely an artifact of question wording.

Interestingly, the diagonal issues of 1976 are no longer diagonal in 1980. The marijuana question was not included in the 1980 survey, but the women's lib thermometer question and the seven-point busing scale were included in both years. Women's lib and busing are horizontal issues in 1980. Both line up parallel to the horizontal axis (busing is slightly inclined in a NW-to-SE direction, but less so than any of the issues in Figure 9.11).

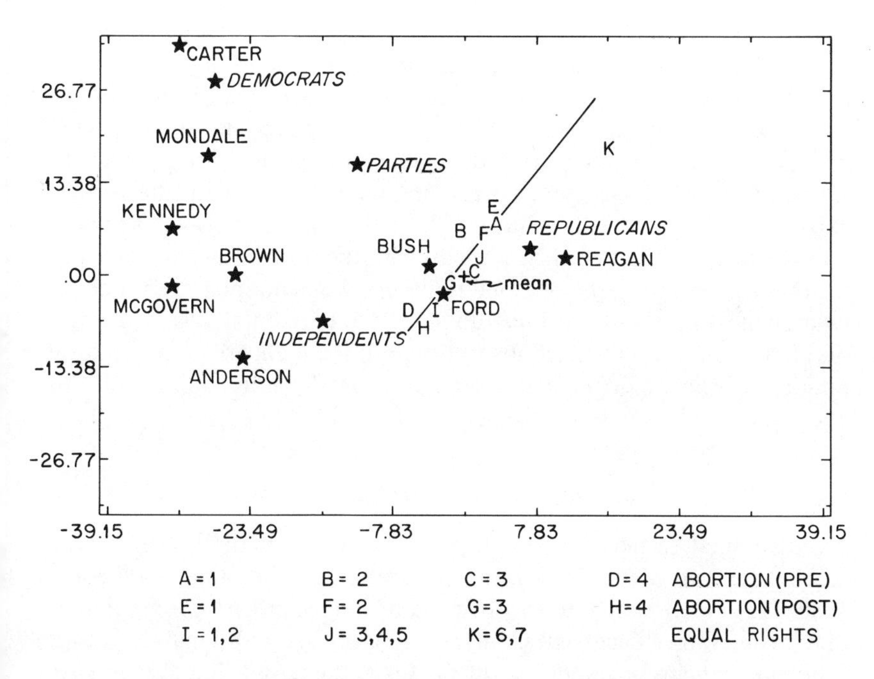

Figure 9.14. 1980 issues: abortion, equal women's rights.

This result is surprising. In 1976, women's lib and busing clearly contained both a social component and an economic component. In 1980, the social element has largely disappeared. We can only speculate as to why this happened. Busing as a tool to integrate schools was immensely unpopular in both years, with a majority of the whole sample selecting the most extreme antibusing position in both 1976 and 1980. The reason why busing is an economic issue in 1980 cannot be due to a shift in opinion on the seven-point scale, because almost none occurred.

That women's lib is an economic issue is particularly surprising in view of the fact that women's rights is a social issue in the same year. At the very least, this result suggests that these are two very different issues.

There is one explanation we can offer for the busing and women's lib results. The horizontal axis is described by economic issues, but these issues are, at the same time, mainstream issues in American politics. Thus, to some extent, our two predictive dimensions may be a horizontal dimension representing mainstream issues and a vertical dimension representing issues that have not yet been absorbed into the mainstream. Conventional versus unconventional issues may be another way to characterize this dichotomy.

This interpretation does not contradict the existence of a social dimension and an economic dimension. Economic issues are largely conventional from the standpoint of the last major party realignment of the 1930s, whereas social issues are of a much more recent vintage. What appears to be happening is that social issues are, at first, relegated to the status of "new" issues and, correspondingly, line up with the vertical axis. After the issue has been around for some time, it becomes absorbed into the mainstream and then lines up with the horizontal axis. We may see that by 1984 the issue of equal rights for women, apparently a newer issue than women's lib, will line up along the horizontal axis. The abortion issue continues to resist absorption into the mainstream of electoral politics. Given the difficulties most politicians have in coping with this issue, this result is not surprising.

9.14 Predictive locations of the candidates in 1980

As mentioned earlier, the within-party orderings of the candidates on each of the two predictive dimensions are largely the same in 1976 and 1980. However, relative to the location of the mean voter, some important changes have occurred. Comparing Figure 9.2 with Figure 9.10, the following conclusions appear evident. First, the term "liberals" is associated with economic and social liberalism in both years. The term "conservatives," however, appears to have moved closer to a middle-of-the-road position on the social dimension. It may be wondered how reliable the estimate of the mean voter's location is in Figure 9.10. Reference to Figure 9.14 suggests that this estimate is not far off. The mean voter's position on the vertical axis in Figure 9.14 places him near the middle of the abortion and women's rights scales. Because Figure 9.14 is based on Figure 9.9 rather than Figure 9.10, we conclude that the term "conservatives" is still associated with a right-of-center position on the social dimension in 1980, but not nearly as extreme a position as in 1976.

This conclusion is supported by the high average thermometer score given to "conservatives" in 1980 (see Table 9.9). It appears not only that conservatives are better liked in 1980 as compared with 1976 but also that the reason for this is a growing tendency to associate conservatives with middle-of-the-road views on social issues.

Perhaps the biggest change in 1980 is in Reagan's position on the social dimension. Although still more conservative socially and economically than any other Republican, Reagan is much closer to the social mean of the electorate than in 1976. We attribute most of this shift to the same cause identified for the shift of the term "conservatives." Referring to Figure 9.14, we see that the medians for the more extreme social views (i.e., A, E, and K) are all above Reagan's position. In short, there seems to be a belief that Reagan is not an extremist on social issues, relative to the voters. The raw data support this view. On the abortion (preelection) scale, for example, the average position given Reagan by the voters is 2.1, as compared with 2.8 for the voters themselves.

However, problems arise in trying to explain why Carter and Mondale are socially more conservative than Reagan. The data support the view that, as in 1976, Carter is socially the most conservative Democrat, with Mondale's position on the social dimension biased by being Carter's running mate (and having served almost four years as his vice-president). However, Carter is simply too far away from the social mean for this to be the sole explanation of his location. We hypothesize that unspecified valence issues have upwardly biased his location on the social dimension.

The "meanness" issue was very important in the 1980 presidential campaign, with Carter being accused of unfairly attacking Reagan by suggesting that he was, in Reagan's words, a combination of "Scrooge and the Mad Bomber." On the other hand, Reagan used this issue to great advantage, suggesting that he was too nice a person to be guilty of any of these charges. Obviously, our leadership dimension misses a lot of this issue. Thus, as in 1976 for the case of Wallace, we find a certain degree of error in the vertical axis locations because of unspecified valence issues. It may well be that Reagan's location on the social dimension is closer to the mean voter than would be the case if the "meanness" issue were incorporated in the valence dimension.

9.15 Conclusions about the 1980 presidential election

The similarities between the 1976 and 1980 presidential elections are striking. In both years, an economic predictive dimension and a social predictive dimension underlie voter attitudes toward the candidates. In both years, the major difference between Republicans and Democrats exists on the economic dimension rather than the social dimension. This holds true for candidates and voters alike. The terms "liberal" and "conservative," when applied to voters, refer to the economic definitions of these terms. When applied to candidates, liberalism and conservatism also take on a social meaning. The social definition of conservatism appears to have "softened" somewhat in relation to the 1976 election, but it remains true that as candidate labels, the two ideologies are distinct in both economic and social terms.

In addition, the economic typecasting discussed in relation to the 1976 election remains in force in 1980. Only Anderson, a renegade Republican, is close to being perceived as an economic liberal. Still, even in

Figure 9.9, he is economically to the right of every Democrat (though just barely to the right of Brown). For a candidate advocating a tax of 50 cents per gallon on gasoline, this is significant. As with Rockefeller in 1976, there is a limit to how liberal (economically) a Republican can be perceived as being.

Finally, Carter had a twofold disadvantage in 1980 with respect to Reagan. Carter was farther from the mean voter than Reagan. However, in contrast to 1976, Carter's disadvantage in the predictive space was only made worse by his poor evaluation on the valence dimension. Interestingly, a mock election between Carter and Reagan in 1976, using the policy and nonpolicy model to predict choice for all voters, indicates that Reagan would have lost if he had run against Carter four years earlier. Reagan appears fortunate not to have won the nomination that year.

Finally, we wish to stress the historical continuity of our results. Earlier work on the 1968 and 1972 presidential elections, using the same methodology employed in this chapter, suggests that our results are equally descriptive of these earlier elections. This means that at least since 1968, the predictive basis of American presidential elections has been substantially unchanged. The "social issue" is commonly identified as making its first appearance in the 1968 presidential election. We speculate that between 1932 and 1968, American presidential elections were based largely on the economic left–right dimension, with foreign policy constituting a second predictive dimension from time to time. This foreign policy dimension would appear to be an internationalist–isolationist scale during the earlier part of this period, being replaced later on by a toughness-toward-the-Soviets scale.

9.16 Final conclusions

This chapter has demonstrated that the general model of elections developed in Chapters 4 and 5 has strong empirical support. Voters do view candidates as occupying positions in an underlying predictive space. Further, for at least the last two presidential elections (and probably the last four), this predictive space has been defined by an economic left–right dimension and a social left–right dimension. Candidate locations do not vary a great deal from one election to the next, suggesting that the dynamics of presidential campaigns consist of efforts to alter the connections that voters make between predictive locations and candidate issue positions.

It is important to keep in mind that what we are deriving are *voter* maps of political figures. Thus, to find that Republican politicians are perceived as uniformly more conservative on the economic dimension than Democratic politicians is to learn something about how voters view politicians of the two major American political parties. Whereas it may be true that on an "objective" basis, Nelson Rockefeller is more liberal economically than his positions in Figures 9.1 and 9.2 suggest, what matters in elections is what the voters perceive to be true. This point is consistent with our emphasis throughout the book that voter perceptions are the key to understanding election outcomes.

We have not reported empirical results on how voters link predictive locations with candidate issue positions. Appendix 9.2 describes the methodology appropriate for measuring these linkages. This is obviously an important topic for future research.

We have had reasonable success at predicting reported voting decisions on the basis of the combined policy and nonpolicy model developed in Chapter 5. In 1976, the combined model predicts reported voting behavior better than the pure policy model. The pure policy model performs somewhat better than the combined model in 1980. However, the combined model is a good predictor in both years.

Finally, we have seen that in 1976, the nonpolicy values of the major-party candidates played a crucial role in the election outcome. These results lead us to conclude that the election theory developed in this book offers significant insights into the American electoral process.

This chapter concludes the theoretical and empirical development in the book. In the final chapter we shall offer some concluding observations about the spatial theory of voting.

Appendix 9.1: A methodology for statistical analysis of thermometer scores

In this appendix we explain the statistical model underlying the empirical results reported in Chapter 9. In order to increase reader comprehension, we limit ourselves to the case of two predictive dimensions.

Assumption 1: There are two predictive dimensions. Let $\boldsymbol{\pi}_j = (\pi_{j1}, \pi_{j2})'$ denote the coordinates of the jth politician on these policy-oriented dimensions. Let $\mathbf{z}_m = (z_{m1}, z_{m2})'$ denote the coordinates of the mth respondent on these same two dimensions.

Assumption 2: There is one valence dimension that candidates can be mapped on using other data or subjective judgments by the investigator. This dimension may represent a single nonpolicy issue, such as candidate ability, or it may represent a common factor underlying a set of nonpolicy issues. Let V_j denote politician j's position on this valence dimension ($j=1,\ldots,p$).

Assumption 3: Let T_{jm} denote the mth respondent's thermometer score for candidate j. This score depends on both policy and nonpolicy factors. Assume that $T_{jm}=c_{jm}-P_{jm}$, where the term P_{jm} depends on π_{j1}, π_{j2}, z_{m1}, z_{m2}, and V_j, and c_{jm} depends only on the nonsystematic factors that are uncorrelated with T_{jm} and P_{jm}. In other words, c_{jm} is independent of the positions of politician j and respondent m. Both P_{jm} and c_{jm} are *unobservable,* but the variance of the c_{jm} in the voter population is estimable.

Assumption 4: Let $r>0$ denote a parameter that determines the sensitivity of thermometer rankings to differences in P_{jm}. The method handles $r=1$, 2, or 4. Assume that

$$P_{jm}=[(\pi_{j1}-z_{m1})^2+(\pi_{j2}-z_{m2})^2+aV_j]^{1/r} \tag{A9.1}$$

The procedures for $r=2$ (the value used for the empirical results of Chapter 9) and $r=4$ build on those for $r=1$, which is the one that is easiest to explain. For $r=1$,

$$\begin{aligned} T_{jm} &= c_{jm}-\|\boldsymbol{\pi}_j-\mathbf{z}_m\|^2-aV_j \\ &= c_{jm}-\boldsymbol{\pi}_j'\boldsymbol{\pi}_j+2\boldsymbol{\pi}_j'\mathbf{z}_m-\mathbf{z}_m'\mathbf{z}_m-aV_j \end{aligned} \tag{A9.2}$$

where $\mathbf{z}_m=(z_{m1},z_{m2})'$.

Assumption 5: Assume that c_{jm} is uncorrelated with c_{km} for $j\neq k$ in the population from which the sample is drawn. Assume also that c_{jm} is uncorrelated with z_{m1} and z_{m2}. Denote the variance of c_{jm} by ψ_j^2.

Assumption 6: The variance-covariance matrix of $\mathbf{z}_m$ is diagonal. Denote this matrix by

$$\Sigma=\begin{bmatrix} \sigma_1^2 & 0 \\ 0 & \sigma_2^2 \end{bmatrix}$$

Let $\boldsymbol{\mu}_z$ denote the expected value of $\mathbf{z}_m$.

Step 1: Select one politician whose scores will be subtracted from the others' scores in order to make the differences conform to a linear model in $\mathbf{z}_m$. The choice of which politician is to be used is arbitrary.

A zero subscript will now be used to designate the politician whose scores are subtracted from the others. Because the assignment of the origin is arbitrary, set the origin of the predictive space at $\boldsymbol{\pi}_0$ so that

$\boldsymbol{\pi}_0 = \mathbf{0}$ in expression (A9.2). The empirical results in this chapter are based on setting the origin at the mean $\mathbf{z}_i$. The choice of where to set the origin is a decision for the investigator to make. In the current context, setting $\boldsymbol{\pi}_0 = \mathbf{0}$ simplifies the algebra, in which case

$$T_{jm} - T_{0m} = c_{jm} - c_{0m} - \boldsymbol{\pi}_j' \boldsymbol{\pi}_j - a(V_j - V_0) + 2\boldsymbol{\pi}_j' \mathbf{z}_m \tag{A9.3}$$

Step 2: The sample mean score for the jth politician is $\bar{T}_j = N^{-1} \sum_{m=1}^{N} T_{jm}$. Subtract $\bar{T}_j - \bar{T}_0$ from $T_{jm} - T_{0m}$ for each $j = 1, \ldots, p$ and $m = 1, \ldots, N$. Let

$$Y_{jm} = T_{jm} - T_{0m} - (\bar{T}_j - \bar{T}_0) \tag{A9.4}$$

Step 3: Compute the sample variance-covariance matrix of the Y_{jm}, averaging over the respondents. This $p \times p$ matrix converges in probability to the population variance-covariance matrix (as $N \to \infty$)

$$\Sigma_y = 4\pi' \Sigma \pi + \psi_0^2 \mathbf{1}\mathbf{1}' + \Psi \tag{A9.5}$$

where $\pi = (\boldsymbol{\pi}_1, \ldots, \boldsymbol{\pi}_p)$ is a $2 \times p$ matrix of candidate positions, $\mathbf{1}$ is a p-dimensional column vector of *ones*, and

$$\Psi = \begin{bmatrix} \psi_1^2 & & 0 \\ & \ddots & \\ 0 & & \psi_p^2 \end{bmatrix} \tag{A9.6}$$

is a diagonal matrix of variances of the c_{jm}.

Step 4: The covariance matrix (A9.5) can be written as $\Lambda C \Lambda' + \Psi$, where Λ is the $p \times 3$ matrix $(2\pi', \mathbf{1})$, and C is the 3×3 diagonal matrix

$$C = \begin{bmatrix} \sigma_1^2 & & 0 \\ & \sigma_2^2 & \\ 0 & & \psi_0^2 \end{bmatrix} \tag{A9.7}$$

Because the symmetric square-root matrix of $\Lambda C \Lambda'$ is $\Lambda C^{1/2}$, a *factor analysis* of the sample variance-covariance matrix of the Y_{jm} yields an *estimate* of the matrix $\Lambda C^{1/2} \Gamma$, where Γ is an unknown orthogonal rotation matrix. The factor analysis subroutine in the program yields a maximum-likelihood estimate of $\Lambda C^{1/2} \Gamma$. The variances ψ_j^2 are also estimated. The next sequence of steps in the procedure estimates the parameters of Γ, C, and $\boldsymbol{\mu}_z$. We shall not number the remaining steps.

A brief note is in order at this point concerning the indentifiability of Γ. Multiplying any row or column of Γ by -1 leaves it orthogonal. Because of this, the candidate map has certain ambiguities. These ambiguities consist of 90° rotations and reflections across either axis.

To estimate Γ, note that it can be written as the product of three orthogonal matrices as follows: $\Gamma = \Gamma_3 \Gamma_2 \Gamma_1$, where

$$\Gamma_1 = \begin{bmatrix} 1 & 0 & 0 \\ 0 & \cos\delta_1 & -\sin\delta_1 \\ 0 & \sin\delta_1 & \cos\delta_1 \end{bmatrix} \tag{A9.8}$$

$$\Gamma_2 = \begin{bmatrix} \cos\delta_2 & 0 & -\sin\delta_2 \\ 0 & 1 & 0 \\ \sin\delta_2 & 0 & \cos\delta_2 \end{bmatrix} \tag{A9.9}$$

$$\Gamma_3 = \begin{bmatrix} \cos\delta_3 & -\sin\delta_3 & 0 \\ \sin\delta_3 & \cos\delta_3 & 0 \\ 0 & 0 & 1 \end{bmatrix} \tag{A9.10}$$

The first ordinary-least-squares fit estimates Γ_1 and Γ_2 using the fact that the third column of Λ is the vector **1**. This fit also yields an estimate of ψ_0^2, the variance of c_{0m} in the population.

The second least-squares fit estimates $\Gamma_3, \sigma_1^2, \sigma_2^2$, and the valence weight a, using $\{\bar{T}_j - \bar{T}_0\}$ as the values of the dependent variable.

Multiplying $\Lambda C^{1/2}$ on the right by Γ_3 leaves the third column unchanged; that is, $\Lambda C^{1/2}\Gamma_3$ is $\psi_0 \mathbf{1}$, the third column of $\Gamma C^{1/2}$. Because $\Gamma = \Gamma_3 \Gamma_2 \Gamma_1$, multiplying our estimate of $\Lambda C^{1/2}\Gamma$ on the *right* by $\Gamma_1' \Gamma_2' = (\Gamma_2 \Gamma_1)^{-1}$ yields a matrix whose third column is an estimate[1] of $\psi_0 \mathbf{1}$. Let $M = (m_{jk}) = \Lambda C^{1/2}\Gamma$. Then we have the linear model

$$1 = \beta_1 m_{j1} + \beta_2 m_{j2} + \beta_3 m_{j3} \tag{A9.11}$$

for $j = 1, \ldots, p$, where

$$\beta_1 = (\sin\delta_2)/\psi_0$$

$$\beta_2 = (\sin\delta_1 \cos\delta_2)/\psi_0$$

and

$$\beta_3 = (\cos\delta_1 \cos\delta_2)/\psi_0 \tag{A9.12}$$

because

$$\Gamma_1'\Gamma_2' = \begin{bmatrix} \cos\delta_2 & 0 & \sin\delta_2 \\ -\sin\delta_1 \sin\delta_2 & \cos\delta_1 & \sin\delta_1 \cos\delta_2 \\ -\cos\delta_1 \sin\delta_2 & -\sin\delta_1 & \cos\delta_1 \cos\delta_2 \end{bmatrix} \tag{A9.13}$$

The parameters β_1, β_2, and β_3 are estimated by fitting the p equations

[1] We do not estimate ψ_0 this way, but the scalar can be used as a check of the other estimator.

given by (A9.11) by least squares using the estimates $\hat{m}_{jk}$ obtained by the factor analysis, that is, the elements of the estimate of $\Lambda C^{1/2}\Gamma$.

Having obtained the estimates $\hat{\beta}_1$, $\hat{\beta}_2$, and $\hat{\beta}_3$ in this way, we estimate ψ_0^2 by $\hat{\psi}_0^2 = 1/(\hat{\beta}_1^2 + \hat{\beta}_2^2 + \hat{\beta}_3^2)$. Then $\hat{\psi}_0 \hat{\beta}_1$ estimates $\sin \delta_2$, and $\hat{\beta}_2/\hat{\beta}_3$ estimates $\tan \delta_1$. From these we obtain estimates of $\cos \delta_2$ and $\sin \delta_1$ through the identities $\cos \delta_2 = \pm (1 - \sin^2 \delta_2)^{1/2}$ and $\sin \delta_1 = \pm (1 - \cos^2 \delta_1)^{1/2}$. The choice of sign is arbitrary, because the various choices represent reflections and 90° rotations of the map.

Once these quantities have been estimated, we have estimates $\hat{\Gamma}_1$ and $\hat{\Gamma}_2$. The matrix $\hat{M}\hat{\Gamma}_1'\hat{\Gamma}_2'$ is formed to estimate $\Lambda C^{1/2}\Gamma_3$. By deleting the third column of $\hat{M}\hat{\Gamma}_1'\Gamma_2'$, which estimates $\psi_0 \mathbf{1}$, we have an estimate of $2\pi' W^{1/2} R$, where

$$R = \begin{bmatrix} \cos \delta_3 & -\sin \delta_3 \\ \sin \delta_3 & \cos \delta_3 \end{bmatrix} \tag{A9.14}$$

is a 2×2 rotation matrix, and W is a diagonal matrix with diagonal elements σ_1^2 and σ_2^2.

Let $N = \pi' W^{1/2} R$, and thus $\pi = W^{-1/2} R N'$, because $R^{-1} = R'$. Let $\mathbf{e}_j = (0, \ldots, 0, 1, 0, \ldots, 0)'$ be a p-dimensional column vector, where the 1 is at the jth position. Then

$$\begin{aligned} \boldsymbol{\pi}_j' \boldsymbol{\pi}_j &= \mathbf{e}_j' N R' W^{-1} R N' \mathbf{e}_j \\ &= \sum_{i=1}^{2} \sigma_i^{-2} \left(\sum_{k=1}^{2} n_{jk} r_{ik} \right)^2 \end{aligned} \tag{A9.15}$$

where $N = (n_{jk})$ and $R = (r_{ik})$. Similarly,

$$\boldsymbol{\pi}_j' \boldsymbol{\mu}_z = \sum_{i=1}^{2} \sigma_i^{-1} \mu_{zi} \left(\sum_{k=1}^{2} n_{jk} r_{ik} \right) \tag{A9.16}$$

These results are combined to set up a regression equation whose dependent variable has the values $\bar{T}_j - \bar{T}_0$ for $j = 1, \ldots, p$.

Assumption 7: The c_{jm} have the same expected value; that is, $E(c_{jm}) = E(c_{0m})$ for each j. Then, from (A9.3), with $V_0 = 0$,

$$E(T_{jm} - T_{0m}) = -\boldsymbol{\pi}_j' \boldsymbol{\pi}_j + 2\boldsymbol{\pi}_j' \boldsymbol{\mu}_z - aV_j \tag{A9.17}$$

Applying (A9.15) and (A9.16) to (A9.17) and gathering terms, using $\hat{n}_{jk}$ in place of the true n_{jk}, it follows that

$$\bar{T}_j - \bar{T}_0 = -\alpha_0 \hat{n}_{j1}^2 - \alpha_1 \hat{n}_{j2}^2 - \alpha_2 \hat{n}_{j1} \hat{n}_{j2} + \alpha_3 \hat{n}_{j1} + \alpha_4 \hat{n}_{j2} - aV_j + \epsilon_j \tag{A9.18}$$

where ϵ_j is an error term, and

$$\alpha_0 = \sigma_1^{-2} \cos^2 \delta_3 + \sigma_2^{-2} \sin^2 \delta_3$$

$$\alpha_1 = \sigma_1^{-2} \sin^2 \delta_3 + \sigma_2^{-2} \cos^2 \delta_3$$

$$\alpha_2 = 2(\sigma_2^{-2} - \sigma_1^{-2}) \sin \delta_3 \cos \delta_3$$

$$\alpha_3 = 2(\sigma_1^{-1} \mu_{z1} \cos \delta_3 + \sigma_2^{-1} \mu_{z2} \sin \delta_3)$$

and

$$\alpha_4 = 2(\sigma_2^{-1} \mu_{z2} \cos \delta_3 - \sigma_1^{-1} \mu_{z1} \sin \delta_3) \quad \text{(A9.19)}$$

Fitting the equation (A9.18) by least squares (regression), estimates of the five α's and a are obtained. Note that $[\bar{T}_j - \bar{T}_0 - E(T_{jm} - T_{0m})]$ has an error of order $1/\sqrt{N}$.

Solving for δ_3, σ_1^{-2}, and σ_2^{-2} by using the first three equations in (A9.19),

$$\tan 2\hat{\delta}_3 = \hat{\alpha}_2 / (\hat{\alpha}_1 - \hat{\alpha}_0)$$

$$2\hat{\sigma}_1^{-2} = \hat{\alpha}_1 + \hat{\alpha}_0 - \hat{\alpha}_2 / \sin 2\hat{\delta}_3$$

and

$$2\hat{\sigma}_2^{-2} = \hat{\alpha}_1 + \hat{\alpha}_0 + \hat{\alpha}_2 / \sin 2\hat{\delta}_3 \quad \text{(A9.20)}$$

provided that $\hat{\alpha}_0 \neq \hat{\alpha}_1$ and $\hat{\delta}_3 \neq 0, \pm\pi/2$. These cases are covered by performing two checks immediately after the regression has been performed: checks for $\hat{\delta}_3 = 0$ and $\hat{\alpha}_0 = \hat{\alpha}_1$.

The coordinates μ_{z1} and μ_{z2} are estimated by combining the α_3 and α_4 equations in (A9.19) using the estimates of δ_3, σ_1^{-2}, and σ_2^{-2} as obtained from the expressions in (A9.20). The parameters of the rotation matrix Γ and C have now been estimated, and so $\hat{\Lambda}$ can be obtained from the estimate of $\Lambda C^{1/2} \Gamma$ obtained from the factor analysis. The estimated $\boldsymbol{\pi}_j$ are taken from $\hat{\Lambda}$.

Estimating the z_{m1} *and* z_{m2}: It is easy to estimate z_{m1} and z_{m2} for each respondent using the $\hat{\boldsymbol{\pi}}_j$ and $\hat{a}$. Let $u_j = c_{jm} - c_{0m}$ and

$$y_j = -\hat{\boldsymbol{\pi}}_j' \hat{\boldsymbol{\pi}}_j - \hat{a}(V_j - V_0) \quad \text{(A9.21)}$$

From (A9.3),

$$T_{jm} - T_{0m} = y_j + 2\hat{\pi}_{j1} z_{m1} + 2\hat{\pi}_{j2} z_{m2} + u_j \quad \text{(A9.22)}$$

for each m. Equation (A9.22) is a linear model with three independent variables $\{y_j, \hat{\pi}_{j1}, \hat{\pi}_{j2}\}$, an error u_j, a zero intercept, and the dependent variable $\{T_{jm} - T_{0m}\}$. A least-squares fit of (A9.22) yields estimates of z_{m1} and z_{m2}. Because the sample size is p, these estimates are noisy for most surveys.

Appendix 9.2: Estimating the voter translation coefficients

In this appendix we shall describe the methodology that enables us to estimate the translation coefficients of the voters (i.e., the v_{ij}'s). We shall also discuss the survey data needed to obtain these estimates.

The linear mapping model of Chapter 4 can be reexpressed as

$$\theta_{ijp} - b_{ij} = \mathbf{v}'_{ij}\boldsymbol{\pi}_p + \epsilon_{ijp} \tag{A9.23}$$

where θ_{ijp} is the ith voter's perception of the pth politician's position on issue j $(i=1,\ldots,N;\ j=1,\ldots,J;\ p=1,\ldots,M)$. Voter i's perception of the status quo policy on issue j is b_{ij}. The vector $\mathbf{v}'_{ij}=(v_{ij1},\ldots,v_{ijm})$ is i's vector of translation weights that map positions on each of the m predictive dimensions $(m<M)$ into positions on issue j. The vector $\boldsymbol{\pi}_p=(\pi_{p1},\ldots,\pi_{pm})'$ is the position of politician p on the m predictive dimensions. Finally, ϵ_{ijp} is a zero-mean random error whose distribution is independent of $\mathbf{v}_{ij}$ and $\boldsymbol{\pi}_p$.

Assume that v_{ijk} is a random variable for $i=1,\ldots,N$, $j=1,\ldots,J$, and $k=1,\ldots,m$. Assume also that the v_{ijk} are distributed independently for i and k, so that $\text{Cov}(v_{ijk},v_{rst})=0$ for $i\neq r$, $k\neq t$. In addition, assume that $\text{Var}(v_{ij1})=\cdots=\text{Var}(v_{ijm})$. Because the units of π_{pk} are undefined, set $\text{Var}(v_{ijk})=1$ for each k with no loss of generality. Finally, assume that $\text{Cov}(\epsilon_{ijp},\epsilon_{ijq})=0$ for $p\neq q$.

With these assumptions, we can employ factor analysis to estimate the v_{ijk}'s of the voters. We can also estimate the $\mathbf{z}_i$'s of the voters and the $\boldsymbol{\pi}_p$'s of the candidates. In contrast to the methodology in Appendix 9.1, however, we cannot estimate the angle of rotation in the predictive space. We are also unable to include a valence dimension in the analysis.

From the foregoing assumptions it is easily demonstrated that the covariance of $d_{ijp}=\theta_{ijp}-b_{ij}$ and $d_{ijq}=\theta_{ijq}-b_{ij}$ is

$$\begin{aligned}\text{Cov}(d_{ijp},d_{ijq}) &= \boldsymbol{\pi}'_p\boldsymbol{\pi}_q \quad \text{if } p\neq q\\ &= \boldsymbol{\pi}'_p\boldsymbol{\pi}_p+\psi_p \quad \text{if } p=q\end{aligned} \tag{A9.24}$$

where $\psi_p=\text{Var}(\epsilon_{ijp})$ is the specific variance of the pth response variate and $\boldsymbol{\pi}_p$ are the loadings of the pth politician on the m underlying dimensions.

In matrix form, $\text{Cov}(d_{ijp},d_{ijq})$ is the (p,q)th element of the $M\times M$ covariance matrix Σ, where

$$\Sigma=\Pi\Pi'+\Psi \tag{A9.25}$$

$\Pi=(\boldsymbol{\pi}_1,\ldots,\boldsymbol{\pi}_M)'$ is the $M\times m$ matrix of loadings of the M politicians on the m underlying dimensions and Ψ is an $M\times M$ diagonal matrix whose

pth diagonal term is ψ_p $(p=1,\ldots,M)$. The diagonal elements of $\Pi\Pi'$ are called the communalities of the responses.

The sample covariance of d_{ijp} and d_{ijq} is

$$s_{pq}=(NJ-1)^{-1}\sum_{j=1}^{J}\sum_{i=1}^{N}(d_{ijp}-\bar{d}_p)(d_{ijq}-\bar{d}_q)$$

where $\bar{d}_k=(NJ)^{-1}\sum_{j=1}^{J}\sum_{i=1}^{N}d_{ijk}$; s_{pq} is an unbiased estimator of the (p,q)th element of Σ. By the law of large numbers, s_{pq} is also a consistent estimator as $N\rightarrow\infty$. Thus, the sample covariance matrix $S=(s_{pq})$ is a consistent, unbiased estimator of Σ. A factor analysis of S will yield a consistent estimator of ΠT, where T is an $m\times m$ orthogonal rotation matrix.

Suppose, for example, that $m=2$. Then any orthogonal rotation matrix is of the form

$$T=\begin{bmatrix}\cos\theta & -\sin\theta\\ \sin\theta & \cos\theta\end{bmatrix}$$

and $\boldsymbol{\pi}_p T$ is a clockwise rotation of $\boldsymbol{\pi}_p$ by the angle θ. Thus, if there are two predictive dimensions, factor analysis will yield an estimate of the candidate positions up to a rotation of the coordinate system. The factor scores v_{ijk} and the specific variances are estimated by standard procedures of the factor analysis.

The $\mathbf{z}_i$'s of the voters can be estimated if we have observations on $\mathbf{y}_i=\mathbf{x}_i-\mathbf{b}_i=(x_{i1}-b_{i1},\ldots,x_{iJ}-b_{iJ})'$ and if we set $A_i=I$ (the matrix of salience weights for the J issues). With the $J\times m$ matrix of factor scores $V_i=(\mathbf{v}_{i1},\ldots,\mathbf{v}_{iJ})'$, where $\mathbf{v}_{ij}=(v_{ij1},\ldots,v_{ijm})'$, we have $\mathbf{z}_i$ by the identity

$$\mathbf{z}_i=(V_i'V_i)^{-1}V_i'\mathbf{y}_i$$

stated in Appendix 4.2.

Disjoint predictive dimensions

The assumption that the v_{ijk} are random variables for all j and k may not be defensible in the case of disjoint predictive dimensions. The results of this chapter indicate that two predictive dimensions underlie American national elections, the first economic and the second social. For all purely economic issues, $v_{ij2}=0$, and for all purely social issues, $v_{ij1}=0$.

Suppose we group issues into three sets: (1) pure economic issues, (2) pure social issues, and (3) issues that involve both predictive dimensions. We can then factor-analyze the covariance of the responses issue by issue to confirm our hypothesis of disjoint predictive dimensions. In other words, for a given issue j, we can factor-analyze the sample covariance matrix whose (p, q)th element is

$$s_{pq} = (N-1)^{-1} \sum_{i=1}^{N} (d_{ijp} - \bar{d}_{jp})(d_{ijq} - \bar{d}_{jq})$$

where $\bar{d}_{jk} = (N)^{-1} \sum_{i=1}^{N} d_{ijk}$. Given our hypothesis, for issues in sets (1) and (2) only one factor (i.e., dimension) should be recovered. For issues in set (3), two factors should be recovered.

By relating the maps obtained by the single-issue factor analyses, it should be possible to identify the pure economic issues from the pure social issues. Each set can then be pooled to obtain two candidate maps, one for candidate positions on the economic dimension and the other for candidate positions on the social dimension.

Data requirements

We need data on θ_{ijp}, b_{ij}, and x_{ij} in order to perform the factor analyses described earlier. The SRC/CPS national election studies include a number of seven-point issue scales on which respondents are asked to place themselves and major political figures. Although these data are ordinal, the sample covariance matrix is the structure to be analyzed, and the degree of distortion created by not allowing respondents to choose points anywhere on a freely defined issue scale is probably not that great.

Interpreting b_{ij} as the status quo policy on issue j, b_{ij} is the ith voter's perception of the incumbent's position on the jth issue scale; x_{ij} is the respondent's own position on the jth issue scale, and θ_{ijp} is i's perception of the pth politician's position on the same issue scale.

Bibliographical notes

Hinich (1978b) and Cahoon, Hinich, and Ordeshook (1978) use the same methodology employed in this chapter to analyze aspects of the 1968 American presidential election. Results for the 1972 presidential election are available from the authors.

Earlier work aimed at testing spatial theory, but based on different methodologies, includes that of Rusk and Weisberg (1972) and Rabinowitz (1973). These two studies apply different nonmetric scaling techniques to thermometer data to derive candidate positions in a Euclidean space. Aldrich and McKelvey (1977) apply a factor-analytic model to seven-point issue data to estimate candidate and voter locations on a common set of issue scales. More recent work by Poole and Rosenthal (1982) applies a metric unfolding technique to thermometer data to produce a Euclidean representation of voters and candidates.

For a fuller discussion of the methodology we describe in Appendix 9.1, see Cahoon (1975). Cahoon, Hinich, and Ordeshook (1975) also contains a discussion of this methodology. The mathematical structure of factor analysis, described in Appendix 9.2, can be found in Morrison (1967).

Finally, data used in this chapter were made available by the Inter-University Consortium for Political and Social Research.

CHAPTER 10

Concluding observations

In this final chapter we shall discuss a few of the central themes of this book. Voter information, outcome stability, and outcome location are all important subjects that we have analyzed. We now wish to sum up our most important findings on these topics and to state freely what we think are the major conclusions that can be drawn from our results. The spatial theory of voting provides important insights into real-world voting, and we should not shrink from saying what they are.

10.1 The role of information in spatial voting models

An important topic in this book is the level of voter information. For committee voting, we have examined a variety of cases. In Chapter 3 we discussed two types of strategic voting - sophisticated voting and vote trading. Both are predicated on high levels of voter information. At the very least, a voter who contemplates either type of behavior must have some knowledge of what will happen if he does not behave strategically. Chapter 3 also took up the subject of agenda power. Here again a high level of information is presumed. A committee chairman who contemplates agenda manipulation for his own benefit must have a good idea of what outcome will otherwise occur.

In the absence of a dominant point, strategic voting and agenda manipulation can produce socially perverse outcomes. But this can occur only if information levels vary greatly among voters. If some voters vote strategically, while others are unaware of what is going on, there is no question that the voters with little or no information can be exploited. Similarly, an agenda setter with complete knowledge of voter preferences can take advantage of a committee whose members are unaware that they are being swindled.

We believe that such instances are the exception and not the rule. If one set of voters has enough knowledge of voter preferences to behave strategically, it is likely that the other voters do as well. Although it is well known that cooperative voting agreements are generally unstable, the ability of minority members to bribe majority members into deserting their coalition provides safeguards against the possibility of majority tyranny. Similarly, if the committee chairman knows enough about voter preferences to manipulate the agenda, it is likely that the committee members can see what he is up to. As seen in Section 3.8, a fiendish agenda setter can be foiled by sophisticated voters.

In Chapter 8 we developed a theory of expectations designed to model situations of imperfect voter information. There we showed that forecasting future vote outcomes under conditions of uncertainty can bring stability to issue-by-issue voting and result in median outcomes on all issues, based on mean voter forecasts. We also saw in Chapter 8 that voter expectations complicate the agenda setter's problem, making it more difficult for him to blackmail the voters into approving exorbitant budgets. These results indicate that low voter information also acts as a restraint on the exploitation of voters.

Chapters 6 and 7 also model situations of imperfect voter information. In Chapter 6, committee members are unsure about how changes in total budget size will affect item-level spending changes. As we saw, if views on this subject are diverse, support increases for small changes as opposed to large changes in total budget size.

Chapter 7 is concerned with electoral uncertainty. However, the results of Sections 7.4 and 7.5 point in the same direction as the central result of Chapter 6. Candidates who are associated in the minds of voters with a high degree of uncertainty, concerning either their predictive location or their expected future policies, are at a relative disadvantage compared with well-known or well-understood candidates. Just as voters are likely to be wary of making big changes in status quo budgets, they are also likely to be wary of making big changes in elected officials. The net result is a preference for the status quo and an unwillingness to approve major shifts in policy.

Of course, our model of predictive dimensions is based on the assumption that candidate information is costly, and so voters will rely on shortcut methods to learn about the candidates. The shortcut method described in Chapter 4 allows individuals to vote rationally without a major investment of resources. The results of Sections 4.8 and 4.9 indicate that the predictive significance of the shorthand labels used to describe candidates is fundamentally linked to voter willingness to accept policy change. Only the anticipation that a change in elected officials will not produce a major change in policies leads voters to prefer a challenger to an incumbent.

In summary, then, we find that low information levels have a stabilizing influence both in mass elections and in committee voting. Further, whereas high levels of voter information can destabilize voting, it is unlikely that they will lead to socially perverse outcomes. Although low information levels are more strongly associated with support for the status quo, a high level of information among all participants in the voting process does not mean that anything can happen. A balance among competing interests will still prevail, and the final vote outcome will not be overly slanted in anyone's favor.

10.2 Stability versus instability in spatial voting models

One of the most difficult questions raised in this book is that of predicting vote outcomes in the absence of a dominant point, particularly in committee voting under conditions of high information. As we have shown, there is no simple answer to this question. Game theory has yet to provide a general solution to this problem, and it is doubtful that one exists. Chapter 8 demonstrates that in some cases, institutions can create stability where it otherwise does not exist. But the opposite can also occur. As shown in Section 8.11, institutions can destroy stability.

The whole question of what constitutes "stability" needs rethinking. Given the rarity of dominant points, one is forced to conclude either that democratic decision processes are racked with instability or that a less restrictive definition of stability is appropriate. Whereas cooperative game theory has accepted the second option, it has yet to provide a generally acceptable alternative.

American politics suggests a different way of viewing the problem. One of the recurring themes both within and between branches of government is the balance of power among decision makers – balance of power referring more to outcomes (i.e., who wins and who loses) than differences in the weights of the players. When the executive branch encroaches too far on congressional prerogatives, forces are set into motion that ultimately redress the imbalance. President Reagan's budget victory in 1981, based on skillful use of the reconciliation feature of the congressional budget process, was perceived by many congressmen as a usurpation of congressional authority. The net result of his victory is that Reagan has had major difficulties with Congress over every succeeding budget. President Nixon's use of impoundment in the early 1970s to control federal spending led to a similar result. The Budget and Impoundment Act of 1974 was an assertion that Congress would not accept an inferior role in the spending process. The War Powers Act of 1973 made the same point in the area of foreign policy.

This history of interbranch rivalry may appear to support the argument that democratic decision processes are inherently unstable. On the other hand, there is an undeniable predictability to interbranch relations. As with the course of a swinging pendulum, it is not difficult to tell where future events will lead. An "imperial" presidency will be followed by a period of stubborn, independent behavior by Congress, which will be followed again by a period of executive-branch ascendancy. These oscillations may be viewed as a type of stability, or at the very least a pattern of predictability.

The same point can be made about intrabranch behavior. Congressional reform cycles follow very much the same pattern described earlier. Concentration of power in the hands of party leaders or committee chairmen, leading to excessive control over policy outcomes, inevitably leads to reform movements that ultimately succeed in dispersing power among a larger set of members. This result, in turn, inevitably leads to complaints about fragmented decision making or congressional stalemate and a successful move to restore some measure of party government. The congressional reforms of the 1970s were designed to break the concentration of power in the hands of southern Democratic committee chairmen that led to the blocking of liberal legislation. The proliferation of subcommittees and the rise of "subcommittee government" was then countered by increasing the powers of the Speaker of the House to enable him to have greater influence over legislation. In contrast, at the turn of the century, the Speaker was seen as using dictatorial powers to dominate legislative outcomes. A congressional revolt in 1910 reduced his role to that of a figurehead.

Whether this cycle that alternates between allowing the few or the many to influence policy is evidence of stability or instability depends on what is meant by stability. Nonetheless, it helps from the standpoint of science to know that winners who win too often or too much are likely to become losers. This is a type of balance that is evident in democratic decision processes. Whether one wishes to view it as a stable or unstable balance is largely a matter of taste. There can be no doubt, however, that the pattern of outcomes produced by this process is regular and predictable.

Perhaps the whole subject of stability has been overemphasized. As long as politics exhibits predictable, explainable patterns, a science of politics can exist. The spatial theory of voting is not dependent on the existence of general equilibrium. It is dependent on logical patterns underlying the behavior of voters and candidates. Even the breakdown-of-equilibrium example of Section 5.4 exhibits a type of predictability. That a predictive location to the right of the other party's candidate is more attractive than a location to the left demonstrates that instabilities can exhibit regular patterns.

10.3 Centrist election outcomes

The last topic that is a major theme of this book is the force exerted by the center of voter opinion over election outcomes. As we have seen, a number of conditions give rise to centrist election outcomes. Probabilistic voting that permits voters to abstain from alienation and indifference makes centrist locations on the predictive dimension attractive labels for the candidates. Widely divergent views of nonspatial candidate characteristics have the same effect. Chapter 4 shows that the expectation of large policy changes under a noncentrist challenger increases support for a centrist incumbent. Chapter 7 shows that either familiarity with the future policies expected of ideologically centrist candidates or a high degree of perceptual uncertainty associated with noncentrist candidates increases the likelihood of a centrist election outcome. In short, we have identified a broad range of conditions under which the center of voter opinion exerts a powerful force over election results.

Chapter 9 demonstrates that the center of voter opinion has played an important role in recent American presidential elections. Jimmy Carter's victory in 1976 over Gerald Ford was possible only because his advantage over Ford on the valence dimension of the campaign compensated for his greater distance from the mean voter's most preferred point in the predictive space. Ronald Reagan's victory over Carter in 1980 was doubly enhanced by his closeness to the center of the predictive space and his advantage over Carter on the valence dimension.

There is no doubt that closeness to the center of the electorate is an important factor (as is the candidate's position on the valence dimension of the campaign) in determining electoral success. Interestingly, Figure 9.3 indicates that even extremist candidates in American elections, such as George Wallace, are relatively close to the middle of the predictive space. No candidate lies anywhere near the horizontal periphery of the electorate (which is much farther from the center than the vertical periphery). This is also true in 1980. Because it is doubtful that equilibrium conditions are ever strictly met in mass electorates, we conclude that the center of voter opinion exerts a force more powerful than our theoretical results indicate.

Of course, there are real-world forces that account for candidates being somewhat distant from the center of the predictive space. The results of Chapter 9 indicate that adopting a major-party label biases voter perceptions of a candidate's location on the economic predictive dimension. Because winning the nomination of one of the two major parties is a prerequisite for success in the general election, a candidate has no choice but to accept a certain disadvantage on the economic dimension. Associations a candidate may have with interest groups such as organized labor or business groups are also likely to convince voters that the candidate is not located at the center of the predictive space. Because such associations are also essential for electoral success, the candidate is again caught in a bind.

The major point is that a candidate's predictive location is a judgment of the voters, not a conscious decision by the candidate. We have argued throughout this book that candidates can affect the way voters link issues with dimensions, but candidates cannot move their predictive locations at will. Further, our empirical results indicate that whatever movement in the candidate's predictive location does occur between election periods is not something the candidate sits down and decides. Obviously, Jimmy Carter did not decide to move himself away from the center of the predictive space between 1976 and 1980. The fact remains that he did move in that direction.

We are left, then, with the conclusion that closeness to the center of the predictive space is an asset in two-candidate elections, but one that voters bestow on candidates rather than the other way around. Still, our empirical results indicate that major American political figures are not far away from the center of the electorate. The political mainstream occupied by Democratic and Republican politicians flows very close to the center of voter opinion.

10.4 Final conclusions

Images of evil agenda setters mercilessly exploiting voters and disliked candidates forced on an unhappy electorate are inaccurate characterizations of voting in free societies. The spatial theory of voting demonstrates that in both mass elections and committee voting, centrist or other outcomes reasonably reflective of voter opinion are to be expected. Although the question of outcome stability remains unanswered, the more important question of predictability can be answered affirmatively. Voting and candidate behavior exhibit logical, explainable patterns that spatial theory can illuminate.

In closing, we hope the reader is convinced that spatial theory is a powerful tool for understanding voting and elections. The theoretical and empirical results of this book are both a statement of what the spatial theory of voting has accomplished and an indication of the numerous possibilities for further development.

Bibliographical notes

Our contention that democratic voting is characterized by forces that keep outcomes reasonably close to the center of voter opinion is shared by some spatial theorists, but not most. Tullock (1967, 1981) is one of those who share our position. Shepsle and Weingast (1981b) argue that institutions create stability in real-world voting systems, but they do not directly address the question of the welfare implications of institutionally induced stability. Ordeshook (1971), Kramer (1977a), and Coughlin (1982) are all concerned with conditions under which election outcomes are Pareto optimal, with the implication in some places that these conditions are not difficult to meet.

The emphasis in the spatial voting literature, however, is on electoral instability and opportunities in committee settings to manipulate vote outcomes. McKelvey (1976, 1979), Romer and Rosenthal (1978), Plott and Levine (1978), and Schofield (1978) are a few of the more recent articles in this vein. Riker (1982) has taken these conclusions to their furthest point, defining a new field termed "heresthetics" to describe the art of manipulating vote outcomes.

References

Aldrich, J., and R. McKelvey. 1977. "A Method of Scaling with Applications to the 1968 and 1972 Presidential Elections." *American Political Science Review* 71:111–30.

Aranson, P., M. Hinich, and P. Ordeshook. 1974. "Election Goals and Strategies: Equivalent and Nonequivalent Candidate Objectives." *American Political Science Review* 68:135–52.

Arrow, K. J. 1963. *Social Choice and Individual Values,* 2nd ed. New Haven: Yale University Press.

1970. *Essays in the Theory of Risk-Bearing.* Amsterdam: Holland.

Bergstrom, T. 1975. "Maximal Elements of Acyclic Relations on Compact Sets." *Journal of Economic Theory* 10:403–4.

Black, D. 1958. *Theory of Committees and Elections.* Cambridge University Press.

Black, D., and R. Newing. 1951. *Committee Decisions with Complementary Valuation.* London: William Hodge.

Brams, S. 1978. *The Presidential Election Game.* New Haven: Yale University Press.

Cahoon, L. 1975. "Locating a Set of Points Using Range Information Only." Ph.D. dissertation, Carnegie-Mellon University.

Cahoon, L., M. Hinich, and P. Ordeshook. 1975. "A Multi-Dimensional Statistical Procedure for Spatial Analysis." Unpublished paper, VPI&SU and Carnegie-Mellon University.

1978. "A Statistical Multidimensional Scaling Method Based on the Spatial Theory of Voting." In *Graphical Representation of Multivariate Data,* edited by P. C. Wang, pp. 243–78. New York: Academic Press.

Campbell, A., P. Converse, W. Miller, and D. Stokes. 1960. *The American Voter.* New York: Wiley; University of Chicago Press edition 1976.

Cohen, L. 1979. "Cyclic Sets in Multidimensional Voting Models." *Journal of Economic Theory* 20:1–12.

Cohen, L., and S. Matthews. 1980. "Constrained Plott Equilibria, Directional Equilibria and Global Cycling Sets." *Review of Economic Studies* 47:975–86.

Coughlin, P. 1982. "Pareto Optimality of Policy Proposals with Probabilistic Voting." *Public Choice* 39:427–33.

Coughlin, P., and M. J. Hinich. (in press). "Necessary and Sufficient Conditions for Single-Peakedness in Public Economic Models." *Journal of Public Economics.*

Davis, O. A., M. H. DeGroot, and M. J. Hinich. 1972. "Social Preference Orderings and Majority Rule." *Econometrica* 40:147–57.

Davis, O. A., and M. J. Hinich. 1966. "A Mathematical Model of Policy Formation in a Democratic Society." In *Mathematical Applications in Political Science, II,* edited by Joseph Bernd, pp. 175–208. Dallas: Southern Methodist University Press.

1967. "Some Results Related to a Mathematical Model of Policy Formation in a Democratic Society." In *Mathematical Applications in Political Science, III,* edited by J. L. Bernd, pp. 14–38. Charlottesville: University of Virginia Press.

1968. "On the Power and Importance of the Mean Preference in a Mathematical Model of Democratic Choice." *Public Choice* 5:59–72.

Davis, O. A., M. J. Hinich, and P. C. Ordeshook. 1970. "An Expository Development of a Mathematical Model of the Electoral Process." *American Political Science Review* 64:426–48.

Denzau, A., and R. Mackay. 1981a. "Structure Induced Equilibrium and Perfect Foresight Expectations." *American Journal of Political Science* 25:762–79.

1981b. "Expectations in Sequential Elections." Unpublished paper, Virginia Tech.

1981c. "On the Role of Expectations in the Creation of Policy Equilibrium." Presented to Southern Economic Meetings, New Orleans.

Denzau, A., and R. Parks. 1975. "The Continuity of Majority Rule Equilibrium." *Econometrica* 43:853–66.

1977. "Public Sector Preferences." *Journal of Economic Theory* 14:454–7.

1979. "Deriving Public Sector Preferences." *Journal of Public Economics* 11:335–54.

Downs, A. 1957. *An Economic Theory of Democracy.* New York: Harper & Row.

Enelow, J. 1981. "Saving Amendments, Killer Amendments, and an Expected Utility Theory of Sophisticated Voting." *Journal of Politics* 43:1062–89.

Enelow, J. M., and M. J. Hinich. 1981. "A New Approach to Voter Uncertainty in the Downsian Spatial Model." *American Journal of Political Science* 25:483–93.

1982a. "Nonspatial Candidate Characteristics and Electoral Competition." *Journal of Politics* 44:115–30.

1982b. "Ideology, Issues, and the Spatial Theory of Elections." *American Political Science Review* 76:493–501.

1983a. "Probabilistic Voting and the Importance of Centrist Ideologies in Democratic Elections." Presented to Public Choice Society meetings, Savannah.

1983b. "Voting One Issue at a Time: The Question of Voter Forecasts." *American Political Science Review* 77:435–45.

1983c. "On Plott's Pairwise Symmetry Condition for Majority Rule Equilibrium." *Public Choice* 40:317–21.

(in press). "Voter Expectations in Multi-Stage Voting Systems: An Equilibrium Result." *American Journal of Political Science.*

Enelow, J., and D. Koehler. 1980. "The Amendment in Legislative Strategy: Sophisticated Voting in the U.S. Congress." *Journal of Politics* 42:396–413.

Farquharson, R. 1969. *Theory of Voting.* New Haven: Yale University Press.

Fiorina, M. P., and C. R. Plott. 1978. "Committee Decisions Under Majority Rule: An Experimental Study." *American Political Science Review* 72:575–97.

Fiorina, M. P., and K. A. Shepsle. 1982. "Equilibrium, Disequilibrium, and the General Possibility of a Science of Politics." In *Political Equilibrium,* edited by P. C. Ordeshook and K. A. Shepsle, pp. 49–64. Boston: Kluwer Nijhoff.

Fishburn, P. C. 1973. *The Theory of Social Choice.* Princeton University Press.

Henderson, J., and R. Quandt. 1971. *Microeconomic Theory: A Mathematical Approach,* 2nd ed. New York: McGraw-Hill.

Hinich, M. J. 1977. "Equilibrium in Spatial Voting: The Median Voter Result Is an Artifact." *Journal of Economic Theory* 16:208–19.

1978a. "Spatial Voting Theory When Voter Perceptions of Candidates Differ." CE 78-11-4, Virginia Tech.

1978b. "Some Evidence on Non-voting Models in the Spatial Theory of Electoral Competition." *Public Choice* 33:83–102.

Hinich, M. J., J. Ledyard, and P. Ordeshook. 1973. "A Theory of Electoral Equilibrium: A Spatial Analysis Based on the Theory of Games." *Journal of Politics* 35:154–93.

Hinich, M. J., and R. Mackay. 1979. "On the Determination of Spending Limitations and Budgetary Ceilings When Voters' Perceptions of the Budgetary Mix Differ." CE 79-7-1, Virginia Tech.

Hinich, M. J., and P. C. Ordeshook. 1969. "Abstentions and Equilibrium in the Electoral Process." *Public Choice* 7:81–106.

1970. "Plurality Maximization vs. Vote Maximization: A Spatial Analysis with Variable Participation." *American Political Science Review* 64:772–91.

1973. "A Sufficient Condition for an Electoral Equilibrium and the Implications of Alternative Empirical Models." *Business and Economic Statistics Section, Proceedings of the American Statistical Association,* pp. 384–7.

1974. "The Electoral College: A Spatial Analysis." *Political Methodology* 1:1–29.

Hinich, M. J., and W. Pollard. 1981. "A New Approach to the Spatial Theory of Electoral Competition." *American Journal of Political Science* 25:323–41.

Hotelling, H. 1929. "Stability in Competition." *Economic Journal* 39:41–57.

Hoyer, R. W., and L. Mayer. 1974. "Comparing Strategies in a Spatial Model of Electoral Competition." *American Journal of Political Science* 18:501–23.

Kadane, J. B., "On Division of the Question." *Public Choice* 13:47–54.

Kessel, John. 1980. *Presidential Campaign Politics.* Homewood, Ill. Dorsey Press.

Key, V. O., Jr. 1966. *The Responsible Electorate.* Cambridge: Harvard University Press.

Kramer, G. 1973. "On a Class of Equilibrium Conditions for Majority Rule." *Econometrica* 41:285–97.

1977a. "A Dynamical Model of Political Equilibrium." *Journal of Economic Theory* 16:310–34.

1977b. "Theories of Political Processes." In *Frontiers of Quantitative Economics, III,* edited by M. Intriligator. New York: North Holland.

1978. "Existence of Electoral Equilibrium." In *Game Theory and Political Science,* edited by P. C. Ordeshook, pp. 375–89. New York University Press.

Levitin, T., and W. Miller. 1979. "Ideological Interpretations of Presidential Elections." *American Political Science Review* 73:751–71.

Luce, D., and H. Raiffa. 1957. Games and Decisions. New York: Wiley.

Mackay, R., and C. Weaver. 1980. "Monopoly Supply and Commodity Bundling in Democratic Processes." Unpublished paper, Virginia Tech.

1981. "Agenda Control by Budget Maximizers in a Multi-Bureau Setting." *Public Choice* 37:447–72.

(in press). "Commodity Bundling and Agenda Control in the Public Sector." *Quarterly Journal of Economics.*

McKelvey, R. D. 1976. "Intransitivities in Multidimensional Voting Models and Some Implications for Agenda Control." *Journal of Economic Theory* 12:472–82.

1979. "General Conditions for Global Intransitivities in Formal Voting Models." *Econometrica* 47:1085–111.

McKelvey, R. D., and R. G. Niemi. 1978. "A Multistage Game Representation of Sophisticated Voting for Binary Procedures." *Journal of Economic Theory* 18:1–22.

McKelvey, R. D., and P. C. Ordeshook. 1976. "Symmetric Spatial Games Without Majority Rule Equilibria." *American Political Science Review* 70:1172–84.

McKelvey, R., P. Ordeshook, and M. Winer. 1978. "The Competitive Solution for *n*-Person Games Without Side Payments." *American Political Science Review* 72:599–615.

Morrison, D. 1967. *Multivariate Statistical Methods,* New York: McGraw-Hill.

Mueller, D. 1979. *Public Choice.* Cambridge University Press.

Niemi, R., and H. Weisberg (editors). 1976. *Controversies in American Voting Behavior.* San Francisco: Freeman.

Ordeshook, P. 1971. "Pareto Optimality and Electoral Competition." *American Political Science Review* 65:1141–5.

1978. (editor). *Game Theory and Political Science.* New York University Press.

Owen, G. 1968. *Game Theory.* Philadelphia: W. B. Saunders.

Page, B. 1976. "The Theory of Political Ambiguity." *American Political Science Review* 70:742–52.

Plott, C. R. 1967. "A Notion of Equilibrium and Its Possibility Under Majority Rule." *American Economic Review* 57:787–806.

1971. "Recent Results in the Theory of Voting." In *Frontiers of Quantitative Economics, I,* edited by M. Intriligator. New York: North Holland.

Plott, C. R., and M. Levine. 1978. "A Model of Agenda Influence on Committee Decisions." *American Economic Review* 68:146–60.

Poole, K., and R. Rosenthal. 1982. "The Estimation of Spatial Voting Models." Unpublished paper, Carnegie-Mellon University.

Rabinowitz, G. 1973. *Spatial Models of Electoral Choice: An Empirical Analysis.* Chapel Hill: Institute for Research in Social Science.

Riker, W. 1980. "Implications from the Disequilibrium of Majority Rule for the Study of Institutions." *American Political Science Review* 74:432–46.

1982. "Political Theory and the Art of Heresthetics." Presented to the American Political Science Association, Denver.

Riker, W., and P. Ordeshook. 1973. *An Introduction to Positive Political Theory.* Englewood Cliffs, N.J.: Prentice-Hall.

Romer, T., and H. Rosenthal. 1978. "Political Resource Allocation, Controlled Agendas, and the Status Quo." *Public Choice* 33:27–43.

Rusk, J., and H. Weisberg. 1972. "Perceptions of Presidential Candidates." *Midwest Journal of Political Science* 16:388–410.

Schofield, N. 1978. "Instability of Simple Dynamic Games." *Review of Economic Studies* 45:575–94.

Schwartz, T. 1977. "Collective Choice, Separation of Issues, and Vote Trading." *American Political Science Review* 71:999–1010.

Shepsle, K. 1972. "The Strategy of Ambiguity: Uncertainty and Electoral Competition." *American Political Science Review* 66:555–68.

1979. "Institutional Arrangements and Equilibrium in Multidimensional Voting Models." *American Journal of Political Science* 23:27–59.

Shepsle, K., and B. Weingast. 1981a. "Structure and Strategy: The Two Faces of Agenda Power." Presented to the American Political Science Association, New York.

1981b. "Structure-induced Equilibrium and Legislative Choice." *Public Choice* 37:503–19.

Simpson, P. B. 1969. "On Defining Areas of Voter Choice: Professor Tullock on Stable Voting." *Quarterly Journal of Economics* 83:478–90.

Sloss, J. 1973. "Stable Outcomes in Majority Rule Voting Games." *Public Choice* 15:19–48.

Slutsky, S. 1979. "Equilibrium Under α-Majority Voting." *Econometrica* 47:1113–25.

Smithies, A. 1941. "Optimum Location in Spatial Competition." *Journal of Political Economy* 49:423–39.

Stokes, D. E. 1963. "Spatial Models of Party Competition." *American Political Science Review* 57:368–77.

Tullock, G. 1967. *Toward a Mathematics of Politics.* Ann Arbor: University of Michigan Press.

1981. "Why So Much Stability?" *Public Choice* 37:189–202.

Wendell, R., and S. Thorson. 1974. "Some Generalizations of Social Decisions Under Majority Rule." *Econometrica* 42:893–912.

Zeckhauser, R. 1969. "Majority Rule with Lotteries on Alternatives." *Quarterly Journal of Economics* 83:696–703.

Answers to selected problems

Chapter 2

2.1 $x_{\text{med}} = 1$

2.2 Persons a, b, and e prefer $y = 2$. Thus, y receives three votes, and z receives two.

2.3 The interval of medians is $1 \leqslant x \leqslant 5$.

2.4 (a) A tie, because b and e prefer $z = 3$, whereas a and d prefer $y = 2$. (b) y wins, because a, b, and e prefer it to $z = -1$.

2.5 $x_{\text{med}} = 26$

Chapter 3

3.2 $\|\mathbf{y} - \mathbf{x}_b\|_{A_b}^2 = 100$ and $\|\mathbf{z} - \mathbf{x}_b\|_{A_b}^2 = r^2$; so $r = 10$

3.3 $r = 10$

3.4 $r = \frac{1}{10}$

3.5 $r = 1$

3.6 $x_{e1}(50) = 69$, $x_{b2}(69) = 22.1$, and $x_{e2}(69) = 51.9$. Thus, the median position on the first vote is 69, and the second vote's median is 51.9. The package of majority rule outcomes is $(69, 51.9)$.

3.7 The median position on the first vote is 50, and the second vote's median is 69. The outcome package is $(69, 50)$.

3.8 B prefers the second agenda, because B prefers $(69, 50)$ to $(69, 51.9)$.

3.9 The median position on project 1 becomes 67.29. The median on a subsequent vote on project 2 is 53.44.

3.10 The majority rule outcome is $(60, 60)$.

3.11 The majority rule outcome is also $(60, 60)$.

3.12 $\mathbf{x}_{\text{med}} = (60, 60)$

3.15 Set the sixth ideal point directly above $\mathbf{x}_5$ so that the figure is symmetric. The point in the middle of the square is then a median in all directions, and this is dominant.

Chapter 4

4.1 (a) $w_{i1}(0) = w_{i2}(0) = 0,\ w_{i1}(1) = 1,\ w_{i2}(1) = -1$
(b) $w_{i1}(0) = w_{i2}(0) = 0,\ w_{i1}(1) = 5,\ w_{i2}(1) = -5$

4.3 $\pi_\theta = (\theta_{i1} - b_{i1})/v_{i1} = (\theta_{i2} - b_{i2})/v_{i2}$

4.4 $\theta_{i1}=0$
4.5 $z_r=z_s=z_t=1$
4.6 $\boldsymbol{\theta}_r=\pi_\theta \mathbf{x}_r$, $\boldsymbol{\theta}_s=\pi_\theta \mathbf{x}_s$, and $\boldsymbol{\theta}_t=\pi_\theta \mathbf{x}_t$; if $\pi_\theta=-1$, for example $\boldsymbol{\theta}_r'=(-0.3,-0.1)$
4.7 $\boldsymbol{\theta}_i'=(-0.333, 0.133)$, $\boldsymbol{\theta}_j'=(-0.233, 0.033)$, and $\boldsymbol{\theta}_k'=(-0.033, 0.133)$; $z_i=-0.52$, $z_j=0.96$, and $z_k=0.71$
4.8 $z_i=-0.32$, $z_j=0.67$, and $z_k=0.3$
4.9 $c=\frac{1}{10}$
4.10 Psi wins if $\theta_{k2}<0$ or $\theta_{k2}>0.2$ and all other values remain the same.
4.11 $\mathbf{z}_i'=(3,0)$

Chapter 5

5.1 (a) The variance is $\sigma_a^2=1$ and $E[u(\tilde{\theta})]=5$.
(b) $\sigma_b^2=4$ and $E[u(\tilde{\theta})]=2$.
5.3 $D_k(\pi_\theta, \pi_\psi)=56(\pi_\psi^2-\pi_\theta^2)-116(\pi_\psi-\pi_\theta)$; $D_k(0,1)=-60$ and $D_k(0,-1)=172$
5.4 $P_k[D_k(0,1)]=0.27$, $P_k[D_k(0,-1)]=0.96$
5.5 $\pi^*=\frac{12}{5}$, $\pi^*=0$
5.6 $\pi^*=\frac{3}{2}$. This type of equilibrium is achieved without the explicit use of a nonpolicy term in the model.

Chapter 6

6.1 $z_i=0$
6.2 $z_i=4$
6.3 $z_i=4$; so i prefers 5 to 1
6.4 $c=\frac{9}{20}$
6.5 $z_i=3$, 2, and $\frac{6}{41}$
6.6 $z_i=\sum_{j=1}^{n} y_{ij}$

Chapter 7

7.1 The expected utility of the lottery is -32. The utility of the average position $\pi_\psi=\frac{7}{4}$ is $-\frac{109}{8}=-13\frac{5}{8}$.
7.3 $z_i>(\pi_\theta+\pi_\psi)/2+3\sigma_\psi^2/(\pi_\theta-\pi_\psi)$
7.4 In general, when $\pi_\theta>\pi_\psi$, the expected utility of $\tilde{\theta}_i$ is greater than that for $\tilde{\psi}_i$ if and only if

$$z_i>(\pi_\theta+\pi_\psi)/2+(\sigma_\theta^2-\sigma_\psi^2)/2(\pi_\theta-\pi_\psi)$$

Thus, the answer is $\sigma_\theta^2<1$.
7.5 $\sigma_\theta^2<2$
7.6 $z_i^*=z_i-b/2$ if $z_i>b/2$. If $-b/2<z_i<b/2$, then $z_i^*=0$. If $z_i<-b/2$, $z_1^*=z_i+b/2$.
7.7 The median z_i^* is (a) $z_{\text{med}}-b/2$ if $z_{\text{med}}>b/2$, (b) zero if $|z_{\text{med}}|<b/2$, and (c) $z_{\text{med}}+b/2$ if $z_{\text{med}}<-b/2$.

Chapter 8

8.1 $x_{a1}(x_2)=138.5-0.9x_2$, $x_{a2}(x_1)=146.5-0.9x_1$

8.2 $x_{b1}(x_2)=101-0.9x_2$, $x_{b2}(x_1)=98.5-0.9x_1$, $x_{c1}(x_2)=182.5-0.9x_2$, $x_{c2}(x_1)=169-0.9x_1$

8.3 $x_{a1}(x_2)=27.3+0.067x_2$, $x_{a2}(x_1)=108+0.2x_1$

8.4 $M_{a1}(x_2,10)=267-1.8x_2$ if $0.9x_2<128.5$; $M_{a1}(x_2,10)=10$ if $0.9x_2\geqslant 128.5$

8.5 $M_{a2}(x_1,10)=283-1.8x_1$ if $0.9x_1<136.5$; $M_{a2}(x_1,10)=10$ if $0.9x_1\geqslant 136.5$

8.7 $B_b(1)=105$

8.8 $k_b(100)=\frac{3}{5}$, $k_b(200)=\frac{7}{9}$

8.9 $B_a^*(65,\frac{1}{2})=157$, $B_b^*(65,\frac{1}{2})=139$, and $B_c^*(65,\frac{1}{2})=349$

8.10 $E[1/(1+\tilde{k})]=24/35$, $E[\tilde{k}/(1+\tilde{k})]=11/35$, and $E[(1+\tilde{k}^2)/(1+\tilde{k})^2]=(27/35)^2$. Thus, $B_\theta^*=67.2$.

8.11 $B_\theta^*=38.3$.

Index